WHAT IS

POETRY?

INTERVIEWS FROM

THE POETRY PROJECT NEWSLETTER

(1983–2009)

EDITED BY ANSELM BERRIGAN

WAVE BOOKS

SEATTLE/NEW YORK

(JUST
KIDDING,
I KNOW
YOU
KNOW)

Published by Wave Books

www.wavepoetry.com

Copyright © 2017

All rights reserved

Wave Books titles are distributed to the trade by

Consortium Book Sales and Distribution

Phone: 800-283-3572 / SAN 631-760X

Library of Congress Cataloging-in-Publication Data

Names: Berrigan, Anselm, editor.

Title: What is poetry? (Just kidding. I know you know):

interviews from the poetry project newsletter (1983–2009)

Description: First edition. | Seattle : Wave Books, [2017]

Identifiers: LCCN 2016035923 | ISBN 9781940696393 (softcover)

Classification: LCC PS135 .W47 2017 | DDC 811/.5409—dc23

LC record available at https://lccn.loc.gov/2016035923

"N.Y. Poetry Scene / Short Form" reprinted from *No Other Way* © 1998
by Charles North, by permission of Hanging Loose Press. A longer version
of "An Interview with Harryette Mullen by Barbara Henning" appears in
*Looking Up Harryette Mullen: Interviews on Sleeping with the Dictionary
and Other Works* (Belladonna* 2011). David Henderson interview copyright
1996 by the author, used with permission. "about" by Jack Collom appears
in *Cold Instant* (Monkey Puzzle Press, 2010). "Surprise Each Other: Anne Waldman
on Collaboration" also appeared in *Vow to Poetry: Essays, Interviews, & Manifestos*
© 2001 by Anne Waldman. Reprinted with permission of The Permissions Company,
Inc. on behalf of Coffee House Press, www.coffeehousepress.com. "Will Alexander:
A Profound Investigation" appears in *Singing in Magnetic Hoofbeat: Essays,
Prose Texts, Interviews and a Lecture 1991–2007.* © 2012 by Will Alexander.
Reprinted with permission of Essay Press.

Designed and composed by Quemadura

Printed in the United States of America

9 8 7 6 5 4 3 2 1

First Edition

FOR

BILL BERKSON

AND

TED GREENWALD

Introduction by Anselm Berrigan   xi

The N.Y. Poetry Scene / Short Form—Charles North   1

Talking with Red Grooms: An Interview by Anne Waldman   8

Translation as Puzzle and Performance:
An Interview with Paul Schmidt by Tim Dlugos   13

The Colors of Consonance: Bernadette Mayer Talks . . . with Ken Jordan   19

Taking Risks Seriously: David Rattray Talks . . . with Ken Jordan   29

Allen Ginsberg & Kenneth Koch: From a Conversation   38

An Interview with Harryette Mullen by Barbara Henning   47

An Interview with David Henderson by Lisa Jarnot   60

An Interview with Alice Notley by Judith Goldman   72

An Interview with John Godfrey by Lisa Jarnot   88

An Interview with Ed Sanders by Lisa Jarnot   103

An Interview with Victor Hernández Cruz by Sheila Alson   118

An Interview with Bernadette Mayer by Lisa Jarnot   130

An Interview with Kenneth Koch by Daniel Kane   140

A Silent Interview with Samuel R. Delany   156

To Buffalo and Back with Renee Gladman:
Interview by Magdalena Zurawski   164

A Conversation with Lorenzo Thomas by Dale Smith   173

An Interview with Fred Moten by Ange Mlinko   184

Lisa Jarnot Interviews Stan Brakhage   191

Interview with Charles North by Ange Mlinko   200

"Surprise Each Other": Anne Waldman on Collaboration by Lisa Birman 209

Interview with Alex Katz by Vincent Katz   219

Adventures in Poetry: An Interview with Larry Fagin by Daniel Kane   229

Tina Darragh Interviewed by Marcella Durand   238

Lewis Warsh Interviewed by Peter Bushyeager   244

Jack Collom Talks . . . with Marcella Durand   251

Anne Waldman Talks . . . with Marcella Durand   261

Edwin Torres Talks . . . with Marcella Durand   275

Harry Mathews Reveals the *Inside Story* to Marcella Durand   286

Brenda Coultas Tells the Truth to Marcella Durand   298

Akilah Oliver Talks to Rachel Levitsky   310

Will Alexander: A Profound Investigation with Marcella Durand   320

Ron Padgett Lifts Off, with Edmund Berrigan   333

Wayne Koestenbaum and Maggie Nelson in Conversation   344

Knowing Isn't Enough: A Conversation with
John Trudell by Brendan Lorber   353

An Interview with Ted Greenwald by Arlo Quint   362

An Interview with Eileen Myles by Greg Fuchs   374

Interview: 10 Questions for Bruce Andrews and
Sally Silvers by erica kaufman   386

INTRODUCTION

The publication of *What is poetry? (Just kidding, I know you know)* coincides with the fiftieth anniversary season of The Poetry Project at St. Mark's Church. The Poetry Project was created in 1966 out of the need for a stable ongoing reading series/gathering point/community center for the overlapping circles of poets in downtown NYC. Those circles included and came to include poets variously associated with the New York School, the Beats, Black Mountain, Umbra, Language writing, and the Nuyoricans—associations which are variously highlighted, fleshed out, made ambiguous, undermined and otherwise reformed in the interviews found herein. In one sense, these groups and their outliers are a source-in-common for the poets and artists this book casts its light upon. But The Poetry Project has always been a site of challenge and respite for individual poets who refuse to take conventional paths, who want live experience with fresh material right now, and who, as Ted Greenwald puts it in his conversation with Arlo Quint, "want the work out front." That's the ethos. It's a near miracle the place has survived and continues to thrive a half-century after a fight at Café Le Metro accidentally collaborated with Lyndon Johnson's Great Society Program, a radical priest named Michael Allen, and some wily poets in organizational furor to get it started (see Miles Champion's essay on the history of The Poetry Project, "Insane Podium," at the Project's website, and Daniel Kane's book *All Poets Welcome: The Lower East Side Poetry Scene in the 1960s* for the longer versions of the story).

These interviews were conducted over the course of a quarter century, beginning in 1983, and becoming a regular feature in the pages of *The Poetry Project Newsletter* in the early 1990s, when the *Newsletter* reached its peak (and still current) length of thirty-two pages and had grown in readership from several hundred to several thousand readers. Part of what spurred the increase in interviews was a shared if unspoken (i.e., without editorial mandate) desire on the part of younger poets involved with and working for The Poetry Project to engage in cross-generational conversations. This impulse translated into interviewing poets and artists who hadn't been given the forum to speak on their own terms about their work, the sources fueling that work, the ongoing questions of how to live and how to live specifically as poets, their respective senses of the past and present becoming future, and their takes on the state of the art. In some cases the early days of The Poetry Project came to the foreground, as well as its later growth and development into a national center in lower Manhattan for poetry as a living, transformative, and at times rapidly changing form of art. Most of these interviews were conducted live and specifically for the *Newsletter*, so going in the interviewer and interviewee had a real sense of who their readers would be: the immediate *Newsletter* readership, who would get the physically modest, staple-bound publication in the mail, and the people who showed up at the Project for weekly (sometimes thrice-weekly) readings, where the newsletter would be available in stacks at the Parish Hall entrance. This overlapping readership was and is rooted in New York City, with a sizeable percentage also composed of readers across the United States, and a small percentage composed of readers in other countries.

For the poets closely involved with The Poetry Project since, and subsequent to, its inception, the interviews were an opportunity to speak directly to a community one could perceive as known, imaginary, expanding, unwieldy, intermittent, formative, desperately necessary, and sometimes peculiarly unsatisfying all at once. Community being the kind of term that often implies everything and nothing simultaneously, with the bottom falling out of the word depending on who happens to be wielding it. Poets can be particularly adept at using and exposing such terms. At the same time the poets and artists interviewed herein are by and large skilled practitioners of spoken language: used to speaking directly, resisting academic jargon, moving off-hand from one subject to another, digressing, making circles, filling them with particulars, casting wide and partial nets to make time, make shapes, and keep moving. They talk to and with the person in the room first, taking charge when given space, highly attuned to idiosyncratic detail, and opening up quickly or gradually to anyone else who might be listening or who might listen eventually. That the poets on both sides of the interviews have intensely varied practices and aesthetics means the range of subjects found within these interviews is necessarily wide and ultimately disorienting to completely list (I know—I tried a few times). But for serious artists—poets especially, given that their basic materials, words and their sounds, are the lifeblood of human communication—the particulars that make up what we decide to call "subjects" are *everything*, however fleeting those particulars may be. A fair number of the poets in these interviews developed as artists under the spotlight of high-level support, scrutiny, argument, and competition. The Poetry Project in the 1960s and '70s wasn't just a place to go give a reading and cross off some list of desired venues. The point was to be exposed, to expose your rawest risk-taking work to a discerning audience, one that would let you know right there whether it's working or not, and to participate in that as communal process. In such light talking about anything and everything related to the art becomes part of that process, making the interview an oddly logical form to put to work in the service of poets.

That said, as forms handled by poets go the interview is a recognizable curiosity—a companion to the work in the name of lateral insight, and one that typically presents a discrete, finished surface. Conversely, a ton of labor goes into each interview: arranging, taping, transcribing, and editing even a short interview is a process that can take weeks or longer. The finished result usually reads quite differently than the unedited transcript, but a transcript, finished or unfinished, is a representation of a conversation that may have been filled with odd rhythms, pauses, rushes of speaking, evidence of garble, nerves, tension, etc. A live interview is a conversation that becomes writing, as opposed to, say, e-mail interviews, which can be informative, but are typically made of writing posing as conversation, without any real stakes or playfulness. *What is poetry? (Just kidding, I know you know)* is a book of interviews that overlaps with certain other categories of book while ultimately eluding those categories. This is not an oral history of The Poetry Project, for instance, though a great deal of information that might qualify as anecdotal history of The Project and its numerous social and artistic contexts can be found within. It's not a scholarly book or a book "about" poetry, though one may find out a great deal about poetry as a living art form flowing through the costume of each interview. It is an anthology of a type, and many readers will naturally jump around the book while reading it, but the book is also a collection of stories filtered through the form of the interview into one longer story made of overlapping circles. As such, it will reward readers who take on the experience of reading it from beginning to end. Characters appear, recede, and pop up again in surprising places. Jobs, death, illness, war, and money problems come up as frequently as references to the arts, and the chronological structure of the book belies a sense of time that often reaches back to the 1960s and earlier, while examining the future from the perspective of that particular day a conversation is taking place. It is not a linear chronicle of an era, but it is a chronicle nonetheless, an assemblage verging on accidental chorus that presents ideas and discussion about poetry in the charged words of the poets, not in unreadable academic speak, and not in insulated literary terms divorced from the broader ground of the world and its inexhaustible complexities. Its necessity is bound up with the casual intensity of its invitation: you won't find many people who speak on and for poetry, or anything else for that matter, in such high and ordinary terms. The ride is for anyone to take.

*

The idea of making a book out of interviews from *The Poetry Project Newsletter* first occurred to me as possible when I was Artistic Director of The Poetry Project in the mid-aughts, and a large number of people who have made it possible for this book to be assembled should be acknowledged, and thanked:

   —Miles Champion, Corina Copp, Corrine Fitzpatrick, and Stacy Syzmaszek, who worked in the Project office with me in 2005 and 2006, when the first giant sheaf of photocopies from the *Newsletter* was put together.

   —The current staff of the Project: Stacy Szymaszek, Simone White, Nicole Wallace, and Laura Henriksen, who have given their blessings to the book and have been invaluable sources of conversation and information while making it easy and entertaining to dig through the Project's archive of past newsletters.

   —The editorial staff and interns at Wave Books, especially Joshua Beckman and Heidi Broadhead, for taking this project on in as supportive a manner as one could hope for, helping to work through the numerous structural and logistical questions such a book poses, and for converting hundreds of pages of photocopies from old *Newsletters* into a workable, editable document—a serious feat.

—Karen Weiser, Elinor Nauen, Joshua Beckman, and Alice Notley, who have provided feedback and editorial insights throughout the manuscript-making process, and who listened patiently as I talked my way through the curious task of making go together a set of interviews that were never intended to "go together," so to speak. And also Charles North, for graciously permitting me to take the title from his terrifically wry, stage-setting "interview" of Paul Violi that opens the collection.

—It would be remiss of me not to acknowledge all of the editors of *The Poetry Project Newsletter* since its initial issue in December, 1972. In its early days the *Newsletter* was a four-page community bulletin board of sorts, its pages filled with reading calendars, workshop descriptions, want ads, glimpses of emerging publications, and the comings and goings of those closest to the daily life of the Project. Some of these issues can be found as PDFs on The Poetry Project's website, by the way (poetryproject.org). As the population of the Project's immediate community grew, so did the size of the *Newsletter*, and with that growth came book reviews, questionnaires, feature pieces, poems, lightning-quick baby interviews, shorter interviews that didn't quite fit this volume, and eventually the ongoing run of longer interviews that this book takes its selection from. At least one other book could be made from all that material, a rougher-hewn, more protean collection of snapshot forms, say. To my mind, the interviews are an extension of all that material, finally, and the numerous editors from Ron Padgett in 1972 to current editor Betsy Fagin have been my quiet partners in the making of this book. Editing the *Newsletter* has always been a behind-the-scenes labor of deadline-love and teeth-gnashing, a classic thankless job, with the design of the thing changing with every new editor. So let their work be applauded, each one:

Ron Padgett 1972–1973, Bill MacKay 1973–1975, Ted Greenwald 1975–1977, Frances LeFevre 1977–1978, Vicki Hudspith 1978–1980, Greg Masters 1980–1983, Lorna Smedman 1983–1984, Tim Dlugos 1984–1985, James Ruggia

1985–1986, Jessica Hagedorn 1986–1987, Tony Towle 1987–1990, Jerome Sala 1990–1991, Lynn Crawford 1991–1992, Jordan Davis 1992–1994, Gillian McCain 1994–1995, Mitch Highfill 1995–1996, Lisa Jarnot 1996–1998, Brenda Coultas & Eleni Sikelianos 1998–1999, Katherine Lederer 1999–2000, Ange Mlinko 2000–2002, Nada Gordon & Gary Sullivan 2002–2003, Marcella Durand 2003–2005, Brendan Lorber 2005–2007, John Coletti 2007–2009, Corina Copp 2009–2011, Paul Foster Johnson 2011–2013, Ted Dodson 2013–2015, Betsy Fagin 2015–2017.

Finally, I wish to thank all of the poets and artists who took part in these interviews. The interviewers worked in service of poetry in making them happen, and all are to be commended. I especially want to acknowledge the efforts of Lisa Jarnot and Marcella Durand, both of whom took it upon themselves during their respective editorial tenures at *The Poetry Project Newsletter* to deepen the knowledge of the larger Poetry Project community and the poetry world at large, and to expand and complicate the definitions, visible and invisible, of said bodies. This book would not be possible without their contributions. As for the poets, painters, filmmakers, and dancers interviewed—these are people whose work I've lived with, learned from, and loved for years. Their work, the groundbreaking capacities of that work, and their respective contributions to this world speak for themselves. To have had the chance to give each of them a little more time and space in the form of this book, and to hopefully draw more attention to their respective bodies of work, has been my total honor and pleasure.

ANSELM BERRIGAN
JUNE 2016

WHAT IS POETRY? (JUST KIDDING, I KNOW YOU KNOW)

THE N.Y. POETRY SCENE / SHORT FORM
ADDRESSED TO PAUL VIOLI

NOVEMBER 1983   NO. 101

Reprinted from *Joe Soap's Canoe*, the New York poetry issue, (edited by Martin Stannard, Suffolk, England) with the following introduction: "To place poetry within a current geography (for the benefit especially of British readers) a message went out appealing for an essay on "the current New York poetry scene." What came back was Charles North's "Short Form," the genesis of which is best described by Paul Violi: "North and I sat down with a tape but I could say nothing worthwhile, let alone write an essay. So Charles put it together in this format, a sort of questionnaire to me, which I left unanswered. In other words, it's all his, and besides he puts the answers in the questions."

Why are we doing this?

What does "scene" mean?

Seriously, if scene means "where it is" and the "it" is poetry, does that mean the reading spots (projects, institutions, coffee-houses, bars, clinics), bookstores that do and don't stock big- and small-press poetry, *quartiers* (Lower East Side, West Village, Upper West Side, Soho), etc.? Or does it mean something vaguer, something like The State of The Art—which could conceivably have little to do with the aforementioned venues (which could, conceivably,

exist in an *ironic* relation to them, i.e., maybe those are precisely *not* where it really is).

To what extent does one's perception of the scene depend on one's aesthetics? A. A great deal.

What is poetry?
(Just kidding, I know you know.)

If "scene" has something to do with health, vitality, quality, and opportunity, characterize the New York Scene.

The N.Y. Scene is clearly a number of scenes, most of which have little to do with New York per se. As we all know, the "New York School" tag which everyone associated with tries to snip off (with only moderate success and properly so) has to do with a state of mind, a sense of *Europe*, and the sense that the world is mad, rather than with this oceanic city.
(Not a question.)

Name some parts of the N.Y. Scene. Which of those, e.g., "original" N.Y. School, St. Mark's, etc., have additional parts, e.g., second and third generations, splinter groups (Bolinas, Naropa), etc.?

Is it logically possible to make any meaningful generalizations about the N.Y. Scene?

How parochial is your view of things (anyone's)? For example, what do you know about the Brooklyn poets apart from the redoubtable Bob Hershon and the *Some Mag* crowd?

Who, apart from present company, are some of the interesting N.Y. poets, keeping in mind that you can't remember all of them at any one point and are likely to offend many?
Do you think in terms of "movements" or factions?

Do the large venues, the 92nd St. Y, the Guggenheim Museum, the Academy of American Poets, have anything whatsoever to do with the N.Y. Scene?

Why is there a sense that the best lack all conviction while the worst are full of polemical intensity, that things have somehow gone awry, and that N.Y.'s fabled energy is more fable, or rather more mere energy, than formerly, or is that only my sense, bound up with my own limited perspective and efforts at selfhood?
(Choose two.)

Do any of the following apply to any, few, or all of the scenes and portions of scenes described (by you, one hopes) above? World-weariness, careerism, art-world madness—speaking of which, when we tried to do this on tape and failed miserably, we did seem to agree that the current state of the Art World, always in the picture for N.Y. poetry at least since the golden-haired fifties, has something to do with what's *wrong* in the poetry world, something like, the loss of "quality," the overpowering of literature by performance (notwithstanding the rightful claims of that brightly lit power-puncher), the much publicized and boring, the excellent and retiring, etc. etc. If I seem to be grinding an axe, that is because it is somehow continually being handed to us at the zenith of dullness.

What is your perception of the national perception, if such a thing can be considered, of the N.Y. Scene? (I have in mind the ridicule in varying degrees received by the N.Y. School Poets, St. Mark's, etc., over the years. Has this changed?)

Here's an interesting one. Do you think John Ashbery together with his acclaim has had a positive or negative effect on attitudes to New York and its poetry? I can see several sides to that. What about the "meteoric" aspect of his rise up the versified heavens?

There are, as I think we said on that selfsame dismal tape, loads of poets in N.Y. who aren't very different from poets elsewhere, as I think is probably the case always. The business of the "prevailing style," the common idea of aim and effect, tone and language, grants and nepotism (just kidding). Could you characterize that style and give some idea of how many poets it applies to, and what all that has to do with N.Y.?

No? Then I guess it's my own idiosyncratic and simplistic way of bringing order to chaos.

How important is St. Mark's city-wide? Nation-wide?
(*Descriptive* linguistics.)

Does big press publishing, centered in N.Y., producing a limited number of poetry books each year which appear in most of the bookstores, having nothing to do with the N.Y. Scene (whereas, for example, *Sun*, *Full Court*, and *Kulchur* Presses do)

How would you change the N.Y. Scene, if you had three wishes?
(Short answer.)

Is N.Y. still the center of the universe?

The "language poetry" phenomenon has one foot in N.Y., which seems proper, the latter being the modern-day Babel. As a lot of us have flirted and more with that sort of writing and continue to be as interested in language as we are in the striving depicted world, would you feel it proper to comment on those of our colleagues in N.Y. who have given themselves over to language without fear?

Is "criticism" a part of the N.Y. Scene?

Is the *N. Y. Review of Books? The N. Y. Times Book Review? N. Y. Magazine?*

Is the continuation of gentrification, "sliver" buildings, condo and co-op conversion, and cynical design?

Speaking of criticism which is a sensitive and important issue, does whatever you said above about it constitute a plea for a more informed and aware response to what's going on in poetry *now*, a profound disappointment at the missed opportunities in the widely read organs, missed opportunities for *poetry* is what I mean, its health, distribution, and ability to excite?

Do you ride the subways to work? how many taxis do you take in a month? do you believe in commuting? do you walk to poetry readings? are there too many readings in this area so that the idea has lost something essential? can there never be enough readings? should poets be helped to produce poetry? do you believe in poetry on the page? is it significant that Schuyler wasn't noticed nationally until well into his fifties? do you think there will be, or is there currently, an Ashbery backlash? is O'Hara likely to go down in history as a Major poet? does the *New Yorker* emanate secretly from Connecticut? does what poets in N.Y. do to earn $ say anything significant about the N.Y. Scene? does anyone in England care about any of these?
(Answer in order.)

What about Third World poetry in N.Y.?

I keep having the feeling that this scene business is fundamentally elusive, essentially so, that it looks different to everyone who looks at it. It probably has to do with age as much as poetics. When you're starting and come here from the Midwest (or The New School) it's one thing, when you've sat through a thousand readings and resented a thousand bookstores for not stocking what you think is important, it's another. Let's title this Disillusion-ment of the Eighties. I know a lot of people *don't* feel that way. It's interesting. Frances (LeFevre) really was someone in a position to have an overview. We should dedicate this to her. I didn't entirely go along with her taste, of course, it was somewhat over on the conventional side in spite of everything, but she was properly removed from each specific scene and somehow clearly saw it as well. This is off-topic. The question is, to what extent does commenting on a poetry scene produce that scene which, until that point, didn't quite exist?

Is this too long already?

Let's return to the Art world/poetry world connection. I assume everyone gives lip service to that. Name some real ways in which the N.Y. poetry scene is as it is because of the way the N.Y. art scene is (not necessarily direct influence, such as, though it's certainly true for some, having painters for friends and lovers causes one to see things in other ways, try to do similar things with words—though *not* to paint with them). Jimmy (S.) titled his short prose piece for the poetics section of the Allen anthology "Poet and Painter Overture"; Ashbery's the art critic and writer of masterpieces such as *Self-Portrait in a Convex Mirror*; O'Hara wrote, curated, mentioned, hung out with, adored; Koch was and is extremely close to; Edwin Denby and Barbara Guest similarly. And of our "younger" poets, Berkson, Berrigan, Padgett, Ratcliffe, Schjeldahl, Yau, Yourgrau, Towle, Shapiro, Welish, Lauterbach, Greenwald, me, you, and others. Writers have married painters, gone on vacation tours with them, enjoyed a cool glass of beer on a sweltering day in front of the N.Y. traffic while talking about everything under the poetic sun. John Yau was and for all I know still is a housepainter. So in one sense, one (rather large, it's true) group keeps alive the poetry/painting connections. Oops, forgot the other way around too, Rivers, Katz, Motherwell, Dine, Freilicher, Winkfield, Bluhm, Guston, Jacquette, Schneeman, Paula North, Dash, Jean Holabird, etc. etc. What about other groups? This isn't what I mean. I mean what Schuyler was, essentially, talking about: the air we breathe. I see it for better and for worse, worse meaning, these days if not before, the Business of Art, the Business of the Meteoric, as well as those other problems tossed off above; better meaning the desire of every poet to do something as beautiful as some of the paintings we see around us every day. And the sense that art is important, part of the scheme of things, easy, or easier, for painters to feel nowadays—the actual importance if any of Schnabel, Salle, et al., being a whole other issue—than for poets to feel. Or is that a wild understatement? So Art, art acts as a kind of emotional resource, the business management side of the

Muse, as well as whatever it performs in the way of specific and general cross-influences, inspirations, and the like. What was the question?

Would you like to reject those questions you feel are too frivolous? Does frivolity have something essential to do with the N.Y. Scene?

For, we know that some poets from more rural, or less frenzied, areas of the country think that New York poets (by which they mean, more or less, the amplified N.Y. School) are, by virtue of being in the grip of the "artificial and curtailed life," subject to a decadence that forces them to the peripheries of life, poetry and the American Way. Don't we?

Speaking of art, why isn't music, N.Y. being a "world-class" concert hall, more important to the N.Y. poetry scene than it is? Or is it? Consider rock, punk, Cage, Thomson, poet/instrumentalists, aspirations towards the condition of music, the poetic equivalent of Muzak, the Drones, hymns to intellectual beauty.

I'm running out of gas, in case you hadn't noticed. Time to end, or go to your questions, or get my typewriter, the manual, fixed. It broke down after page 1 of this, and I see now that the questions got less coherent after I switched to the electric portable, some sort of comment on technology, which brings up a slew of further considerations regarding the influence of environment upon city attitudes, like winter sunlight on an otherwise disengaged scene.

What about "subject matter"?

Be sure to reread your answers.

CHARLES NORTH
JANUARY 1983

TALKING WITH RED GROOMS
AN INTERVIEW BY ANNE WALDMAN

OCTOBER 1984   NO. 108

ANNE WALDMAN: Now say that again.

RED GROOMS: I think that maybe in the twenty-first century there'll be a total
reaction against the twentieth century, and maybe the nineteenth century
will be featured as a star.

AW: Why would that be?

RG: Out of perverseness. Pure perversity. I think that the twentieth century
condemned the nineteenth century until very recently, until the last decade—
and only half of that. And just looking at it in this Bobby Rosenblum's book
[*Nineteenth-Century Art* by Robert Rosenblum and H. W. Janson], it looks
terrific. First of all, it has emotion and sentiment which had largely been out-
lawed, and what's wrong with it? Nothing's wrong with it!

AW: You mean the sensuality?

RG: Yeah. Sensuality and sentiment.

AW: How sentiment?

RG: Romance close to insanity. Really, it's like some of the stuff you just can't
even place into context from a twentieth-century point of view. There is cer-
tain psychological portraiture that looks so off the wall you really have to go
back into literature very deeply. I wouldn't be able to even replace the parts.

I think the two centuries are largely an antithesis of each other and the twentieth century has been a reaction to the nineteenth but the twenty-first will accept that art. How about the acceptance of nineteenth-century literature which may be even more difficult to take in some ways than the art or probably equally as hard?

AW: Well, there are the geniuses: Whitman, Poe, Melville, Dickinson.

RG: Right. But they seem to be modernists like Manet. The Impressionists and so forth seem to be modernists.

AW: They're on the edge.

RG: So I'm really talking about the more radical elements, the elements that were outside, that show the modernist elements of the century. For instance, Rosenblum introduces in this book, in the back, modern paintings. And I personally feel they are a little bit out of place. They feel somehow not "with it" in a way, whereas the real nineteenth-century sentimental stuff seems "right."

AW: Why do you think that would be, because people are more in touch with experience?

RG: I honestly think these trends are a perverseness of human nature.

AW: Who starts that?

RG: In the lifeblood of every civilization these trends seem to extend from the lively thinkers, people that are very alive and thinking about how things look or sound or read.

AW: As a lively thinker yourself you seem to be encompassing quite a range of possibilities, sentimental and otherwise in the paint, ink, and construction and film of this recent show (Marlborough, April 6–May 1), from Geishas to a Yellow Pages construction of Franz Kline to satirical political portraits of Arafat, or "Night of the Generals" which reminds me of Burroughs with its hard satirical bite. Could you talk about your "place" as an artist, how you see it?

RG: Well, I thought that in order to get to a personal "voice" that I wasn't totally "with" the whole concept of modernism as it went on concurrently with—you know—current contemporariness. And so that looking back to any other time or to the nineteenth century (which were the first paintings I knew) was okay. I don't know what it was, but I had preferred that kind of offhand view to going along with the modernist line.

AW: But wasn't it more life itself? Like getting out and strolling down 14th Street, or experiencing a traffic jam . . .

RG: Yeah! Yeah, that's right. Sometimes actual life. People don't necessarily look modern. They just look like a glob of humanity and they may not look slick and fashionable and if so, you have to respond accordingly. As neither does the ocean. The ocean to me looks very nineteenth century. It was probably painted best in that century.

AW: Sometimes after a big dose of your work I'll walk onto 57th Street or whatever and I'm still in a Red Grooms world. Which is what happens when you experience any powerful visuals. Like Fellini, the work opens your eyes, stretches the imagination so you really see reality more intensely—the extremes which are not really exaggerations—facial expressions, a gesture, a wild hairdo. Your perceptions are brilliant, original but also *true*.

RG: But you actually do see my work in it?

AW: In the people most—in their gait, clothing, preoccupations, their colorfulness. Rudy Burckhardt gets some of those humorous qualities—human aspects—in his films.

RG: But I think that what makes me an impure artist or maybe not an artist at all is that I'm totally fascinated with people, and I'm more into the personage than trying to make whatever it is—that sawdust-filled bag of bones or whatever. That's what interests me—that whole psychology. But I love art and I like the formalist stuff and everything of other artists.

AW: Well, you have some of that, too.

RG: But when I'm doing it myself I'm so magnetized by the human psychology. And I enjoy being a voyeur and I really like to try to figure people out and so forth. I've been totally knocked off track by other human beings. At any moment there are powers of persuasion that are overwhelming. In the New York works I've done I have tried to make it a kind of portraiture thing where I was really trying to get the texture of what I thought I saw, particularly in the neurosis of the population, and present it in context with the props—the mailboxes, fireplugs, any texture of the city. I took on certain projects like Bronx and Manhattan because I had a strong vision I couldn't help seeing, feeling.

AW: The subway car is powerful—desperate and amazing.

RG: I don't actually try to make things worse than I think they are. It often surprises me how strongly people react to it. It makes me see it differently too. Almost naively you make a distortion here and there and the impact is terrific on people.

AW: I feel comfortable in the subway.

RG: I always think about New York that it ranks as a world city probably because it's an unself-conscious place and a place of great vitality. The ugliness is not controlled. It's really a sort of bile.

AW: It's organic.

RG: Right. Most American cities can't vie with that because for some reason or other there's a tendency in the States to clean things up. Maybe its proximity to the incoming migrant groups keeps it raw. They can't be overdigested. There's an urgency to life in the city. I live in Chinatown and at this very moment, I can't believe it, there are women out there wearing coolie hats! The tourists should come down and look at this! This is really China, coming to the States, right at this very moment! Every day it's really something. And I think that's great because the worst is the whole prefabricated sort of phoniness where you go somewhere and they have to fabricate the color of the place. In New York you don't have to make that effort.

AW: You talk of New York as being raw and the neurosis being obvious and yet there's a veneer or patina in how people adorn themselves, or hide or cover themselves, and those choices too are incredibly interesting and wild and strange.

RG: It's really the presentation of a true culture, a culture that has not really digested itself yet and is actually in the process of living. I've been to Paris and Paris is great and of course is a great world city and I'd thought at some point, some time ago, that I was too late, and then very much more recently I've looked and I saw, oh, it's fantastic. It's *now*. So I guess a city, an urban place somehow is the repository of humanity, is certainly the register of the culture. And I love Tokyo for the same reason.

AW: Back to the recent work. How about the icons as contrasted to the man or woman-on-the-street characters—the new paintings/constructions of Keaton, Mae West? Are these key figures for you? They're so American and theatrical as works.

RG: Well, it's interesting you call them icons because sometimes I think the only thing I'm interested in is the figure—the bust and head. You think you're putting a lot of imagination into something and basically it's just, as you say, an icon.

AW: It's the contrast to the ordinary caricature.

RG: This is more *still*. It's frozen. I did the Keaton because I was on Martha's Vineyard and I felt like I had "island fever" or something. I felt the lack of a bigger flow of events. We went to see some Keaton films and I did it.

AW: So it would be that simple, seeing a film—

RG: I saw Mae West, too. The bust of Keaton—the building part, the architectural part—had to do with the kind of gingerbread houses in a town called Oak Bluff that's on Martha's Vineyard. The other character in the piece—Ulysses S. Grant—had come there when he was President. I had seen a history book on the area and was impressed that a President had been in this funny town. He'd made a personal appearance or something. It had been a Methodist town, but it was also a blue-collar resort for Boston. I felt I should do something with the gingerbread and wasn't sure exactly what and that's what it turned out to be. That picture. I'd also been reading about Alexander the Great and that's his image on the medallion on the top left corner and Darius, the Persian King, is leading his hordes of elephants on the other side. It has some literary origins. Also I'd discovered a biography of Lauren Bacall which is why she's on there.

TRANSLATION AS PUZZLE AND PERFORMANCE
AN INTERVIEW WITH PAUL SCHMIDT
BY TIM DLUGOS

DECEMBER 1984   NO. 110

Paul Schmidt, who will read his translations at The Poetry Project on December 12, is a full-time translator. His translation of Arthur Rimbaud's collected writing was published in 1980. Today, he's working on a new project—a translation of the complete works of the Russian poet Velimir Khlebnikov. Schmidt has recently begun to translate poems by Pier Paolo Pasolini. His own poems, a new outgrowth of his work as a translator, have recently appeared in *Shenandoah*. Tim Dlugos conducted this interview at Schmidt's apartment in the West Village.

TIM DLUGOS: What's your current project?

PAUL SCHMIDT: My current project is an ongoing project that's been going for the last four years, actually: a commission to translate into English from Russian the complete works of a Russian poet named Velimir Khlebnikov. He is a fascinating poet, a contemporary of Mayakovsky. He was born in 1885 and died in 1922 and is a major figure of Russian and world poetry, but his poetry is very much locked into the language, and for that reason he's scarcely been translated at all, and is really still for most Russians a fairly inaccessible figure. He was a mathematician and sort of a Futurist, conceiving of his work as opening up the future. He wrote a lot, five volumes, and

I'm committed to translating it all. Harvard University is going to publish it; the first volume will be a volume of selections, a kind of introduction to Khlebnikov. There will follow in the next few years about three other volumes.

TD: How are you going about unlocking Khlebnikov's work from the Russian language?

PS: It fascinated me precisely because it posed very serious problems in translation, and made me really rethink what the process of translating poetry is all about. What could you conceivably call translation and what couldn't you; how could you expand the notion? So when he writes a poem that's based on neologisms, various fantastic permutations of a Russian root, how do you go about it? One of the things I've done is to go back and look at Old English and related languages, for example Frisian and older Germanic languages that are very closely related to English, to look at archaic forms of things, because the effect in Russian is very archaic, to look at what might produce the same effect in English.

TD: Do you do that kind of excavation and then use the archaic word itself?

PS: Not the word itself, but in a sense make up my own words basing them on similar forms in the older varieties of English. The one poem I'm thinking about is the one that Khlebnikov is probably best known for, "Incantation by Laughter." He takes the Russian word *smekh*, which means "laughter," and makes up words by using prefixes and suffixes and infixes, which Russian does rather easily. In that one, I went through a number of possible ways of translating, and then started to do this excavating. So that's one possibility. His work varies enormously stylistically, which in a sense makes it difficult. A lot of the early stuff is oriented toward the Russian language and his Slavic background; and the later stuff is international Modernist poetry, of a kind we recognize. He was very influenced, for example, by Walt Whitman, and so you see a very long line, which is unusual in Russian. And then a lot of it is more traditionally metric Russian. But his stuff has variations on meter and irregular meters and line lengths. That's another problem because in Russian, that's rather unusual. Russian poetry is based on very strict form, and the traditional meters of Russian poetry are used to this day conventionally and constantly. So when Khlebnikov distorts them, in Russian it's fairly strong. But when you translate it into American poetry, where we've gotten rid of any sort of conventional metric system at all over the last 85 years, that effect falls flat. So how do you work with that? There are a lot of challenges with it. It drives me crazy sometimes. But I'm learning a lot about poetry, and for me, that's the most valuable thing. It makes me sit down every day and have to consider a lot of very technical questions.

TD: How is the experience different from translating from the French of Rimbaud?

PS: The first difference is that I did the Rimbaud a long time ago. I started doing that when I was 22, and worked at it off and on for about twelve years. This is another part of my life. But as far as the technical difference, with Rimbaud the biggest problem, as always with French, is to deal with the extremely cognate vocabulary; that is, French and English share an enormous number of words whose form is identical but whose pronunciation is different. Often the meanings differ considerably and certainly the poetic effect differs. I had done a lot of the Rimbaud when I had to go back through it and realize that these words are often the wrong choices. Sometimes you can get a kind of Frenchified style, too. With the Rimbaud, there was again the problem that Rimbaud distorted seriously all the rules of French prosody, and out of it he invented the prose poem. The effect in French is quite striking, because historically in French poetry prosody is fairly fixed, certainly in the nineteenth century. How do you achieve that effect in English, where the prose poem doesn't even exist? I mean, we have poetic prose, but the whole notion of a prose poem doesn't have the resonance that it does in French; the background is missing. It's funny; for both Rimbaud and Khlebnikov, there are a lot of links, but the major one that's very helpful in translating is that Whitman was an extraordinary influence on both poets. Rimbaud, in fact, developed his line from reading Whitman in translation, and Khlebnikov developed his from reading Whitman in translation. So there's an American resonance to both poets that for me is very interesting. That's a great connection. A lot of translation is simply the notion of a problem for which there is a more or less elegant solution, almost in the sense of a fancy crossword puzzle or a chess problem. The object is to find the most elegant solution.

TD: How faithful do you feel you need to be to the original structure of a poem?

PS: I don't think you can make any hard and fast rule; at least, I'm not able to make one now, and the times when I've set them I've always come a cropper. My feeling is that every poem poses unique problems that have to be resolved in terms of the poem itself. It does make a difference when you're translating the complete works of a poet, or a major chunk of a poet's work. Then there's a certain internal consistency to find and maintain. Very importantly on the level of lexicon, certain poets use certain words and they mean certain things for that poet, they have a certain resonance that's uniquely theirs. There it's very important to find equivalents for those key words that will have the same resonance in English, or for which you can create the same resonance in English. But in terms of the formal problems any given poem poses . . . I guess to generalize, I'd begin by saying, in what way do the formal qualities of this poem mark themselves off from the language as a whole? How, within the linguistic and cultural tradition of the Russian, say, does this poem stand? And then, to try to say what formal qualities in English would give you the same relationship. For instance, if a poem has end rhymes in the original, is it a pattern that's recognizable in English? If you have a poem that in the original is iambic pentameter in rhymed quatrains, ABAB quatrains, it's a familiar pattern in English. So the problem is, will an English poem in that form give you the same historical resonance that the original does? Sometimes it won't; sometimes it will look too old-fashioned. For example, translating contemporary Russian poetry, where iambic tetrameter in ABAB quatrains is a constant form, if you translate that into English there's nothing contemporary about that at all; it sounds as if it were written fifty years ago, or it can. So you have to vary. Russian, for example, has very regular metrical patterns, stress patterns; where English, by the nature of English, has to distort; that's where you get the effect. So you have to play with it. And then, beyond the formal concerns, you have to find the ... internal consistency of the poem? What I mean is this: for me, translation is a performance. I mean that almost the same way you'd say it about an actor's performance. You're given a text to perform. The text exists on the page. Your responsibility is to transform it; that is, to take a given form and to make it resonate, to bring it alive, in whatever way possible. You have the same leeway and the same constraints that an actor does. And you're called upon in the same way an actor is to create a character. For example, first in Rimbaud and now with Khlebnikov, it's a matter of trying to think what's in that person's head, what was their life like, what elements in their life can you identify with in your own. Always identify, never compare.

TD: Do you really think that that biographical aspect is very important; getting into another person's cultural skin?

PS: I think so; and I don't mean by that some kind of naturalistic Stanislavskian recreation of the character's everyday existence. But I mean the cultural ambiance, and the person's vision of the world. How do they conceive of language? How did they see themselves relating to the world through language? Did they see their language as part of the rest of the language, as cut apart from it, as something private and personal, as something that they had to share? Did they see the entire wealth of their language, dialects and all, as grist for the mill, or did they select very carefully? Have I read the same books they did? That's very important, you always try to find out the reading list in translation. So once you're doing translation, it's sort of a job of literary criticism, because you do some of the same job to analyze the text. Where did it come from? How did they get it? What did they do with what they had?

TD: What you're talking about is much more than the text; it's an exhaustive, if not reliving, then reconstruction of a life.

PS: That was certainly the case with me for Rimbaud, and now in a different mode, with Khlebnikov. There was a point where I was real crazy and thought I *was* Rimbaud, and ran around literally trying to recreate his life. But that certainly gets in the way of poetry. But with the Khlebnikov, it's more a matter of knowing everything I can about his life, the times he lived in, going to Moscow and looking at the places where he lived, visiting people who knew him, his family, for instance. I was very lucky in that my old teacher Roman Jakobson was a good friend of Khlebnikov and Mayakovsky. In fact, I first heard of Khlebnikov through Jakobson. And he would recite poems of Khlebnikov's in the same intonation as Khlebnikov, saying, "This is how I remember Khlebnikov saying this poem." He died about three years ago. But when this whole project came up, the first thing I did was to go up to Cambridge to see him. I said, "Look, they've proposed to me to translate Khlebnikov. What do you think? Is it crazy or should I do it?" "Do it, do it," he said. "No matter what happens, to give Khlebnikov a greater resonance than his voice has now is worth it." Mayakovsky, too . . . I'll be doing readings from Mayakovsky at St. Mark's, and those come from Jakobson. He said, "This is the way Mayakovsky sounded." When I translate Mayakovsky, who was a great reader of his own verse, there the idea of performance is very important, because I translate to perform them myself. It has to sound right, has to get the same acoustic effect that I know the Russian did because I remember Jakobson doing it.

THE COLORS OF CONSONANCE

BERNADETTE MAYER TALKS ABOUT HER NEW BOOK, HER HISTORY, WORKSHOPS, DICTIONARIES, SEX, POLITICS, AND SEEING COLORS

WITH KEN JORDAN

OCTOBER/NOVEMBER 1992   NO. 146

Reviewing *A Bernadette Mayer Reader* in the *San Francisco Chronicle*, Tom Clark called the author a "semi-deity," a description which likely rings true. The publication of the *Reader* provided an excuse to sit with the semi-deity, drink a few beers, turn on the tape recorder, and ask questions. Let's pick up at the point when she told me, with total sincerity, that she is not an opinionated person.

KEN JORDAN: *You're* not an opinionated person?

BERNADETTE MAYER: This is my new stance.

KJ: Since when?

BM: This summer. But I'm assuming I never was. Or I'm hoping.

KJ: How did you come to this startling realization?

BM: I think it's just sensible not to be. But I said this to someone recently and he said, But we *like* your opinions! (*laughs*) Of course, I don't mean about everything. It just doesn't make sense to have opinions about poetry to me anymore. What is the necessity of an opinion?

KJ: Even about *[name of prize-winning poet]*?

BM: Uh-oh! We're poet-bashing now. (*laughs*)

KJ: What was the last really exciting experience you had when reading? I mean extreme, powerful experience, like when you discovered Gertrude Stein?

BM: Well, that doesn't happen so much any more. Does it? Reading Gerard Rizza's poems.

KJ: When *did* you first read Stein?

BM: I know that in 1965 I hadn't read Gertrude Stein. I hadn't even heard of her. This is the funny old story where I was taking Bill Berkson's poetry workshop at The New School. I was a matriculating undergraduate. The government was paying me to go to school, and that was the only reason I was there, because at that point in time they had a thing for orphans where if you stayed in school they paid you $99 a month, which was my rent! So even though I had a nine-to-five job—just like *you* (*with venom*)—I went to school at night. And I had to do it quick because the money ran out when you were 21, 22. Anyway, I gave Bill some writing at one point in that class, and he commented that I was reading too much Gertrude Stein. And I had never read her and never heard of her! So I guess it was shortly after that that I started reading her work.

KJ: Why do you think he said that about your work?

BM: Because I was writing funny things. *I am remembering that I am becoming* . . . you know. I was using a lot of gerunds.

KJ: What was the first Stein you remember reading?

BM: I think one of the first things was *Tender Buttons*, and *Lectures in America*. And then I read *The Making of Americans* shortly after that, which was amazing. I was reading a lot of huge books at the time. The year previous to my returning to school I read all the books that I'd never read but that I wanted to read at that point. All of James Joyce's writing, and *The Cantos*, William Carlos Williams . . . all the *men*! That's all I knew. I spent a year reading all those books because I realized I'd never learned anything in school, except for a little Greek and Latin, and I had one wonderful English teacher, Sister Immaculata, in high school. I learned about poetry from her.

KJ: When you read Stein, did you think Bill Berkson was right?

BM: Yeah, I did. And I was thrilled that there was this writer existing in the world. I started imitating her as much as I possibly could. For a long time I did that, I would write blatant imitations and give them to Bill. One of them is called "Portrait of Mable Dodging the Village Curé." I was really happy that he had that knowledge. He was very sophisticated; he was twenty-six at the time.

KJ: So how did you get to "Corn" from here? You once told me that when you were younger "Corn" was your greatest hit.

BM: Does "Story" come in the book before "Corn"? It does? You know that's wrong.

KJ: Chronologically?

BM: Yeah. It's funny that I did that. It doesn't give a date for "Story"? Gee, what a conniver I am secretly unconsciously being. I guess I wanted "Story" to begin the book. See, the section called Early Poems includes poems that go for a number of years, some of which were written after "Story." But "Corn" was written when I was 19, although most of those strange . . . language poems? (*laughs*) No. Erase that. Don't say language poems . . . They were written when I was 19, that year I was reading all the Joyce. So it's before Gertrude Stein. "François Villon Follows the Thin Lion" and all those works were written before that.

KJ: Really? But you dedicated that poem to Bill Berkson . . .

BM: Yeah, but only after the fact. See, a lot of the dedications I put in the book . . . I figured if I'm going to have this beautiful book that spans a period of time, I want to put a lot of dedications into it. That poem in particular was never published before this book, but it was written in Bill's workshop. Bill had given us an assignment to somehow explain to us what distortion is in poetry. I don't remember what his explanation of what it is was, but as soon as he said the word . . . He actually asked me in class, and I was very shy and didn't like to answer questions (*laughs*) . . . and he made me say what I thought distortion in poetry was, and I said it could be using a lot of very thin letters or using a lot of very fat letters. You know? So then I wrote the poem "François Villon" because it has a lot of *i's* and *l's* in it, but they are also mixed up with a lot of *o's*, and the word "oolfoos" has all those *o's* in it. So the fat letters are really standing out against the thin letters. Right? So it was really inspired by this question, and that's why it's dedicated to him.

KJ: This was still before reading Stein?

BM: Well, it's hard to know. I think I took his class twice.

KJ: What about "Yellow-Orange"? (*quoting:*) "my jig was a sage ear"

BM: Yeah. That was definitely written before I was back in school. It would be interesting to make a pile of the back-in-school poems as opposed to the not-in-school poems, which are probably a lot wilder, in some sense. But at that point in time I was just studying language—when I wasn't reading—as if it were that the letters were objects, and I was beginning to realize that I saw each letter as a particular color, with consistent colors for every letter of the alphabet, and that I had always done this. I never really *knew* before that I had always done this.

KJ: What colors were which letters?

BM: I've drawn the alphabet in all its colors for people, like *A* is red, *B* is pink, *D* is black, *C* . . . I skipped *C*? *C* is sort of yellow, tannish yellow. *E* is green, *F* is bluish gray, *G* is brown . . . and it just goes on! I came to realize that I had been doing this since I was a child, but I never thought everybody didn't do this. Realizing it was just a matter of talking to people and finding that that didn't happen to them.

KJ: And that led you to think more about letters as objects . . .

BM: And shapes. Each word being a particular vision in terms of its shapes and colors. So I was interested in words like "oolfoos," and words like "Salma-gundi," and funny words like that. But I wasn't interested in them for their absence of meaning. I was interested in them as if they were sculptures, physical objects.

KJ: I know it's strange to reconstruct it like this, but what were you thinking when you were writing poems like "Corn" and "Pope John," when so few people were writing in that way.

BM: How did it work? Well, I'd constantly be reading a dictionary while I was writing, and looking at etymologies. So all those things were going on together with the physical aspects of the words and the colors of the letters. It was really like making abstract sculptures or something like that. I mean there was a part of me at that point in time that didn't think I could write a great love poem. I didn't know how to do it.

KJ: Did you try?

BM: I don't think I ever really did. Though when I was even younger, when I was 17, I used to try to write poems about the situation in my household, all the fighting that was taking place between my grandfather and the people who shared my house. So they were more literal kinds of poems, and they're in *Ceremony Latin*, at least the ones I would ever dare show the world. But I didn't think I was a good enough writer, or a knowledgeable enough person, to write about these big, major things. Of course I wanted to write about death too, given my history.

KJ: Your history? (*points to the tape recorder as audience*)

BM: ... of my parents dying when I was so young. They were both dead by the time I was 14, and then my uncle who became my guardian died when I was 17. So it was like a real barrage of death. And I couldn't write about it at all. I mean I guess the normal impulse for someone would be then to write about all those things, right? But I just knew that I didn't have the talent or the skills to do it.

KJ: So "Corn" ...

BM: That's a real dictionary poem. "Corn is small hard seed" comes right out of my dictionary! And then you start wandering a little further up or down in the dictionary from looking up the word "corn," you see the little Corn Islands and things like that. And that's all it is. And I was making up things, like "Corn from Delft / Is good for Elves." But that's somehow etymologically related to some of the surrounding words.

KJ: Did you think about possible readers at all?

BM: Probably not. I mean, I was just practicing. I was apprenticing myself to poetry, I wasn't really thinking about people reading it.

KJ: In the early poems you just wrote down facts you could know with certainty, dictionary definitions, simple fantasy, stuff like that, and you stayed away from writing about more ambiguous emotional experience. How did you walk into writing about your own personal experience?

BM: There's actually a very factual answer to that question . . . That's true, but it wasn't a matter of choice that I didn't write about those other things, really. *Memory* is the ultimate factual book, right? It's all data. I don't get into emotions in *Memory*, really. There wasn't time to keep these journals every day, and to shoot a roll of film as well, and then doing regular things like having a job and eating and sleeping and stuff like that. But after I wrote that book something happened, and I realized that I had gotten on the edge, you know, and I went to see a psychiatrist. And it was through him, actually, that I started writing the other books like *Studying Hunger*. That was written all during the time I was seeing this psychiatrist. He bought me two journals so he could always have one and I could always have one to write in between our sessions. That way he could read what I'd written since the last time we saw each other. I hate this word, but I think he was facilitating *Studying Hunger*. *Memory* was then being published as a book when I was seeing him, and he wrote the little introduction to it, David Rubinfine. I couldn't have written *Studying Hunger* if I hadn't been working with him, I don't think, because I really thought I was an insane person, I was still experiencing such strong responses to my parents' deaths, and stuff like that. And sometimes it would be so overwhelming that I couldn't . . . what couldn't I do? In the end there was nothing I couldn't do, but I couldn't perceive myself as a sane human being. Or whatever. And I always realized that I had been treated weirdly by the people that I knew, or as if I was odd. You know, I said odd things, or . . . I was convinced that I was crazy. And he convinced me that I was not. And in the meanwhile we summoned up all these ghosts. I chose the form for *Studying Hunger* after seeing him for a while.

KJ: What kind of therapy was it?

BM: It was Freudian psychoanalysis! And it was free! He was a friend of my great lover Ed Bowes, they knew each other through the movie business. I said I could pay him $10 a session, or $20. I tried to up the figure as much as possible, but I didn't have any money at the time. Never did, did I? Finally he said, that's ridiculous, accepting $10 from you would be meaningless to me, and probably difficult for you, so let's just do it for free. I saw him for five years.

KJ: It was also in the early '70s that you led the infamous workshop at St. Mark's which had much to do with the development of the notorious Language movement.

BM: That workshop started in 1971 and it lasted for four years, until '75, and I encountered the people who'd eventually start the Language school around '72. Charles Bernstein, Peter Seaton, Nick Piombino, Bruce Andrews, and some others were in that workshop. It was the first workshop I ever gave at St. Mark's, and I was terrified of teaching. I was only 26 and didn't think I could teach anything, or conduct a workshop either, so I did a tremendous amount of over-preparing, if there is such a thing. I gave two workshops: one about the Dadaists, and one about Wittgenstein. Then there were people coming to the workshop saying, shouting at me from the back of the room, What does *Wittgenstein* have to do with poetry?

KJ: When the young Language folks were in the workshop, what was the dynamic like?

BM: It was great. It was over that period of years that we made the experiments list. Then, after a while, the workshop became a true collaboration. The very last year that I was doing it I wasn't even doing it anymore. We had a rotating leadership, so that every week somebody in the workshop would do something else. People came up with different experiments, and it would go on for four or five hours. We talked a lot about theory, Jacques Lacan, semiotics, and stuff like that. Though theory didn't have much to do with the way I had evolved as a writer, I was very interested in all those things. They were much more interesting then than they are at the moment, you know.

KJ: Turning back to the *Reader*, after selections from *Studying Hunger* are poems like "Carlton Fisk is My Ideal" and "Eve of Easter." Did you make a deliberate decision to try and to write a poem in which one speaks about one's emotions in a more conventional sense?

BM: Yeah. Those poems were influenced by other writers I was reading at the time. I was very interested in the idea that such a thing as clarity could exist in a poem, and that maybe at that point in time I was capable of creating some clarity in my work. (*laughs*) When I was writing these poems was when I was called a failed experimentalist by . . . I'm not going to tell you who! But that hit me kind of hard. Also, I was very close to Clark Coolidge by then, and at that point we were both working in very different directions. And Clark . . . I don't think he hated these poems, but he was getting a little worried: what was I doing this kind of writing for? (*laughs*)

KJ: During that first workshop at St. Mark's I assume the issue of "clarity" and "sincere expression" came up for discussion.

BM: At that point in time, everybody was trying to avoid doing it. But I always assumed that eventually, someday, that I *would learn how* to do it. But most people were trying to avoid that as practically anathema . . . That's why I like to have no opinions. (*chuckle*) One of the responses to the *Reader* that I've gotten from people is that they like the variousness of the kinds of writing that are in it. I think everybody must know this already—I hope they do— that one person can write in many different ways. You can even do them all in one night! The great thing about accumulating practice and time as a writer is that you reach a point where you can do *many* things. I get that really thrilling feeling when I'm writing that there are many things possible, and it's especially fun to approach writing completely blankly—and then see what happens.

KJ: Jordan asked me to keep this interview to about 1,500 words, and we're already past 2,500, but I wanted to include something about the *Sonnets* . . .

BM: Lee Ann Brown wanted to publish a book, but she didn't know *what* book, so I started to go through the poems again and I realized that I had been writing the sonnets all the time. How I got involved in writing them is probably through Catullus, even though Catullus never wrote any sonnets, as far as we know. But because of his way of expressing things in poems there always was a structure that involved a conclusion of some kind. I don't think I like any of the poets of the past who wrote sonnets, do I? Oh, of course I do. Paul Goodman. He writes the most amazing sonnets. That was a thing that inspired me to write them too, and here are Paul Goodman and Catullus always writing about sex. Sex works really well in the sonnet form. And of course Shakespeare, we don't have to mention him, but another sex poet. Before I even realized I was writing sonnets I had rewritten some of Shakespeare's sonnets to my own liking, you know, changing some of the "master of my passion" to, in my sonnet, at very least into the "master/mistress." Sonnets always seemed interesting just because of the way they let you think within the poem. Sonnets permit you to think in a way that other poems might not. You couldn't think in the same way given another really strict form. You don't think in a sestina the way you think in a sonnet. I like the idea of fooling around with the question of beginnings and middles and endings, those concepts one always hates in writing, especially in fiction, and the sonnet has them. The traditional form of the sonnet is to set up the scene, and then develop it in the middle, and come to a conclusion in the end couplet. And that's really stupid. That's not the way we think; but it is structurally fascinating to do it. To not do it while also doing it. I'm not sure how that's done, but if you're always aware that you're doing that, and you're not doing it at the same time ... As soon as I published the *Sonnets*, I started getting letters from all these funny places inviting me to be in something like a new formalist anthology. They just want to seize on anybody who writes sonnets, and they don't realize what the *Sonnets* really are is not that at all. I sent some to one, but I think they rejected them. Women formalists, something like that. A *real* minority.

KJ: You've never been aggressive about pushing your work. Over the years, it seemed that whenever you had the chance to publish with a more established publisher, instead of sending the politically considered manuscript of poems meant for the largest audience, you'd tend to send 500-page single-spaced journals.

BM: (*laughs*) That's ended my relationship with many publishers! But I usually send the thing that I want most to be published at that moment. And when I went through all my manuscripts for New Directions, I decided that at this moment the thing I want most to be published are the complete *Studying Hunger Journals*, which of course are all prose—400 some odd pages.

KJ: Single-spaced?

BM: No ... well, parts are! And on legal-sized paper! But Barbara Epler at New Directions and I agreed beforehand that there was no chance in the world that they would do that.

KJ: But in the past you thought that other publishers would?

BM: Well, yeah. Because ... why did I think that? Well, why not? But Barbara and I agreed that this book would be something like a selected works. You see, that's what I've learned. Because when I responded to Barbara's first request I said I'll send you a list of possible manuscripts, and you decide which one you think is most likely to get published. So I'm very mellow now. (*laughs*)

KJ: We're almost at the end of the interview and we've barely touched upon politics and sex.

BM: And money.

KJ: Can great poetry change the world?

BM: I've been told that I'm a fool to believe that, but I do ... I noticed when I was looking at the bluelines of the *Reader* that I never put in the more strongly political poems, and perhaps one of the reasons for that is they're tremendously dated. They don't seem to work anymore. So that's something I don't think I've learned how to do yet—write a really effective political poem. Unless the nature of the poems *themselves* could be political, which apparently it does seem to some people.

TAKING RISKS SERIOUSLY
DAVID RATTRAY TALKS ABOUT THE WORTHWHILE LIFE, FLYING THROUGH THE AIR, SOME INVISIBLE VIRTUES OF RECEIVED CLASSICS, AND A ROOM FULL OF IRAQI CAB DRIVERS WITH KEN JORDAN

FEBRUARY/MARCH 1993   NO. 148

Poet and translator David Rattray has been an almost legendary figure since City Lights published his translations in the ubiquitous *Artaud Anthology* of the mid-'60s. He is certainly one of our most knowledgeable—it would be fair to say "learned" and "erudite"—scholars on the dissolute wing of the avant-garde; which, of course, includes some of its most vital practitioners. His collected stories and essays, *How I Became One of the Invisible*, has recently been issued by Semiotext(e), and it was on the occasion of that publication that we met in his Alphabet City apartment.

KEN JORDAN: Were this a *People* magazine interview, at some point you'd be asked: just how does one become one of the invisible?

DAVID RATTRAY: "One of the invisible" really means a member of the invisible secret Utopia. It means somebody who is in this world but not really of this world. It is the antithesis of what they vulgarly call exposure.

KJ: Invisible to whom?

DR: Invisible to whatever that is reflected in the glaring eye that gives you

exposure, such as Channel 5, the NEA, and publications and trade publishers and a review in the *New York Times* . . .

KJ: They used to call this the underground.

DR: One of the first really good books that I ever read was given to me by my grandmother, who wanted to pass something good along to me: Ralph Ellison's *Invisible Man*. But that doesn't have anything directly to do with being somebody that would have been an underground artist thirty years ago.

KJ: Maybe it does.

DR: Maybe it does.

KJ: You can see where it might.

DR: If I'd never had any kind of education I probably would have ended up being some sort of an outsider artist in a jail or an insane asylum making cartoons with little texts . . .

KJ: If you hadn't had an education?

DR: But because I did have an education I didn't just reject the whole thing wholesale and say that every one of the professors and all the received classics was just a crock, what many of my respected contemporaries did. I didn't do that at all. Rather, I found in the works of many of the accepted and received classics that they had something valuable, beautiful, and real to communicate that was definitively worth listening to. So I found that my definition of the invisible could be enlarged to include figures such as John Hall Wheelock, a poet writing in a late nineteenth-century vein, who I quote in the book. A man like that is also part of the underground. Not every one of them has to be on the lam!

KJ: You were an undergraduate at Dartmouth?

DR: I went to the Classics Department there, and we read very intensively in Greek and Latin literature. I worked on that a lot, so it got into my blood and my bones. I read it to this day. But the one who brought it all together for me in the end was a wild man named Jack Hirschman, who is still well known as a poet.

KJ: He was a professor there?

DR: He was an instructor in the English department. He didn't do too well there because he wasn't just an academic, but with the students he did really well because he was a wonderful man, a fireball of energy, and he had all these great things for us to read.

KJ: Like what?

DR: Like John Wieners, for starters. Like Malcolm Lowry, Jean Genet, and William Burroughs. We'd never heard of these things. We got our initiation from Jack Hirschman. Artaud . . . I was sent to Artaud by Jack Hirschman. It was like living in the Book of Revelations.

KJ: And then where did that send you?

DR: It sent me straight to the wilds of Southern Mexico, where this poet friend, Van Buskirk, and I had a plan to smuggle vast quantities of marijuana into the United States. And we thought we would be able to live off the proceeds from selling it. It was like that movie, *The Treasure of the Sierra Madre*. It had a comically pathetic ending. We didn't get busted. We succeeded in bringing into this country something like a half a pound—some wretched amount—of rather mediocre Mexican pot. It didn't amount to a hill of beans! We brought that in at the risk of life and limb. I mean, not only did we expose ourselves to being murdered by Mexican gangsters or the police. We were friends with our landlord, the police commander where we lived. And he was a raving maniac, a very interesting man, a dope addict—I described him in great detail in the book. But if we hadn't been killed in that fashion, we had the US Immigration, the Customs Service, and the Texas Rangers to overcome.

KJ: Did you go straight from Dartmouth to Mexico?

DR: I first went from Dartmouth to France for two years on a Fulbright Fellowship, and I got a degree from the Sorbonne. I took it seriously and did well, I really learned a lot.

KJ: What were you studying?

DR: Still Latin and Greek, and we did some French studies, like Flaubert.

KJ: So the standard classics . . .

DR: Exactly. They were the received classics. But while I was there a poet named Harold Norse introduced me to the reading of William Burroughs. I've never met Burroughs, but I've read and admired him since 1958. Harold Norse gave me his copy of *Naked Lunch*, and I read it in one night, and it completely changed my life.

KJ: Why would you say that?

DR: Well, it gave me a whole perception of what is real and what is unreal, involving our culture and the things we were striving for. Burroughs had a very clear perception of that. He often used to think of how certain substances, both the standard ones like heroin and cocaine, and various mysterious other ones like yage in South America, and so on, have that specific ability to kill the editor that's in there in your optic nerves that prevents you from actually seeing things as they really are. Burroughs was always a visually oriented guy, and so for him it's always what you *see*. He was literally a *visionary* and a *seer*. So he's thinking about what you see. And, obviously, 99 percent of what we see isn't really what's there. The editor that's in the optic nerve and other places in the brain that's receiving signals is sort of fudging things to help us survive, to cope better. But because it helps us cope, it also conceals from us the true nature of what we're looking at. There's a barrier between us and reality, and Burroughs was extremely keen on breaking down that barrier, and peeling away that dirty film between us and reality. And time and again he was thinking of heroin and various other things as ways to get rid of the affective garbage between us and what we really see. *Naked Lunch* and *The Soft Machine*, these were the first ones that I gravitated towards. And I did gravitate towards them, big time. I was very, very attracted to Burroughs' vision and understanding of things.

KJ: Of course, so much a part of Burroughs' vision has to do with a heavily romanticized vision of life as an outsider, as a gangster . . .

DR: Well, you should have seen me in the early '60s!

KJ: I'm curious . . .

DR: In my black suit. I had this black suit and black wraparound sunglasses, which I wore at all times. The breast pocket of the black suit was for my kit, which held all my drug paraphernalia ... I was really quite a card, moving from one club to another listening to jazz, which was because of Van, who opened my ears to jazz. I embraced that romantic vision wholeheartedly.

KJ: It's a big leap from Dartmouth.

DR: I thought I was just jumping through a hoop that's in mid-air and coming out the other side. I remember it vividly as an experience just like that. You know, the Living Theatre had a thing towards the end of *Paradise Now*, they'd make a human pyramid, and those who dared could climb up onto the top of this pyramid and do a swan dive—it was called flying—and they would just leap off with their arms outspread like wings and fly into the waiting arms clasped together of the people in the audience who were waiting for them to come flying through the air towards the seats.

KJ: Did you jump?

DR: Of course. And flying was exactly what I thought I was doing when I stepped out of the academic world, out of that cocoon, to spread my wings and fly. And it included stepping into a way of living that involved the daily risk of life and limb and the systematic destruction of everything that a middle-class upbringing in East Hampton, Long Island implied, and was supposed to lead to. I was supposed to become a professor of literature at an Ivy League college somewhere, married to a girl that'd come to East Hampton in the summertime, and it was all going to be very nice. My mother couldn't, for the life of her, understand what was wrong. She had no problem with me reading Jean Genet or the Marquis de Sade or Marcel Proust or anybody else, but ...

KJ: She just didn't want you to take it seriously!

DR: Exactly. I could pursue my intellectual interest to my heart's content, but to live in a way that seemed to be implied by the things that really touched me most deeply, and made me feel that this was where I had to go—that was something that I can't blame my mother for not approving of! No one of her class and time could possibly have understood.

KJ: *How I Became One of the Invisible* brings together different kinds of writing—fiction, memoirs, and discursive essays—but it's wonderful the way the book coheres, because at its center are your interests and your sensibility, which is so specific and particular.

DR: I would say that this book really is a poetic autobiography. Whether it's stories of what happened in my life, as a young man and then later, or essays about books and writers that I considered or translated, the book always has to do with whatever it is that poetry is trying to find and communicate. I think that idea of finding and communicating is very important. Somebody recently asked me to define poetry, and I think it can be defined—people say that it can't, but I believe that it can. I think a simple one-phrase definition of poetry is: the invention of life or reality through language. To invent reality through words, this is what poetry does. And it isn't such a highfalutin thing as such a definition might make it seem. I also think that if poetry isn't capable of keeping a roomful of Iraqi cab drivers enthralled for an hour, then it isn't worth a goddamn thing. It must make people want to dance, or to make love, or to sing. It must fill them with the impulses to do something real in life; it must stimulate their imagination and their mind; it must entertain them and give them something to think about and provide them with some solid information. I believe that good poets and good poems do this.

KJ: The book includes essays about writers who you've translated, including Artaud, Crevel, Gilbert-LeComte. What is it that attracted you to these figures?

DR: I *identified* with all of these people. I have a personal sense of identification with them because they shared that search to invent life through language, and it's a very dangerous and a tricky kind of search. Because you don't really know whether it's real. These guys were out on what Ken Kesey always used to call an edge—out on the edge—they were edge people. People who write on the edge of craziness or death or some kind of final confrontation with a recognition of the absolute emptiness and void of everything. Maybe nothing is real. Those people lived with that all the time, and so have

I—all my life. And this isn't a before and after story. I'm living with it now. So I really identified with them. I felt a kinship with figures as different from each other as Émile Nelligan and Artaud and some of the other people that I talk about. Even ones that were spectacularly different from me, or at least the way that I conceive of myself. But those are my subjects because I feel that in a way they're my ancestors, my predecessors, my heroes.

KJ: What is it that brings them to the edge?

DR: Because they're stripped of the coping mechanisms that make for balanced living. In some cases this has happened to them situationally, because of the world in which we live; in other cases, maybe they willfully and perversely chose to embrace this. It happens differently to different people. But even the most well-balanced and sane people in the world can be confronted with some of these problems, and there really is not an answer to them. There really isn't any way to cope!

KJ: Of course, what makes these writers so fascinating to read is their commitment to write from the "edge" with such a determined honesty.

DR: To be honest in a real, absolute way is almost to be prophetic. And if you can be prophetic—though not too many people can be for very long at any time in their lives—but if at least that prophetic note is struck a few times, then it's gonna upset the applecart. And if that applecart is not upset, then conscious life just can't go on! This injection of irrationality and craziness and disorder into the ordered life is what regenerates life in general. Without it, we're going to get a hieratically ordered system, such as they had for many years in ancient Egypt, and among the Mayas, and so on. I think it could come very easily to us here, and probably will—thanks to IBM and all of these great, uniform institutions. A very important part of what the poet is supposed to be doing is upset the applecart. Because, after all, the applecart is just an endless series of indigestible meals and social commitments that are useless and probably shouldn't even be honored, and futile, pointless conversations and gestures, and then, finally, to die abandoned and treated like a piece of garbage by people in white coats who are no more civilized or conscientious than sanitation workers. That's what the applecart means to me. And when a poet's voice, a poet's imagination, is able to touch people enough so that they will change that, of course it's upsetting the applecart. I think that poetry has a real kind of . . . I wouldn't say preachy kind of a function, but it definitely is there to support and encourage people to realize that there's a worthwhile life out there to be lived. A way of living that is there—that all you have to do is invent it. It's available to all of us.

KJ: When you say a "worthwhile life," and when Pat Robertson says a "worthwhile life," you're talking about two very different things. Would Artaud have been talking about a "worthwhile life"?

DR: Oh yes. He would have said, a life that is free. He would have said, without any organs. A body that didn't have any organs, meaning that all those biological imperatives, and, I suppose, social imperatives. Artaud, after he'd been sick with cancer long enough, was dreaming of a way to live that was pure and free and enlightened. And I think I can relate to that. In my book, when I was talking about cutting loose from those kinds of bonds, I quoted this poet Albers Von Flauten, whose diary of 1822 sums it up in just a rhyming quatrain:

> To taste of nothing but the flesh of light
> Forever whole and sweet
> To drink of waters that refresh
> But never drive the blood to heat

And I think that that kind of a life is really there, it just has to be invented.

KJ: And so the purpose of poetry . . .

DR: Is to help people invent their lives—through language!

KJ: And at the same time to subvert all that keeps one from living a real life.

DR: Yes, exactly. Even sometimes in a destructive way. I certainly don't think that the lessons in living that you can get from reading certain kinds of literature, including many pages by William Burroughs and Jean Genet, are all that edifying in a constructive way. But they help destroy, they help break it down. I remember the Marquis de Sade saying to someone—and of course he was always constructing these little imaginary debates—he said to this imaginary opponent: You build. You're always building. I destroy! I simplify! And many of these corrosive pages of the great or underground classics help to destroy—they're not very edifying or uplifting. They're good for people because they help to destroy something that needs to be destroyed, that needs to be subverted.

KJ: Would you say that there's more that needs to be destroyed today than when you started out thirty years ago?

DR: Oh, no doubt!

ALLEN GINSBERG & KENNETH KOCH
FROM A CONVERSATION
The Poetry Project's 1995 Symposium

OCTOBER/NOVEMBER 1995   NO. 158

The following is an excerpt from a much longer discussion:

What pre-twentieth-century poet do you think wrote valuable work, neglected by anthologists?

ALLEN GINSBERG: Christopher Smart. "Rejoice in the Lamb" was not published until the 1920s or so. It was written during the time of Dr. Johnson and is an 80-page poem of which you'll see in anthologies only the one & a half pages of "For I will consider my Cat Jeoffry." Everybody knows that one? But there's eighty more pages that are much more brilliant than that covering Kabbalah, the Hebrew alphabet, the Greek alphabet, minerals, ecology, written (mythically) three verses a day in Bethlehem Mental Hospital. Bedlam. Then there's Edward Carpenter. He was the tutor to Queen Victoria's children in the nineteenth century. Later on he was an outspoken gay activist, visited Walt Whitman, was very much influenced by Whitman and wrote a huge book of poems called *Towards Democracy* that really has some brilliant poems in it, particularly a description of a train journey between Paris and Turin, and a fantastic 1880's visionary theosophical poem called

"The Secret of Time and Satan," which is so brilliant and the acme of late Victorian romanticism. And I remember hearing it read to me by the grand-son of President Chester A. Arthur, Gavin Arthur, who was one of the elegant old men in San Francisco during the '60s. He read it to me and Robert Creeley, and we were both completely knocked out so I went and found, there is a one-volume version of *Towards Democracy*, this Whitmanic long verse line assemblage. It's nowhere near as good as Whitman, but there are a couple of stand out poems that are just knockouts and there aren't that many really good poems written in long verse lines as models. So I would like to say something about the twentieth century. One great poet who's not very well known: Marsden Hartley as poet, rarely anthologized. But when I went to visit William Carlos Williams in the early '50s and asked what other models of open form verse there were, he recommended not Carl Rakosi, not Charles Reznikoff, but of all people, Marsden Hartley the painter. And there is a volume of Hartley's poetry that's now out on Black Sparrow Press. So there are two poems, "Lewiston Is a Pleasant Place" (description of his home town), and "Family Album in Red Plush"; classics, I would say.

What famous poets do you think have been overrated?

AG: Me, ha ha ha. Old ones, I don't know, as a poet I haven't seen much of Emerson that I liked. Longfellow, obviously, but then maybe somebody will come back to Longfellow . . .

KENNETH KOCH: Can I answer the same question? One problem with antholo-gies is that you don't get enough of the good stuff and then some of the good stuff you don't ever get, like Smart's whole poem. But I think Byron's "Don Juan" is one of the three greatest poems in the English language and you can't get it in a short space so you never get it in anthologies. I'm not sure how many people read it. And the same is true of Spenser's "Faerie Queene," which you can't get in an anthology. Also some of the best poetry in the Renaissance, which is saying a lot, is Christopher Marlowe's plays, particu-larly in *Tamburlaine*, which you never get in an anthology. So that's the problem of anthologies is that they're collections of appetizers and you don't get the main course often. I just discovered an Italian poet I'd never read before, an eighteenth-century poet, he's very disgraceful, he's the most pornographic poet I've ever read. But he writes sonnets, he's very very good. His name is Baffo. Guillaume Apollinaire wrote an essay about him and translated his poems. I've been trying to translate them but they're just about impossible because he writes in Venetian dialect. Anyway, that's just some sort of a novelty in poetry, the works of Baffo. He has a great name, doesn't he? In the twentieth century, I think that one of the best American poets is a man named John Wheelwright, whom almost nobody reads. Aside from John Ashbery and Fairfield Porter, I hardly know anybody else who's ever read him, though his books were published. There was a collected poems published by New Directions.

AG: Rexroth liked Wheelwright, and promoted his memory in San Francisco.

KK: There's also a poet named David Schubert, a twentieth-century poet, another one who died young like Wheelwright. There's an anthology of Schubert's work which was brought out by Ted Weiss, he's very good. The poetry of Thomas Hardy is not read as much as it should be. I mean it's terribly good, but when one says "should" about poetry, one really doesn't know what one is talking about. That is to say, Hardy should occupy as much space as a lot of poets who occupy more. Paul Valéry said on the subject that it's not true that nobody likes poetry. There are lots and lots of people who like poetry, but there are very few people for whom poetry is necessary. So for those for whom it's necessary, they ought to read Hardy. Oh, poets who have been overrated. Oh fame is so brief and so peculiar, it's very hard to tell. I don't think Allen's overrated. I'm not going to mention anyone in the twentieth century, there are quite a few who have been overrated. What do you think of I. A. Richards' statement that . . . why am I asking you questions?

AG: Well!

KK: I. A. Richards' statement that the music of poetry is intellectual, that's a stunner, isn't it?

AG: Yeah. Bunting's view was that the primary element should be the melopoeia, the music. Pound's was phanopoeia, the image on the mind's eye. Now what does Richards say?

KK: That the music of poetry was primarily intellectual.

AG: That the ideas, or the logopoeia is the music, so to speak?

KK: I think so, yeah. Look, if you change the meaning slightly, I'll give you an example: I was told when I was a baby poet, that the most beautiful line in the English language is "Shall I compare thee to a summer's day." And people talk about the "ays." Well if you change day to bay, there's no music left; "Shall I compare thee to a summer's bay?" There's nothing there, so the music is partly intellectual.

Have Beat poets written Beat poems?

AG: What distinguishes Beat poetry from other contemporary forms? My first thought was, all the Beat poets smoked pot.

KK: All I remember about Beat poetry is that I wrote a little play called *The Election*, which was a parody of Jack Gelber's play, *The Connection*. *The Connection* was all about people down at the Living Theatre sitting around waiting for the dope to come, and my play was all about people sitting around waiting for the vote to come. This was in 1960, and we had Nixon and Eisenhower and Kennedy on stage and Allen was in the—do you remember being in this play?

AG: No, I was smoking too much pot. I had short term memory loss, ha ha.

KK: It starts off with some guy, the poet who supposedly has written this play; it's a play within a play within a play. And Allen plays the poet's friend, and he's supposed to be—this was a time of the Beatniks, and I had the Ur-Beatnik there, so I wanted to use him. So Allen was actually in the first show, and then dropped out and we got somebody else, but I well remember the dress rehearsal, when I said to Allen, Allen was coming on like Lionel Barrymore. "Why do you, WHY do you . . . tell me this?" And I said, "Allen, can't you be a little more beat?" And do you remember what you said to me, you said, "Kenneth, are you trying to typecast me?" (*laughs*) Anyway, that's my main memory of the Beat movement.

Have poets of the New York School written New York School poems?

KK: Well, that's for a critic to decide. I mean if a critic wants to create a school where there was none, that's ok. That is to say, there was no school because there was no manifesto . . .

AG: Personism, there was Personism.

KK: Frank wrote that as a joke.

AG: Yeah, but it wound up being a big, serious manifesto. And, you know, it was taken so by critics.

KK: I know. By whom?

AG: Critics.

KK: I didn't hear anything.

AG: Alright. Did you see any common theme or form?

KK: In the early work of John Ashbery, Frank O'Hara, and Kenneth Koch, yes.

AG: And Schuyler?

KK: Schuyler came in a little later, but I saw the same things. But I saw it more clearly in the beginning. We were pretty much alike (in certain ways) for about five or seven years.

AG: What was the likeness? What was the common element?

KK: We paid a lot of attention to the surface of the poem, to the language. I can't speak for these guys, John would deny everything I said, since he's always claiming there is no New York School, and I suppose there isn't. But anyway, what I wanted was for every line to be exciting and for every two lines to be exciting and I was always finding out what I was saying in the poem by writing the poem. I never knew in advance. And we were all interested in music and dance and opera and painting particularly. We all knew French, we were influenced by French poetry. Mainly I think we were influenced by each other. I was at Harvard with John and he said to me one day that he just read Alfred Jarry, and he decided that our work should be crazier, so we took that to heart. We sort of thought that you guys were a little too close to the ordinary reality, but then we all got to be friends anyway.

AG: What I thought was the common element was the French wildness or craziness, but applied in a very common way to personal relationships, friendships, hyperbole among tea party friends. And gossip . . .

KK: That's particularly true of Frank. I think your poetry was closest to Frank's in that respect. The main thing it had in common was that it was colloquial, it was talk and it wasn't the dreary stuff which everybody was publishing.

AG: I thought the common element was interest in Williams and the vernacular and idiom. That's what Frank said, and that's what was the common element between the Beat school, the Projected Verse people, Black Mountain and the New York School and the North West's [Gary] Snyder and [Philip] Whalen. Everybody had some reference to the transformation of the diction and the rhythms into vernacular rhythms and/or spoken cadences and idiomatic diction.

KK: There was something about the subject matter. The academic poets were always taking some small thing like a drug store or the bus or some little incident and building this big structure around it that it represented everything. We all had that in common, that we didn't do that. That was nice. As far as the public goes, it was Allen that got us all on the good list of poets because after *Howl* came out, Allen was one of the most sought after men in America. And I remember when you were interviewed for the *New York Times* and you gave a list of fifteen poets that everybody should read and you were kind enough to include us on it so we got a step up there.

AG: Well I thought it was a united front against the academic poets to promote a vernacular revolution in American poetry beginning with spoken idiom against academic official complicated metaphor that had a logical structure derived from the study of Dante . . .

KK: Couldn't we talk about the differences a little bit, just to be a little more straightforward here?

AG: Ok. Well you were ga-ga.

KK: You must've thought sometimes, that at least some of the work of the poets of the New York School was a little bit off the subject and irresponsible, and silly and effete and so on.

AG: Yes. I did often, yeah.

KK: How mad did it make you?

AG: Not very mad.

KK: Do you know what the New York poets sort of felt might be a limitation on you guys?

AG: Yeah. Too parochial. Americanist in a kind of, not vulgar, but a kind of provincial way. Not sufficiently exposed to Roussel, Jarry, and others. And too much narcissistic, involved in each other's self-mythologization, to the exclusion of other people, and maybe a little too vulgar in the handling of fuck, shit, piss, motherfucker, and all that.

KK: Ok. Anyway, I thought that you put the words on the subject matter a little too fast, so that you don't get any of the mysterious evocative powers that the words have if you let them alone a little bit. So that you could make a social criticism absolutely dazzling but it remained a social criticism. It didn't set out for the stars or anything. I'm aware that it's very hard to do them both at the same time. You said that you regretted that there were the poetry wars and I always thought that it was a great idea except that we didn't win decisively enough. Well, why did you think the poetry wars were a bad idea?

AG: Well I have this little boy scout idea that they would all accept this new genius that was coming in and acknowledging it.

KK: How did that work out?

AG: Well Robert Lowell did, you know he was the head of the academics. He did accept Williams and start changing his style, and he was very fond of Gregory, and friendly with me, finally. But now you've got the Academy of American Poets in one place, and St. Mark's in another.

Do you think "first thought, best thought" is still a valid approach to writing poems? Why or why not?

AG: I think it's a valid approach. I don't know if it's the final finish.

KK: It's not always the best thought, obviously. I remember once I was at some reading for *Poetry* magazine in Chicago, and somebody came up from the newspaper and said, "Mr. Koch, can you write poems spontaneously?" Now can you imagine any other way to write? I mean, how else would you have to write? You sort of wait, what would you do, go looking for the words in a dictionary?

AG: You use a rhyming dictionary, a dictionary of antonyms and synonyms and you figure out your main image in advance and then you work it out.

KK: No, I think the first thought is always the first thought, and it's great, but then you have to revise.

AG: You revise much?

KK: All the time.

AG: I didn't know that.

KK: You told me once about twenty years ago, God help us, or thirty years ago that you had decided that because you were a poet, everything you wrote was poetry, so you didn't revise.

AG: No, no, I cut and I eliminate poems that I think are not poems, but mostly it's intact, except that I revise also. But I depend on the first inscription for structure and basic ideas, and anything I abstract or didn't really explain, then try to fill in like a bureaucratic form, you know, instead of saying I walked the streets, I'll say I walked on 7th Street, walked on a bottle strewn curb of 7th Street.

KK: I want to say one other thing about that. Years ago, I wrote a poem that I wasn't quite satisfied with, and it began, "Oh this is like a day in Bergen Norway." And I showed it to Frank and he said, "It's good, Kenneth." I said, "No it's not quite right." He said, "Why don't you take out the 'in'." That was very good advice, so the line became, "This is like a day Bergen Norway." That's all.

AN INTERVIEW WITH HARRYETTE MULLEN
BY BARBARA HENNING

OCTOBER/NOVEMBER 1996   NO. 162

When Harryette Mullen and I discussed this interview in June, at first we considered a fast techno-sophisticated e-mail interview. Both of us, however, preferred the summer pace of snail mail. Our initial plan was to exchange postcards. Postcards are great for questions, quips, and slogans, but not for an in-depth response. As the interview unfolded, I was sending postcard questions and Harryette was responding mostly with letters. One of the disadvantages of using the US Post Office is the indefinite delay for carrying. I almost always mailed a card the day before Harryette responded. The result was a rather disjointed exchange from which the following is excerpted.

6/16/96 Dear Harryette . . . Before we first met at the Nuyorican in 1990, Lorenzo [Thomas] had told me so many wonderful things about your writing . . . I was so pleased when you sent me *Trimmings*. Since then I've used it in almost all of my writing workshops. Could you begin by talking about the processes involved in writing this poem? And what in your reading-writing-speaking life brought you to consider femininity and language in this way? . . . I guess these are enough questions to generate a series of postcards. Love & all that. Barbara

June 17, 1996 Dear Barbara. Your idea of a postcard interview, especially in the era of fax machines and e-mail, strikes me as charming and irresistible. I'm responding to your suggestion with this letter initiating my end of the correspondence. Although I do use a computer to write, and I have access to a fax machine at work, I'm not hooked up to a modem, and I've never used e-mail. I also don't own a television, which to Angelenos seems especially perverse. Sooner or later I might acquire the TV and VCR that are essential equipment for any contemporary cultural critic, yet I can't help thinking that to watch television while living in Los Angeles is redundant. I want to thank you for the review of *Muse & Drudge* that you wrote for the *Poetry Project Newsletter*. You generously quoted many lines from my work in the review, but I appreciated most your critical insight into the poem's appropriation of Sappho's lyric as Sapphire's blues. Not only do you alert readers to my textual appropriation and transformation of Sappho's lines and tropes, such as "a handsome man" or "I sleep alone" (using Diane Rayor's translation of Sappho's poetry into American English), but also you point toward an urgent concern that the poem works through: tradition and its rupture, the continuities and discontinuities of cultural transmission, the dissemination and preservation of language, of speech and writing, of meaning itself.

Given the stress some critics have put on the way the lines "skirt the edges of meaning," I would assert that I intend the poem to be meaningful: to allow, or suggest, to open up, or insinuate possible meanings, even in those places where the poem drifts between intentional utterance and improvisational wordplay, between comprehensible statements and the pleasures of sound itself. In one quatrain, "a strict sect's / hystereotypist hypercorrects / the next vexed hex / erects its noppy text," I allude to the discourse of the Christian Right and right-wing populists of the Republican party, while also recalling the speech of Dixiecrat George Wallace, who used to pronounce "détente" as the "the taunt."

The lines "hip chicks ad glib / flip the script" refer to the performance of female rappers, specifically Salt-N-Pepa, who used rap as AIDS education through their song, "Let's Talk About Sex." When I sought a line to complete the quatrain that fit the rhythmic and phonemic patterning of the other three lines I'd written, "tighter than Dick's hat band" popped into my head, as an automatic simile that I'd heard throughout my childhood whether my mother or grandmother referred to tight clothing, or tight situations. But it was only in the context of the lines about female rappers, whose tight distichs (couplets) inform my own improvisational approach to rhythm and rhyme in this poem, that I grasped, for the first time, the origin of this folk simile: a metaphorical description of a condom. I saw a continuum, in terms of "oral tradition" or "verbal performance style" from my own matrilineal heritage—in a religious, lower-middle-class family that spoke of sexuality through metaphor, circumlocution, and euphemism—to the bold public style of today's women rappers. The poem embraces all of that, while also using language as verbal scat. Print and electronic media, as well as orality, provide my materials.

It would be fair to say that lines like "divine sunrises / Osiris's irises / his splendid mistress / is his sis Isis" strike the reader as something close to pure word-and-sound-play, but this verse also alludes to the project of Afrocentrism. Even a relentlessly language-centered quatrain like "mutter patter simper blubber / . . . / mumbo-jumbo palaver gibber blunder" is intended to comment on the loss of indigenous languages of enslaved Africans, while its recurring sound patterns also suggest homophones of kinship terms *mother father sister brother*, thus setting up an analogy between loss of language and loss of kinship. Similarly, the admittedly nonsensical lines "marry at a hotel, annul 'em / nary hep male rose sullen / let alley roam, yell melon / dull normal fellow hammers omelette" play on my own name, Harryette Romell Mullen, by echoing and scrambling the phonemes sounded in the name.

This poem, despite random, arbitrary, even nonsensical elements, is saturated with the intentionality of the writer. I am aware that the poem presents difficulties for any reader, because of its specific and topical references to subculture and mass culture, its shredded, embedded, and buried allusions, its drift between meaning and sound, as well as its abrupt shifts in tone or emotional affect. These effects all contribute to what Peter Hudson, a black Canadian who reviewed the book in *Afro News*, called the poem's "restless, unsettled nature" and "the overall irreverence and off-key eloquence that characterize the work."

I'm imagining that this letter and your first postcard will cross somewhere over the Midwest, and our "snail mail" interview will have begun. I'll write you again from Boulder, where I'll be spending a week at Naropa. As hectic as life gets, snail's pace seems just right to me!

Best, Harryette

June 21, 1996 #1 Hi Barbara, got your card today, just as I was pushing myself out of the door to turn in my grades at UCLA. So I'm finally free to get on with summer. Time to pack whatever clean clothes I can find & get my head in gear for poets' summer camp at Naropa. Yes, that was a good night at Nuyorican. My sister & I'd planned to meet at NYC. We had no idea we'd find Lorenzo there visiting from TX. He & I are both veterans of that state's Artists in Schools program back in the 1980s. He was active on a lot of different cultural fronts, on the local, national, and international levels, including working on poetry programs with Pacifica Radio, writing music criticism and helping to organize blues festivals, working in the schools, and attending literary and academic conferences from Austin to Amsterdam. His work's had a lasting impact on me. He had ties to Umbra, NY School & Language writing & belongs to a global community of poets. He offered a different model than the homegrown TX regionalists.

Love, Harryette

June 21, 1996 #2 Dear Barbara, that postcard you sent with Beaton's photo of Stein & Toklas, with kinky black wire dangling over Alice's head, gets to the point of *Trimmings*' origins: my reading of *Tender Buttons* and *Melanctha*. The pleasure & horror of those two works especially stirred me up, riled me, got me thinking about the effects of race & sexuality in language. I'm starting a letter I'll try to send before I go to Boulder.

Love, Harryette

6-22-96 Dear Barbara, I remember that the first time I tried to read Stein, I really couldn't stand it. It was boring & repetitious in a way that I found obnoxious. Years later, after I'd been reading more intensively and thinking more critically about language, when I returned to Stein, especially *Tender Buttons*, I was astonished at the freshness of her language, which still seems innovative and intriguingly enigmatic. What really struck me was the complexity of meaning found in the utter simplicity of her syntax. It reminded me of sophisticated baby talk, and I am very interested in baby talk, a marginal language used mainly by women and children. *Tender Buttons* appeals to me because it so thoroughly defamiliarizes the domestic, making familiar "objects, rooms, food" seem strange and new, as does the simple, everyday language used to describe common things. As critic Elisabeth Frost has noted, my poetic language is more public and social, less private and hermetic than Stein's. Louis Cabri and Jeff Derksen also have commented that the language in *Trimmings* is less a disjunctive idiolect, more a layering and juxtaposing of communolects.

Trimmings was in part a reflection on the marginality of women and of "the feminine" in language. (As well as a reflection on the feminization and marginalization of poetry, and certainly my own marginality as a black woman in relation to the dominant cultural construction of the feminine.) It is a "minor" genre, the prose poem. It's also a list poem which I thought of as a form congenial to women, who are always making lists. Of course, the catalogues (of heroes, ships, and so forth) in epic poems evoke a masculine tradition, not to mention David Letterman's lists. However, a whole poem composed of a list of women's garments, undergarments, & accessories certainly seems marginal & minor, perhaps even frivolous & trivial. Actually it was an inside joke for me to begin *Trimmings* with "a belt" since a convention of epic poetry is to begin "in the middle." So that joke I was having with myself was about the epic poem versus the little list poem, which has become a workshop cliché: in this case a list of feminine apparel.

Writing the poem also involved a process of making lists. First, I made a list of words referring to anything worn by women. Each word on that list became the topic of a prose poem. (I started with clothing, then decided to include accessories. There were a few things I decided not to write about, such as wigs, dentures, and so forth.) Then I made more lists by free associating from words on the first list. I generated lists of words that might be synonyms (pants/jeans/slacks/britches), homonyms (duds/duds, skirt/skirt), puns or homophones (furbelow, suede/swayed), or that had some metaphorical, metonymical, or rhyming connection (blouse/dart/sleeve/heart, pearl/mother, flapper/shimmy/chemise), or words that were on the same page of the diction-ary (chemise/chemist). I would improvise a possible sequence of words, seeing what the lists might suggest in the way of a minimal narrative, a metaphor, an association, or pun.

Each prose poem is a unit of the "long poem" that is itself a list, with each item described figuratively, as in true riddles. I also quickly understood that the structure of the poem was like a hologram. Each prose poem basically does the same thing as all the rest, since whatever the trope, it is the woman's body that appears consistently in every figure as the tenor of which clothing is the vehicle. This simply extends and elaborates a metonymical tendency already present in everyday usage: "skirt" and "petticoat" also commonly refer to women as well as to clothing worn by women. I also borrow or recycle language and/or syntactical structures from a variety of folk and mass culture genres, including: riddle, nursery rhyme, fairy tale, prayer, television commer-cial, cliché, tabloid headline, and weather report, as well as from specifically African-American forms including the blues and the dozens. Love & Rockets, Harryette.

6/27/96 Dear Harryette—hello from my office in Brooklyn. I loved reading your letter which did arrive before my two postcards . . . In *Muse & Drudge* . . . I always knew when I was an outsider, looking in from another cultural experience or even from my own purposeful alienation from everyday television and advertising . . . I'd get one line, lose the next, then a meaning would come through that had only resonated before and then . . . lv Barbara

6/29/96 Dear Harryette . . . You speak of your "layering and juxtaposing of communolects." In my own work, I think of quilting and women's work as a kind of *feminine écriture*, a way of gaining authority and smashing oppressive authority, in a quiet subversive way. Your process of writing this poem by beginning with lists and generating other lists and improvising on these is quite different than composition by waiting for "inspiration" or "deep feeling." Could you speak about the effects—if any—Oulipo methods have had on your practice. again . . . Barbara

2:54 PM 7/15/96 Dear Barbara, Wow! Three cards and lots of questions to think about! I'll try to consolidate my responses, and address as many of your questions as I can in this letter. You asked about community. Definitely the idea of community is important to me, and specific communities of speakers, readers, writers, artists, critics, and intellectuals have certainly influenced how I think and how I use language. Most fundamentally, some persistent aspects of my identity and my work have been determined by my community of origin. The southern black community of my childhood made both literary and oral traditions of poetry immediately available to me as a significant aspect of everyday life and of communal rituals. For me, the black community was organized primarily around the institutions of school and church, particularly since my mother is a teacher and my maternal grandfather was a Baptist minister.

Our family stressed the value of education and literacy. Books and book knowledge were revered in our household. At the same time, it was apparent that the love of language prevailed also among folks in the black community who were less connected to books and literacy. One's knowledge and verbal skill were always subject to being tested in practical situations and everyday encounters, when it was important to be able to interact with people, whether or not they were highly educated or deeply literate. This community valued anyone with strong skills in oratory, storytelling, poetry, song, and verbal contests of various sorts. It was okay to be bookish, but you also had to be able to talk the talk. Playing the dozens, signifying, capping, sounding: all of these forms of verbal dueling were ways we learned to use language, wit, and humor to defend ourselves against verbal aggression. Every child had a large repertoire of formulaic greetings, insults, taunts, and retorts, which often exploited the mnemonic force of rhyme and rhythm.

"What's cooking, good looking?"

"Ain't nothing cooking but the beans
in the pot,
and they wouldn't be, if the water
wasn't hot."

As children, we memorized poetry for school and church programs, and we recited folk poetry on playgrounds and in backyards as we jumped rope and played other games. We not only repeated these conventional utterances from the folk tradition, but we also invented new rhymes and songs.

I remember my first real job, at fourteen, working for minimum wage as a waitress at a camp for rich white kids. All of the kitchen and dining staff were black, while the owners of the camp and all of the counselors and campers were white. The white folks were kept completely separate from the colored folks who were there to serve them. They slept in bright, airy cottages with hand painted tile in the bathrooms. (We knew this because we could earn a little extra money by cleaning their cabins between the two summer camping sessions.) We were housed in crude shacks with concrete showers that were infested with scorpions. We used to invent satirical verses about our bosses that we sang on the way to and from work each day.

"Miss Johnson's such a dried out hag,
her mouth looks like a drawstring bag."

I remember also that the men who tended the grounds, and the women who laundered our uniforms, were all Mexican or Mexican American people who spoke little or no English. While we were not permitted to speak to the white campers, some of whom were the same age I was, I always exchanged a polite greeting in Spanish with the men who did the mowing and trimming, and the women who took in our crumpled piles of food-and-sweat-stained uniforms and handed back to us neatly folded, clean, starched dresses and aprons for the next day's work.

The linguistic, regional, and cultural differences marked by southern dialect, black English, Spanish, and Spanglish are fundamental to how I think about language, and how I work with language in poetry. My attraction to the minor and the marginal, to the flavor of difference in language, has something to do with this sense of heteroglossia that was part of the environment of my childhood in Texas. The southern dialect was both familiar and foreign to me, since I grew up in working-class and middle-class black communities in the South, and in a family divided between people from the North and people from the South, all of whom were educated speakers of standard English.

The heterogeneity of these various communities has influenced me, often in complex, unpredictable, and subliminal ways. I think of myself and my writing as being marginal to all of the different communities that have contributed to the poetic idiom of my work, but at the same time it is important to me that I work in the interstices, where I occupy the gap that separates one from the other; or where there might be overlapping boundaries, I work in that space of overlap or intersection. I have spent much of my life in transit from one community to another, and as a result I often feel marginal to them all. Yet

I also feel something in common with people who are very different from one another. I try in my work to make my marginality productive. By necessity, the margin has become a positive space where I am free to do my work. This concern is at the heart of *Muse & Drudge*, a poem that deliberately addresses a diverse audience of readers, with the expectation that no single reader will comprehend every line or will catch every allusion.

My association with communities of intellectuals—a result of my experience as a student and teacher in universities, as well as my practice as a poet—has given me an aesthetic and critical language with which to examine and interrogate my other connections and experiences. I do see my work as a poet and as a critic overlapping, intersecting, and reinforcing each other in various ways. Ideas for poetry often come from the critical reading and writing that I do in other contexts. Race and gender theory clearly have influenced my work as a poet, especially in my last three books. Sociolinguistics, ethnography, and folklore have also been influential disciplines which I sought out through elective courses during my undergraduate years at the University of Texas at Austin . . .

Oulipo has been important to me because of this group's systematic cataloguing and exuberant invention of textual operations and literary techniques. I was interested in Oulipo's vigorous exploration of the ludic aspects of writing, as well as their theory and practice as intellectuals and artists. In Oulipo's erudite tongue-in-cheek manifestos I found a pleasurable convergence of work and play. The first time I used Oulipo constraints in a creative writing course was at Cornell, where my students initially resisted because they thought these guys were elitist, and because my students cherished the romantic idea of poetry as the inspired expression of a uniquely perceptive individual. Yet what I found useful, as a poet and as a creative writing teacher, was Oulipo's demystification of creative process and aesthetic technique. Their idea of "potential literature" liberates the writer to concentrate on the process, rather than the product, of writing.

Far from being elitist, they make the creative process more accessible as they deflate the divine afflatus of artistic inspiration. A formal constraint, such as a

lipogram, gives the writer a definite problem to tackle. I find it far more diffi-
cult to face a blank page, hoping for inspiration, than it is to seek solutions to
a specific problem such as writing a poem about a rose without using any of
the alphabets in the word R-O-S-E. This was the example I used to demon-
strate to my class the pragmatic virtue of Oulipian constraints. In order to
make the formal challenge more user-friendly, I encouraged my students to
use and then lose the constraint at different points in the creative process. My
example of such a two-step process resulted in one of the quatrains in *Muse &*
Drudge. I began with a lipogram, which was used to generate a lexicon for the
poem. Then the constraint was dropped, allowing any alphabets to enter the
composition. I actually wrote two brief poems. One was a Z-shaped lipogram/
calligram I called "Z-Rose." Words and phrases generated with the constraint
("pink pajama" "zig-zag" "living ink") were then cannibalized for the second,
unconstrained poem, which became a stanza of *Muse & Drudge*.

O rose so drowsy in
my flower bed your pink
pajamas zig-zag into
fluent dreams of living ink

I have found that using constraints in this way expands the possibilities for
improvisation, as various textual operations may be tried at different points
in the writing process. Such flexibility makes it possible to use even the most
severe constraint, without fear of it being too rigid, mechanical, or stifling
to the writer's individuality. Rather, it simply gives the writer a more eclectic
array of aesthetic tools. This was helpful, I think, to students intimidated by
Georges Perec's amazing feats of writing first a lipogrammic novel without
the letter "e" and then a univocalic novel in which "e" is the only vowel.

You've asked about the poem as women's work, as piece work, like quilting.
Those ideas are consonant with my own methods and metaphors of writing.
The poem also comments on quilting/writing as artists' work, and as a meta-
phor of tradition as the interaction of continuity and discontinuity.

stop running from the gift
slow down to catch up with it
knots mend the string quilt
of kente stripped when kin split

My paternal grandmother was an accomplished quilter. One of my treasures is a quilt she made, using the "cathedral window" pattern, which resembles a stained glass window. The list poems, *Trimmings* and *S*PeRM**K*T*, as well as the stanza form of *Muse & Drudge*, allowed me to make a kind of long poem composed of discrete units, so that in effect, I could write brief manageable poems that were parts of a longer work that was the book-length poem. The discreet units, stanzas or paragraphs, form various patterns like the pieces of a quilt. I could start anywhere, proceed in no particular order, writing whenever I had the chance and the energy. With my wardrobe and supermarket lists, my tidy prose paragraphs, my quatrains of blues songs and jump rope rhymes composed of recycled representations of black women, I could continually end and begin, without feeling the trauma of endings, the fear and uncertainty of beginnings. My own consolation in the face of rupture, a writing through the gaps and silences. Love & Rockets, Harryette. P.S. I didn't know it was so long. I'm trying out a new laptop.

7/7/96 Dear Harryette, I'm on the Staten Island Ferry with a friend who is looking for an apartment in this neighborhood with a history of hotels & rooming houses, now little apartments, inexpensive and transient. The ferry ride is beautiful and calm compared to the subway. I think I've sent you a lot of questions which you'll find when you get home from New Mexico. If I didn't ask already: I find that I work with fragments in part because I'm so busy. Does the urban bustle affect your turning to fragments? Lost in thought-parts and found-in-arranging. Does this mean anything to you? Lv Barbara

7:44 PM 7/29/96 Dear Barbara, . . .Writing in fragments seems to be a very contemporary response to the postmodern distraction, the channel-surfing attention span, our fractured sense of time, on the one hand. People I know, poets and academics, are writing literally on the fly, taking their laptops aboard airplanes. That's what we share with the business passenger working on a spreadsheet or annual report. On the other hand, when I think of poetry in fragments, I also think of Sappho, whose work comes to us, like classic Greek art and architecture, as enigmatic shards and evocative ruins. Given the human capacity to destroy civilization "with the touch of a button" the same way we microwave lean cuisine, ancient ruins stand as a figure for the obliteration of ourselves and our own culture. We imagine that some extraterrestrial archaeologists might someday examine our fragments, and wonder what manner of beings we were. In some contemporary work, including my own, the artist is engaged in a kind of archaeology of the detritus of consumer culture, the artifacts of the electronic age. That's why I immediately recognized Tyree Guyton's Heidelberg Houses, in Detroit, as visual art equivalent of what I was trying to do in *Muse & Drudge*. David Hammons has a similar approach to recycled resources. I'm also inspired by the work of Leonardo Drew, which is more abstract, but still carries the emotional charge of abandoned and reclaimed materials.

8/9/96 Dear Harryette, Tyree Guyton's project is dear to my heart, too—coming from Detroit's devastation, an artistic reassemblage. Maybe that's one of the reasons your work means so much to me, *Muse & Drudge* is a Detroit-like project. Attached is the text from our clipped and quilted interview. If there is anything you want to add or delete, drop me a note and I'll try to make the changes. It's been a very thought-provoking interview for me and I've enjoyed the whole process—it's been a thread through my whole summer. Thanks so much, Harryette. Lv. Barbara

AN INTERVIEW WITH DAVID HENDERSON
BY LISA JARNOT

DECEMBER/JANUARY 1996   NO. 163

David Henderson is the author of *Felix of the Silent Forest*, *De Mayor of Harlem*, *The Low East*, and *'Scuse Me While I Kiss the Sky: Jimi Hendrix, Voodoo Child*. He has a new collection of poetry, *Neo-California*, forthcoming next year. I talked with David at his apartment on East 14th Street on August 8, 1996. The following is an excerpt of our conversation.

LISA JARNOT: David, you started editing *Umbra* magazine in 1961. How old were you when that happened?

DAVID HENDERSON: I was a young teenager. I came to the workshop and they were putting together a magazine and somehow they made me the editor, one of the editors, I wasn't *the* editor. I think we had three editors. I was hanging at the Deux Mégots and met Calvin Hernton and the Deux Mégots crowd—like Carol Bergé and Jackson Mac Low. My friend was Eddie Krasnow. He was a painter but he wrote poetry. I was going to the New School at night and these guys were in my class. They were mostly married guys who lived in the suburbs. So we would hang out in the Village after class and then somehow we found out about the Deux Mégots open readings and we would go there but we were all afraid to read. It was intimidating, you know. But anyway, I met Calvin there. Calvin was just off the boat, from Mississippi or

somewhere, some southern college where he had been teaching and read this great poem, you know? So I went over and said man, that was a great poem, and we became friends, drank beer, and talked about writing. Calvin came over to me one day and said "these writers are putting together a magazine, and they're having a meeting, and I want you to come, let's go." So I went, and they had all these black writers, and it was astounding. Because in the early '60s, there was LeRoi Jones—who was—I'm trying to figure out where he stood in terms of Allen Ginsberg and I guess to my mind at the time he was at least equal to Allen—but I was more interested in Ted Joans, who I'd never met but I would see him in the Village and I was very in awe of him. And then Richard Wright and Ralph Ellison, but I didn't even know where they were, and quickly discovered that Richard Wright was in Paris. So there were all these black writers. And I met Tom Dent, Lloyd Addison, Lorenzo Thomas, and Clarence Major. Tom Dent was the organizer, and there were like fifteen writers—Asaman Byron, Norman Pritchard, Joe Johnson, Charles Patterson, James Thompson (who is now Abba Elethea), Alvin Simon, Steve Cannon, Lennox and Maryanne Raphael, and Jerry Summers. Ishmael Reed and Winnie Stowers showed up a bit later, as did Al Haynes and George Hayes. And we sat there and we were all just gassed at each other's presence and we said "well we want to do a workshop and do a magazine." Subsequently they somehow decided that I was an editor.

LJ: So you had already been writing poetry at this point?

DH: I'd been writing more prose than poetry, but I had written poetry. I published a poem in something called *The Black American* that came out of Harlem, and which actually was still coming out in the '90s, but then they changed the title, and it had by that point become a tabloid. At first, when I published in it, it was a small magazine that looked like *Jet* magazine and they had paid me $5. Anyway, I had published a poem, which was like a big deal, right? And then we started to put together this magazine and have workshops where everyone would read. I was writing more prose—and poetry—but mostly prose. But I had these poems and they [the workshop] were very enthusiastic; they thought these poems were good, and we listened to everyone's poems and they were all really relevant, you know? It was amazing because it wasn't about "is this a good poem?" or "does it have iambic pentameter?" or "the rhyme scheme is great." They were all poems really about intensity—not all of them were about social things—but a lot of them were about being black, or being an outsider, which is exactly what we were. We were on the Lower East Side, and over on Avenue C and 2nd Street, in this small apartment. And we came out with a couple of issues over a period of two years. It was really important. We went all over and did readings as a group and we all hung together. It was great, and I remember we would go out to the suburbs and read for these middle-class black people and they would hate us and we would hate them—but it wasn't like "hate" hate, it was like, "wow, these people are really out of it," and they would say, "wow, they are really out of it" and we would drink up all their liquor and read the poems and it was a lot of fun actually. So anyway, that's *Umbra*, and subsequently when *Umbra* stopped functioning, I went to California. No, actually, before I went to California, I took it over for some reason. It was just kind of sitting there, and the people who were supposed to be editing it hadn't come out with an issue; they didn't manage to get it out. So I subsequently put together another group. Len Chandler was involved in it, and Nancy Chandler, and Merble Reagon, Barbara Christian, Marilyn Lowen, and a whole bunch of people who were essentially people from the New York chapter of SNCC more or less. Then I went to California where Victor Hernández Cruz, Jorge Aguirre, and Barbara Christian and I put out *Umbra/Latin Soul*, the last *Umbra*.

LJ: What year was that?

DH: 1970.

LJ: What about the St. Mark's scene? Did you spend time at The Poetry Project before you left for the West Coast?

DH: Here's the story of St. Mark's. St. Mark's came out of Le Metro readings, right? The Deux Mégots readings went to Le Metro and then those readings went to St. Mark's. Le Metro now is called the Telephone Bar. And Le Metro was a downstairs café and they had the open readings there. By that time I was disgusted with the open readings and I didn't participate much. During that time, we used to read three or four times a week, and the open readings—I thought that they had gotten kind of stodgy or something. But I was hanging out with these people, these anarchists, and we had a loft building on 2nd Street. But a lot of the Umbra poets still went to Le Metro and read, and there was an incident there with Tom Dent and Ishmael Reed— there was some brawl. I don't remember who got hit. I think it might have been Tom, but Ishmael was involved. And then the poets all walked out, and said where the fuck are we going to read now? you know? And these guys— Bob Ernstthal who used to run the Bread and Puppet Theatre, Allen Hoffman and Paul Prensky, and some others—we had this building. I mean we had three floors over what became the Tin Palace. It was 2 East 2nd Street. I said come and read over at the loft. And the readings came over there, and they were there for about three months, and the readings were there every Monday, and it was like a transition. And then the Church came in and the readings went to the Church, and that was the whole thing. And actually, that whole episode Ishmael Reed wrote about in the first issue of the *East Village Other*—one of the stories on the front page about the whole transition from Le Metro to what we called the Bowery Poets Co-op. So we had the readings there and then it went to St. Mark's and that was an interesting time. They had this group called the Motherfuckers, right? This is so funny because this was after Amiri [Baraka] got busted in Newark in the Newark riots. Amiri wrote this poem . . . I used to know the whole poem, but it had this line "up against the wall motherfuckers, this is a stick up." He was telling people in Newark to go into car dealerships and take the cars, because "they're yours," you know. So this group named themselves the Motherfuckers, after the poem, right? And I never could understand these people—or where they came from or where they went—but they were like the people who are really heavily pierced who sit in Tompkins Square Park. They would stand there in St. Mark's. They would just be there in a group and they were very anti-social. I never got to know any of them. Maybe somebody did. I don't know who did, probably Jim Brodey got to know them. But they were the Motherfuckers. They were there from the beginning at the Church as I recall. And they were kind of antagonistic, but in a fairly unantagonistic way.

LJ: One of the things I'm interested in is the way your work engages the geography of the Lower East Side. You seem like a New York School poet in some ways—I'm using that term very loosely. But I know that you spent a lot of time in California too. Do you feel like an East Coast poet or a West Coast poet?

DH: I'm a New York poet, you know, I've written a lot of poems about being in New York, right? But I've been other places—I have a lot of poems about California. I wrote this poem called "Berkeley Trees" which talked about New York and it talked about the California poets who I got to know, like Snyder, who I always thought was the best, absolutely the best. And di Prima, who always mystified me, and then there were all these Asian American poets like Lawson Inada, Kitty Chu, who I thought was really a good poet. And then I got involved in Third World Communications in San Francisco, and Roberto Vargas, who I thought was really the quintessential poet. And Victor Hernández Cruz also made the move to California and was involved in that scene. I believe that after [Nicolás] Guillén and [Pablo] Neruda he is the great Latino poet of the Americas. Bob Kaufman was very important to all these poets on the West Coast too. I noticed, however, that the poets who were involved in the Beat Generation seemed to have another kind of agenda, which I tried to decipher, but there always seemed to be a distinction between them and the other poets, especially black poets, and it took me a long time to get a handle on it. I realized when I went to the Beat show at the Whitney that the Beats and their whole time line were still being formulated in the early 1960s. Now looking back I can see how it was shaped, especially with the positioning of Amiri Baraka, and the handling of the poetic genius of Bob Kaufman, and the disinheritance of Ted Joans, and the submergence of jazz.

LJ: Part of what I wanted to talk to you about was the political in terms of poetry, what the relation is between poetry and the political world. How much does poetry fit into politics for you?

DH: Very much so. But then what politics are you talking about? It certainly wasn't right-wing politics; it was more the politics of inclusion, because Umbra was very involved in the Civil Rights Movement. A lot of the people in Umbra were involved in SNCC in terms of civil rights. So James Meredith came to our workshop, and Charlayne Hunter, and Andy Young. Straight from the movement. And I went down there and worked with the Free Southern Theatre, and we did a poetry show, and we drove all over. And then when I came to California, that was considered post-Civil Rights, which was a really funny period because the Voting Rights Act had been passed, and I had been involved in all that post-Kennedy shit. The assassination of President Kennedy was major shit, especially combined with Malcolm X's assassination a few months later. And so I think by 1970 people had thought there was a new day, and just like Reconstruction after the Civil War, there were all these really innovative programs happening, but at the same time all the seeds to dismantle these programs were also showing up at the same time. And one of the reasons that I left New York was when Adam Clayton Powell got drummed out of Congress. That totally disgusted me because he was one of the most important legislators ever—it was like 66 pieces of progressive legislation he was responsible for. So, as I said, while 1970 was like the Reconstruction, a lot of things were coming into play, but a lot of things were going out. So the seeds were there for Nixon. There was always this tension between—for us black people on the Lower East Side—our politics and the politics of the white Left. A lot of people from Umbra went back South. And some people went into academia, which was a buy-out. So I quickly got out of that, but I certainly felt tainted by that. It was a strange time. But I think the tension between the white Left and the black liberation movement became very pronounced. Because the black liberation movement was about civil rights, but it was also about international politics, about what was called the third world. And the whole third world thing is something that I got involved with in California because there were all these people from Asia and Latin America and the American South Sea Island protectorates and all these people were there, right? And the only context we really had was the people of color thing and the third world thing, which Richard Wright had done the early work on. And then I saw how Richard Wright's concept had been totally co-opted by the *New York Times*—by the establishment—so that third world was about economics or the living standard of a particular country of color. But Wright's work with the third world was about a heightened (even cosmic) consciousness from being involved in Asia, Africa, or Latin America as well as the West and the balance between those elements therefore forming a third world. It was a time when I was just learning about all of these places from people who were from these places and therefore learning a lot about neocolonialism. In California we were involved in multiculturalism very early on and multiculturalism is really a way of talking about third world Americans, people of color, and it was always a wedge into what had become the monoculture. It was never meant to be what it has become. But of course you become aware that these things become co-opted into the structure of whatever gambit you make. So then you think of what the next gambit is going to be and if you can make this gambit, how is it going to play out and how can you protect it? You can't protect it. You can't protect the gambits, and you can't protect your leaders or pop heroes. I mean there's not even the thought of it. So Bob Marley for me was major because here was a guy who was so important and most people were like fans, but they had nothing to do with whether he would survive or not. But anyway, I was also in California at the same time that Roberto Vargas put together a group from the Mission and they went down to Nicaragua and fought in the Revolution. And Roberto became First Secretary and I wrote a poem about it. I went and visited him in Washington when he was First Secretary and that was very funny. We had dinner with his family and he was having a lot of fun. Which was great, because I think at a certain point poets should do something like that. I mean there's this whole Western tradition of being in despair and you commit suicide or something.

LJ: So you think poets should be politically active?

DH: Better than killing themselves or some bullshit. There's too much drinking alone, trying to write the great poem.

LJ: What about young writers today? Do you think that the Umbra scene has influenced up and coming writers? Do you see that kind of political activity or social consciousness in young writers?

DH: I don't think that any of the Umbra writers tried to organize like the Beat Generation did and try to make it into this whole "thing." A lot of younger writers say, "oh, there was *Umbra*, right?" And umbra means mystery and obfuscation anyway, so you don't really talk about it, all you do is name the people who were in it and how many works came out of Umbra, and it's an astounding amount. In 1994 we were at the National Black Arts Festival and Ishmael Reed said that over fifty books have come out of *Umbra*, some huge number of books have come out of *Umbra* in poetry and prose and plays and stuff.

LJ: When you think of young people who are writing in New York today, or even on the West Coast, do you see that kind of organized thing happening? I mean who are the younger writers you're interested in?

DH: I don't know; that's such a strange question. I like Paul Beatty. I think that Tracie Morris is a genius. I think she's brilliant. I can't off the top say that this one young writer is great.

LJ: Do you go to readings at the Nuyorican Cafe?

DH: Not much. The slams are not particularly my cup of tea. Julie Patton is really good, but I don't really follow that scene very much.

LJ: I guess I'm interested in how much things have changed, or have they changed? Have the writers changed? Has the context in which the writers write changed? I'm interested in the way you perceive that.

DH: You know, I'm going to say that part of it is this whole business of the writing schools. The writing schools—their whole increasing involvement in academia and writing—to me it makes things tremendously complicated because then I tend to say well, okay, I'm a non-academic writer and I don't want to be identified academically, because they look to me like Cabals, and it's more about power and influence. I mean I was in this bookstore earlier today over on 6th Avenue and I was looking at these journals, and almost every English department has their journal which they distribute. To me that's complicated it. So a lot of the young writers I don't know where they're coming from. Maybe it has to do with this Language business or poststructuralism stuff, which I never thought was good for anyone except for critics who really got off on it, or for academics addicted to reading who got off on that kind of non-stuff. But I never thought that it had a lot to do with writing, especially in terms of writing involving personal and social liberation.

LJ: What about music? You work with song in your writing. And you've been a documenter; you've written a biography of Jimi Hendrix. What do you think the relationship is between poetry and music? Is that essential for you?

DH: When I was in Newark the last time with Amina and Amiri, Amina said "David, 'keep on pushing.' I want you to do a reading so you can read that poem again." And I used to read that poem a lot. This was in the '60s. And I never thought of it as a big deal at the time, but in retrospect from what people say I guess apparently it must show that the black writers at the time didn't recognize Rhythm & Blues. But I use R&B in my songs, in my poems. So I guess that was the deal. But Langston Hughes liked that; he understood it because he used the blues. But when he was coming up the blues was the pop music of the time. So I dealt with R&B, it was as simple as that. I mean I used to sing. When I was a kid I used to sing R&B. We had a group. There's this book called *They All Sang on the Street Corner*, and it's a great book about many of the people—the groups—that sang on the street corners. And that's what we did. And people said okay, that's a gang—you're a gang. No, we were a gang because at that point living in a place that was like Howard Beach, if you didn't have any people with you, you were in trouble. Because the white kids didn't really like us, living in a project in the outer boroughs.

But essentially what we did was sing, like hunter-gatherers. So we sang all the way up until I left home. Then I really didn't sing anymore, for a long time until I went to California, and then we had a group there. I had a band in California. And we did something I have the video of, at San Francisco State, we did it for the Poetry Center. We did some gigs. But I've always been involved with music and with musicians.

LJ: Well what do you think makes a poem a good poem? Do you think music is part of it?

DH: The thing is that everyone has a good poem, everyone has at least one good poem. I mean I don't care who they are. I mean if you've been writing at it for a while, you know. So it's not really about the poem then is it? Or is it? I mean it's not like "Howl," right. You say, okay, do you have a good poem? And you say, yeah, I have "Howl." But you know, read "Second April" [by Bob Kaufman]. Read *Solitudes Crowded with Loneliness*. Kaufman kills them. You talk about a poem, Kaufman has the poems. I remember we had this poetry reading for Bob at the Fillmore East in 1966. I thought that Kaufman was dead. I think that we announced that he was dead. I think that Eileen said he heard that and he laughed, which is beautiful, because Bob, in terms of Zen, and in terms of "surreal"—he was so much of that. He had gone beyond all that shit I guess in a way. But he wrote these poems and they were great and he believed in poetry. So many of the younger poets in San Francisco, they loved Bob and many of them hung with Bob. So if you can write a poem like "Second April," then that's significant. And then okay, has anybody done that? And if anyone has, is it possible to be able to perceive it out of the great mass of poetry that there is. I don't know, because it seems to me that there's a lot of self-promotion—to what point? I don't understand the point. The self-promotion could be, alright, you could get a university professorship, you could win an award, you could get a grant, and that all seems to me to be competitive in the academic sense, but that has nothing to do with poetry.

LJ: So David, what advice would you give to young poets?

DH: And now you're working for the *Today Show*, right? You're speaking in sound bytes. I don't have any advice that I can think of off the top. It depends on what the context is. When I taught the workshop [at The Poetry Project], which was great, these were poets who were essentially writing for themselves and trying to become better, and I thought that was great. The advice that I had for them was the same advice that I have for myself, and I was glad for them, so that I could finally give myself some good advice in a good context. Okay—some people there wanted to write longer works of fiction, which I encouraged, because I think that poets write great prose, and I don't see the great difference between prose and poetry, and that was kind of the way I titled my workshop—for people doing manuscripts in poetry or prose—and I always talked about how they go back and forth between each other. And so I said, if you're going to be a writer—well are you going to be a writer first of all? Do you want to do this? Or do you just want to write for yourself?—which is great, I think that a lot of people do this. I've discovered a lot of people say "Oh, you're a poet. Well, I've written some poems." And people have written some poems, and some of them are pretty good. But pretty good to whom? It doesn't even matter. If it means something to them, or to someone that they love, then that's as good as it gets. Then maybe you'll write "The Waste Land" or something, maybe you'll be T. S. Eliot. My advice to poets is not to get hung up on poetry, but to appreciate poetry because it's the greatest form whatsoever because technically there's no reward. And then there are all these poets who are not called poets like songwriters and like rappers, right? Whole landscapes of poetry are not even recognized. So what's my advice to younger poets? Write your poems and try to find another form of writing. I mean you say "younger poets," and I assume that they want to distinguish themselves in some way as poets, but I think the best thing about being a poet is forming other relationships with other writers and getting into some interesting subjects and following them through, and looking at them poetically.

LJ: David, have the chickens come home to roost? What's the future of America? Are things going to get better or worse?

DH: The chickens are coming home to roost because of what America did geopolitically, like in Iraq. A former ally, then it's manipulated into a situation where the US bombs the shit out of them, and kills a lot of women and children, or they try to starve people out. So "the chickens come home to roost" means that all the evil that was perpetrated overseas to protect the American way of life—well, it's going to be hard to elude the anger that has been inculcated in generations of a lot of people of color all over. I'm very afraid of the aftermath, or the blowback from American foreign policy. Are things going to get better or worse? I think a lot depends on the poets, if the poets can get it together. That's what I said when I made those remarks at St. Mark's State of the Art Symposium. I think the poets can either do it or not do it, but I don't think they are going to do it by looking at themselves as so distinct. As I was saying, when I was researching Marley and Hendrix, the poets always had great information, the poets always had great leads, and they put things together in a way that nobody else did, and they knew what was important and what wasn't and they were always good. Jim Brodey— great insights, did a pretty good interview with Hendrix at a difficult time, which I reprinted in the new edition of the Hendrix book in its entirety. So I think it's up to the poets because the poets are the leaders of the artists. Because you get the visual artists and the musicians, and they're directly tied into the weirdest shit. The dancers are always going to be beautiful—I like the dancers—but they're not political. So I think it's the poets. And for the life of me I don't understand why you don't have poems about the Welfare Act. Not your doctrinaire leftist poem about "rise up people and overthrow the means of production," and all that crazy shit. I think we have to bargain for a position in this society based on what we know, and I think that poets know all that there is to know—is there any more that one needs to know? I don't think so. Then it becomes "let's make a deal." And the poets are not even talking about that, and since they lead the artists, if they're not talking about it, then nothing's happening.

AN INTERVIEW WITH ALICE NOTLEY
BY JUDITH GOLDMAN

FEBRUARY/MARCH 1997   NO. 164

In late September I called Alice Notley in her Paris apartment, requesting to do an interview by correspondence with her. We exchanged three letters each over the next two months. Our letters cover works produced by Notley in the 1990s, including *The Scarlet Cabinet* (with Douglas Oliver), *Close to me & Closer . . . (The Language of Heaven)* and *Désamère, The Descent of Alette,* and *Mysteries of Small Houses.* Each of these outstanding recent books tells a story (at times, more than one), forms a discrete relationship to narrativity, and develops its own music. The following text is composed of excerpts from our correspondence.

10/2/96

JUDITH GOLDMAN: At your workshop at The Poetry Project last spring, you talked about voice, about saying I in a poem, using that I to shape the way you talk about yourself, and the way the I unifies the poem. You asked, at one point, "Is there an actual I who is exactly myself?" You also problematized narrative during the workshop, saying that narrative is an outside (false) structure that people use to jail their pasts. Do you see narrative as self-romanticizing—as though the I the story falls to becomes too large(?) or too idealized to be the "exactly [one]self"?

ALICE NOTLEY: In that workshop last May, I was presenting considerations and techniques associated with a manuscript I'd just finished called *Mysteries*

of Small Houses. The project of *Mysteries* was to "re-center the I." I'd been writing narratives with fictional characters for a number of years and suddenly saw "I" as a challenge and a mystery. I wanted to investigate the basic I (I mostly uncorrupted) as closely as possible. Basic I is terrifying of course. It really exists, but we seem to construct everything—our world, our social forms, our narratives, and our anti-narratives—in order to keep it hidden. I wanted to find "my self"—as the only self I could investigate—in the context of my past in order to determine its constancy, or lack of it, across the years. I thus had to re-see my life. I tried for a scary honesty; I wanted to be frightened by my own existence. Be as alive as I am and not be in other people's ideas of life-shapes or other people's theories about the non-existence of the self. Yes, I think narratives of the self are often self-romanticizing, but not because they make the I too large, rather because they make it too small and not precisely individual enough. I think each I is both huge and unique. As for voice, I probably talked about how the voice comes from the depths of the unique body and the unique self and each person's voice—taking voice to be both sound and style—is different. For example, I can tell the difference between each person's poems, no matter how imitative or downright bad they are, after a few sessions of an ongoing workshop. Why is that?

JG: Describing your own writing, you said, "I remember everything; it isn't past, it's wild," and further stated that names tame things that shouldn't be tamed. How do you free your writing from the constriction of narration? Do you feel that you have to de-narrativize or unname certain memories as part of your poetic process? Do you ever find that words in and of themselves are conducive to narration and find it difficult to free them from coalescing into already recognizable forms? Does a poem represent a process of organizing the self?

AN: The quotation—"I remember everything; it isn't past, it's wild"—is from the first poem in *Mysteries of Small Houses*. It's called "Would Want to Be in My Wildlife." It's a kind of introduction to the process of the book. That is, in order to write it I went into a sort of hypnotic trance, which really wasn't very different from my normal writing state, though it felt new and exciting anyway. I think perhaps I went deeper into that state than usual, in order to remember things. But I find that there is a particular state to write from in which I am free from the constrictions you mention, free from stories as I already know them and also free from my current tag words. In the case of *Mysteries* I tried to find my four-year-old self and to re-enter the house where I lived when I was four, because it seemed that when I was that age I was both most natural and most good. I identified essential self with that age—the problem then became, what was the purpose, if any, of my later experience? As you may have gathered, I'm always inventing a new way in to writing poetry. I suppose that's how I manage to keep such things as shape and narrative and vocabulary fresh for myself. As for your final question in this sequence, I don't try to organize my self so much as to find it over and over, though I often try to organize what I think about things.

JG: Your newest published works, particularly *The Descent of Alette*, as well as *Désamère* and, *Close to me & Closer . . . (The Language of Heaven)* are very much concerned with storytelling. These are phenomenally intricate texts that, as you state in your preface to *Close to me*, "anyone can understand." Did you specifically think of these books as a project of producing texts that anyone can understand? Or perhaps better said, who are or who aren't these texts for? What is the poet's (social/political) responsibility to articulate the memories of the self and the wildness or presentness of the memories as represented by an I? How are the narratives that these recent works present different from narratives that you consider too structured or, to put it bluntly, dead?

AN: I wrote *Alette* in particular for everyone, or at least for the sort of people who ride and take shelter in the New York City subways. I wrote *Close to me* . . . to demonstrate the aptness of the non-intellectual voice for speaking of profound things. I wrote *Désamère* as an eco-warning: I'm not afraid of the ecological cliché especially as the situation becomes more and more drastic.

But I *always* want to write poems anyone can understand. And I always have wanted to. Even in my most "difficult" works I've always tried to include some more generally attractive aspects—a highly defined, seductive musical shape, or jokes, patter, color. I think that so-called popular poetry underestimates the verbal intelligence of so-called ordinary people, who in turn haven't been properly taught poetry in school. Meanwhile so many people's careers in the academy and in poetry seem to depend on their obfuscating poetry, making it seem as theoretical and intellectual as possible. The consequence is that ordinary people think they can't understand poetry, and popular poetry talks down to them, these people who in bars, on streetcorners, and at kitchen tables conduct sophisticated verbal dealings daily, tell stories at least as well as any professor of literature, get at each other with words in the most subtle ways. My books are for anyone, anyone who feels like taking the chance and the time. Of course that still won't be a lot of people. In relation to political/social responsibility in *Mysteries of Small Houses*: If I say that the self is wild and free and vast, is the real, but is only realized apart from the social and political restrictions we're always laying on each other—the implications are obvious: Let's get this dead weight off that smothers self-realization, catches us up in economic situations that are globally harmful to others and to the planet, enslaves us to one or another doctrine. As for how my narratives are different from "dead" ones: For one thing the music is different each time. When I invent a new music for my poem, I insure that I won't tell a story I've already told or that I can predict. And then there's the "matter" or subject of my books—it's always something that makes me shaky and that I can't deal with adequately. I won't be able to cover it, I won't be able to kill it.

JG: In your workshop, you also discussed language-based or text-based writing that uses words instead of ideas as "amusing," but superficial. How/why did you stop writing language-based poetry (if that is how you would describe some of your earlier work)?

AN: I don't think I've ever written language-based poetry as such. I've always had too much to say. Too much happens to me personally, and more, there's what's happening to the world . . . There's too much to talk about, to deal with. I'm not interested in "language" when there's so much danger in the air. I sometimes use "language" to help me get to what I want to say or to an area of feeling or responsibility. The words, coming both from my depths and from the outer world with its urgencies, help me locate my poem.

JG: On a more simple autobiographical note, do you consider yourself an expatriate? Is there a community of writers in Paris that you identify with? Do you ever feel nostalgic about or homesick for the States/New York City?

AN: People keep asking me the expatriate question. It always surprises me because of that word, which has daddy inside it and all sorts of loyalties and localisms. I don't consider myself a patriot or an expatriate; I'm here, I'm staying, my French is still terrible. I've mostly been looking at the US from Paris, in that sudden new way available from being outside it, but I'd prefer to be looking at the world now. Though the US is where my professional life is and will be. But the world is effectively dropping more and more boundaries, becoming one thing. There isn't a real community of writers here that I identify with. I identify with a national (American) and finally international community of writers that exists in the air, in books and magazines and letters; that's been the case for a long time, since before I moved to Paris. I'm afraid I don't miss New York much, I lived there too long, but I very much miss certain friends. What I do miss is the Southwest and Needles, the desert—very sharply sometimes. But the experience of being in another culture is continuously . . . pungent. I like Paris because of the French, the French working people, shop people, are smart and politically informed and witty and contrary to popular opinion, very nice. And then there are negative things to notice, the language to grapple with, another history—it's something to do! In New York I'd gotten so I wasn't sensitive to anything new there.

JG: In the next few questions, I want to concentrate on how you figure yourself as a feminist, and how you constitute your poetics as a woman (or how being a woman informs your poetics). How does mothering fit into your poetics? What about the poetics of everyday life?

AN: I'm not interested in a poetics of mothering or in mothering, nurturance, procreation, even creation *per se*. I'm interested in being the mother of my own children—whom I also see as my very close friends. I'm interested in the status of the mother in society, which I take to be pretty low, like that of the poet, since there's no pay for it unless you do it for someone else's kid. And I'm not interested in a poetics of everyday life—I really can't stand the phrase. I used it in the title of an essay ("Notes on 'The Poetry of Everyday Life'") because I was assigned it, but the essay is about enlarging or even transcending our notions of what that is. I'm interested in a poetry that's as inclusive as possible. And I found out very early on in my career that much of my experience was excluded from poetry up to that time. For example, it's astonishing to be trying to get on as a poet while bearing and rearing a child, realizing that there are only a handful of poems in the language that deal with your state of mind and urgencies. Sylvia Plath sometimes refers to being a mother and was one of the few examples available to me of a poet-mother. Her last poems though brilliant are sick. I have no idea why she's an icon of feminism. She's a dreadful example for any young mother who needs courage. Are we all supposed to kill ourselves and endanger the lives of our children? I felt as if I had to invent out of air a way of speaking of my experience as a mother: that was at first. Later I had to invent forms to contain my children's voices since they were never not where I was even while writing. I quite enjoyed the latter—inventing the poem "January" and those talky poems that took place at 101 St. Mark's Place; but sometimes while I was writing the earlier work I felt quite desperate.

JG: How do you feel reading magazines with your work and work by your sons in them? What correspondences or lack thereof do you see between your work and their work?

AN: I'm pleased that my sons are both poets. Poetry is an honorable, exacting, necessary occupation. I can't think of a better one. It isn't surprising to me that someone might pick it up from his parents, or rather pick up insights into why it's necessary and how it's done. Because, of course, poetry isn't about who's the best poet. It's about continuing the tradition of poetry, making sure its "services"—spiritual, intellectual—remain available to people. I read their poems to see what I can pick up from them. They're more in touch with certain kinds of things—new sounds—than I am. I of course am wiser than them due to my great age.

JG: What about your relationship, as a woman writer, to male poets? (I guess also both contemporaries/poets in history.) Are there particular female poets in history who have greatly influenced you? What about contemporaries?

AN: I've had very good relationships with a lot of male writers; I've also had a problematic relationship with poetry's politics, institutions, ideas as to what poetry should be, etc., due to being a woman. Both have always existed simultaneously and sometimes intertwined. Ted [Berrigan]'s influence on me was profoundly benign and necessary. I'm not sure what poet I would be now if I hadn't met him. When I first knew him he was a little skeptical about women poets. He wasn't sure that he liked the poetry of the women poets he knew about as much as he liked the men's poetry, partly because women were denied involvement in the parts of life that seemed to give poetry its edge. He quite quickly changed his tack though. It seems to me now that he recognized my talent before I did and fostered it as much as he could—to the extent of insisting we leave England in 1974, when he didn't really want to, because he thought I needed to be around American poets and similarly insisting on leaving Chicago in 1975 to get me to New York and the poets there. I think he recognized before we did that Anne [Waldman], Bernadette [Mayer], Maureen [Owen], and others and I constituted a real generation of poets and a new kind of voice. Ted really cared about poetry.

But I had consistent support from the very beginning of my poetry from men such as Bob Creeley, Anselm Hollo, Tom Clark, and Phil Whalen, and a little later Edwin Denby. I felt that Doug [Oliver] was seriously interested in my poetry from our first meeting in 1973. Likewise I don't remember a lot of gender problems at The Poetry Project. In the years I lived in New York, the Project was most often run by a woman. It was a woman-friendly institution, though we fought a lot about everything, so we probably fought about gender too—it's hard to remember. For me the gender problems arise when I'm not allowed to speak: men will dominate the room, the subject, the theory, the panel. They like to compete and only like to compete with each other. Women poets still, thus, get goddessed. Men lead movements and argue with each other over the present and future of poetry, insuring that they get more space in the so-called discourse. It's like they're still doing all the real thinking. We're geniuses, they say, and then go back to arguing with each other. Somehow we don't have any power, so we never get attacked. It's also a fact that the ways in which poetry gets published, discussed, and accepted into the academy or whatever are ways invented by men: book publication, magazines and magazine formats, forums for discussion, standards of discussion, standards of publication, not to mention the whole idea of a literary movement, the academy, the avant-garde are all male forms. There's a sort of male-ish bossiness and proprietorship that never quite gets shaken. And the notion that this is the only way, that it's always been this way, that no one invented it.

JG: I just read *At Night the States* and was really amazed at how you achieved both a presentation of fragments—in their sharpness (an almost 'indecent,' insistent, implicit fragility)—and also a wholeness, a body going through time, meaning a body of thought, going through time . . . I have been thinking a lot about elegies—in a way, I always trip over ideas about elegies and the "deadness" of figures whenever I write—maybe this is a kind of music for me? You're imparting a kind of life after death—a very real one; your self as an intrusion upon coldness, dis-aliveness or pathetic reanimations were an amazing address/redress of elegy . . . Do you feel that this is akin to what you were doing in *Close to me*, with your father? I think that book is not as "ghost-oriented" . . .

AN: The short poems in *At Night the States* have always been difficult to read aloud, mostly because the audience doesn't know how to take them. The audience can't figure out whether to applaud or not. I find that interesting, thinking about it now. There may be some special value in poetry that the applause mechanism can't intrude on. Anyway, in these poems, as is obvious, I was intent on going on, going through. I wrote them with no thought as to their qualities; I scarcely thought of them as poems. I looked at the folder of them about a year after I'd completed them and was struck by the fact that they *were* poems, that I didn't know of any like them, and that they might possibly be of real use to someone else. Around that time I wrote the title poem, which is quite different, and then I had a book. Writing *Close to me* was very different; I'm not sure the two compare. You see, I've been talking to my father for a long time now. He may be so alive to me that notions of elegy don't relate to the writings he figures in. I began having dreams in the mid-'80s in which he told me things and gave me instructions. Several of these dreams were involved in the inception of *Alette*, in which he is, of course, the owl. But when I began *Close to me*, I felt that he was talking to me. Period. Not dead, no elegy. I wanted to try to get close to death as a state, and he was my guide but he wasn't dead, not the way Ted is dead in *At Night the States*.

11/10/96

JG: The way you define what being a poet does as a service really means a lot to me. I feel strongly that being a poet is political, that it fulfills an important subversive political function. Of course I'd also like to see a changing social framework, and think I have seen experimental writing meet with somewhat more success in the world at large on its own terms and poets partially earn a living or get recognition by it. In general, when this happens, I characterize it not as an annexation (like a dilution), but a victory ... This all relates to what you say in your talk, "The 'Feminine' Epic," when you describe what led you to write *Alette*. How do you reconcile thinking about social problems systemically—like national culpability and "needing an epic"—but also as related to "godlike forces," like accidents or problems in causality? Or that the repercussions of actions might exceed or defeat the intentions behind them? Is *Alette* a kind of purposive accident, a use of "godlike forces" that make accidents, tripping up "human" (or nationalist) intentions? In "The 'Feminine' Epic," you say you want to tell a "continuous story." One reason I find this so important is because of the tradition of Romantic ellipse that continues even now—as a lacuna where all the action happens, or at least, the *crisis* happens. We're supposed to know it already; it's in the social script, even though it's semi-unsayable or sublime. The necessity of continuity means the story might not go as planned, i.e., pay attention! And that nothing is unspeakable.

AN: You seem to be proposing a difference between what can be understood through reason and what keeps happening without anyone's foreseeing it, as if reason were the human-species quality and disruption or the unforeseen or the inspired, the godlike. I think that reason is also part of the godlike, that being able to see things whole and with detachment is as assuredly godlike as creating or initiating something unexpected. Life seems to be about the two together, in the sense that it couldn't exist without both, would be stationary without disruption and chaotic without rational analysis, so they are both of god, whatever that is. My epic is an accident—as is everything else I write— in that it turned out entirely differently from how I sort of foresaw it. I don't plan on the accident, so in that sense it isn't a purposive accident—I don't anticipate the surprises or I wouldn't be surprised, I guess. I don't try to trip up human intentions, I'm not interested in subversion: I'm very blatant.

JG: What I also like about "continuous story" is that you don't say the whole story—as if it were something that could be exhausted or that you would want to finish and exhaust. That poetry is a place for story, against the other narratives of narrative works like novels, because of the epic form. *Alette* is set apart from the work of many contemporary writers who investigate an aesthetic of breakage and fragments. Do you feel that there is some contradiction in the singularity of continuity? Can a singular story be told or is the story of it, the narrativity of it, something that joins others to it, that binds them, as you say in giving "some of the guilt back to the national community"?

AN: The singularity of continuity is entirely appropriate to the way I know and perceive. Mostly I wanted to see if I could tell that kind of story; I'm interested in trying out as many possibilities of poetry as possible and in being as skilled as I can be. Telling that kind of story seemed to be difficult, so I thought I'd better try it. Writing in fragments and with breakage seems to me to be easy, although sometimes I feel like doing that anyway. I don't like to rule anything out. The measure of *Alette* isn't based on the unification of a chorus: the two relevant pieces from *Beginning with a Stain* are, and some, maybe a lot, of *White Phosphorus* is, but *Alette* is in a virtually unified voice. It's a woman's epic because I wrote it and because its protagonist is a woman; and of course a "singular story can be told" because I did so, though I propose it as a gift for anyone who wants it, who thinks it applies to them or simply would like to read it. I very much like the relation of protagonist and chorus, as in classical Greek drama and in oratorio, but I don't believe we're always all in the chorus except in some impossible overview. That isn't how a life works; anyone is singular and somewhat plural and at perhaps the most crucial moments anyone is very very single.

JG: Does it seem like part of what you are doing is unifying voices whose growth was stunted and whose (voice)body was fragmented and scattered the moment it began to gain strength? What I'm interested in here is another political issue at stake in poetry that you discuss in your epic talk, which is not just the marginality of poets' lives in American society, but also in choosing the identity of poet as a political stance, as an activism in itself, as united with and sharing common elements with other subversive/constructive activities. Do you see it as your service ("And what if I owe an epic?") to bring out what might be private knowledge and force it into a public domain, as well as bringing out a part of communal knowledge that doesn't surface very often, that is constantly being hidden? To force what are, in a way, new things into narrativity?

AN: Again, I don't feel that I'm unifying voices; I'm more trying to represent them. You refer to "choosing the identity of poet as a political stance, as an activism in itself . . ." A couple of things there. I'm never quite sure that I chose the identity of poet, I feel more as if it chose me, or at least as if it gradually happened that I got co-opted by it. There was a point at which I found myself too fascinated by poetry to do anything else. I do think that it can be an activism and that it doesn't have to have a political subject to be that. I think the poems I wrote in *When I Was Alive*, an out-of-print book consisting of imitations of dead male poets but coming out of the most in-between moments of a woman's life, bespeaks as much activism as *White Phosphorus* does. What you stand for is often more important than what you struggle against. How to live as opposed to how to fight.

JG: As you say, "We live in that total international multicultural natureless world" but do we really live in it in terms of the command that you speak of? What I'm trying to get at, here, I guess, is change, and how poetry works as a force in the world to make change happen. Is it a matter of changing how things are represented or of changing the quality of life itself? I guess it's possible to relate this to experimental poetry's assuming more of the reader to begin with . . . as you said in letter #1, much popular poetry doesn't assume enough intelligence.

AN: I think all poets—myself included—tend to exaggerate the evil they might do with their poems. All poetry is marginalized, not just experimental poetry. I find it hard to imagine an international corporate poem, unless there came to be a market for such a poem, but there's really no market for any poetry. Well I suppose there will be a multinational form of the *New Yorker* poem, maybe there already is. What I'm much more interested in is keeping up with the way the world is changing and both resisting its changes—since few of them seem positive right now—and, understanding that the young are necessarily embroiled in those changes, being exceedingly sympathetic to what's going on. Poetry itself doesn't make things happen, it's more subtle than that. Poetry's part of everything that's happening culturally. It also sends itself into the future, when a certain poetry might be finally appreciated. But I think that rather than overtly change things it accompanies, comforts, gives courage, amuses, stimulates, etc. Partly *Alette* is that with which you compare your own experience. Poetry is poetry by being all of its selves though, even its doggerel self. I honestly don't think of myself as an experimental poet, because I don't think in such terms much, well I did say *New Yorker* poem. I write usually what it seems to me poetry needs next; I suppose that's why all my works look different from each other and I suppose that's what lands me in the experimental category.

JG: In your talk on the epic, when you discuss the "natureless world" in terms of *Désamère* ("There's no one to kill because the machine of natural obliteration can't be stopped"), does that mean we have to work in a closed economy of social value towards representation? I'm asking you this because for a moment there you seemed to present a kind of closure that was pretty bleak . . . when in fact your recent work, take *Alette* for example, often seems to articulate its own world, its own power structures and environment—as good can happen in them, and as open: they are surreal, while referentially and politically engaged; they are symbolically and minutely concerned . . .

AN: Regarding "There's no one to kill, etc." and "natureless world," and "do we work in a closed set and fight in a closed economy . . ."—that's not even the point. The point is much worse, I fear. I wrote *Alette* before *Désamère* [although *Alette* was published after *Désamère*], it's not more recent. The question of the future of the planet explodes all theories of a suitable poetics, suitable representation and so on. That kind of discussion becomes irrelevant. I'm never going to support inept poetry, but frankly when I read the facts about global warming or overpopulation I really don't care how one's *supposed* to write the poem. If a whole world is being destroyed, I don't think it matters as to whether it's correct to "imagine" that destruction or to attack it from a vantage of realistic depiction and overt reaction. Either will do, as long as we're talking about the problem.

JG: You ask: "Why did I want to write about a woman of action if women don't act and if I don't really approve of deeds?" You also talk about women's deeds being "symbolic action." But I think that a lot of what you are doing is making what is usually viewed as symbolic really literal, or active. In talking about poetry accomplishing spiritual/intellectual services or tasks, would you say that the task you set for yourself in *Alette* was to externalize dreams and not to take them as just dream language that symbolizes something in "real" life relationships, but other possible, forceful narratives that don't stand in for something else, but are what they are?

AN: I think dreams are partly a way of thinking and that the figures and actions in dreams tend to be symbols, but of much more than relationships. They can stand for qualities, abstractions, hard-to-define ideas the way that gods and goddesses and their actions do in myths. But they're hard to pin down so also, as you say, they are what they are, and sometimes they are, I think, only being a story, as if to amuse the dreamer. People like to be told mythical stories because there's both a story and all that resonance.

JG: Could you talk a little bit about your trance technique poetics, and finding your one I? I only know about your process from the workshop tapes and what you told me in letter #1 . . . I think people might be really interested in this, and how it relates to the techniques of H. D., Robert Duncan, even Rimbaud . . . and the hypnogogic. How do you define trance writing in terms of poetics? What does this have to do with writing a feminine epic and making the heroine put what is underground on the surface and fight it out there? How does the epic connect with what might be considered its opposite, your personal autobiographical work? If the autobiographical poems are different than that, how are they different? (A difference in uncovering the musics?)

AN: I don't think I used the trance technique exactly when I was writing

Alette. For that work I would use dreams I'd had at night or would try to fall asleep briefly during the day or simply close my eyes and try to see something, follow a chain of imagery. If I was using dreams, I would try to choose details quickly or make the decision to use the material at all quickly —I was trying to be as automatic as possible. I didn't use those techniques for *Close to me* and *Désamère*: with the former I didn't have to do anything special for my father's voice to start speaking in my mind; for the third section of the latter I concentrated on images gathering under my eyelids— aren't such images called eidetic?—and forming their own plots. I discovered a different sort of technique in the process of writing *Mysteries of Small Houses*, a sort of deep relaxation which made my limbs tingle and was very pleasant. I discovered, from doing some reading, I was probably practicing a mild form of self-hypnosis, so I began to employ a few of the certified self-hypnosis techniques, concentrating on a landscape, making my arm heavy, counting backwards and so on. In terms of poetics, I guess I'd say that this process is not very different from the one I ordinarily associate with writing poetry. You go into a sort of trance to write; you shut out much of the world so that only the poem is transpiring and if you're getting materials from your environment it's only transpiring in terms of your poem. As far as *Alette* and what's underground coming to the surface, I was interested first of all in the liberation of people from the dreary exigencies of "chartered" unnatural tyrannized lives, by throwing open the possibility of psychological liberation— this can't be the only way humans have lived, so much is repressed—not desires, but all sorts of possibilities and potentials. I don't know how the epic books and the autobiographical book connect, except that the latter also contains story elements and also creates a background for the writing of the other kind of work, a naturalistic parallel.

JG: I also really value what you said in your first letter to me about doctrinaireness: "finding some reflection of it [in poems] of what they've [people in the academy] been taught to think or its lack." Are there other poets in particular whose terms create helpful different frameworks for you to talk about poetic/social issues, that you think work around, through, or with dominant ideas about deconstruction/post-modernity that are so doctrinaire?

AN: At the moment I work most in conjunction with Doug. We're interested in the same kinds of forms and share many of the same concerns, but speak so differently from each other, being American and English, that we're enriched by the different textures of our languages. And also the differing textures of the ways in which we think. I also always want to know what people like Ron Padgett, Lorenzo Thomas, Anne Waldman, Anselm Hollo, etc. think about things. I continue to be interested in the work of Leslie Scalapino, Eileen Myles, Joanne Kyger, Lyn Hejinian. I want to know how mature minds are dealing with what's going on in the world. And I'm waiting to see what the very young will come up with in terms of forms and techniques. Anselm and Edmund are both quite interesting at the moment. As is Alicia Wing, say. I also feel as if I'm picking up on some things that Ted was doing at the end of his life that have sort of lain dormant since his death. I think that there's been a dearth of intelligent commentary on his work and that his later work has been ignored—but that's good for me, I can steal from it with no one watching.

AN INTERVIEW WITH JOHN GODFREY
BY LISA JARNOT

APRIL/MAY 1997   NO. 165

John Godfrey lives on the Lower East Side in Manhattan. He is the author of *Dabble: Poems 1966–1980* (Full Court Press, 1982), *Where the Weather Suits My Clothes* (Z Press, 1984), and *Midnight on Your Left* (The Figures, 1988). He is a registered nurse and currently works with pediatric AIDS patients. The following interview was conducted on January 19, 1997, at John's apartment on East 12th Street.

LISA JARNOT: When we talked on the phone a couple weeks ago you mentioned having gone to Buffalo, but you'd been at Princeton before that, with other poets like John Thorpe and Lewis MacAdams?

JOHN GODFREY: To tell you the truth, John Thorpe was hardly there at all. I think he disappeared after one semester. He came and went. His father was a professor in the English Department at Princeton. John at that time was to me a type—the boarding school beatnik. I didn't formally "go to Buffalo." After lasting it out and graduating from Princeton in 1967 I went west and worked on a ranch in Crook County, Wyoming, and returned in the fall to the East at loose ends and waiting for the draft. Because Lewis MacAdams, my first connection to poetry activities, was in graduate school at SUNY Buffalo, I went up and out there. The living was cheap. I was there from

October 1967 to April 1968. I met Jack Clarke and Duncan McNaughton
that way. Phoebe MacAdams and Genie McNaughton were equally close
friends to me at that time. John Wieners was there, and, of course, Creeley.
Like most of us, something got me into writing when I was high school age,
and it was a schoolteacher. Because I'd spent five or six years going to a
small-town Vermont school, and my parents moved to Albany, New York.
I took a scholarship exam to this place called The Albany Academy, this
military school—it was kind of weird—it was like Ivy League military, and
I got in. And I didn't know how to write shit. It was like ninth grade, and
you wrote book reports. I was horrible. And I had an English teacher who
straightened me out quickly. He was the typical old-school type of guy—
probably about 35, on the effete side, like most private school teachers would
be expected to be. He was the kind of guy everyone was very fond of—jocks
were fond of him, smart guys were fond of him. That happened consistently
through high school, where a teacher of English—where there was a certain
fascination with that person who gave me a lot of encouragement. This hap-
pened again in Dallas, where I attended the last three years of high school,
again as a scholarship boy at a private school. There were two English teach-
ers there who helped and encouraged me. By the way, I went to Princeton for
free. Says something about my father's income. But anyway, I was interested
in writing. My father also wrote, and expressed himself in words a lot. But
when I got to college the world was not what it was soon to be—there wasn't
a huge draft going on, there wasn't a lot of noise about Viet Nam. Although
there was noise, it was mainly civil rights. My mind was blown. I was so
happy to be away from home and I was really going away to school because
I wanted to join the upper-middle class. And that lasted about half a year,
and during that time I was writing poems, without any motivation really.
And then I suddenly identified with it for reasons that had to do a lot with
being in the wrong place at the wrong time. I wasn't happy to go to that par-
ticular college.

LJ: Did you have influences as a poet—were there poets that you were reading?

JG: Well, from the very start, the biggest influence, and it still remains, is Shakespeare. I mean that's the best stuff you get to read in high school, and the way I was educated, you started in the ninth grade, you were reading Shakespeare. And you were memorizing the famous soliloquies. And those famous soliloquies are righteously famous. I use a lot of the patterns that just became ingrained from reading Shakespeare at that age. Mainly I mean Shakespeare will have a speech in which a person deals with a present moment on about five or six levels, and he weaves together observations leading to events, all in a speech, and it isn't a very long speech—they're magnificent. But when I was blundering around, not knowing shit as a freshman in college, when it came to poetry or something like it, I was listening to a lot of blues and folk, and I was getting an ear, because I hadn't had music as a kid at home. I listened to the radio, but I didn't have records. I had a roommate who had a record player, so I had the opportunity to purchase records and listen to them. This roommate had the Folkways folk anthology, and I got into Lightnin' Hopkins lyrics, and Bob Dylan. I'd just discovered Bob Dylan at the age of eighteen when he had one record and I was attracted to raggedyness. But I wrote things in isolation until I was almost twenty years old. And there was this guy, a dear friend, Lewis MacAdams, who had gone to the same high school and been a year ahead of me, and was also a year ahead of me in college, who dressed very flamboyantly, with capes, and Spanish hats, and things that he would never have worn in Dallas, who was active on the college literary magazine. There was a group that was very up to date, inspired by Burroughs and Kerouac, and so on. And Lewis MacAdams, whose poetry I love, introduced me to all of this stuff. He loaned me books, he introduced me to this very straight seeming classmate of mine, John Koethe, who was way ahead of me. To that point I had dug up the Don Allen anthology. I knew Ginsberg's *Howl* and *Kaddish*, and had an interest in Bob Kaufman, who, by the way, did not impress the poets I got to know in the East Village at the time. All of a sudden I was reading Jones/ Baraka's *Dead Lecturer*, Wieners' *Hotel Wentley Poems* and *Ace of Penta-*

cles, Duncan, Ashbery, and Berrigan. So all of a sudden my life changed, and I totally disengaged in a lot of ways from where I was. I came to New York occasionally with great trepidation. There were a lot of people walking around stoned on methedrine and they were very intimidating, and they were very prejudiced. I came from a lower-middle-class background, but I was a little shy and whatnot, and they all assumed that I had to be some rich guy, or some upper-middle-class guy. It was very funny when Ted Berrigan finally figured out what my background was, and the age of my parents. We became very brotherly behind that, because he in fact would have been like the third oldest in my family, after initially having been quite biased against me on the background issue. Anyway, MacAdams turned me on to all of the books and to a number of people, and they seemed like such real things— the bohemian in the East Village. And so venerable. There wasn't one of them over twenty-five except Berrigan, but they seemed so venerable. And I would come to New York and want to show them my poems. See when you really start thinking now, "yeah, that's what it's been all this time, I'm a poet," you start writing and all of a sudden you realize, "jeez, I've only written twenty poems." You have this feeling that you want to have a big stack of pages next to you, and so you do it. I mean I probably wrote two poems a day for about three years. I used to get very upset if I couldn't sit down and write something. The reality of it was not interesting. I was interested in the enthusiasm and the fact that—well, you know the feeling—if you're a poet and you have a certain thing that you know that you can do, doing it is probably like an expert on an instrument who practices all the time just because there is so much pleasure in being able to do it. I don't really feel that way now; I don't have time to be so self-centered with respect to poetry. It's equally interesting to do it though; when you get into a groove, it's great. Not only is it possible to write on so many different levels at the same time, it's possible to find out things about the way that you work on all those different levels too.

LJ: What were the poems like, your early poems?

JG: I think I'm too embarrassed to try to remember. Well, I've never known a poet whose first poems were not "poor me, I'm so lonely." I've seen it, I've snuck around, I've found it . . . You know, you never leave a friend who's a poet alone in your apartment to go out for cigarettes because he's going to start looking through your poems. Some people are going to sniff underwear or find your porn, but poets are going to try to find your most recent poems that you don't want to show them. The young Jim Brodey was incredible. He would walk in your place, talk, lean over your desk, start looking at things, push them aside, and you'd say, "hey man, get the fuck away." But what I wrote then? Yeah, I started out with the same "pity me" type of thing and then I sort of realized that if all I was really familiar with was academic/ scholarly treatments of modern poetry, I had to get something beyond that, but that was also something that was going on. I mean by that time, I'm nineteen years old, you have to study so much of Eliot, you'd get some Pound also, but they seemed fairly far away. So a lot of what kicked in at that time was that kind of self-consciousness that Bob Dylan brought to what had formerly been a kind of bland lyrics. Yeah, and Bob Dylan became a big influence, not so much in the way he was doing it, but in the spirit of it, which was, for one thing, to challenge constantly the people who had been interested in him. Every time he came out with an album you ran out to get it and listen to it because you realized that he was going to shake somebody off. That was the attitude a lot and what we all aspired to at that time in the '60s to be doing was to be out from under—out from under the deductive. Academics works like bad science. Academics kind of deduces rather than using induction. Induction maybe has to do a lot with phenomenology or something like that, if you want to be real philosophical. Especially in the '60s, the idea of entering new kinds of matter into all kinds of art works had a lot to do with that—these things are here—they should be noticed and added to the data that is used in art. But you know, very quickly, the first two things that knocked me down were being loaned *The Tennis Court Oath* [by John Ashbery], and *The Sonnets* [by Ted Berrigan], which were only out for like two years at that time. In fact, the copy I had was the C Press edition of *The Sonnets* that was loaned to me by John Koethe. I never gave it back to him and I still have it. I'm more of a sap than an intellectual, and Ted's sonnets had an analytic quality, but at the same time I was aware of the sentimental Irishman in them. Ted maintained that quality for me all the way. And, having this ear for disjunctive things, one of the appealing things about Bob Dylan was that we weren't thinking of things in terms of the linear, like you do today, the lingo was different. You know, all these non sequiturs and abrupt turns of direction were interesting. *The Sonnets* were like that, *The Tennis Court Oath* used a lot of that. I didn't understand shit about how it might be done, how those guys might have done it, but my gut took me in that direction. You know, I try to avoid in my own stuff getting into connecting dots, or having something that has a narrative flow that is narrow. I like to suggest that it's sort of like a movie. I also have to say that one of the big influences from that time was having seen *A Married Woman*, the Godard movie, which just knocked me out, because it does what I aspired to, which is to give you different angles on something concrete, and at the same time have something abstract going on, either in what the voices are saying and then making the impression through the use of all these weird still life angles that there's something going on, so that you're thinking also on a conceptual basis. And all these things going on at the same time, and not being a linear thing. It's sort of like picking details and not worrying whether they make a totally coherent picture. It's maybe hard to convince someone who wasn't there because they weren't born yet, but everything that was going on in America in the '60s was very aware that some kind of threshold had been crossed and the way people thought, the way people lived, everything was being challenged, up in the air, everything was new and there was a belief in answers. So much for answers, huh? It was more a depressing than a hopeful time.

LJ: Well how do things seem now?

JG: Now? Terrible. From what I do so many hours a week, and think about a lot, I'm into a different kind of narrow world. But you know, if you've got knowledge of how classism and racism and sexism work in a city like this, that's far more important to me than anything that's going on in arts or poetry, to say the least.

LJ: Maybe we should talk about that. You're working about sixty hours a week as a nurse. So what's a typical day for you?

JG: I get up at 4:30. It's kind of weird, but when you get used to it it's cool. It's just another time to get up. I exercise a bit, eat quickly. I'm in my car at a little after 6:00 and I drive out to Bayside to this office and I open the place up. And I have to do a lot of paperwork. Every kid I have for a patient has a chart, and there are hundreds of pages—all of these items that I have to keep up to date, and a lot of them legal, with the Department of Health. I'll do paperwork until about 8:00 and then I might work on a couple of visits from the day before. I have to write up a lot of details on these visit reports, because what I'm doing is more or less a clinic visit in the home, between clinic visits to the doctor. And I'm keeping a running account of how a patient is doing, especially when they are taking medications and there are issues of compliance with multiple medications, expiration dates, storage details, food restrictions, and dangers of drug resistance with regard to all the preceding. Because I deal with people who lie a lot, the best of them lie to me a lot. It's very interesting. I have to deal with people who have no reason to like me, and I'm a likeable enough guy. The kids and I get along great, but I'm dealing a lot with adults who have control of how these kids are going to live and who are dreadfully undereducated, and because they live in complete segregation, aside from television exposure, they have no idea of what is expected of them when they go out into the white-dominated world, whether it's a hospital or welfare, or something like that. They become very defensive; they have ways of coping that aren't always in the best interests of the kids. So, I'm in my office and by 8:00 I'm starting to use the phone, I make dozens of phone calls—I talk to doctors and all my patients. Then at about 10:30 or 11:00 I get in my car and I make four or five visits in Brooklyn, and I cover Bushwick and BedStuy, a little bit of Crown Heights, the downhill part of Park Slope, and Sunset Park. I'm out there making visits until 6:00, and if things come up, I might be out there until 7:00. I get home, I eat, stare at my navel, and go to bed.

LJ: So what you do is physical evaluations of the kids?

JG: Yeah, a lot of it is strictly clinical, but a lot of it gets into all kinds of stuff. I mean most of my visits I aim for an hour or an hour and fifteen minutes, but I'm there for an hour and a half. Something comes up, something's really wrong, or I'm going to run some kind of test I can do in the field. It's very hard, but it's also very gratifying because I get to learn so much. I've learned so much physiology. I've learned how to do a very quick, very thorough head to toe examination. I have no trouble with kids. I think poetry is a very good background for dealing with children in the first place, as we know from guys like Jack Collom and so on. If you're a little wacky and you're dealing with kids who have maybe a delay, but they're not bad on receptive language, you can find out a lot by joking with them and being ridiculous and absurd. They have difficulty knowing what's real and what's not anyway because they're children. And one way to learn what is real is to learn what isn't real—and absurd language use is not real, and they begin to get a certain value for when you're really communicating real things. You know this is a really great job—having always been fascinated by Céline's writings as much as anyone's. In the 1930s there were all these fantastic things happening in fiction. I mean think of it—you have Faulkner, you have Céline, you have Williams, you have all these people writing these great novels, all of them trying to be fearless in confronting really the big things, the human condition, all this ugliness. And Céline especially with his nose stuck in the underclass, portraying himself in a way that wasn't quite true. He was sort of an upper-middle-class guy who happened to be slumming. Not slumming, I mean all of a sudden you find yourself in the slums, you're not slumming—you're in the slums.

LJ: When do you write poems?

JG: Whenever I feel like it. I chip away at it. I used to have a fetish about pens, and then it became a fetish about sketchbooks, and now I just use a legal pad. I keep it around and I chip away at things. When I put them on my computer then I print out a thing to look at and it becomes a little more together. What I react to becomes a little more together. I always wrote longhand and you never knew what it really was until you typed it, which I dreaded doing because I don't type well and for that reason I usually wrote as short as possible, because I knew that sooner or later I'd have to use the typewriter. I mean when I first started out, there weren't even xerox machines. You had to type everything over again to send it to somebody; it was a drag.

LJ: Do you ever think about writing a long, sustained, "epic" poem?

JG: Never. I used to do sonnet sequences and shit like that. I never published those. That was a phase of mine up to about 1970. At that point I felt like I had something going on inside, like I was ready to step out of an apprentice mentality. My *Music of the Curbs* represents to me the time when I stepped out, poems from 1970 to about 1974. I kept them to myself for extended periods of time. I felt like I was woodshedding. I was more interested in certain poems than in certain poets, and I began reaching back in time. A big influence since the mid-'60s had been a Penguin edition Baudelaire, now out of print. The translations were by this Brit don Francis Scarfe, and the translations were all in prose small type at the bottom of the page. No attempt was made to fudge around with relative prosody between the English and the French versions. Also the Rexroth translations of Reverdy by New Directions, beautiful renderings of a Cubist silence and elegiac sentiments. Apollinaire's *Zone*, also elegiac—since that time translations have increasingly abounded. I have most of Apollinaire and Reverdy. I don't really know what to do with them from my soul, I'm such an American. Which leads me to my final real source of inspiration at that time, Whitman's *The Sleepers*. These four things, poets, poems have been the four corners of everything I've done, if you forgive me the attitudinizing and druggy dreck that got into my work at times. Also, Ted Berrigan had a lot of great

ideas. I hadn't the faintest idea until years later how he'd actually done
The Sonnets. I mean what he did was using the clerical facility you get with
methedrine he would take lines that were actually cut out on small pieces of
paper and then rearrange them. And that was one part of it, but the real part
of it was that Ted would wait until it looked right. He wouldn't try to be able
to defend it verbally. He wouldn't try to make anything more of that than
what it was—it looked right, and that was when you were through with it.
And I liked that a lot. That was very important to me that there was noth-
ing to measure, except for whether the person doing it thought it was right.
To paraphrase the great Yogi Berra, writing a poem is 90 percent instinct,
and the other half is aesthetics. And if it wasn't right to anybody else in the
whole fucking world, then well, go figure—do you really want to do this, or
are you going to commit yourself to doing something that no one is inter-
ested in? Speaking about collections and stuff like that, in my heart of hearts
I think that if you're young and you're a poet, then you ought to go off and
do it and come back in about 25 years and show me. If you get too hung up
on production, you kind of take away from the idealistic quality of being a
writer which is sheerly to commence and progress and discover. I'd like to
say—I'm not trying to be politically correct—but I think it's interesting that
in the group of people just showing up in New York under the age of 30, the
most interesting writers I know of right now are women. I sort of think that
women find more interesting things to have as their subject of honesty. Right
now it seems that the inheritance is being manipulated in the most interest-
ing way by young women, and usually from a much more intellectual use of
writing than was true twenty or thirty years ago.

LJ: Do you set up a system of rules for the prose poems that you write? Are
there any constraints that you use?

JG: Yeah. I started using a trick at a time when I hadn't been writing because
I'd been studying a number of different things. I tried real hard to stop being
a poet for a few years in order to have other interests for a couple of reasons.
I was changing gears and no one really seemed to like what I was doing and I

was kind of depressed, did some travelling, and was diverting myself in weird ways that still continue. Then I'm in school; I'm writing like four papers a week, about things I'm interested in but I'd rather just learn about it rather than have to write it up, and they're all scientific and medical, and I say to myself, "you know, what the fuck? Every time you walk down the street things go through your brain like they always used to—you're a fucking poet. Why don't you do it?" Then I'd answer, well I don't have any time. And then I rationalized that if I could sit down and pull off these papers, then I should try sitting down and pulling off a poem in that kind of time constraint. Now when you do something with an academic demand placed on you, you sit down and you don't think in the least about being inspired, or about how careful you're going to be in writing it. So that when I said okay, now is when I have to go sit down and write a poem and I don't fucking feel like it, there's no trigger. So I got an idea. Since I was well acquainted with Thai language at this time and I have this one dictionary which happens to be for Thai people to learn English—all the entries being in Thai language. I'd think of a word in Thai language, open to that page, and take the English definitions that were given for Thai people in order to learn English, and choose words in the order they appeared on two open pages up to whatever number I happened to pick—19, 26, whatever, many words. And then I would write a sentence or a phrase using each one in order. I got this idea because Bob Dylan used to in the early '60s write all in rhymes, and he would hit the most weird combinations. You could tell that he was being taken into an imaginative direction by having to get to a rhyme. And I decided that I was going to try to do that with these lists of words. And then I would come up with this stuff. Now if I look at those poems, I can't for the life of me remember which were the words that I had to work with, and some of them are totally nothing words, but it just was a way to start pulling things out of my head. And I still do it, simply because I am still able to get things to pop off in all kinds of different directions.

LJ: Yeah, Robert Duncan used to do that with a Japanese dictionary. He would pick phrases from the Japanese dictionary and then arrange his lectures based on the information from that.

JG: I didn't know that. You know, when you use these arbitrary things it's amazing how what you come up with may have the consistency of something that doesn't have that much arbitrariness and that's what the beauty of the arbitrary was. John Ashbery was very effective 35 years ago in his use of the arbitrary. He could make something just come out of infinity into this place that seemed to have had some kind of finiteness about it, something concrete about it. He just pulled in this thing that didn't belong there and made it fit. I mean your mind would make it fit and it would bounce you into this place that just had nothing to do with our conventions of thinking, of logic. Logic isn't really very sound. I've been thinking about it a lot; I've been reading a lot of science writing and dealing with the scientific method. But I'm not interested in analytic thinking about the writing of poetry, or theory, semiotics. I'm not into any science of language or linguistics. Riffing isn't very scientific. There's a complete break between my science in medicine and my writing.

LJ: But your work life, your nursing life, is starting to come up in the subject matter of your poetry.

JG: Well actually, you know, I loved living in the East Village a long time ago because it was a ghetto and I lived in some very bad places and I was interested in what I could find out about how the people who belonged there lived. I mean in those days you could be one of a dozen white people living on a block that had 3500 people on it and observing what went on and hearing what went on from the next door and upstairs, and all around you, always fascinated me a lot. But I never got into too many kitchens. I was hanging out with guys in that neighborhood doing drugs, and I got into their homes and saw what went down. I've always had this nosiness about people who live in this kind of neighborhood. Now, I'm in the kitchens of these certain people who've always fascinated me. I deal with a lot of nasty places, and it's hard to describe. It is very poetic. I'm inside all the places that I've lived next door to. That affects me when I'm writing a lot more than any-thing that has to do with what actual role I'm doing out there. I mean if you spend all day in elevators in housing projects in Brooklyn, that's a lot of your visual information and your tone information. I always did this. I'd be writ-ing a poem but at the same time I'd be coming and going from Avenue C and 8th Street, thirty years ago. It's like paint, what goes through your brain when you're walking around is like paint. You're going to use it when you do your work.

LJ: It's interesting to talk about being out in the world and doing the things that you're doing as a thing that's useful to people, but I wonder, does poetry function in the same way? Do you think it's useful to people? I mean obvi-ously it's not helpful on the same scale as what you do with your job.

JG: If you want to start thinking about the utility of what one does in one's life you're crazy. I mean, the most honest reaction to what goes on in the world is to say nothing fucking matters. No matter what you do, the world is not very manageable. So you live in it, and nothing is really manageable—your per-sonal life isn't, and all kinds of other things aren't, so why should there be a purpose to everything you do of a kind where you're saying, "this matters to so and so." Poetry, I never give it a thought. I find it kind of charming that people will have symposiums discussing the role of poetry. I mean the role of poetry for poets? I mean, what the hell? Poetry is like DNA or fingerprints, and that's what you aspire to. You aspire to realizing your DNA when you write, and that's not easy to find out and you try to approach it more and more as you go along. And when you're very young you're probably going to be impressed by so many things that you're doing these kind of malaprop imitations, which in themselves are very good, because your imitation failed because your DNA was showing. And you attempt to try to get to this kind of pure DNA state in your writing. What that has to do with anybody else, go figure. Why should it be interesting to someone else? If it is, great.

LJ: Do you think that all the DNA is showing in your work?

JG: Oh no. I might hit it from time to time on a given day. I mean I don't sit around thinking about this very much.

LJ: Are there people who you think of as your contemporaries as writers?

JG: Well sure. It would be hard not to since we've known each other for so long. Let's put it this way, of my particular generation, it was the women in that group who had some kind of priority and seemed to have the seniority also. It was almost like they had their own little hegemonies—there was Anne Waldman, followed after a few years by Bernadette [Mayer] through her workshop, and Alice [Notley] through her workshop. I think of them as my contemporaries. I'm coeval with them, but I don't think the rest of the world thinks of us as any kind of crew. I mean I haven't had that much exposure. I was never an insider on the Project scene. I'm, like, in the middle of the left lane most of my life. As a kid my older siblings even spoke of me as an independent type. But there are a number of people who give me good feedback. And to be honest with you, I have read a lot, especially magazines, and I'll read my friends' books, but I don't study poetry. I read poetry, and this and that and the other happens in my head, but when I'm writing, I'm sort of cut off from any sense of preparation for the act of writing. I go with what's happening. It's more a matter of you sit down and try to do what you can. There may not be much there on that day and sometimes that's the best day to catch yourself. Music always pushes me. Jazz gives me ideals, you could put it, not of technique, but of outlook. I contemplate music for inspiration far more than I do poetry. Coltrane's *Ascension* and *Interstellar Space* —I love Rashied Ali's drumming—a lot of Don Cherry, late Monk with Charlie Rouse—who, if you ask me, was the tenor who knew how to play *Monk*—and also Bartók's string quartets, all of 'em. These I take to the desert island along with those four poetry mainstays. Incidentally, here's a music beauty tip: *Chants Sacré Melchites, Hymnes à la Vierge*, sung by Sister Marie Keyrouz, a Lebanese Maronite nun. The hymns are in Latin, Greek, and Arabic, mixed in the same hymn. The hymns are from the early Byzantine Church liturgy. Harmonium Mundi disks are expensive, but this one will take you, well, to interstellar regions. When it comes to my own work, I try not to like everything I write, but of course I end up doing that. You know, you get so involved in things you can't see them anymore. And there are a lot of times when I think, Jesus, I have a lot of ideas that are not conducive to writing wonderful poems. You know, my idea of writing in the first place is not conducive to writing a wonderful poem. And I see things where I think— you know how it is, on the wrong day you think it's all been a waste of time and I regret having gotten myself to the place where I find myself writing this, that, or the other way. I spot weaknesses or I have habits of dealing with ironies that are not that discernible, especially if they have to do with feeling. Sometimes I think that I don't communicate feeling in a way that is as deep as the feeling. You know you get into these little snits, and then on other days you say, "why the fuck don't I get the Nobel Prize tomorrow?" It's a weird game. It's very hard to know what relative place you are at every time you look at things, like Heisenberg's indeterminacy, and what always happens of course is that it's a bad day and you've got to give a reading. So it's a little like being the pitcher who's in the bullpen and says, man, today I've got nothing. And he goes out and throws the no-hitter. And after the game they say to him, "how did you feel before the game?" And he says, "man, I felt horrible." You give a poetry reading and for five minutes people shake your hands and the next thing you know you're looking around for the two or three friends who want to go and have drinks. It's not like you're going to get mobbed out the door with bulbs flashing. I would kind of hate that. And I'm glad I've never had to deal with celebrity—that would be kind of dreadful.

AN INTERVIEW WITH ED SANDERS
BY LISA JARNOT

OCTOBER/NOVEMBER 1997   NO. 166

Ed Sanders is a poet, musician, editor, historian, and activist. His most recent publication, *1968: A History in Verse*, was published this year by Black Sparrow Press. This interview was conducted at the Naropa Institute in Boulder, Colorado on July 12, 1997 and at the Cedar Bar in New York City on July 23, 1997.

LISA JARNOT: I want to talk to you about Allen Ginsberg. Partly, what was your relationship with Allen like?

ED SANDERS: I was a senior in high school and read *Howl* and I bought *Howl* actually at the University of Missouri Bookstore on a fraternity weekend. And it seemed like, as a young man, about everything I'd been looking for in terms of a model for writing poetry and combining poetry with your personal life in a way I thought would be appropriate, although I was living in the Midwest, in a '50s type all-American environment. Then I moved to New York later and saw him from afar. I attended poetry readings at places like the Gaslight on MacDougal Street or the Living Theater on 14th Street. I saw him read as I did other poets—Edward Dahlberg, Kerouac, Corso; I saw Frank O'Hara read. So wherever I could go to find poets that I admired to watch them read I went, but I never considered introducing myself or try-

ing to be part of it; I was just a witness. And I was going to New York University trying to study languages so I didn't really meet Allen until 1963 when he came back from a long stay in India and Japan and Cambodia, Viet Nam, and other places—he went to the Vancouver Poetry Festival—and then he came back. And before that I had corresponded with him. I sent him *Fuck You: A Magazine of the Arts* in India and he liked it and sent me this really important poem, "The Change," where he kind of changed spiritual directions and came to terms with his body on a train in Japan after visiting Joanne Kyger and Gary Snyder on the way back to Vancouver. So anyway, from 1963 on, when I formally met him, and he took me to a party at Robert and Mary Frank's house, I began hanging out with him any time we were around in the same area until he died 34 years later. We had many, many capers and adventures and he called all the time and we saw each other now and then. A number of people could say the same thing. He was part of my life, and part of my family's life. He was part of the household. He gave us advice, a lot of advice. And you know, he'd give advice on what kind of furniture to have in your kitchen; he was very much a teacher.

LJ: What do you think his significance is historically?

ES: Well I think he's left behind a body of a lot of wonderful poetry going back to his early days, like a Byron or an Emily Dickinson or a Shelley. There are poems that are quite on the Whitman/Poe level of skill. Another way is as an educator. Someone told me his Blake lectures alone are 3000 typed pages— his analysis of Blake is quite bright and brilliant. And I think that's one of the reasons some of the academics were so hostile to him, because he was like a walking Encyclopaedia Britannica of Western poetry, and also Eastern poetry and Chinese poetry, so he knew very much. He's a scholar is all I'm saying, and this scholarliness is a legacy. And then his politics are a legacy. He was originally to be a labor lawyer. His mother was a Communist and his father was a Social Democrat and out of that came Allen, always hungering to celebrate the regular people, but with a sense that not that many poets are "great" or that there is a winnowing out and judgment that occurs unfortunately among those people that create, as to a hierarchy of "value" or "genius" of their labors. So he was very active in that and very capable of looking quite snooty and judgmental, and he had a lot of anger in him that he, like all men I guess, was trying to control by writing his own personal *Iliad* and *Odyssey*. His poems are like this epic of coming to terms with violence. But anyway, he has a lasting legacy. He was an American genius. They didn't put Lord Byron into Westminster Abbey until 1968, so it may take some decades. He may go through what I call a "Poe job"—they may savage him for a while before he can re-emerge.

LJ: Do you think that poets have to take on more responsibility now that Allen's gone?

ES: Allen had a natural metabolism that was very, very elevated. He's such a difficult role model to emulate because of his enormous psychic and actual energy, and he was not, in ways that he would let on, having the cycles of manic depression that other famous poets did, going all the way back to William Cowper, and forward to Robert Lowell, or Anne Sexton, or other poets. His energy cycle was always above the *y*-axis, so it's difficult. In my own feeble way I try to emulate his political activity with my vow to go out in a blaze of leaflets. Not only do you have to tend to the current stages, you have to set the stage, the soil, the ground—to use an agricultural metaphor—for the future. Every thirty or forty years a big social attempt is made to make things better for working people. You can go back to 1825, 1848, 1870, 1905, 1917, the '30s and '40s, and then later the '60s. Personally, now that I'm middle aged, I think that part of my goal is to help set the soil for the next period of stress where there is an attempt to make an improvement for working people, a genre that I think includes poets.

LJ: Do you think there are particular things that poets need to know or to put forward into the world?

ES: Two different things, right? "Need to know" and "need to put forward." What was that Ezra Pound thing as to what a poet should do? It's like get a dictionary and learn the meaning of words. And again, that's a metaphor for the curiosity that a poet should have. And if you don't have the curiosity, you should train yourself to have that level of curiosity where you are always researching the world, and if we're talking about Allen, that's a great example of what he was like. He was the first Jack the Clipper I ever met—always handing me swatches of clippings, and making clippings and systematic filings on issues and subjects part of his life. In my own archives I have some of his files that he would give to me so I could do some work on them too. I have these manila folders with his handwriting and then the various subjects. So you have to prepare yourself and always study many different things. And therefore it makes the planning of personal time very important. Poets tend to be Bacchic sometimes. They can don the fox skin masks of the Bassarids and go dancing off into partying. So the idea is—since poets tend to travel a lot—to travel with portable research systems. Gary Snyder does that. I'm always impressed with the way he studies while he travels, studies books and his ecological studies. And so, I think poets, without being preachy, without succumbing to doggerel, should present issues and opinions, revving up the culture for the next "cycle of improvement" I call it, or revolutionary period, hopefully without violence.

LJ: How much does research overlap what Allen did? I know he did a lot of research on the CIA.

ES: I'm not as overt. I do a lot of almost secret research into cases. I've done a lot of research helping elected officials in investigating things, such as illegal dumping by organized crime. And with respect to the CIA I've done a lot of gathering of files and information for the last 27 years on certain cases, quietly, because I believe that there is a class of killers, and I would say serial killers, that were attracted to clandestine government work. These guys— many of them from the post–World War II era are retired and old—some of them I think may still be in place. Allen's thing began in 1965 when the federal narcotics agents tried to get a bunch of people to set Allen up, and get him busted, and Allen started looking into the connection between the CIA and the government and illegal drug dealing, and came to kind of realize that

a portion of the people trying to control it and to make arrests were sell-
ing it. So it became like a scene out of Brecht's *Rise and Fall of the City of
Mahagonny*. You know, it turned out that a portion of the CIA were selling
drugs and doing illegal things to raise money. So Allen, with his "CIA
Calypso Blues" and his speaking out in public are emblems of deportment
for a poet. I don't know if any of us can do it with his verve. That's why it's
too bad on one level that he didn't become a labor lawyer. He knew how to
work the bureaucracy to get something done. There are examples in his life
that, hundreds of examples, where he used his uncanny ability to analyze a
bureaucracy to find out whom to call. I've come to his house in the '60s and
'70s and seen him on the phone, say, to somebody in the governor's office.
You know, most of us would say, well I better write a letter to the paper,
but Allen would try to call Governor Rockefeller and speak to him directly.
So he would try to call Clinton for instance, and maybe get right through.
So the idea is to overcome shyness. You have to beg your psyche to emulate
some of the better aspects of Ginsberg's public deportment.

LJ: When you were writing *1968: A History in Verse* was there information
that you left out of it because you felt like you shouldn't publish it?

ES: Well, if you write about a year and there are many, many things—there's
not room. When you create a book-length poem and then you have files and
boxes of things that possibly you could use, but you have to make choices.
Sometimes you leave things out because they're too similar to other things
you write about that are more emblematic. Mine is a kind of allegory for
American civilization, the 1968 book, it speaks to the best aspects of Amer-
ica, of which there are plenty, but also horrible aspects, of which there are a
number. It's almost an allegorical thing, archetypal, so I had to make some
decisions. Yeah, but it's true, because I knew many things that I left out, and
there were some things that I left out for reasons of privacy, but I didn't put
in a lot of material that would be deemed controversial, but you know, per-
sonal information about other people that would just be like trash. You
know like the section "Greta Garbo's Mouth" where I was going to do this

gossip sheet. Janis Joplin sometimes told me about her erotic life—she would fill me in, in great detail. I left that out of the book. Why tell all just because Tell tells you to tell? I did leave things out that didn't make sense to put in.

LJ: Do you think that you learned a lot about yourself from that project? I mean you learned what the FBI knew about you, right?

ES: Yes. I was always too shy to read my FBI files and I finally read through them. Well, you live your own life. You have your own time track and your little portable zone—your body and ten feet around your body that you travel in life with—and through that year you go interact with the people that come into that ten foot zone by phone calls, by vision, by conversations, whatever—that's your experience of that year. So if you want to make a year more living—that's why I use the image of creating a living structure—if you start bringing in other things, and other strands of information about what other people were doing at the same time, it does help you to fill in, to understand the broader picture. So doing that kind of research is like a three-dimensional sculpture. It's a sculptural thing where the year becomes like a living sculpture and the other aspects of the sculpture are outside your zone, and it helps you to understand. So yes, if you're asking did it help me understand what I did or my own experiences the answer is a resounding yes, for sure. I tracked a bunch of people—I call them time tracks, where you track—the analogy would be like a multitrack recording studio where you have 24 tracks and each one is going along in time with an instrument or something happening on it, and for a whole book of poetry—a multitrack book—yeah, you have parallel tracking and every once in a while you bring information from these parallel tracks into the book, into the flow of the book where it makes sense. So then it's like a 24-track mix, and you bring some things to the foreground and submerge other things at different points in the flow of time. So you're like a maestro, or to use that metaphor, you're like a recording engineer that's mixing and bringing some things out at one point and pulling them back at other points.

LJ: How much of that comes out of Olson?

ES: Well, Olson was kind of pre-electronic, but he had some good ideas. He was the first guy I knew that cared about wetlands. In the '60s there was this thing called urban renewal where they were determined to do away with poverty, and one of the things the antipoverty program did was tear down buildings and build new buildings. And doing that does a couple of things. It gives jobs to the construction business, and to the paving business, and it creates jobs. But in the town where Olson lived, Gloucester, they were attempting to fill in some of these tidal wetlands which he would walk by—he was a walker. He loved to walk in the town he was writing about, so he didn't want these beautiful tidal oceanic wetlands to be destroyed, and the same way with the interesting old houses, the federal or Greek revival from the nineteenth century that they would tear down to put up a parking lot. And he would fight against that. But his techniques I followed a lot, and some of his writing techniques such as the shamanic rev-up method of writing, where he would study things, study his files and get kind of revved up, and then a transmission occurs and you write this stuff down. That's a definite possible method for writing certain sections of a work that contains history—where you have a bunch of files and notes and you study them carefully, and then you get what Robert Duncan called your "body tones"—you get your muscularity and your bios revved up like a drag racer, and then out comes this poetry. That can be useful in historic poetry; it can distill the essence of a thing. So I owe something to him. And also all his observations in "Projective Verse," which is now a manifesto that's from 1950, so it's 47 years old, but like good writing it often has useful material for the present, and his perception that one insight must lead directly to another, and his metaphor of the poem as a high-energy construct, where the mind receives energy, or it's like a high-energy grid, so that the mind reading it receives this energy as it proceeds down the page. So what that's saying is to charge your language with energy, to work on it so that it doesn't have any points where it doesn't discharge that energy, or that élan, or dare we use the word beauty. It's kind of a macho image really. Why not have part of your poems without any energy at all and just sort of like a tidal pool? Of course a tidal pool's full of life forms—crustaceans and sea urchins and pieces of kelp, and eaten claws of lobsters. Anyway Olson wrote this poem called "Maximus from Dogtown I" which completely revised my thinking on how poetry could be written because I'd been influenced a lot by the long-lined "Howl" and Olson was much more systematically mythological than Ginsberg. He had Egyptian elements and all kinds of mythic elements in his story about this guy who wrestles a bull in Dogtown Meadow and the bull's like this symbol of the universe. And finally the bull kills this guy because it grows up. Anyway, you'd have to read the poem. So, I read that, and then I started putting out *Fuck You: A Magazine of the Arts* and I started writing to Olson, sending issues. And he wrote back. And he had read "Poem from Jail" which is a mythopoetic thing. The basic structure of it is a re-creation of the Demeter/Persephone myth in the nuclear era, against the background of a doomsday machine. Olson's the only one who ever picked up on that. He understood its mythology, that a lot of it was borrowed from Hesiod's *Theogony* which we both loved, and I knew by heart because I'd just taken a course at NYU in Hesiod's *Theogony*, so I had that thing memorized, almost. So Olson wrote me letters. He wrote me about fifty or sixty letters treating me like an equal. I was a 22-year-old kid. I didn't even know Ginsberg yet. I knew nobody. I was afraid of becoming intimate with these heroes.

LJ: How much does New York School writing influence your work? I mean we're talking about Olson and Ginsberg, but you were also a major part of the New York School, being on the Lower East Side, and hanging out with Ted Berrigan . . .

ES: And Frank O'Hara. I didn't see O'Hara very much, but he was very supportive. And Ashbery was very supportive when I was a young man. We would have some conversations. He wanted me to put together a book of poetry and he encouraged me, that he would help get it published under that foundation that was set up after Frank died. And when I was arrested for *Fuck You: A Magazine of the Arts*, Ashbery appeared in court, as did Kenneth Koch, to be expert witnesses. They weren't called on to testify, but they were there, Kenneth Koch holding a tennis racket and John Ashbery in the front row of the state supreme court in lower Manhattan in the summer of 1967. So, how much was the influence? Quite a bit, O'Hara particularly—those city walking poems—of which Ron Padgett is also a master—of the gazing around while you're walking—it's a variety of the Buddhist pacing meditation type of thing that Gary Snyder picked up on in *Mountains and Rivers without End*, the idea of walking through an environment and observing, and Apollinaire walking through Paris. And picking up information as you're walking and buying your Gauloises and checking out the new *Art Forum* and saying hello to a friend, that idea of using your body where your body and your heartbeat is part of it. That was an important lesson to me—that it wasn't just Zen monks that could pace their white sand gardens in Kyoto—but it was also Frank O'Hara on the way to work at the Museum of Modern Art. That was an incident where you could create poetry. And then of course Ted Berrigan and I were close friends for a number of years, and his writing was an influence. I often thought I sounded just like Ted, I often emulated his speech patterns and the way he looked at things.

LJ: So how did you manage to end up on the Lower East Side, from the Midwest?

ES: Well New York University was in Washington Square Park and there were all these interesting types that hung out in Washington Square Park, especially early in the morning in the summertime. I was living at the Hotel Colburne off Washington Square in a little 17-dollar-a-week room there in the summer of 1959. I'd go to Washington Square while all the street sweepers were there and all these bohemians were hanging out, guys with names like Billy Budd, stuff I've written about in Volume I of *Tales of Beatnik Glory*—"Vulture Egg Matzoh Brei" is the story that deals with that. But they kept talking about this thing called "the East Side." So one day I took a walk with some people to get some peyote and there was the East Side and the West Side and there was this no man's/no woman's land there that they literally sprinted through, just between Broadway and 1st Avenue—and then you were at this other place called the East Side where I quickly learned there were all these cheap apartments, and all these painters with things in the storefronts.

LJ: So you were studying classics at that point. Did you go to NYU to do that?

ES: No. I went there because it had a good graduate program in rocket science and I wanted to be a rocket scientist or physicist at one point because 1958 when I first went to NYU was the time that Alan Shepard went overhead, the Mercury Program. For a lonely, young, insecure poet boy from the Midwest it seemed like a kind of nice loner thing to do, go up in a rocket and orbit the earth. So that was the reason I went to NYU. But my mother had passed away in 1957 and my mother had always said that a gentleman knew Greek and Latin. So in high school I took Latin, and I wasn't very skilled at it, but it helped me. So in honor of my mother who passed away when I was in high school I decided to take Greek. I had thought I should take Russian, because obviously they were the competitors and they were going into space also, but anyway I decided to take Greek. It's a difficult language to get going in but I quickly started to study Greek poetry. Almost immediately they make you take an *Iliad* and *Odyssey* course, which really changed my life. And then I had some really good teachers at NYU—Dr. Bluma Trell was one of them. I took a Greek lyric poetry class with her where she was able to explain these meters. We're not talking iambic pentameter—but very complicated and var-iegated meters. So I was able to, through her, jump right into Sappho and Simonides and Anacreon and Stesichorus—a lot of Greek poets that opened me up to meter. So after a while I decided to change my major to classics and that's what I graduated in ultimately in 1964. I took a lot of mathematics but I really wasn't cut out to be a rocket scientist.

LJ: What about the origins of your political consciousness?

ES: My parents were like Stevensonian Democrats in a very conservative area and they were always volunteering for things. Like in the '50s there was a big drive in America to do away with one-room schoolhouses and have consoli-dated school districts on the grounds you could get a better education. My parents were involved in that and reorganizing school districts. When Roosevelt died my parents went out on the front steps of our house and we all wept. So Roosevelt was like a hero to my parents' generation. My parents would sneer at Joseph McCarthy and the McCarthy hearings. I knew about people like Norman Thomas and I knew a little bit about the '30s, because even in the '40s where I was raised in a rural area of Missouri, hobos would come because we were a quarter mile from the train tracks. The rule was that they weren't allowed in the house, but we were to feed them. So it was a knowledge of the '30s and memories of the horror of the '30s were very ingrained in the consciousness of my family. So then when I got to New York I picked up issues of a great publication of the time called *I. F. Stone's Weekly* which taught me that there's a subsurface to everything; you can't believe what you see on television or what you hear on the radio or read in the newspapers. There's always a subtext, there's always a reason, there's always an underlying set of muscles and sinews that are really explaining what's going on. Then I got exposed to things like the *Monthly Review* which was a socialist publication and I began to follow the Cuban Revolution through the *Monthly Review* and there were other left-wing publications I began to read and I slowly began to read and study things. Now I had no idea—they didn't talk about Buchenwald back in Missouri, so when in the late '50s the photographs from Buchenwald began to appear in books which I would look at in the 8th Street Bookshop. I really couldn't afford these books, but I would see these concentration camp pictures and I'd already started studying Ezra Pound and I didn't realize what the deal was. So finally I realized why people were so upset with Ezra Pound—I understood by seeing these wasted bodies in boxcars that I was not told at all about in the Midwest. So I had this sense of what one country can do to another by looking at these horrible concentration camp pictures. So I began to evolve and to become a Social Democrat, and I point out in my book on 1968 that it took 1968 in all its moil and toil and boil to realize that that's really where I was. I believed in voting. Like Sweden in 1968 voted to have 25 percent of their economy controlled in the interests of the people, by the state, and I realized that I believed in that, and the nationalization of certain key industries, while allowing for some entrepreneurial activity, what they called a mixed economy. And I realized that's what I believed in when I was running through the tear gas of Chicago with Allen Ginsberg.

LJ: How did the Fugs fit into all of that?

ES: We really didn't. The Fugs were formed in 1964 out of my bookstore. And we didn't grow out of the political culture of the late '60s so much as out of the Civil Rights and Happening movements. And my bookstore was just a block away from where Claes Oldenburg had his storefront and those happenings and stuff. I had this little kosher meat market that I rented and left the "strictly kosher" sign up. It's gone now, it's a community garden. And Tuli Kupferberg lived above an egg store next door and we got to talking and one thing led to another and we decided to form a poetry group and he thought of the title the Fugs. The Peace Eye for a while was a very famous hang out place, like there'd be Nico or Donovan. People would, visiting poets would come by, Jerry Rothenberg, whoever was in town. And Allen lived just down the street at 408 East 10th. It was half a block away. And there were all these bars on Avenue B. Mazur's, Stanley's, and then there was the Charles Theatre which had all the avant-garde films—Jonas Mekas, Ron Rice, the Taylor Mead movies. So there was a four-block area of culture, and it was a hangout and then we formed the Fugs there and I put out *Fuck You: A Magazine of the Arts* in the back room. The exact spot last summer was a zucchini barrel. They made better use of the space probably. So anyway, the Fugs grew out of the labor union songs of the '30s and "We Shall Overcome" of Pete Seeger and out of the three-chord Protestant hymns that were transformed into civil rights songs. And out of jazz poetry and out of Bird and bebop and early rock and roll. 1964 when we were formed, that was "Mustang Sally," Roy Orbison's "Pretty Woman," and the Beatles' "I Want to Hold Your Hand." Those were the things that were happening—early Beach Boys, Dylan hadn't gone folk rock yet. That's how we came out. We came out of those concepts of a happening. You'd go to these galleries and there'd be people jumping up and down in barrels full of grapes and then somebody naked covering their head with pieces of ticker tape. And you could call that art. Easy rules—all you had to do was bring youthful genius and will. For all the flaws of the early Fugs we had pretty good timing, and a lot of energy, and we were quite confident in ourselves. And we were all poets, so we could whip out these songs that well, we're not talking Schumann here or Schubert. Because of the recording equipment they were able to capture these things. These things we did one take only, as wild young men looking at each other. We didn't know that you were supposed to face the microphone. So these things we did had a certain life for 32 years.

LJ: Did you have training as a musician?

ES: Well, training, sure—in the '50s all young men and women took their five years of piano. My mother bought a piano at my aunt's auction when she died and brought it home, a baby grand, and took it apart in the living room. She was quite skilled with her hands, and she rebuilt it, fixed hammers and got it all organized and I remember that piano all over our living room rug and she put that piano back together, had it tuned so that we could take piano lessons. So I took piano lessons. Then I studied drums for a while with the woman who was a drummer for the Kansas City Philharmonic. I used to go to Kansas City for a lot of stuff. Kansas City was jazz, so we would go there to these clubs so that we could dance with black girls and Mexican girls. I didn't even know it was jazz. It was just this wonderful music that you could be interracial and sneak liquor bottles into the club when you were a teenager. They never asked for identification in Kansas City. So I got exposed to a lot of jazz. And then we would go to country-western shows in Kansas City. I would see Roy Acuff; I'd see country acts. And then there was the big arena shows in '55 at the Kansas City municipal auditorium where I saw great shows of Bill Haley. I saw Chuck Berry. I saw Bo Diddley. I saw LaVern Baker. And then of course the mating teenage lust game conducted to the Christian emblems of Elvis Presley and the Clovers. So we were exposed to this rock and roll tied to country and western, Hank Williams. And then as soon as I got to New York I got exposed to the Civil Rights music, "We Shall Overcome" and "Down by the Riverside." I went on a lot of peace walks and took part in civil rights stuff. I didn't know about things like Erik Satie or Debussy at that stage. Oh yeah. And I left out the Christian church. My mother was very religious. She taught a Sunday school class for high school kids. And I went to church. I was exposed to all these Christian three-chord hymns; I knew all of them, still do. That was a big boon when we were starting writing popular songs and realizing that they were just fast versions of Christian hymn structures.

LJ: The Fugs were in Europe recently. What was your sense of the political scene there?

ES: We were in Italy for three weeks in the spring. The Center Left is in control of Italy. Berlusconi, the right-wing populist media magnate, was tossed from power and so the cutbacks in medical care and cutbacks in social programs are over for now. And it's true of a number of places in Europe where the right wing has begun to ebb, such as in England with the Labor Party winning. Sweden of course, which has always been a social democracy. Denmark is the most left of all those advanced countries. Austria is still under the control of the Social Democrats, and even the Social Democrats in Germany could theoretically take over. But anyway the point is, their politics were quite grand and I was impressed with the country; the economy was booming. Allen died while we were in Europe and that was a great, sad experience, a national time of mourning. It was all over the newspapers, and on the national television and radio networks. I broke down weeping on Italian national radio. And oddly enough just an hour before he died, we got back from a gig in Milan and we had heard that he was pretty ill and we toasted his soul, just about 45 minutes before he actually passed away. But Italy was glorious other than that great sadness. I recommend it to painters and poets.

LJ: What are you working on now?

ES: I'm preparing a lot of galleys and stuff for European publications. *Tales of Beatnik Glory* Volume 1, Volume 2, and the new one Volume 3 are coming out in Italy and Austria. I've got to teach a course in Vienna in September called "The Poetry and Life of Allen Ginsberg," so I'm preparing for that. I've got to find something to do, another book. Maybe I'll finish *Tales of Beatnik Glory* Volume 4; I've sort of begun it. I thought about writing a novel, a short novel. And I have this play called *Cassandra*—I thought I would polish it up a little bit, change it, and try to get it produced somewhere. And I have to hang around to see that *1968: A History in Verse* gets a fair listen. It's designed to be read quietly in a room. It's not really designed to be performed. Of all my books it's the one most deliberately designed to be just sort of studied. My other book, the biography in verse of Chekhov is also designed to be read quietly in somebody's house or room. With Allen's passing I've decided to read more and not be so driven and calm down a little bit, and not be so clingy to my possessions and boxes of files. You realize how impermanent—because here's a guy who because of his congestive heart condition and other reasons had to get this big fancy loft and a place to put his things up in, and he had just unpacked when he passed. So you really can't cling to anything. So that's my program at this point—do a little writing and do a lot of reading. And that's about it. Except for my little newspaper which eats up a lot of time. Just getting used to post-Ginsberg life.

AN INTERVIEW WITH VICTOR HERNÁNDEZ CRUZ
BY SHEILA ALSON

DECEMBER/JANUARY 1998 NO. 167

Victor Hernández Cruz is a writer currently living in Aguas Buenas, Puerto Rico, his birth-place (1949) and residence until the age of five at which time his family migrated to New York City. He was raised in New York City and wrote *Snaps*, his highly acclaimed first book of poetry, in New York at age 19. He subsequently moved to the West Coast and published numerous other collections of poetry and prose including *Panoramas* which has just been released from Coffee House Press. In November, 1995, while he was visiting New York City, I interviewed Victor in a Chinese restaurant in the Union Square area—one block from Washington Irving's birthplace. When the restaurant's vacuum cleaners got too loud, we moved to the Barnes & Noble café and finished the conversation surrounded by looming portraits of literary figures including Nabokov who joined the conversation.

SHEILA ALSON: How have the multicultural influences within you affected your poetics?

VICTOR HERNÁNDEZ CRUZ: The interesting thing about the word multicultural is that they use it different in the North than they use it in Latin America. Here in the North they say multicultural or multiculturals as to signify or to designate cultures that are separate standing one next to the other. In the Caribbean, within certain layers of the society, or "classes" if you will, the

different cultural energies, expressions, and ways of looking at the world have merged or even melted, or have become, through their contact and connection with each other, something new, unique, and different. So that when you say multicultural (we say also multiracial), consequently you have to see that as being multispirited and multimelodious different things coming together not because they want to stay separate or fight for their own separate identity, but because they have come together in such ways that they become something different, totally different. In the Caribbean we can identify, for instance, specifically African Caribbean culture or a culture that comes more from Spain. But in the music we can definitely identify and feel that the culture of Africa and the culture of Spain have come together through instruments and instrumentation not just the instruments playing one next to each other, but that the chord structures changed how the music is played in relationship to a new element, the guitar and/or the drum for the other side. In the island of Puerto Rico, we tend to think in terms of three races/one culture, three psychologies, three ways of behaviors, three ways of looking at the world, three tempers coming together to make another one that's none of those three, but is the result of those three the Puerto Rican nation as a cultural unit. How do I express what Octavio Paz and some other Mexican writers speak about? The Other. What the mestizaje of the Americas has created is that now the other is also within us. So I am also both the conquistador and the native. I am both the Indian and the Spanish. I am both this what you see and also the mulatto culture of my whole island. The other is also within me. So I don't feel a separateness from that which I see as other outside of me, but a way of bringing it in, or that I know a percentage of that which is out there also makes me up as a human being.

SA: Sort of the union of opposites?

VHC: It could be union of opposites. But I suppose it's what might happen in the United States where there's some sharp separation between people, and they don't see themselves within each other. Perhaps that's beginning to change in certain regions of the country or circles of the country where that doesn't apply. It's much more like a real communication and a real blending. Maybe forms of music here are definitely that—the jazz coming from certain British and French marching bands, layers of African tempos that were originally placed on that and singsong types of attitude (call and response) that were placed upon that. So you can say jazz, in a sense, is a hybrid music mostly cultivated by African Americans. It also has another element in it.

SA: You also earlier talked about the experience of moving here to New York City when you were five years old.

VHC: That trip—that migration experience was like moving from one age to the next, at that time. I don't know if that would be true for today. Because of the widespread use of television now, someone can move from the mountains of the Himalayas today to the States and not have the same cultural shock as I had between moving from a small town in Puerto Rico to New York in the early '50s. Television sends the image of other cultures, of other geographic spaces into each other. So we know what Tibet looks like from watching TV. People who live in the mountains of Tibet know what the Empire State Building looks like or the Manhattan skyline. But we didn't have no television at that time. It was the early '50s. Television was starting to become popularly used in the States. So you can imagine the small province we were in. We had no visual sense of where we were going. No atmospheric sense. No geographic sense. We came right from the small towns into the most industrialized and developed city in the world, which was New York at the time. So it was more than a geographic move. It was a move of the psyche. It was a move of going from one time zone into another without any preparation. It was a different kind of shock. I don't think people would experience that anymore with television and popular media the way it is now widespread.

SA: So that was once more bringing in that element of contrast into your experience?

VHC: Yes. And having that element of contrast or having memory of otherness, memory of other space, memory of other geographies. It kind of never leaves you, especially when you come when you're about five. You have these strong visual, sensorial impressions of the place of your birth. And also you continue to speak Spanish for a while. It always is a substratum of thinking. It's always a contrast. It's always present. It's always like a substratum in your mind, being in one place and thinking of another. As I expressed to you, to me it's like living in the center of metaphors, in its artistic way of comparing one thing to the other. To extract more meaning out of both places or of both objects or whatever you're comparing. In this case, if you compare New York to the mountainous region in a tropicality, then you are doing what might be considered opposites. But we're living in opposites. We're living in a contradiction, within that Puerto Rican diaspora that I grew up. It was that constantly being in a pendulum between hot and cold, between mountain and building. Between staying here or not staying here. Because it was always a debate on whether or not in fact we were going to stay here. Every year there was always talk about getting back to the place of our origin. And there was this development in this tempo that was starting in that direction and then those plans would always fall through. There was never enough money for the whole family to go back, we'd just have to wait one more year. So it was a constant thing of never really settling the mind on, "This is it, this is our new home and we're here forever." So, finally my family did move back. All of my family moved back. Except an aunt that I have in the Bronx, but that's it. That tendency was for real. It was demonstrated now by the fact that they have moved back. So I grew up with that anxiety.

SA: That's an interesting part of what sets up that tension for you in your own sort of psyche, which is ultimately where the poem comes from—which is also the situation with your family and their indecision about where they really were. So they really were in both places in a sense.

VHC: Consequently, the poetry that I did, given that it does take things out of place, has been accused by critics of being surrealistic at times. When in fact there is nothing really illogical that happens in my poetry. I contrast unlikely things. A pineapple in snow, palm trees in Manhattan, things of that sort. And it goes on to other more abstract elements. That constant going back and forth can create interesting content. It doesn't stay immediate. It brings the local situation into an international play. Going back to a Caribbean island is then going back to a historical truth. San Juan was a city 100 years before the pilgrims landed on Plymouth Rock. It's going back to Columbus coming on boats, which is the whole culture of Spain coming here on boats. The medieval period. The Mediterranean element, the Moorish element, the Jewish element, the Gypsy element. All of the other cultural elements that came with the voyages of exploration, that come to the island of Puerto Rico, which I can think about, but from the point of a Manhattan window, are then expanding from the immediate into international geospace, historically and mythologically, within a single poem. So that the poem is always an exploration of those possibilities of history. And a search for it, and a clarification of it in my mind is like unweaving the quilt.

SA: So some of your poems, I noticed, when I was reading *Red Beans*, were explicitly historical explorations. Then I noticed that there were other poems that didn't have that as the major content or as the major focus, but had some other experience as the major focus. They seemed at the same time to be also historic explorations in the methodology, in the form, in the structure.

VHC: I either get to the historical via the personal or I start from the historical and get back to the personal. Either way I have to get back to something much more interesting than a singular person. So I have to write a historical poem or a collective poem. Now for me, language is the most collective thing there is because it is what everybody speaks. So when I'm writing alone, I'm like in a festival of communication with other people. So I never really feel that I'm alone. It is precisely when I write that I most get filled with the idea of my relationship with other people and my relationship to history, to objects, to mountains and to buildings, to streets, to cities. That's exactly when I think most of the world. For me it's more like a festival—writing. It's more in the sense of a carnival, which is a public event, where everyone participates—there are no spectators. You cannot go there and be an audience. You either have to sing or dance, or march, or move, do something, which is part of the process.

SA: So what is the process for you? What do you do? Every writer has their own particular personal ritual or personal process that they do when they're sitting down to write.

VHC: I have to write within this continuous search for history, unraveling Caribbean history. I cannot write just anything that pops into my mind unless I can take it back to an encounter with a larger space, with a larger mythological or historical space. So I'm constantly looking for that. So my mind is already prepared for that. It's not just a writing that's done at random. I try to control that imagery, those ideas that come through the mind in a flurry as much as possible. I try to control it to make the language say exactly what I want it to say, to describe what I want it to describe. It is that which is of interest to me. It's about the Caribbean and the way of being human from that position and about the migration experience of Caribbean people. Those are the important things to me in writing. I don't know if that's clear.

SA: Part of what you do for yourself is you write when your mind or your psyche is in that place where you're making that connection, that historical or mythical connection.

VHC: Writing is also reading, it's also sensitivity to words, it's also something that you practice. Since everything you write you do not publish. I think writing is something that comes after long struggles of practicing and doing it and throwing a lot of stuff away. To write clearly is very difficult. When we read something that reads smoothly, that reads clearly, that person spent a lot of time to achieve that. You don't write smoothly and clearly very fast. If you write very fast, it gets kind of bumpy and kind of slow, the language is rugged—the language is rough. To me, writing is always centering in the fact that one has an affinity with the sound of language, with words and with meaning. And second, that one has something to say. Not necessarily something new to say, but something ongoing to say. That one can become part of the process, the experience of writing. That one can write with literature or against literature—with some poets or against some poets, within the epic or the age. That one lives with the resources at hand which would then be particular to you. There is a particular way of blending or twisting or using the words, but it's all interpretation of what's present and available here. It's not so much its originality, but it's our manner of contributing to an evolution of literature, which is what I do. I don't sing. I'm not in the popular tradition of declaiming. My memory is real bad. I am a reader and writer of literature. One of the ways I came to writing was the fascination with reading and also with hearing stories in all senses. Hearing guitar singing, and people reciting. Primarily it was my interest in words and literature and books, ideas all coming together. There's a delicate balance that comes together. One's sensitivity to language and one's content or information—stream, warehouse, river. Then the technical aspects of language. The actual doing of it, the grammar. Knowing how to write a clear sentence, a noun, an adverb to describe your verb, pronouns, and knowing when to stop and put a period or comma, for the sake of clarity. Using dictionaries, thesauruses, and contemplating words over the years. Keeping a word book. Circling words you don't know. Words that have flavor for me; words that are more like vegetable; words that are like machines and words that are more technical-conceptual. It's three different areas that I try to put words into. All of that is part of writing. It's living with language and words and ways to express and using different forms to be able to do it. Like haikus and coplas in Spanish. Some sonnets and spoofs, where I try to make the words rhyme. Using a multiplicity of styles and forms to express that river that's constantly flowing through you. What one has to really know is that poetic inspiration is there as destiny and that there's no other choice but to write. You might write through "peace and storm" and you write through richness and poverty. So you know that this is your destiny since there's nothing else that can erase it. A habit that you have of being sensually analytical.

SA: Talking about the craft aspect of the language, how would you say that those influences have impacted the craft?

VHC: After a while they go hand in hand. I forgot who it was that said—I don't know if it was Creeley or somebody—that "the form is made by the content." Perhaps Creeley might have gotten that from William Carlos Williams. William Carlos Williams assessed the ideas were in objects. Every step we take gives us our anatomy—sets up our thoughts—the reality that we're living the language that's all around us. The objects, the ideas within those objects, that form can then be your style. So it goes hand in hand. The forms that I'm about, the little town that I come from in the Caribbean—the migration experience—the New York City experience all became blended as one. They each have a different tempo. The tempo of New York is different than the tempo of Aguas Buenas. The poems that are created could be different. It doesn't have to be the same. If I have the strength of mind to be this one person that a variety of things are happening to, then I don't have to say that I'm different here than I am over there in terms of what interests me and what I may be interested in writing. You see what I'm saying?

SA: You mean in terms of form?

VHC: In terms of clarity also. If you're going to be in a confused situation it's good to write about it in a clear way. If you can write about chaos in a clear way then you can communicate. And if you write about chaos in a chaotic fashion, then you're going to see it in the writing. It's going to be too mushy. The reader is not in tune with the object that's in front of them and having that personal relationship with it. In terms of how you might describe something. What it means to you, what it does to you—your emotions and sensations about it. I think that's what Williams is about. He was able to do that—to feel that in his poetry. It just came out in a very natural kind of way. In terms of my craft, I try to do that as much as possible. I try to let this person that's inside, that's centered in spirit, come out with a certain content that's also similar to the language. The content and language, that there's no disagreement with content and language. You can have wonderful content but be out of step with your language. Your imagination can be way up ahead of your technical skills. You can be very florid, and full, and pregnant all over the place but it's not taking anyone anywhere. Balance comes with time. To have that time, that progression and that evolution, you must have that initial seed. That sensitivity to language to begin with. I don't think that's something that can be acquired. You can't buy that in Woolworth's. You can't take a series of vitamins and achieve it or live a series of experiences and come through it and have that ability. You have to have that in you.

SA: Was there anything else you wanted to talk about?

VHC: I just wanted to round out some thoughts I had on bilingualism. I came here with a specific language intact when I was five years old. If we're to believe Edward Sapir, the linguist, we know that language is intact at the age of five. That's about the same age I got to New York City, with the Spanish intact. I grew up stereophonically with the introduction of English. So I was speaking a pretty much broken English. At a certain point, I think the English started to erase the Spanish since this is the environment that I was in. English was all around me. Phonetically, the sounds of Spanish were always with me. I fell back in the writing of it and the reading of it. In my teens when I was 18 or 19, I gained specific consciousness about not losing the Spanish and vigorously practiced and studied and concentrated on maintaining it, keeping it in balance with the English. By that time I'd been writing in English. I was doing a funny thing because I grew up around people who recited poetry orally. This poetry was coplas in rhyming form. I began writing these coplas—rhyming Spanish poems—using English words. This was a ridiculous thing. For one, English doesn't rhyme as readily as Spanish. You rhyme in Spanish at random or by accident, by chance. So those first poems I threw away and went out to look for a more immediate language. A more urban language, a more current language.

SA: When you were writing those rhyming poems, for you, was it a conscious effort to replicate a Spanish form that you knew or was it just because it was within your experience?

VHC: No. I was too young for it to be a conscious effort. I just think I was just coming out of some circumstances where it was present. That's what they were and that's how I hung out from them. That's how I proceeded from them into doing the task of sitting down, putting one word next to the other. It's just something that was. As a habit you have grown up with. Landing the English—erasing the sense of a flowery Spanish, a rhyming tradition from the Spanish. Reading William Carlos Williams and Lorca—*Poet in New York*. That helped me with my footing with the English language to write more in Americanese. It became more like New York City kind of poetry. All the different influences of the different "accents" I call them. There's black English in the housing projects, Polish English, Irish English, Yiddish English, words for things that were all kind of coming together to create a neighborhood language for me that I was able to use. My first two books, especially, and grounding me into a momentum with the language that then opened up into a sense of the American language, a more national kind of sense of it. Just growing and handling it better and becoming more crowded with content. The Spanish always has kept in the background a certain kind of awkwardness in my English. It's hard to describe, but somehow it's there. Sometimes my structure in prose, especially. I can say syntax-wise it's a Spanish structure. I can tell by the ordering of things. So when I write in Spanish they tell me that a verb has to go in reverse. You probably got that from English. So I am doing the same thing in both languages.

SA: Do you see that in your poetry as well?

VHC: Yes, I see it in my poetry. But it's an awkwardness that I see as being fruitful and useful. It creates possibilities for the language, because it's still within clarity and it's still understood. I'm still using the language well. It just has a tinge to it. I want it always to be part of my character.

SA: So there's actually an intention that has come in your own writing process to retain that flavor in your language, not trying to erase it.

VHC: Yes. Now it's intention. Before it was unconscious. I have grasped what was spontaneous. And I've been able to keep it up in a kind of controlled setting. Sort of like a linguistic fascism. Controlling the anarchy of language. Language, pretty much gets hordes of people out of control. And you have to control it. You have to control it by imposing these strict laws of flavor. It has to have this flavor.

SA: One way that you might control it is that when you see it appearing, you keep it there.

VHC: I keep it there. I insist on it there. But I don't use so much Spanish words in my English poetry anymore. Julio Ortega, the Peruvian critic, said that the Spanish language has become English poetry in my work. I'm thinking in Spanish and to an extent, writing in English. Because of this bilingual drama, that I live, I'm very much aware of that drama as it lives in history and literature. I've been reading some of the writers who are linguistic immigrants such as Nabokov, the Russian, Joseph Conrad, Kosiński, Samuel Beckett, writers who have migrated linguistically to other languages. I was looking at an essay that appeared in the *New Yorker* on Joseph Conrad, how his sentence structures come to the verge of being bad English in *Heart of Darkness*. All throughout his life he had this struggle with the language. Nabokov insists on using these tremendously out of the way, big words that you don't readily use in everyday language. You see that in all his books. I don't know if you've read *Ada*, where you have to go to the dictionary constantly. Why is this writer doing this? Is it because he wants to show his profound vocabulary or because he's also a writer who's coming into the English language via dictionaries, and via a struggle to be correct in it and not go out of the way as opposed to most American writers who would write in simple immediate language? Sort of like Williams who also wanted the language to be made up of immediate spaces and experiences rather than to be abstracted and far away. I've been reading a lot of bilingual literature as inspiration, as a resource for my own writing. Some people choose this exile. Puerto Ricans were immigrants through conditions beyond us, economic conditions, when we encountered this English. Through a man like Joseph Conrad, it was a personal choice that he made as an adult. In my case, it's the reverse. I'm back now in Puerto Rico writing in Spanish and also writing in English but separating the two languages because I don't necessarily write in Spanglish. I see some faults in that, not that there's not valid literature that has come along in the Spanglish mode. Bilingualism is the history of literature. To use another language, in practice and in spirit and in reading and in translation. Writing is constant translation to me. No matter what the situation, nor how provincial it might get. To me it always is that. The greatest writers come from those encounters with not just other cultures, but with other languages. I had briefly mentioned that I thought it was important to learn one language before going on to the other. In this country you grow up bilingually. You can also grow up with accessibility to languages, but you only learn a percentage of each. If you don't round out in either one, instead of becoming bilingual you could become nonolingual and I think that's something that we're experiencing in the schools in New York City and Los Angeles and San Francisco and Miami. A whole generation of Latin American kids are actually in a state of confusion because of this language thing.

SA: What did you just say? You become what?

VHC: Nonolingual. A word that means no language. It is best to be centered in one language which expresses your physical and psychological needs, for it to have accompanied your total growth into a person. When a foreign language is imposed upon a people it causes confusion. Two languages constantly floating next to each other can become very taxing on the person on the street. Bilingualism is a great gift in the hands of the writer, but it could create chaos in the population as a whole. In poetry what is important is the spirit of what you are saying and its proximity to music, the cadence of your concept, the things you feel in rhythm. We are really language. That's what the Bible says. Spanish or English. What is important is how the blood is circulating. The salt of the air in the vision.

AN INTERVIEW WITH BERNADETTE MAYER
BY LISA JARNOT

FEBRUARY/MARCH 1998   NO. 168

Bernadette Mayer is the author of numerous books of poetry, including three forthcoming publications—*Another Smashed Pinecone* (United Artists), *Studying Hunger Journals* (Hard Press), and a yet to be titled collection from New Directions. Over the last thirty years her work and ideas have played an essential part in the development of experimental poetry in the United States. This interview was conducted in her apartment on East 4th Street in Manhattan on December 1, 1997.

LISA JARNOT: Do you remember the first poem you ever wrote?

BERNADETTE MAYER: Well, actually the first poem that I ever wrote was a poem that I wrote for an assignment, about leaves. We had this assignment at school, that was our homework. So I wrote this great poem about leaves. I think it's not extant anymore.

LJ: Did it rhyme?

BM: No. It was a good poem though. I got an A.

LJ: So that was in Brooklyn?

BM: No, that was in New Rochelle.

LJ: So that was when you were in college. You were an undergraduate?

BM: Yeah. I didn't really start writing until I was about 17.

LJ: So how did you get from New Rochelle to the Lower East Side?

BM: Well, that was very fast actually. New Rochelle is horrible, as you might imagine. At the time it was a Catholic women's college, and they threw me out. But they couldn't figure out why. Their reason was because I read Freud, and they didn't allow their psychology majors to read Freud until their senior year because it might be a threat to their faith. And I wore sandals. I broke all of their rules. But the real reason was that I wanted to get out of there. I only went there to please my mother. And then, you know, everybody in my family died and I left New Rochelle as soon as my uncle died, because there was no more reason to stay there. I hated it. And for two weeks I went to Barnard, and that was like a two-hour trip from Brooklyn to Barnard. Forget it. So then I moved to the Lower East Side.

LJ: Did you know people here or did you just move here?

BM: No. I just moved here because I knew it was inexpensive.

LJ: When did you first meet poets?

BM: At the New School. I took a class with Bill Berkson and I met all these poets. Frances LeFevre was in my class, and Michael Brownstein. And then I starting hanging out with Peter Schjeldahl and then he introduced me to Ted Berrigan. And then Kenward Elmslie used to have big parties at the time, with big boxes of rolled joints and stuff. That was 1965 maybe.

LJ: Did you spend time with visual artists?

BM: Well I used to edit *0 to 9* magazine with Vito Acconci. We didn't really hang out with the visual artists though, we just published them.

LJ: What was the idea behind *0 to 9*?

BM: It was pretty much the same idea that there is behind any magazine—to create a great environment for our own work and to publish all the things that we both loved to see published. So we started publishing the works of Robert Smithson, and the journals of Jasper Johns. You know, these really interesting things, but I don't think too many people were publishing them at the moment, or at least we never read them.

LJ: How much were you influenced by New York School writing?

BM: Well, you know, I had this incredible resistance to any New York writing. I really didn't want to be influenced by it. So I wasn't. I guess I am now, but I wasn't then. We had such a strong resistance that I was going out with Ted Berrigan for a while and Ted and Ron would do these collaborations and send them to *0 to 9* and we would never publish them. We published one called "Furtive Days." But we would never publish them and I guess it was because of their style or something. I really couldn't figure out why it was. I used to go to a lot of those avant-garde concert performance events with John Cage and Yoko Ono. They were pretty amazing. I always liked those. I think they influenced me much more than any of the writing.

LJ: What did you think of the poets on the Lower East Side?

BM: I was very inspired. I was so happy to be around poets all the time. And then I was reading. I embarked upon this project of reading all of the long books. That was my theory—I could just read a lot of long poetry books that I had never read.

LJ: So which ones did you read?

BM: I read *The Cantos*, and all of T. S. Eliot. I didn't have too much to do. After I fell in love with Ed Bowes, we lived in Syracuse for a while and then I got pregnant and Ed got thrown out of school, and his parents freaked out and they sent him to a psychiatrist in Ardsley. So I had nothing to do for about a year and I had enough money to pay my rent, so I just read all these books. And I used to listen to WBAI at night and write.

LJ: What do you think of Eliot? Was he an influence on you?

BM: No. Never. I'm sorry, I wasn't impressed by Eliot.

LJ: What was the best thing you read?

BM: Well, it was around that time that Bill Berkson told me I was writing too much like Gertrude Stein, whom I had never heard of. So I started reading Gertrude Stein and that was pretty inspiring. I guess I liked her work and I also liked reading philosophy. Like all those amazing philosophy books. Like Kierkegaard and Heidegger and all the great philosophy books. Much better than going to school.

LJ: How old were you?

BM: I was 19. We used to order all our books from Blackwell's in London because they were cheaper. So we would send these great long lists to Blackwell's, and get back these bills for like $30 and we'd get amazing books. And I read all the works of William Carlos Williams. I read Djuna Barnes and that was interesting. I mean I'm sure I read a lot of things.

LJ: What do you think has changed in the poetry world since the '60s?

BM: Well. It went through this period of being very social, and now it's much less social.

LJ: Maybe it's because people work more.

BM: Yeah, I think so. Jobs. Like it used to be very easy to live without a job. But now when I teach a workshop all of my students have jobs. Like real nine-to-five jobs. So that's changed. And I think more people are writing. And what's changed a lot is that there are more women writers. When I was first writing we only knew of a few women poets, like Barbara Guest and Diane di Prima. So it's great to see more women writers. That's why I was so honored to read with Barbara Guest. And I remember when I met Diane di Prima, which was also amazing—to meet your childhood heroes.

LJ: Right. That's one good thing about being a poet.

BM: Yeah. Like if you start a magazine or a reading series you have an excuse to write to almost anybody. I mean literally anybody, so that's the reason to do it. That's why we did it. We started our magazine so we could write stupid letters to Robert Smithson. And we were so honored to write to Jasper Johns. I mean nobody was inaccessible. Everybody wanted to publish their work. It was great. It still is actually. I mean I get on the phone now and call up anybody and invite them to give a lecture and chat with them. It's a great privilege.

LJ: What about the '70s and '80s scene in New York? What about the Language scene? You were at the church.

BM: 1971 was when I did the workshop and a lot of the Language people were in the workshop, secretly learning what they needed to know. We used to talk about Lacan. It was a great workshop.

LJ: What did you think of Language writing?

BM: Well, I encouraged it. I never thought it would reach these proportions. I always thought it was a great idea. I'm for all kinds of writing. I never knew Language poetry would become so exclusive. I mean Language poetry is fine, but it's one kind of poetry. Someone said to a friend of mine recently, "Your book is filled with all different kinds of poetry." I mean, why not? Are you supposed to write only one kind of poetry? I don't think so. I love Louis Zukofsky's translations of Catullus, which are not translations, they're just mimicking the sound of the Latin, and they're beautiful, they're great. What Americans really seem to find difficult is when something doesn't make sense. They find it really hard and boring, what's it all about? It seems like you can just enjoy the sounds of words without any other meaning rearing its ugly head. Why bother. Who cares? It's just that people watch TV and they're made to think that things are very simple and clear, because that's the way they are on TV And everyone thinks that everything should be that way.

LJ: Do you think your relation to the poetry scene has changed? Do you feel more at ease? I mean, as an "established" poet.

BM: In the world of the St. Mark's Church poetry scene it's easier to exist. Years ago when you walked into St. Mark's Church it was like a pickup scene. I mean the difference is that now I really know how I feel about poetry, and that I really love listening to poetry. In the beginning I didn't really know that. I mean I guess I did, but I didn't know that I did. So it's really great. A lot of readings that we go to, I'd prefer to be invisible and just listen to the work. I wish there was a poetry series on TV so you could listen to poetry all day long; the social scene doesn't really make it at all. It used to be much more fun. People used to make love in the church belfry and on the pews. You know, it was a lot of fun. What was more interesting about the '60s, that doesn't seem to be true now, is that sex was more predominant. Unless maybe I'm just missing it. So I'm still regressive in that sense, like when I tell my kids about various types of birth control, and then I suddenly realize that they can't make love without the fear of getting AIDS or something. I mean, and sex is totally different than it used to be. I guess a lot of people really don't pay attention.

LJ: What do you think of monogamy?

BM: Oh, I think it sucks. Yeah, I'm against monogamy. That's an easy one. Always have been. But you know, people in the world don't feel that way. Even in the '60s, people used to go around saying how great faithfulness was. And like if a couple stays together and celebrates their 50th wedding anniversary everyone thinks that's a great thing. I think it's a terrible thing, especially for women. I think it's an awful thing, but nobody will admit it. It's like a moral issue. I mean monogamy works if the woman is really content to do all the cooking and cleaning and be a housewife, and then it works. And that's why there are all those couples who celebrate their 50th wedding anniversary. I mean I can't believe that's what they have to do.

LJ: What about marriage?

BM: I'm against marriage. The only reason I'll get married now is if someone needs a green card and will pay me a lot of money. Then I'll do it.

LJ: What's your idea of utopia?

BM: Well it's all in that book. [*Utopia*, United Artists, 1984]

LJ: It seems like a lot of your early projects are about consciousness, exploring that. What did you think you were going to find out by doing that?

BM: Good question. I've always been interested in the brain and consciousness. I mean it's amazing that I had a cerebral hemorrhage and now I see all these neurologists and am concerned with all those things in a different way. I think it's great actually. I shouldn't say that. I learned in the hospital that you're not supposed to think a cerebral hemorrhage is interesting in any way. Otherwise you get accused of having a sense of unreality. One nurse actually said to me, "you don't realize what happened to you."

LJ: What do you think of the medical system?

BM: I think we should all be able to use our health insurance to see homeopaths if we want to. I think the medical system stinks. And I think doctors must take a course in medical school on how not to tell the truth and how not to answer questions. Because if you ask the doctors a question, they won't tell you they don't know, because that's against the rules. A doctor is not supposed to not know something. So they just make up some phony answer which is not true. And I can't find a neurologist who knows about dreams. I mean I finally found one in a book, but in real life never. And I guess I've been spoiled by seeing a psychiatrist who was a doctor, and he was a neurologist, and I was totally spoiled. I could just ask him whatever question I wanted and he would actually answer, and if he didn't know he would say I don't know. It's a very simple thing to say. But the only valuable thing a neurologist has ever told me is this one guy said in medical school he was told to take PABA to remember dreams. And that works for a while.

LJ: And you've been having dreams again?

BM: Yeah. I have them if I take this drug called Xanax—it induces dreams—but that's problematic because how can you take that much Xanax? And that's the only way I can remember dreams, so one day I hope to come up with another solution.

LJ: Do you still use information from your dreams in poems? Have you been incorporating that?

BM: Yeah I can, but at the moment I don't because I don't have enough memory of dreams to do it. I mean it used to be an integral part of my work, but at the moment I'm writing mostly about reality. (*laughs*)

LJ: When you were in the hospital, how did the doctors and nurses react to the fact that you were a poet?

BM: Oh. Amazingly. They would say to me all the time, "say something poetic." They never used the word poetry as a noun. "Do something poetic." And they would hover over my shoulder when I was using the computer to see what I typed. Well, those weren't the doctors, they were the cognitive therapists.

LJ: Do you think that you figured out anything about consciousness from having that experience?

BM: Oh yeah, definitely. But what I've mainly figured out is that really fascinating things have been happening to me for the last three years, and nobody asks me about them. Nobody seems to care. I can't get a straight answer from anybody.

LJ: You mean like doctors?

BM: Yeah. I mean they all think I'm imagining it. I saw some optometrist and I told him I couldn't read because I was seeing weird squiggly orange and green shapes on the page, and he looked at me askance, to put it nicely, and then about six months later he said, "yeah, I think probably you were right about what you said because I just read it in a book." So it's been very frustrating. I mean it would be great if somebody was really interested in what was happening to me, and if it continues the way it is now, I'm going to be forced to write a book about it, which I don't think is the book I want to write. But I would love to talk about it. I mean when I first left the hospital I was desperate for someone to talk to and I really thought that was a possible thing, and somebody had told me that if you put some kind of statement or question on the Internet that you'll find a person—that it's inevitable, you'll have to find a person. So I did that and the only response I got was from this doctor who said, "if you can't remember your dreams, it's important not to forget your aspirations." (*laughs*) And he signed it, Doctor So-and-So. I mean my collection of silly statements about dreams is endless. So it would be nice to know a doctor, it would be nice to know a neurologist, it would be nice to be able to ask questions and have them answered. I mean it's tiring to be the person who has all these thoughts and they don't go anywhere and nobody seems to care about them. I know I'm complaining.

LJ: You're writing again. How has your writing changed?

BM: It's changed a lot. I feel like a different person. I was thinking I should have a new name, and to start a new kind of writing. At the moment I'm writing these epigrams, and it's amazing. I started writing epigrams because Lee Ann Brown created this game where there were a pile of form cards and a pile of content cards. And every time I would draw out a form card it would be an epigram. So I started writing all these epigrams, and then I realized that it was very easy to write them, and all I had to do was close my eyes and think about anything at all. And epigrams are an amazing form because they're so brief. So that's what I'm doing now. And/or writing a book about the iguana maybe.

LJ: The iguana in the other room?

BM: Yes. Well it's hard not to. He's right next to my desk.

LJ: What are the projects that you haven't done yet that you'd like to do?

BM: Uh. I'd like to get rich. You mean writing projects?

LJ: Yeah, writing projects.

BM: I don't know. Good question. While I was in the hospital I had this dream that—I mean it persisted for about a year too, and I thought it was real— that in *The Desires of Mothers to Please Others in Letters* [Hard Press, 1993], I had written a poem for each prose piece, and that if people read that, they would learn how to write poetry. So, maybe that's a project. (*laughs*) I've written so many poems, they're everywhere. I don't know exactly where they are everywhere, but everywhere I look I find more poems. So, it would be nice to find all the poems.

LJ: That's a good project. What about experiments? Are there writing experiments that are still useful for you from the original experiments list?

BM: I like doing the free associative experiment, where you write whatever.

LJ: How did those experiment lists come about?

BM: We put them together in my first workshop. The workshop students and I put them together. There's a project I'd like to do, but it's not exactly a writing project. But I'd like computers to be able to record everything you think and see. To be like the brain, and to write that out. And apparently eventually computers will be able to do this. That Wim Wenders movie *[Until] the End of the World* is sort of like that. And somebody said to me, "who would read it?" But I'm thinking that I would read it. I would love to read it. Like if you had all these documents of everybody's experience. It would be amazing.

LJ: That's kind of like a high-tech Olson project. Scanning and mapping.

BM: And then you could just take part of it and publish it in a poetry magazine. I like taking prose works and changing them into poetry and vice versa. Well, I just want to make some money. I want to start a wildlife refuge. Those are my plans. I know exactly where to do it but I don't have the cash.

LJ: Where?

BM: In East Chatham, where we can build those wooden walkways over the pond and over the swamp, and people can walk on them and observe. We can bring the beavers back. Beavers and herons and all kinds of wildlife. So that's my aspiration. See I remembered my aspirations.

AN INTERVIEW WITH KENNETH KOCH
BY DANIEL KANE

FEBRUARY/MARCH 1999   NO. 173

On October 12, 1998, I interviewed Kenneth Koch in his apartment in Morningside Heights. I was especially interested in the role of poetry readings, and how readings helped to generate a sense of community on the Lower East Side in the '60s and '70s.

KENNETH KOCH: Before you got here, I was trying to think of the best poetry reading I ever heard. I was driving in from eastern Long Island, with John Ashbery in the car, and he read me "The Skaters." That's the best poetry reading I've ever heard. The second best reading I ever heard was one that Frank O'Hara gave at some gallery—in fact, this was the first time I heard him read. He read "Poem for the Chinese New Year." I heard something in Frank's voice, a kind of tone that clarified something for me, so that was a terrific reading for me. Those were the two best ones I ever heard.

DANIEL KANE: The first one was rather exclusive!

KK: Yes, I would say so! (*laughs*)

DK: On the Lower East Side reading scene, though, it seems that O'Hara was the main figure of the so-called New York School who was actively associated with other poets in that neighborhood. O'Hara lived on East 9th Street

near Avenue A, he was friends with LeRoi Jones (now Amiri Baraka), Allen Ginsberg, and other downtown poets.

KK: How many readings did Frank give in that neighborhood?

DK: Well, I know O'Hara read at least once or twice at the 5 Spot, and he certainly attended at least a couple of readings at the Le Metro series on 2nd Avenue. In 1961, O'Hara also participated in a series of benefit readings for Amiri Baraka's and Diane di Prima's magazine, *The Floating Bear*.

KK: On the whole subject of poetry readings, I must admit I'm kind of skeptical, because I'm not sure that much has ever happened because of poetry readings. I like to read poems in books. Don't you?

DK: I do.

KK: More than you like to hear them?

DK: For the most part. Though sometimes hearing the poet read changes the way I think or "hear" the poem when I read it later in the book. The first time I saw John Ashbery read was before I had read much of his work. To be honest with you, I was bored beyond belief. Then I read a bunch of his stuff over the next few years, and started very slowly picking up on it. Then I saw him read again, and he read differently, I'm sure of it. It didn't have *that* much to do with the fact that I'd been reading him more carefully. The way he read the second time, the way he phrased certain lines, affected me enormously in terms of how I went on to read his poetry.

KK: I think the only time I had that experience was with Frank's reading. There are very few people I like to hear read. I like to hear Ron Padgett read.

DK: I remember hearing Ann Lauterbach read before I ever read her poetry. As she was reading, her hands started moving and dancing in front of her—it seemed as if she were approximating the words visually by sculpting them in the air with her hands. I thought it was all quite thrilling. When she was done, I dashed off and bought her book *Clamor*.

KK: A reading that did have a big influence on me, I now remember, was one which was held up at Columbia University that Allen Ginsberg did, in the late 1960s, with John Hollander. It was during the Vietnam War, and I had not written a political poem since I was a teenager. I was impressed by Allen's straightforwardness, which is something I got from the reading I think even more than I could have from reading his poems on the page. In person, Allen displayed how straightforward he was about everything. He read a lot of "political" poems about the war, and I thought, "Why am I not writing about this war, which I object to so much?" And I didn't like what was happening to my students, what was happening to anybody, so I started to write my poem "The Pleasures of Peace" as a direct result of being inspired by that Ginsberg reading. I worked on this poem for more than a year, maybe two years. It was very hard for me to work on a poem about the war. You know sometimes your body rejects an artificial heart? Well, my poetry rejected everything about the war, everything that was about suffering. So it turned out to be a poem about the pleasures of the peace movement. That poem, though unlike Allen's poems, was due to his reading.

DK: I was looking through the reading lists for St. Mark's Poetry Project, from 1966 to 1971, and noticed the Project had all sorts of benefits for political causes. There were benefits for the Catonsville Nine, the Berkeley Defense Fund, various drug-bust release readings, and so on. Did you see your aesthetics, which for the most part do not include overtly political content, fitting in somehow with the political excitement going on at the Poetry Project?

KK: I remember being always willing to read my poetry for what I thought was a good cause, whether or not my poetry spoke about the cause. And it usually didn't. That's about it. I was happy to read against the war even before I wrote "The Pleasures of Peace." If people wanted me to read something about roller coasters to show that poets were against the war, I would always do it. But I don't know much about the "scene" at St. Mark's. I was never really a part of that scene. By the time it got to be something that I took part in with any regularity I was already sort of an old-timer.

DK: I do get the sense though that you and Ashbery and O'Hara and James Schuyler are seen, in a strange sort of way, as spiritual founding fathers of the Poetry Project.

KK: The Poetry Project didn't have anything to do with the formation of my poetry, or John's or Frank's or Jimmy's, so far as I know, though I have been inspired by reading there; I always like to read there. The audience is so smart. That is to say, they're smart in this particular way that they're up on what's going on in poetry. It's like being a scientist talking to other scientists, and you're excited because they have the same kind of laboratory you have. I was slightly afraid sometimes to read new work at the Poetry Project, because I was afraid things would be swiped. Everybody is on this high frequency there! I had a very funny time with Ted Berrigan about that. I read there one year—my series "In Bed," about a hundred short poems, all with "bed" in the title. So I read it at St. Mark's, and within a couple of months I got a little book from Ted Berrigan, and it had a little poem in it called "By the Seashore" or something like that. And the entire poem is "There is a crab / in my bed." And I thought, "Oh shit!" I didn't say anything to Ted, but I happened to be talking to Anne Waldman about something, and I mentioned this to her and she said "Oh!" She was very happy, she would get to reproach Ted with it. But I said, "Don't tell Ted," and she said "Oh, no no no." But she couldn't help but tell Ted. And Ted wrote me a letter assuring me that this was not true, that he'd written the poem four years before my "In Bed" poems. Alice Notley later told me, "Kenneth, I know that for sure. I'm the crab!"

DK: What do you think the effect of the Don Allen anthology, *The New American Poetry*, was on your career, especially in the way it classified you, among others, as a "New York Poet"?

KK: I have no idea. I don't even know what my career is. I got a little, tiny bit famous for writing *Wishes, Lies and Dreams*. I got asked all around the country to talk about teaching children to write poetry, but my poetry . . . I don't know about my career. Poetry books in this country are sometimes reviewed and sometimes not. It's very hard to know what makes a career. The best thing that happened to me was having John Ashbery and Frank O'Hara as friends. To have two poets who delight you and scare you to death is the best thing that I ever got. I don't know what that anthology did for anyone's career. Frank's career, outside a small audience, seemed to start after his death. I don't think it did anything for my career, or Ashbery's. Ashbery's big academic career started very oddly, with *Self-Portrait in a Convex Mirror*. All that glorious early work was more or less ignored. Very strange!

DK: *The New American Poetry* certainly had an enormous effect among the group of poets who looked towards you and your friends as superheroes.

KK: Is that where Ted found out about us?

DK: Well, according to his journals and letters, Berrigan indicated that he came across your work initially through the Allen anthology, which he first read in Oklahoma. He said that he "came to O'Hara last," and then, from O'Hara, he read through the whole New York School group more carefully, and then he decided that the New York School section of that anthology was the most exciting section. I thought that was curious, especially when you consider all the class issues involved—a working-class, bearlike guy from Rhode Island and Oklahoma, living in low-rent Lower East Side, picking up on what seemed to be a relatively genteel, Harvard-educated, sophisticated Hamptons gang.

KK: I didn't understand anything you just said! What are you talking about, "Hamptons gang"?

DK: All right, forget it. I guess what I really want to know is: what does Berrigan have to do with creating this idea of a "second generation" New York School?

KK: You're asking me things I don't know anything about! The New York School has always been such a shadowy thing. I was aware that there were these terrific talented kids downtown who really liked John and Frank and me and particularly liked John and Frank. I was aware of that, and then after a while it seemed that Ted Berrigan was sort of the daddy of the downtown poets, taking care of everybody and showing them what it was like to be a poet. I taught a number of those guys in various places. I taught Ron here [at Columbia]. David Shapiro was my student too. At The New School I had Tony Towle as a student, and Bill Berkson, and then at Wagner College even Ted came as my student. Ted pointed out to me something very interesting. He said, "Kenneth, do you know every time you mention Paul Valéry you go like this?" (*puts his right hand on top of his head*) I thought that was very astute of him. I was very embarrassed, so I stopped doing that. Joe Ceravolo was my student at The New School. That's a pleasure for a teacher, to have a brilliant student like that who had hardly written a poem before. I was interested in the existence of more New York School poets. I decided to teach at the New School not only because I wanted a job, but I really thought I knew a *secret* about poetry that nobody knew except John and Frank and me. I knew about this new aesthetic, this new way to write poetry, and I wanted to spread it around, because I thought it was *dumb* to think that these other bad poets were writing poetry. I taught with a lot of enthusiasm . . . I really had a mission to make this aesthetic clear to people. I liked this idea of there being more New York poets.

DK: I notice you use the word "aesthetic" as in "I wanted to teach this aesthetic." I'm curious—how would you define that aesthetic?

KK: Well, let me tell you a few assignments I used at the New School. I had people read William Carlos Williams and imitate him. This was to get them rid of meter, rhyme, and fancy subject matter. Ordinary American language, spoken language. I had them write poems about their dreams. I had them write stream-of-consciousness . . . this was to get their unconscious stuff into their poetry. I had everybody write short plays, prose poems, transform an article in a newspaper into a poem, and I had them write sestinas. I wanted my students to break away from "poetry" poetry, and sort of . . . it was something I thought was French. I was very influenced by Max Jacob. Do you know his work? You should read him. From Jacob I learned how to be comic and lyrical at the same time. That was quite a discovery. It helped the determination to get rid of Eliot, and depression, and despair, and inky-dinky meter. I read a critic that I make fun of in my poem "Fresh Air" who said that iambic pentameter was the only "honest" English meter. So, getting back to your question of what is the New York School aesthetic … I don't know, just a lot of fresh air, to have fun with poetry, to use the unconscious, to use the spoken language, to pay attention to the surface of the language.

DK: Your poem "Fresh Air" seems to have set up a distinction between so-called "outsider" or "avant-garde" poetry and "academic" poetry. What is "academic" poetry?

KK: It changes. The academic poetry I was ridiculing then has mainly—but not entirely—gone away. Now there are new kinds of bad poetry that you could call "academic." The kind in "Fresh Air" is by now old-fashioned, like iceboxes—the new kinds of academic poetry are like bad refrigerators. The academic poetry that I made fun of in "Fresh Air" had a heavy dose of myth. It was all these American poets of the '40s and '50s who had gone through their Yeats shots and Eliot shots, and they all had the fever of the bone, the skeleton, Odysseus, all that stuff. Now it's funny what academic poetry has turned into. I've always wanted to write more poems like "Fresh Air," but I didn't have the incentive. After a while, there didn't seem to be a discernible enemy. There were too many enemies. But bad poetry never goes away. Then there was this whole period—it's still with us, I think—of the whole "workshop" kind of poem. "Grandpa dies on the way to the garage," or "I'm having a love affair with a student," or something. At the time I wrote "Fresh Air," academic poetry was the poetry that was in Donald Hall, Robert Pack, and Louis Simpson's book *New British and American Poets*. It was Snodgrass, Ciardi … That anthology was one of my major inspirations for writing my poem "Fresh Air." That's where I got the idea that all this poetry was about the myth, the missus, and the midterms.

DK: In the Donald Allen anthology, Allen stated that all the poets in the book shared a common debt to Pound and Williams. Why was Pound acceptable to so many of the "downtown" poets whereas Eliot, especially the later Eliot, wasn't?

KK: Particularly in *The Cantos*, when they're good, Pound has this very quirky way of talking, very conversational. He gives you all these pleasures—a very flat, spoken style mixed in with unexpected quotes and other languages. I think I and John and Frank were all influenced by Pound's way of referring to all kinds of things all at once. But Pound did it to make some kind of point, whereas I think we did it because we just liked the splash of it, having everything in. That's true for me, anyway—I liked having the whole world in my poems. Strangely enough, one can get that from Pound and from Eliot.

DK: The way you're talking about Pound reminds me of *The Pisan Cantos* when Pound brings in voices of the black soldiers, like in "Canto LXXX": "Ain' committed no federal crime, jes a slaight misdemeanor." I imagine that kind of incorporation of marginalized or "non-literary" speech—a practice which Pound shared with Williams—possibly made Pound especially interesting to the avant-garde poets living in New York during the 1960s.

KK: Even take a line in *The Cantos* like "Nancy, where art thou?" Or "white-chested martin, goddamnit!" Even if Pound's context is to say that civilization stinks, there's all this fun, lively language in it. As Frank said, "If you're not writing about the tremendous excitement and richness of life, you may as well not be doing it." Like O'Hara's poem "Second Avenue," whatever it's saying it's full of everything in the world. That's what is so great about it, so exciting about it.

DK: I wanted to ask you about The New School readings that you organized in the early to mid-1960s. I'm interested in these because they ran concurrently to Les Deux Mégots and Le Metro readings—two Lower East Side reading series which many poets feel were the real predecessors for the Poetry Project. The New School readings included many of the same readers who read regularly in the Lower East Side—John Wieners, who read at Le Metro a number of times, also read at The New School. Did you have an overall vision for The New School readings, and did you sense a shared purpose between your reading series and the series I've mentioned?

KK: I just tried to get the best poets I could, and the variety I wanted. I had Auden, and Marianne Moore, and then some of my guys. I wanted to mix them up. I just remembered I had Robert Lowell read at the New School, as well. I think that the Poetry Project at a certain point opened its gates to more people than I thought they would. They had a reading with Lowell and Ginsberg—why not?

DK: That was Larry Fagin's idea. In an interview with Bob Holman, Larry said, "A lot of the wacky imagery was via Ashbery-O'Hara-Koch to Padgett-Berrigan-Gallup (the *C* magazine crowd). They were the healthiest thing that came along. They took the earlier wackiness and made it even more contemporary. At times almost insipid, and at other times even more contemporary. Delirious swooning. Absolute drivel. There's no need for it now, it's been done." Does that make any sense to you?

KK: It makes sense as an utterance of Larry. He likes to sum things up! (*laughs*) I don't know what he means by "contemporary," and I also don't know whether chattiness or wackiness is no longer needed now. Does Larry mean that Frank O'Hara says "Wonderbread" and that Dick Gallup says "Wonderbread with raisins in it"?

DK: Perhaps some poets associated with the second generation are a little more inclusive of rough edges and behavior. For example, in many of Berrigan's poems we're privy to his really unhealthy eating habits. We know about his many Pepsis, his prodigious speed consumption, his milkshakes and hamburgers. This is opposed to the haute cuisine feel generated by an Ashbery or Schuyler poem—I'm thinking of lines from Schuyler's poems now, where he refers to "pâté maison" and the "concord grape season." At the same time, Berrigan maintains a sense of lightness and sophistication that is often associated with the New York School aesthetic.

KK: Well, John and Frank and I went to Harvard. We were all put on the assembly line to be proper fellows, and to get a good, solid, classical education and to be responsible citizens. Most of the downtown poets weren't on that track. That's another thing about their being younger than we were—we had something to react against that was very strong, and very total. What was going on in the literary magazines was absolutely awful, there weren't any good magazines around. But schools of poetry hardly matter—it's friendship and individual talent.

DK: Since you mentioned friendship, I'd like to talk about how writers like Ron Padgett and Ted Berrigan picked up on the magazine *Locus Solus*, particularly the issue you edited which was made up entirely of collaborations. What are your memories of that collaborative issue in terms of how people responded to it and in light of what we're discussing here regarding a kind of avant-garde tradition? Why collaborations?

KK: Ah! There's a question I can answer. I know that Ron and Ted liked to collaborate, and if their book *Bean Spasms* was in any way influenced by that issue of *Locus Solus*, then I'm very glad I did it. I love that book. I was very interested in collaborating because I had done a lot of collaborations with John Ashbery. We did a series of sestinas called "The Bestiary." We did a whole lot of poems in Paris and in Rome. We'd sit around in a lot of nice places like the garden of the Rodin Museum in Paris and write these poems with crazy rules. Like, there has to be something contrary to fact in every line, as well as the word "silver" and a small animal. I found the act of collaboration inspiring. It was something the French taught me—Breton, Éluard.

DK: I'm interested in collaboration especially when looking at the early years of the Poetry Project. Everyone there seemed to be very much involved with ideas of anonymity, appropriation, and collaboration. Many of the earlier issues of *The World* are made up almost entirely of collaborations where the author is at best a shadowy figure. The question "who wrote what line" was often treated as a kind of game in these magazines. It's also interesting to look at the idea and implication of collaborations in the context of poetry in the 1950s and early 1960s. After all, this was a time where you had a "great poet" like Dylan Thomas presented to you on the radio, reading with that profoundly operatic voice of his. I mean, this was *Dylan Thomas*. It seems that your issue of *Locus Solus*, and the later collaborative activity coming out of the Poetry Project and writers like Padgett and Berrigan, really stood in opposition to that kind of presentation.

KK: There's a quote at the beginning of that issue—Harry Mathews found it—from Lautréamont: "La poésie doit être faite par tous. Non par un. Pauvre Hugo! Pauvre Racine! Pauvre Coppée! Pauvre Corneille! Pauvre Boileau! Pauvre Scarron! Tics, tics, et tics." [Poetry must be made by everybody. Not by one. Poor Hugo! Poor Racine! (etc.)]

DK: Do you think you were doing anything subversive by putting out this issue?

KK: Well, I felt that the teaching and this editing and all the writing I did were for the same interesting cause. Poetry should be exciting and interesting and beautiful and surprising—yes, I was uncomfortable with what poets were seemed to be supposed to do. Collaboration was certainly carried on at St. Mark's. I performed there with Allen Ginsberg, and we improvised sestinas, haiku, rhymed couplets, all kinds of things. That was an event which could only be possible at St. Mark's.

DK: Why was that only possible at St. Mark's?

KK: Where else could it happen? Certain things can only happen at St. Mark's —I think the classiest things go on there, but totally without pretentiousness. Pretension does not seem to get into the church for one reason or another. It's always just poetry. It's a great place to read.

DK: Ted Berrigan, who read and socialized often at the Poetry Project, had taken classes with you and credited you with helping him move away from blatant O'Hara impersonations towards something else. In his diary, Berrigan wrote, "Frank opened all the doors for me. For a while he was a very bad influence on me, because I started getting too close, it was seeming too easy for me, and then Kenneth Koch kindly pointed out to me that Frank was being a very bad influence."

KK: I do remember saying at one point, when everybody seemed to be imitating Frank, that Frank invented this wonderful way of just putting down on paper everything that was going on in his head. This works very well if you have lots of interesting things in your head. But most of the people doing it, Berrigan *not* included, weren't as interesting, so that style could be a problem. I think I was thinking about some West Coast poets who wrote things like "It's

4:15 / have to have a toke. / Walk down the street, / look at a necktie."
I mean, so what!

DK: You know, one thing I wanted to ask you about was your involvement
with Ed Sanders, who was one of the kings of the Lower East Side; he edited
the legendary *Fuck You: A Magazine of the Arts*, he ran the bookstore The
Peace Eye, he formed the band The Fugs. Regarding Sanders' arrest on
obscenity charges for distributing material including his own mimeograph
magazine *Fuck You: A Magazine of the Arts*, Sanders told me he remembered
you and John Ashbery were character witnesses for him. You were called to
testify on a day you were playing tennis, and apparently had to rush down-
town and present your case on Sanders' behalf while holding onto your ten-
nis racket. Do you remember this?

KK: Ed Sanders was one of the good guys. How could anything be more
absurd than being arrested because you have certain books in your book-
store? It was very funny because Ed called me up and asked me about being
a character reference. *Fuck You: A Magazine of the Arts* was not something
I subscribed to but I read a lot of them and thought it was very funny. I
remember Sanders distributed a great questionnaire which asked all the
downtown poets about their buggering habits. I liked very much the maga-
zine's big solicitation for people to volunteer for a filming of a Mongolian
cluster fuck. This turned out to be a key issue of the trial. I was annoyed
with the magazine a few times though, especially when I was on the list of
people Gerard Malanga fucked—I certainly wasn't one of those people!
John and I agreed to be character witnesses. The trial kept getting delayed.
Ed had a civil liberties lawyer who kept on waiting to get a good judge.
Every month or so I'd get a phone call saying, "This might be the day for
your appearance. Be ready." I was told to wear a Brooks Brothers suit. On
one particular day I was aware I might be called down to testify, but I was
scheduled to play tennis. At the tennis court, a big announcement came over
the loudspeakers on all the Central Park courts. "Kenneth Cock! Kenneth
Cock!" I jumped into my gray flannel suit and grabbed my tennis racket.

John Ashbery was already there. They were just starting the trial. They dismissed the case. Here's why. This was after the big *SCREW* magazine case, in which I think the decision had been made that obscenity could only be against the law if it encouraged other people to engage in it. So, our lawyer had sort of tricked the opposition lawyer into concentrating his case entirely on the solicitation of people to be filmed during *Mongolian Cluster Fuck*. Now, the judge was someone with a sense of humor and a brain, and our lawyer had explained to him, "You don't really believe that they're going to make a movie called *Mongolian Cluster Fuck*! What is that? Obviously, this is a joke, so this doesn't fall under the purview of the law." So the judge explained this to the other lawyer and dismissed the case. I had prepared a list of about ten things I thought were socially redeeming about *Fuck You*, but I never got a chance to state what they were.

DK: I remember one of the first things I saw going through back issues of *Fuck You* was a form one could fill out indicating a willingness to participate in a "Fuck-In" against the Vietnam War. There was a box you were supposed to check adjacent to a line which read, "Yes, I will fuck-in." But you also had an option—you could check the line which read, "Preferring to eat dick, I will suck-in."

KK: (*laughs*) That's good!

DK: In *Out of This World*, Anne Waldman talks about the Poetry Project as a New York School center. In terms of the way the reading scene in that neighborhood changed, it seems that it had a lot to do with the poets in the younger crowd—many of whom you taught at Columbia and other places—taking responsibility for running readings at the Project, whereas in the past a slightly older crowd organized readings at places like Le Metro and the earlier reading series at Les Deux Mégots. You organized earlier reading series at places like the 5 Spot near Cooper Square.

KK: Larry Rivers organized the readings there—he knew a lot of jazz musicians. I thought reading poetry to jazz, which the Beat poets and Rexroth out on the West Coast were doing, was absolutely absurd because the beat of music is so much stronger than that of poetry that you could read the telephone book to music and it would sound good. I did that once. The other thing I thought was, "Hey, I want to do that too!"

DK: You read the telephone book to music at the 5 Spot?

KK: Yes, just a little bit of it. Not the night Billie Holiday sang between my sets. That was another night. But John Ashbery never read there. And Frank disdained it—he may have read once, I don't remember. I was the one who had the most enthusiasm for the jazz-poetry nights. I read about three times. One night I read, and Larry was sitting with some painters, among them Mark Rothko. I read my poems, and Larry said, "What do you think?" Rothko replied, "Why don't these poets make any sense?" For the last two readings I had, Larry got Mal Waldron and his trio. These guys sort of objected to the setup. It was mainly funny things I read. I read my short play, "Bertha," a ten-minute play about the queen of Norway who's getting old and bored and decides that she'll conquer Norway again and liven things up. Larry said the jazz musicians were very serious, but he guaranteed them that they'd get their soul back after they stopped accompanying me. I had a lot of fun doing that, and I thought I'd achieve instant fame. Instead, after the second time I did it, Larry told me, "There's a guy in the back that wants to talk to you." He offered me a job as a master of ceremonies at a downtown gay nightclub. I said, "No, I don't think I can handle that." One night after a reading, the drummer said, "That was great man. Where do you get your material?" That was terrific. The last night I read, Billie Holiday came, because Mal was her accompanist. Billie was there at the bar. Mal introduced me to her, and she said to me, "Man, your stuff is just crazy!" I believed—or hoped—that meant "good." That night the audience prevailed upon Billie to sing—it was the night Frank O'Hara would write about in his poem "The Day Lady Died." She almost had no voice—it was like a great old wine that almost tastes like water. Then I got up and read again. The evening ended, except for Frank's poem. What a gift for the immediate! Frank could write fast—he could sit down in the middle of a party and write a poem, and if you went over and talked to him he'd put what you just said into the poem. Amazing. I tried to do that but I had no success at all.

DK: Why were you and other writers associated with the New York School so fond of comic strip characters—Ashbery and his use of Popeye in the poem "Farm Implements and Rutabagas in a Landscape," or Joe Brainard's various Superman and Nancy drawings. Were cartoons part of the fresh air in art and poetry that we were talking about earlier?

KK: It was the main form of art in my life for ten years—in Cincinnati, when I was growing up. I felt a lot closer to Popeye, the Gumps, Orphan Annie, than to other kinds of art. John and I were doing stuff with cartoon figures at least as early as Roy Lichtenstein did, but nobody knew that. That's because we were doing it with language, and Lichtenstein was doing it with visual images. *C* magazine had wonderful cartoon issues, with great Joe Brainard illustrations. Before we stop talking, I'd like to ask you some things. To what extent does it seem to you that such interactions as were going on downtown then are going on there now? Are things made more difficult by factors like high rents and careerism among poets?

DK: Well, I suppose many people living downtown now can't afford to live without having to work forty or fifty hours a week, and even then it's really difficult. Also, maybe the poetry world nowadays is even more fragmented into competing schools and cliques than it was in the past. In the past, the Umbra group, which was composed primarily of black poets, was certainly an important part of the overall Lower East Side poetic community— Ishmael Reed, David Henderson, Lorenzo Thomas, all hanging out with people like Ted Berrigan, Ron Padgett, Taylor Mead, and George Economou at Le Metro.

KK: I'm asking you what's going on now, though, because people come up to me and say, "Oh, the '50s must have been so great, what's happening now?" And I don't know what's happening now.

DK: Maybe the kind of glamour and excitement around poetry is happening now, but we might need twenty or thirty years of mythologizing to recognize it. I am acquainted with the writing of very good poets who seem to be part of a social group that is somewhat centered around the Poetry Project and other reading series at places like the Zinc Bar on West Houston. Just looking at these poets and their publishing and reading practices, one can see that they're all helping each other, promoting each other, and so on. Does that mean that thirty years from now, critics and academics will write about these poets' small-press chapbooks, their online conversations, their romances? It will be curious to see what happens.

A SILENT INTERVIEW WITH SAMUEL R. DELANY

JUNE 1999   NO. 175

In your autobiography, *The Motion of Light in Water*, you state that you are "neither black nor white . . . male nor female. And [you are] that most ambiguous of citizens, the writer." What roles does or will that most ambiguous of citizens play in our public or private culture(s), or in our potential utopias?

You'll remember, in *The Motion of Light in Water*, I present it as an *error* in my thinking that I got trapped into when I was at an emotional nadir—and on my way to a nervous breakdown that eventually landed me in a mental hospital.

Only when I began to get it back together and was in the midst of the kind of thinking that got me *out* of the hospital and, at 23, back into the world—and that started me writing again—did I realize that I was "a black man, a gay man, a writer"; that these were specific, if complex, categories. As categories, they were social impositions—not essences. They were what had always already *given* me my identity; and an identity was something to be examined, interrogated, analyzed: Vigilance and, sometimes, resistance were the conditions of being able to function.

Now people desperately love all that wonderful-sounding ambiguity—just as I desperately desired it when I was beaten and confused and exhausted by life and overwork. "I belong to no category; I straddle them all . . ." It sounds

romantic—decadent, but somehow still transcendent. When we pursue such ambiguity, mistakenly we feel it's a way to escape social accountability. That we crave it is the sign of just how wounding the categories can be or have been. Still, espousing that ambiguity was and is a way of saying: "Not me . . . I'm above all that, outside of it, not a part of it."

What I learned is that precisely when one says "I'm not a part," one is most trapped by one's identity, most paralyzed and most limited; that's the sign one has given up, given in; that you are precisely *not* in a condition of freedom— but of entrapment. Saying "I am not a part" is very different from saying "Because I am a part, I will not participate in *that* manner." The first is delusion. The second is power—which is inimical to the cry of powerlessness that you quote.

In *Longer Views*, your collection of essays, you name a dozen poets whose work you have enjoyed over the last few years. How has poetry influenced your work? What is the connection, for you, between, say, poetry and science fiction writing?

Auden's on my mind: Yesterday someone sent me an audiotape of a TV program that featured Auden, which I watched on *Camera Three* in 1953 when I was eleven years old. The show in which Auden was interviewed made a great impression on me as a child.

One of my best friends in elementary school was named Johnny Kronenberger, whose father, Louis Kronenberger, had collaborated with Auden on *The Oxford Book of Aphorisms*. From time to time Auden babysat for Johnny and his sister Liza. So, by the time I was eleven, I already knew of Auden and knew he was a famous poet—that, indeed, he was queer and lived with Chester Kallman. (The kids at my New York private school were quite a bunch of gossips.) With great glee, Johnny had described to me Chester's imitations of Diana Trilling at his parents' annual Christmas party.

I listened to the soundtrack of the programs just last night—for the first time in 45 years. Having heard the voice of Jim Macandrew, the spokesperson for *Camera Three* (in the 1950s he was the poor man's Alistair Cooke), for the first time since I entered puberty, what I was most aware of last night was how people use poetry for their own purposes—which may or may not have anything to do with what the poet is interested in, writing his or her poem.

In 1953, Macandrew was probably somewhere between 38 and 42. He'd just missed out, doubtless, on the New Criticism, and probably regarded it as a suspicious order of recent academic nonsense—the way someone who'd graduated college in the fifties might have regarded poststructuralist literal theory ten or fifteen years ago. Interviewing Auden, clearly he had an intellectual agenda already in place. What I realized last night, however, which had completely escaped me at 11, was that his only interest in Auden was how Auden was going to validate that agenda. Equally clearly, he couldn't imagine Auden himself having any other interest than to validate it. With every "question/ statement" Macandrew poses, his point is that the historical purpose of the poet has been to provide images of heroes for the nation. Clearly that's what Homer did. Clearly that's what Shakespeare did. Thus, that's what Auden must be doing, too. ("The poet must speak from a position of strength . . ." he begins by declaring): "Okay, Mr. Auden, tell our audience just how *you* go about doing this." And whenever Auden tries, however politely, to move the conversation toward something that might actually be interesting about poetry (at one point, while describing how technology changes the structure of the personal act, Auden explains that pressing a button to drop a bomb is far different from Achilles fighting a one-to-one combat with Hector), Macandrew diligently takes it back to this narrow and striated notion: "Of course the people *must* find a hero in the midst of something technological. They might pick the tail gunner of the plane that dropped the bomb on Japan twelve years ago. But the poet wouldn't be interested in the tail gunner, of course."

Realizing he's been completely misunderstood, Auden declares: "Oh, he *might* . . ."

Today Macandrew sounds unbelievably clunky, dated—and dictatorial: He knows what poetry is for, and that's all he's interested in hearing about. At the same time, the establishment critical position was that the purpose of poets was to write great poems about great political leaders; and the fact that no poet whom anyone actually wanted to read was even vaguely interested in doing anything like this was a sign of the decadent times in which we lived.

While there are *more* poets today, and people have become *somewhat* more comfortable with them, conversing with them, hearing them read, and perhaps a little more polite to them, I don't know whether the fundamental situation has changed. We find lines that we love and quote them out of context—only to reread the entire poem a decade later and discover that the poet was telling us that is something we must *never* do or think!

The very brilliance of expression was the poet's attempt to allegorize its seductiveness as a dangerous idea.

In his essay, "Writing," Auden tells us:

> The English-speaking peoples have always felt that the difference between poetic speech and the conventional speech of everyday should be kept very small, and, whenever poets have felt that the gap between poetic and ordinary speech was growing too wide, there has been a stylistic revolution to bring them closer again.

By the time, a dozen years after watching him on *Camera Three*, I too had begun to write, Auden's work was there to help make me aware that the language labors that produce poetry were not very different from those necessary for prose.

That fundamental closeness between poetry and prose in English is what allowed me to see poets laboring over their poems and to put like labor into my prose. What differentiates the two are the discourses that control the way in which they're read. Though there's some, of course, there's much less difference in the way the two are written than it would otherwise seem.

Can art—poetry, say—really change people?

A communal task that art accomplishes—particularly the verbal arts of fiction and poetry—is to help with the shifts of discourse that must occur for there to be meaningful historical change.

Because it *is* a communal task, because no *single* work of art can accomplish such a discursive shift by itself, the artist (responsible only for her or his own work) *doesn't* have to worry about preaching. It's far more effective to look at a situation and dramatize in however complex allegorical terms you'd like what it is you've seen.

For the same reason that poets and artists don't have to worry about preaching, the general public doesn't need to worry about censorship. "For poetry makes nothing happen," Auden wrote in his elegy for Yeats. That privileged lack-of-power of the single work of art—the single poem, say—is precisely what, I feel, Auden was getting at.

Many works of art taken together, however, through the very process by which we learn to read them, establish discourses—establish discourses of the possible, discourses of the probable, discourses of desire. Discourses are the conceptual tools with which we socially construct our world, materially and imaginatively.

List your favorite utopias.

I don't very much like utopias as a form. I much prefer science fiction—which, as a genre, is fundamentally anti-utopian (and equally anti-dystopian) in its thinking. I suspect, indeed, that's why science fiction has largely displaced utopian fiction as a genre. Again, Auden is the one who spelled out the explanation for us, in *Horae Canonicae*, and again in some of his essays in *The Dyer's Hand.*

For city lovers, the city is the site of New Jerusalem—the site of knowledge, sophistication, freedom of action, as well as of all true learning and culture—while for the urban-oriented temperament the country is the superstition-, disease-, fire-, flood-, and earthquake-ridden Land of the Flies, where life is harsh and brutal and all society is bound by the chains of gossip and village opinion. For country lovers, the land is Arcadia and the city is, rather, the dirty, shabby, mechanized, and inhuman place where everyone wears the same uniform and does the same meaningless tasks in a quintessentially boring setting: Brave New World. As Auden points out, the decision as to whether you are more comfortable in the city or the country is largely a matter of temperament and/or habitation. It is not a matter of objective facts. You pay for the culture, variety, and freedom of cities by having to toil in Brave New World. You pay for the beauties of nature by having to live in a relatively small-minded and oppressive township.

Science fiction—unlike utopia/dystopia—has traditionally taken its images from all four forms; Junk City and the Empire of the Afternoon have joined with New Jerusalem, Brave New World, Arcadia, and the Land of the Flies, and integrated them into single visions of a rich and complex world. (After all, temperaments change, sometimes hour by hour.) The best and most characteristic science fiction novels (Bester's *The Stars My Destination*, Pangborn's *A Mirror for Observers*, Harness's *The Paradox Men*, Sturgeon's *More Than Human* ...) allegorize complex possible relations among all four. More recently, since cyberpunk, two more image clusters have added themselves to the mix: Both Techno-Junk City and the Empire of the Afternoon (the decadent, *beautifully* polluted landscape) have joined the New Jerusalem, Brave New World, Arcadia, and the Land of the Flies. Such complexity—the hallmark of science fictional thinking—leaves the simplistic templates of utopia/dystopia far behind.

If only because of their insufferable and insulting arrogance, I don't think there's a place anymore for the time-hogging utopian monologist. Rather we need to encourage a polyvocalic politics, through dialogue and an appreciation of multiple perspectives, which is what science fiction as a genre does and by science fiction I specifically do not mean speculative fiction, which is, at least today, a monologic imposition by which one or another academic tries to privilege the particular science fiction she (or he) most prefers (cyberpunk, social, feminist, or what-have-you), at the expense of the overall genre's range and richness, a range and richness which makes the individual novels and stories in any or all of those parenthetical subcategories signify in a dialogic and polyvocalic process.

Define silence.

I won't try to define it, because silence—at least in the way it interests me—is one of those objects that resists definition. But I can make some descriptive statements about it so that we might be more likely to recognize it the next time we encounter it in one of its many forms.

Today silence is in a rather beleaguered state.

Silence is the necessary context in which, alone, information can signify—in short, it's the opposite of "noise."

As such, it's seldom, if ever, neutral. It's pervaded by assumptions, by expectations, by discourses—what the poet Osip Mandelstam (born the same year as our Zora Neale Hurston, 1891) called *shum vremeni*, "the hubbub [or buzz; or swoosh] of time." As such, silence is the only state in which the *shum* that pervades it can be studied.

Since Wagner at least, silence has been considered the proper mode in which to appreciate the work of art: Wagner was the first major artist to forbid talking in the theater during his concerts and operas. He began the custom of not applauding between movements of a symphony, sonata, concerto, suite, or string quartet. Also, he was the first person, during performances of his operas at Bayreuth, to turn off the house lights in the theater and have illumination only on the stage.

Silence.

Darkness.

For better or worse, this aligns art more closely with death: It moves us formally toward a merger with the unknown.

Carnival, circus, and social festival are the lively arts that fight the morbidity of that early modernism/late romanticism. They are the arts around which one is expected to make noise, point, cry out, "Oh, look!" then buy cotton candy from a passing vendor, and generally have a life, while artists satirize it in simultaneous distortions, as clown, acrobat, and animal trainer—with silly prizes to the people for random effort and skill.

But, whether one is looking at comic books or construing philosophy, silence is still the state in which the best reading takes place; not to mention the writing—or revising—of a story or a poem.

MARCH 8, 1999, NEW YORK CITY

TO BUFFALO AND BACK WITH RENEE GLADMAN
INTERVIEW BY MAGDALENA ZURAWSKI

DECEMBER/JANUARY 2000   NO. 177

Renee Gladman is a young poet from San Francisco. She has had two chapbooks published, *Arlem* (Idiom Books) and *Not Right Now* (Second Story Books), and her first perfect bound book, *Juice*, is forthcoming from Kelsey Street Press. She was the editor of *Clamour*, a journal for experimental writing for queer women of color, and is currently publishing a series of chapbooks by emerging writers through her press, Leroy. I conducted this interview with Renee during her trip to the East Coast in October. The interview was done in a diner during a road trip to Buffalo, where we read together with Jordan Davis at the Corner Shop gallery, and in the car on our way back to NYC.

MAGDALENA ZURAWSKI: You manage to write a shitload. I'm extremely impressed by that especially because you work full time. I mean, you have two chapbooks and a full-length book coming out. Not to mention a few works in progress and a press. And you're only 28.

RENEE GLADMAN: Well in 1996 I started writing about being out in the city and coming home half the person and having to sort of fill in the parts that you lost during the day. That was the starting point of the writing . . .

RG: Let's just not go to Buffalo. Let's just sit at this table all day . . .

MZ: And talk about how shitty jobs are.

(*Renee laughs*)

RG: I actually have a good job in a lot of ways. But back to the question. So then I would recreate this sort of narrator in the city.

MZ: You'd come home and recreate what you lost?

RG: Yeah. I realized that that was the basis of my approach to writing. The sense of being out during the day, in the city, having a series of experiences and then returning home having lost my sense of self or having had a sense of a cohesive self tested. So I would come home and write these narrative pieces that are sort of re-creations of this narrator in the city. My writing has changed a lot over the last couple of years, but it's still this kind of thing of the person in the city. And the negotiation of self-recognition in the home, in the street, and then back in the home.

MZ: I was reading *Not Right Now* last night and it definitely struck me as the "I" trying to defend itself against the world. It's interesting that it's a first-person narrative, but the "I" isn't really pointed to at all. It's as if the rest of the narrative is taking apart the "I." And the "I" is trying to absorb what's going on around it without being eaten by the surroundings.

RG: The work prior to *Not Right Now* and including *Not Right Now* is a series of short prose blocks that were glimpses at attempts at being a person in the city. And I think that after that, in the *Juice* manuscript, I sort of decided to take that for granted. After I wrote all of them, I realized they were all about loss. I didn't realize that before. It's weird because I didn't approach any of the pieces thinking that I was going to write about specific kinds of loss, but it's like some kind of transition happened between making these attempts at being a person. It's like once you accept the fact of the person then the experience becomes the center of the question.

MZ: The fact of the person?

RG: Existing. The fact of the person existing. If anyone would ask me what my writing is about, I would say it's about the problem of the person.

MZ: And what would be your next statement after that?

RG: The problem of the person period. And then they would say, what the hell do you mean by that?

MZ: That's what I just said.

RG: Right. And then I would say, um, this thing about recognizing oneself and communicating this self that one recognizes to another person. And then having the other person see that and see you next week and be able to see the same person. And then for you to be able to recognize consistencies in the other person and be able to recognize them. But I feel like that is usually not very successful and then the narrator does something that doesn't make sense or sees something that doesn't make sense and then to me that's the problem . . .

MZ: That's the sentence in your writing that seems to come out of left field.

RG: Yeah.

MZ: Those are my favorite parts. I've been meaning to ask you (because you write prose) do you consider yourself an experimental poet or an experimental prose writer?

RG: Does it matter? It's just names. I don't think the distinction between prose and poetry is very important. I think what connects everyone is this interest in language. I just wonder if when people go to write, if they have this idea of difficulties in their minds in the way that I do. I say the difficulties and then people surprise me by saying, well what do you mean by the difficulties? But I would call myself a poet then because that's my definition of poet. One who is negotiating their space in the world in language. What does a writer do? Who wants to be a writer? In any case, I use the writing to deal with philosophical issues. That's what happens for me in writing. I have these philosophical dilemmas. It's getting late. Should we go to Buffalo?

Car ride from Buffalo to NYC:

MZ: I'm doing 78 mph at the request of Renee Gladman, who is hoping to arrive in New York by 7 p.m.

MZ: All right Renee. It's Sunday and we have nothing on tape.

RG: We've got plenty on tape. We need to frame the interview.

MZ: Why don't you ask me why I'm interviewing you?

RG: But I have a question, "Who cares, Maggie, about this interview, why?"

MZ: Well, I can't say that anyone cares about it. Well, I care. But why are we having this interview?

RG: Yeah.

MZ: I wanted to do this interview because I think your work and your publishing activities represent at least one view, one angle of what our generation is interested in or becoming interested in and I thought it was important to put that in a public space. I'm especially interested in how identity politics and experimental writing are less complicated to put together in one space for our generation.

RG: You think they're less complicated?

MZ: I think that people who are interested in experimental writing are less anxious or more interested in dealing with identity issues at the level of language than people of our previous generation. And I think your magazine *Clamour* is one example of our generation trying to negotiate that. What made you start that magazine?

RG: Before I answer that question, I'm not convinced that our generation is necessarily dealing with identity politics any more than previous generations did. I think that our generation is more interested in narrative. The "I" and the possibilities of the "I" have returned. And I think it has a lot to do with where we are in time. I think that in the '60s and the '70s it was time to put the self away and try to deal with more theoretical aspects of writing.

MZ: For what reason?

RG: Well, I'm thinking the Language poetry movement is all white for the most part and I guess there was some feminism, which I guess is kind of identity politics. But I don't think that there were a whole lot of other negotiations that needed to be made. I think that the difference now is that there seem to be more writers in general and there seem to be more writers of color and queer writers who are operating in the experimental communities.

MZ: Maybe that's what I'm trying to say. The strategies that Language poetry brought into writing are being used to discuss or to address issues that maybe so-called identity writing was dealing with previously. It's bringing the conversation to a new place.

RG: The past confuses me. I'm surprised or confused that experiment has been historically relegated to white writers. I think historically writers of color felt this need to give history, to put stories where there were none or where they had been denied. And that was going on. But I feel like we've reached this point where the tone of the stories are set. Now I feel secure enough in the past that it's time to sort of interrogate what it means to try to tell those stories. What it means to try and express one's identity and I feel like all writing is identity based because it's perspective. I think that experimental writing is the perfect situation for people who have existed in this country on the margins. Because there is no narrative, there's not an accepted narrative or a clear narrative of origin. I feel like that allows for some play or some kind of investigation. And I'm surprised there aren't more writers of color, queer writers who are involved in experimentation.

MZ: What do you think prevents that from happening?

RG: I thought a lot about that. I think it's because the avant-garde has its origin among white writers. I don't think that anything that has its origin in white culture is ever going to be suddenly diversified. Historically I can't think of anything that has moved from being a 'white thing' to being multiracial or multicultural. So I think that as long as people are identifying experimental writing as a white activity then there's going to be the sense of, 'if I do that I'm not paying attention to my origins' or 'I'm denying my non-white or non-straight identities.' That's partly why I started *Clamour*. Because I had this fantasy that I was going to start some kind of movement because I knew enough queer women whose texts were challenging in some way that sort of took them from the mainstream and my idea was that I would compile these writers and present it and that other queer writers in particular writers of color would look at that and say 'o this reminds me of something that I'm thinking about' or 'this is an interesting way to approach something that's very difficult.' Maybe it's more rewarding to try to enact the difficulties as opposed to just speaking directly about them. I think experimentation is necessary in marginal communities. I think there are inherent complications in presenting yourself as a cohesive person that is recognizable to other people and the self. I think that being a black dyke for instance makes that very complicated. It makes me feel a bit like an alien, and I think the alien position makes the problem of the person even more problematic. I think that existing in a culture and in a language that doesn't always affirm your existence makes you pay attention to narrative.

MZ: That's a good answer.

RG: Oh, thank you. What I just said though makes me wonder if I actually think it's necessary to complicate narrative further because of my various identities.

MZ: Knowing your work I don't find that it complicates narrative. I think it just forefronts certain issues of narrative, certain issues in writing narrative.

RG: Yeah. I don't actually think that my narrative is very complicated at all. I think the narrator has a pretty easy time speaking. I think what happens is that her perspective on what happens or what she sees or the possibility of experience is questioned.

MZ: I wanted to go back to talking about publications and how you're talking about *Clamour* as being an attempt to form a community. How do you see your new chapbook press, Leroy, in relation to the issues you just spoke about? Or what's your fantasy with Leroy?

RG: My fantasy with Leroy is a more mature one. I'm trying not to have an agenda. But there are two things that I'm aiming for. No way could I be a publisher without publishing the Other. That wouldn't make any sense. Considering my issues, I really have no choice. If I'm going to publish, then the majority of the people that I publish will be people of color or queer people or people who are negotiating some kind of challenge living under the . . . What's a better word for 'dominant paradigm' these days?

MZ: The oppressors? (*Renee laughs*)

RG: The second thing is that I'm kind of a researcher. It's a puzzle for me to figure out how to represent what I see as good writing in the avant-garde among our generation. Or almost our generation. And so it's not that I only want to publish people of color but I want to present a more varied perspective. With Leroy I'm trying out different things. Because I felt really trapped by my *Clamour* agenda. It felt really good to be able to publish a boy. I'm also interested in publishing writers whose work isn't out there as it should be. And so those are my fantasies.

MZ: How large a run do you do of the chapbook?

RG: Right now I'm doing 200. I ask the author for about 75 to 80 names or addresses of people they want to receive their chapbooks. I give the author about twenty and then I have a group of people who as a publisher I send the chapbook to. I sell the rest in order to at least try to make back the cost of printing.

MZ: How do you fund Leroy?

RG: Funding for this program comes from my savings account.

MZ: One more question. Going back to what you were saying about the white origins of experimental writing. I was wondering what got you interested in the avant-garde? What roped you in?

RG: I think my reason for becoming interested in experimental writing, specifically Rosmarie Waldrop, Lyn Hejinian, Mei-mei Berssenbrugge, and Ntozake Shange, who were the first experimental writers that I encountered is that I wanted to be philosophical. I was a philosophy major, studying Western philosophy it was more of a clamp on my mind than it was any kind of opening. So when I started reading experimental poetry it was like I found something. A way to take control of the way I wanted to think about the world. Because I couldn't read Heidegger and feel comfortable that I was included in his philosophical ponderings. And I don't think that I was. My feeling at the time was that I was studying my erasure in some ways. And so finding these other writers who were preoccupied with thought as it occurred in real time. Or in writing. That was perfect for me.

MZ: Your entry into those texts didn't feel problematic? You didn't feel erased?

RG: No. I didn't read them and feel like I could relate to the experience. But I felt an allegiance to the ways of questioning personal experience. I think in general I just decided that literature was a better place for thinking than philosophy.

MZ: The people that you're mentioning aren't really writing in a way that desires the reader to be reflected in the text.

RG: That's true. But the community around the writing didn't reflect me. I embraced a community where there were at the time only two black women.

MZ: Do you feel like that's changing?

RG: Yes. I feel like it's changing a lot. Maybe that's because of the people who are around in San Francisco. Maybe it's just a coincidence. Maybe there just needed to be more time for people to realize that this was happening and that it was a possibility. I think Language poetry was very important and I think approaching language or writing and language from this theoretical perspective is really interesting now for people who have an investment in the person or a narrative. Which is funny because my understanding of Language poetry is that they wanted to remove this sense of the authoritative "I" and focus on the sentence as a unit and deal with meaning in that way.

MZ: One of the projects of Language poetry was to challenge the authority of the poetic "I." It makes sense for that work to be done and now for people to deal with the possibility of a disenfranchised "I" in narrative.

RG: Yeah. I think that our generation has inherited many schools and our situation is requiring different approaches from us. I think that all of these different traditions are impacting our work in a way that couldn't have then. But I'm still trying to figure out why there are more writers of color now.

MZ: Actually, what I wanted to talk about is related to that issue. It has to do with the production of experimental texts. Often experimental texts are on small presses that aren't carried in the average bookstore or taught at most universities. Just from talking to people I've gathered that one's first encounter with experimental poetry or writing is often in connection with one's expensive post-secondary education.

RG: Right. The question is how would these books get to other communities.

MZ: It's even difficult to find these texts in more traditional colleges or universities. Most schools are conservative. Most universities are white.

RG: And so you think that because those communities themselves are not diverse then . . .

MZ: Then the distribution is less diverse. But since there seem to be more experimental writers of color, maybe there are more people of color gaining access to university educations.

RG: Yeah. Maybe that's true. But I'm surprised that a lot of the black publications don't include more experimental writing because I think that people at black colleges must know about Wilson Harris and Nathaniel Mackey and Harryette Mullen. But it hasn't quite crossed over.

MZ: Maybe that's true of experimental writing in general.

RG: Yeah. I think so.

MZ: You see it crossing over slowly. I've been surprised lately, seeing experimental writers pop up in traditional venues. Although maybe there's no such thing as experimental writing. That's a whole other conversation in itself. I mean, what's avant-garde. I think the avant has pretty much left the garde.

RG: Yeah. I know. To me it's less an intentional experimentation than a reproduction of complications. It's fucking hard to be a cohesive person in 1999. It really is. It makes sense to me that it's reflected in writing.

A CONVERSATION WITH LORENZO THOMAS
BY DALE SMITH

APRIL/MAY 2000   NO. 179

Lorenzo Thomas is Associate Professor of English at the University of Houston–Downtown. His collections of poetry include *Chances Are Few*, *The Bathers*, and *There Are Witnesses*. *Extraordinary Measures*, a critical and historical study of twentieth-century African American literature, was published this spring by the University of Alabama Press. Dale Smith spoke with Lorenzo on the lawn of the Texas State Capitol during a break at the 4th Annual Texas Book Festival.

DALE SMITH: You've written political, or culturally critical, poems in the past. Do you still use the poem as a political tool?

LORENZO THOMAS: Right now I have been writing a number of poems about my family, things I remember about them from my childhood. Aunts and uncles, you know, who had interesting history, immigrant history, it seems to me, when they were younger, had all kinds of amazing adventures in this country long before I was born. And, I don't know, I guess it's a function of age and memory that I feel like going back and reconstructing snippets of things I heard when I was a child, and writing poetry based on that. I don't know if that says anything about the particular moment that we're in. I used to write poetry that people considered very political, though I don't consider

all of it to be so. But everything has a social context to it. I don't think that these [recent] poems are different really. They each have a political comment based on what those people, my aunts and uncles, analyzed as the place they were living in, and the actions that they took accordingly. I'm publishing, maybe, what I know of the actions. But if you read further into it, or if you read closely, you can see that they were reacting to a situation, and that reaction was in some sense a political reaction. Though I am not saying the personal is political, because that's nonsense. Politics is the conscious response to the social setting you find yourself in. "Anything I do is political because it's me"—that's not what I mean. These were immigrant black folks who had to make a way in this country, which at that time was not particularly a good country for black folks, immigrants or native born. And so I think part of what I've been doing in these poems is trying to understand what those stories I heard as a child really meant. The prose things I've been working on, the book that comes out in February, *Extraordinary Measures*, goes back and looks at William Stanley Braithwaite, Fenton Johnson, Margaret Walker [and others]. I went back and started with the teens, with [Paul Laurence] Dunbar and Fenton Johnson, because, again, I had the desire, reading this for experience. I know my life, and everything that happened with my life, but I'm fascinated to know what happened before I was here. And I guess I was also looking at people like Braithwaite and Fenton Johnson as being poets who faced the same issues and problems that I faced and did something in response to those. So Fenton Johnson in particular is, I would say, the first African American modernist poet. And I wanted to know how he became that. How did he become the first black poet to be published in *Poetry* magazine? How did he become a featured writer in Alfred Kreymborg's *Others* magazine, and I think maybe for a while, the only black poet who was, you know, part of that circle? What did that mean to him? So I think that's one of the things I wanted to look at because in some ways that spoke to the situation I find myself in often.

DS: What did you find out about Fenton Johnson?

LT: I found out that he was an excellent poet and a horribly naive politician who eventually was driven into silence by the FBI. He turns up under FBI surveillance as a radical dissident because of magazines he was publishing. They weren't poetry magazines. They were magazines intended for the general public, discussing the issues of World War I, segregation and the Jim Crow laws and their relationship to this country that's fighting to make the world safe for Democracy, [even though] black people can't vote or walk the streets safely in the United States. So he's approaching those issues, but unlike W. E. B. Du Bois, at the *Crisis*, who has 100,000 readers who are members of the NAACP, Fenton Johnson has a thousand readers and is publishing his magazine out of his pocket. He can't stand up to the FBI.

DS: So what happened?

LT: What happens is he shuts up, is what happens. So that's, you know, a kind of a horrible story. It's not the only story of that type but it is a story that is fascinating to me. And I wanted to know more about that. And what I found out in looking at that is the situation Fenton Johnson faced during the World War I period is very much like what happened later on to somebody like Melvin B. Tolson during the World War II period. Tolson had a newspaper column called "Caviar and Cabbages," in a weekly black newspaper called *The Washington Tribune*. He has these poems of that era—"Rendezvous with America" is a very beautiful poem—that are very kind of upbeat in a sense—you know, songs in praise of democracy and all that. And I was interested to see how he reconciles all this. He knows better. He's lived in Texas in a segregated town. Lynchings go on around him. There's all kinds of labor strife going on in the very defense factories where black folks work, thinking, well hey, are black workers going to get a decent payday here, or does the same system continue while once again we fight to save the world democracies, fighting for freedom as Franklin Delano Roosevelt was talking about it? So I wanted to understand Tolson. How does he articulate this? Essentially what he does is he writes on two levels. One level is praising the promise of America as a democratic society and the other level is pointing out the shortcomings. And those are both interwoven into the same poems, and they certainly are the subject matter of his newspaper columns. Langston Hughes is much the same. "I, too, sing America" is Langston Hughes doing exactly that. On one level it praises the promise of democracy in American society while very pointedly pointing out our objections to the reality which has never matched the rhetoric, even today. So essentially what I discovered going back to look at that, was that those are analogous to the 1960s when the civil rights movement began to change into something else, the Black Arts Movement and things like that. Those issues were very real in the '60s. And what I learned in going back and doing the research is that's not the first time it happened, and unfortunately, it probably will not be the last time, because the forces that desire inequality in this society do not rest. They are at work doing evil all the time. So it's our business to pay attention. I think that going back and seeing how earlier thinkers, intellectuals or writers tried to deal with the situation can be instructive for us. We can look at where they fell off the tracks, or were pushed, and in most cases it's what's pushed, in this country's history. I think that can be instructive. I'm very dismayed when I talk to people today who think that everything started in 1980 and have no apparent interest in going back and looking at the history here and understanding what happened, what's still happening. Early on in the 1960s I was paying attention not only to African American poets, of course. Ted Greenwald and I made a very conscious, careful study of Ezra Pound. We read everything we had heard about him. At the same time I made a very careful study, for me anyway, of a number of Surrealist writers, and talked to people like Ron Padgett who of course knew a lot more about it. Ron is a translator of French, so he knows what he's talking about.

DS: What did you learn from these writers?

LT: I learned a great deal from them. And then of course, that thing the French Surrealist writers lead you to looking at is the Négritude writers, who are sort of lumped in that same category with the Surrealists. So they are Surrealists with a difference, and the difference is not merely skin color, or melanin. The difference is also a political difference. As disaffected as André Breton or Louis Aragon might have been, the black African and West Indian students—they're both of course [Léopold Sédar] Senghor and Aimé Césaire —have yet another dimension of disaffection or disaffiliation that's expressed in their work as people of African descent living in a colonial situation. Certainly there are, in terms of the poetry, some affinities—technical affinities— between what the French Surrealists are doing and what the Négritude poets are doing. The Négritude poets learned from the French Surrealists, but then they also learned from the Harlem Renaissance [poets] Claude McKay, Langston Hughes, and Countee Cullen. Césaire and Senghor were totally excited when in the 1930s they come across Eugène Jolas and his translations for *Transition* magazine of Claude McKay and Countee Cullen. You can follow also the African poets who were writing in Portuguese, [like] Francisco José Tenreiro from the Cape Verde Islands, who writes very much in Portuguese but in the style of Langston Hughes. And these poets, the Portuguese-African poets, are of course, first excited by their elders, who are people like Senghor, and from there they too discover the poets of the Harlem Renaissance writing in English, and that excites them. And they, you know, create Marcelino dos Santos from Mozambique, and people like that. So all those things were very interesting to me and the people I was working with in the '60s in New York, people like Ted Greenwald and Ron Padgett, at Umbra Askia Muhammad Touré and David Henderson and Black Arts writers Larry Neal, Steve Kent, Amiri Baraka, and all those people. Everybody was very much interested in knowing who came before us regardless of what their nationality or race might have been, though we might have been more interested in some people than others, individually. But that was the thing, we wanted to know who came before us. What, if anything, did we have in common in terms of the situations that we faced and the situations they faced, which is, I think, what study is about. It's not about being ignorant. How can you be a poet and be ignorant?

DS: You mean there were things that happened before 1980?

LT: Yeah, (*laughter*) just a few.

DS: So *Extraordinary Measures* is an investigation of a neglected past?

LT: This is a collection of essays that covers the entire twentieth century in terms of starting with a poet like Fenton Johnson, in the teens, and coming up to commenting on some people that really start publishing in the '80s, people like Harryette Mullen and Paul Beatty, who I think are continuing some tremendous, great work. And again, I'm trying to trace the connections of those poets to the forebears, the people who've set patterns that they are now developing, expanding and moving onward. Because I think we have too much of a love of novelty in the United States.

DS: What do you mean by that?

LT: Well, it's something that Jackson Mac Low warned me about many years ago. He pointed out to me that originality is not by itself a quality to be adored. Just because something is novel or original doesn't make it worthwhile. But in the United States we highly prize novelty and newness. I live in a city where you can't find a building from before 1883. This is also a city that has torn down skyscrapers that were built in the 1960s, mainly because they're too old.

DS: They're also replacing the stadium . . .

LT: Yeah, and replacing the baseball stadium for the same reason. It's too old. (*laughter*) It was built 30 years ago. And given a society like that I think the artist who does not pay attention to what the past was about is really aiding and abetting what I heard a poet this morning talk about (Dani Apodaca), [who said] the United States is a nation of amnesiacs. And that's the truth. Our concern for novelty and so-called originality or newness leads us to become a nation of cultural amnesiacs.

DS: It also seems that our stories, told through the media, come as a series of Columbines, or other high-stress news events, crossing the screen and then fading out with no follow-up or judgment.

LT: There's no shadow cast at all. Everything is a brand new story. It lasts for three weeks and then it's dead. You can't find a newspaper anywhere in the country that will even run a sidebar giving you a history of one of these trouble-spots. It's like, hey, this is a brand new word, remember it for the next few weeks, and it will be replaced by something else. Like what Orwell writes about in *1984*, where there's, you know, a memory hole and the files go down the memory hole and that's the end of it, and we conjure up something new. Sounds like what happened last month except the names are different. I don't think attention to the past destroys the poet's ability to say something new, or to be innovative. I don't believe the cliché either that you have to know the rules before you can break them. I think that's nonsense. But I do think you have to have a cultural memory. No matter what you want to do in terms of innovation you must have some sense of what came before this moment. There was a statement that Haki Madhubuti made several years ago in a moment of severe disappointment at what was happening with the racial situation in the United States. He said, why is it every twenty years black people have to do the same thing all over again. Right? Well part of it is the intransigence of the society and the evildoers within it, who never cease. The other is not paying enough attention to the past, so that you have constantly people who think they're doing something brand new when in fact they're doing something that was tried before. And because it was tried before doesn't mean that you don't do it again. But you should have some awareness of what happened the last time this tactic was employed.

DS: As a teacher of poetry you probably see poems that are technically well written but without a deeper cultural understanding.

LT: Oh, yeah. I think that poetry like anything else can be looked at as the creation of a wonderful, artistic object. If you're interested in lamps or coffee tables—if that's all you require of them—great. Well, lamps, you might want to have lamps that work. Certainly people have and can produce that, and it's just marvelous to look at beautiful objects. They really don't say much or really illumine anything for anybody, and that I think is certainly what you want to avoid. Unfortunately, like anything else, it's very easy to get into that. You write something that someone seems to enjoy and then the tendency is, well, do it one more time. But I think sometimes that's not the question. Why did people enjoy this one? Is it because it simply reinforces what they already believe, is it because it was the word of the moment, or is it because I actually managed to say something that was useful? And saying something that is useful in a poem, because I did it this morning, does not necessarily mean that writing the same thing again tomorrow is going to be useful tomorrow. Again, I think that's why, as a poet, we take responsibility for the whole history of the art form that we're doing. Nobody else is responsible for it except us. We have to know it if no one else does.

DS: Has knowing the history of the poem deepened your own practice?

LT: I don't know. I would hope so. In terms of craft I would say, to go back to our lamps and coffee tables, craft is just a matter of saying, well here I have before me eleven tools and I know how to do three things with each tool. Now there are some people who know how to do four or five things. This is entirely apart from having anything to say. Am I going to contribute anything to the development of my life-affirming discourse, which are issues that are beyond the so-called question of craft? I think the two are connected. I think that a good example is the longest movie that Leni Riefenstahl made, *Olympia*. She also did *Triumph of the Will*. And in *Olympia*, Riefenstahl invented the way that sports is still broadcast on television. Thirty cameras, slow-mo, stop-action, etc., etc. She did all that in the 1930s. She invented the cinematic vocabulary of sports broadcasting. Well, it's marvelous technically. There's no better example of film editing that you can show anyone. But the whole point of it was to glorify the theory of the Aryan racial supremacy of Adolf Hitler and the Third Reich. That's the reality of it. So you have brilliant technique in the service of a rather dangerous social and political idea. Are the two connected? Yes they are. Can they be separated out again? That's the big question, which again brings you back to looking at a writer like Ezra Pound, for example. It's the same thing. There are technical lessons that you can learn from reading him, starting with *A Lume Spento* from 1909 and going forward to *Rock-Drill* in *The Cantos*. You can learn lots of things, technically. And every poet writing in English, I think, has. Every poet who started writing before 1980 anyway. (*laughter*) Does that mean that you also imbibe Pound's social and political ideas? Well, yeah, you have. Have you bought them? Maybe not, but you have to be certainly consciously aware of that possibility. How much of the idea does the technique reflect and vice versa? I don't know the answer to that. I wouldn't even speculate. Each case is different. There is an answer there but I just don't know enough yet to frame one.

DS: Who were your teachers?

LT: The other poets that I knew in the formal workshops or the collectives—or just who I was hanging out with. I think that Ted Berrigan had a workshop that traveled with him, but it wasn't really a workshop. It was just hanging out with Ted. It was a workshop if you want to think about it a certain way because everybody learned something from Ted. You couldn't stand five minutes in Berrigan's company without learning something valuable. In school I was much more concerned about the literature teachers I had who taught me well. I read everything and I didn't do so well in courses that were not my major. But those were people who thought that you had to know early English writing and you had to know Victorian writing and you had to know Modernism. You had to know everything, was their attitude. Which was fine with me. I just loved to read everything that they put in front of me. And I guess, in terms of what I was saying earlier about knowing the history of the art, that's what I got from my literature teachers. But if you're talking about visual arts, painting or sculpture, or you're talking about music, no one in her right mind would suggest that a musician should not know the whole history of music. It doesn't matter at all what they want to do. Right?

DS: You'd want to listen to it all anyway. You'd want to buy every record you could get your hands on.

LT: Yeah. So you can sample it. (*laughter*) I met a few poets who don't read anything except their own stuff. I don't know how they survive as people, but I think that, again, one of the concepts of the Black Arts Movement was to read and explore. And one of the things that happened in the Black Arts Movement is that everyone realized that we had gone to school and we had these marvelous literature professors who had made us read everything, but they hadn't made us read any black people. So we had to go back and do that. And that was the main thrust of the Black Arts Movement. We said, hey, we've got to go back and rediscover and reclaim all this material. It's there, it's in the library. It's on the street too. And that was what we were about, going back and finding it and reclaiming it, because again, when you start talking about a culture, the artist is the custodian of the culture. No one else is. Baraka says if you lose your culture you're in bad shape. This doesn't mean venerating it as an idol, or spending millions of dollars at auctions to buy rubbish, which is another expression of things going haywire. That's not what I'm talking about. I'm talking about what Robert Creeley at one point referred to when he was asked about tradition. He said, well, tradition is what is still useful. You see? And we're constantly making choices. But there are people who think that tradition is some kind of catechism or regimen that is imposed by some panel of experts somewhere. That's not the deal.

DS: It seems too that, since tradition is either ignored or, at the other extreme, commodified and marketed as an experience of high culture, people who work in the arts find themselves in a difficult position, because the public view of the artist doesn't match his or her living practice.

LT: I think that in some ways artists invent their audiences, but I don't think it's something that can be clearly seen, or that pays off in the short-term. Certainly, the poets who started writing in the late 1940s and early 1950s have had a fantastic impact on the mind of America, like Allen Ginsberg, or even an older poet like Melvin Tolson, who is only now beginning to be appreciated for what he does. The changes are real and can be seen if you stop now and look back. Whether anybody could actually see those in the 1970s or 1965, I don't know. You can go to the library and look at *Time* magazine and see. It's an interesting research project. I don't know if anybody could actually pinpoint what had happened, or when it happened, but from this vantage point we know it happened. The world came to be more like they wanted it to be than it was then. That's what I mean when I say the artist invents his or her own audience. The world comes to be more like what we want it to be than it is when we started.

DS: It also became more economically and socially restrictive.

LT: Yeah, well, artists are not the only minds at work. (*laughter*)

DS: It would be interesting to see what those minds were up to in the late 1940s.

LT: Well, among other things, they were inventing cybernetics, the computer— ENIAC and UNIVAC. That's what some other minds were doing in the late '40s. And they were doing it based on what the defense needs of World War II had been, which then became the rationale for postwar civilian society, with voices like those of the poets and painters saying, wait a minute, or howling, in protest.

NOVEMBER 1999
AUSTIN, TEXAS

AN INTERVIEW WITH FRED MOTEN
BY ANGE MLINKO

OCTOBER/NOVEMBER 2000   NO. 181

Fred Moten's chapbook *Arkansas* was published by Pressed Wafer last spring. He is Assistant Professor of Performance Studies at New York University's Tisch School of Performing Arts. The following transcript is excerpted from an interview conducted on July 8, 2000, in New York City.

ANGE MLINKO: So you grew up in Arkansas?

FRED MOTEN: I grew up in Las Vegas. But the community that I was from in Las Vegas, many of the people were sort of first-generation immigrants I guess you could say, from Arkansas. So it was almost as if Arkansas had been transplanted to Vegas.

AM: How did that happen?

FM: Well, Vegas had, because of the casinos and because of the Nevada test site where they used to test nuclear bombs, opportunities for unskilled labor who were pretty low paid. And so, at the very tail end of the so-called Great Migration when people started moving west instead of just up north to Chicago, Vegas was one of the places where people moved, along with LA and the Bay Area. And also, there is a big Air Force base in Vegas, and a lot of black folks who were in the army or in the air force stopped through there

and saw things there. So there was a pretty old and established black community in Las Vegas that my mom was a part of. And a lot of people even from the same little town in Arkansas that she was from. We used to go home—well, when I use the word "home," I mean Arkansas even though I was brought up in Vegas—we would go home for Christmas a lot and I spent summers in Arkansas.

AM: You're always coming back to your past, particularly your mother, in your work.

FM: Yeah, she was the biggest influence on my life, because my father and her were divorced when I was about eleven—and even when he was around she was the major influence for me. In every way. Not only in terms of the sounds that I'm trying to get at, but politics and the music I loved I was introduced to by her. So she's in everything I write, in my scholarly stuff too. I'm sure that that will always be the case.

AM: Well, one of the things that I found in my research was this introduction you wrote to an issue of *Women & Performance: A Journal of Feminist Theory*. In it, you mention anima, and it hit me that there's a strong anima in your poems, via the women you invoke and implore. In fact, being exiled from the anima seems to be an abiding fear.

FM: I think that that's a huge thing. The first place where I really began to think a lot about anima was from reading [Amiri] Baraka, and reading specifically this essay that he wrote called "The Burton Green Affair," and it's about Burton Green, this jazz pianist . . . he played sort of what got called free jazz at the time, in the mid-'60s. And at the very moment when Baraka was sort of becoming more and more militantly black nationalist, he was faced with trying to determine and trying to understand the political significance of free jazz. He, I think, really felt that it was the soundtrack for a sort of revolution that they thought—everyone thought—was just around the corner. So the fact that a white musician, a white pianist, was playing this music with black musicians was a real problem for Baraka. There's a complicated way he had to try and separate out the pianist from these two saxophone players, Marion Brown and Pharoah Sanders. And the term anima, spirit, breath—in the essay, Baraka comes up with that as a way of trying to distinguish between the sound that the horns were producing and the kind of more percussive and punctuated sound that the piano was playing. Ultimately in the essay everything gets confused and convoluted, and the sort of racial determinations he's trying to make don't really work. Part of the confusion that shows up in that essay has to do with the fact that anima does get coded, or is coded in certain ways as feminine. And the ideology of black nationalism at that moment was structured in such a way as to try and distance the feminine. Baraka had a certain moment when the feminine, and homosexuality, were associated with a kind of Europeanness that he was trying to break away from. And I always felt this was the problem. Partly because the most significant influences in my life were women: my mom, my grandma, the music that they played and listened to. You know, it seems like every morning I was listening to Ella Fitzgerald, Sarah Vaughan, and that voice was the voice that was in some ways always in my head and the one that I was always trying to capture and figure out how to incorporate into what I was doing. And what I began to realize as I was going through school is that this is a phenomenon not just unique to me. That, especially I think in Afro-American culture, there's this tremendous tension between the black male artist trying to establish a kind of manhood, trying to establish a kind of masculinity which is supposed to correspond to a certain kind of political force. But, at the same time, I was trying to figure out some way to assimilate this feminine sound, this feminine spirit, which has this tremendous aesthetic weight, but which also has this tremendous amount of political weight too. And so all of my work, poetry and the other theoretical stuff too, has been trying to think about this. And of course, you know, once I met Laura, my wife—that only complicates it and enriches it.

AM: I was recently saying to someone, that discourse tries to be masculine and totalizing, and poetry is feminized with its negative capability and not-knowing, and discourse is always trying to minimize or even replace poetry . . .

FM: Well, it's repressed, you know, is what I think. I mean, there's an animus of critical theory, which is desperately trying to repress the feminine. But it can't really do it, and the stuff that I most admire is the stuff in which the failure to repress the feminine is most pronounced. Well, let me put it a little differently. There are some folks in whose work I see this profound failure to repress the feminine, and so in a way, for me, that becomes an avenue into their work—but more or less by accident, not necessarily a function of their intentions or desires. And then there are folks who I think are making a real attempt to actively embrace it, and they're even better, you know? Take Baraka's prose works from the mid- to late-'60s. He's someone who I think of as as much a political theorist as I do a poet. (And I want to make it clear that he's, as far as I'm concerned, great. And I probably disagree with some of those essays, but there's no way I could be doing any of the stuff I do without him having been there first.) But he is someone who's operating at the level of this insistent kind of repression of the feminine, and it comes back to haunt his work in ways that are really intense, and the most beautiful moments in his work are precisely when they come back to haunt the work. In that essay, for instance, that I was talking about before, "The Burton Green Affair," on the one hand he wants to talk about the horn players as the embodiment of a kind of black masculinity, but the way that those horns must have sounded that night could never be separated from a sound that has been traditionally associated with the feminine, you know, the horn screaming, and just the sound of a tenor horn anyway. That sound is what animates his essay. But this happens all the time, it seems to me, in his work. So that's a place where maybe he's trying to put something away, put something back, put it down, but it keeps coming back, and it's good that it does, and it produces amazing stuff. And then, somebody like Derrida let's say, is somebody who I think is much more intensely aware of what it means to try and actively embrace this femininity, thematically and in terms of the way he writes, and that produces great insight and beauty, as far as I'm concerned, too. But they're two different kinds, two different effects. There is a whole bunch of folks one could think of along those lines, and—though I might have indicated before that maybe the active embrace of the feminine produces better stuff, I probably would take that back, I don't know.

AM: So you think a little repression is good for art? (*laughing*)

FM: Well, I mean, I think it depends on what you're looking at and I just wouldn't want to make the blanket statement that this one is always going to produce better art. It's not an easy thing. I'm sure that there's a tremendous amount of repression, you know, going on in my stuff too. It's not some simple thing where I'm totally aware.

AM: How could you be, if it's poetry?

FM: Exactly!

AM: I know you write about Afro-American performance studies. But the one time I saw you read, you weren't performative. You have a beautiful reading voice, but you don't declaim your work or engage in any—I don't even know what the word is—improvisational techniques?

FM: Well, I mean, part of it is, I'm just really new to reading, and maybe as I get more, you know, get older and more confident with it I'll become a little more animated, I guess you could say. But also at the same time, I really want to emphasize what I read, the music that I'm trying to infuse in the poetry—if I can do what I'm trying to do—the music is in there without me having to amplify it in some exaggerated way. And, all our music and all of those speech patterns and so forth, I want that stuff to be in there and on the page. Bill Corbett reading, for me, is a model to which I sort of aspire. I mean, I think he's a lot more animated than me, you know, he takes, sucks in all this air and lets it out in all these amazing ways—I remember hearing him read this poem called "Anthem," which is like, to me, his greatest hit. I love that poem. And that ability to both let ride with the music on the page and also breathe something new into it, to sort of bring those two things together is an ambition. What I'm interested in critically in Afro-American literature and performance is discerning how this tremendous amount of political content is all bound up with emotional content, sexual content, and how that plays itself out in moments in which you can't pinpoint a discernable meaning. So part of what's at stake is to be able to make a distinction between content and meaning. Like when James Brown screams, that has content, but you can't pinpoint and say, well the scream means this, and it would be silly to do that. But then at the same time you wouldn't want to discount that content too, so to try and have that content is really important, and this is part of that tradition. And also, not just content, but sentiment, you know? And I've been trying to write these critical books, and one of them, the title of it—I have the title but half the book isn't written yet—is *The Sentimental Avant-Garde*. And that's basically the general sense in which I think about, especially the Afro-American part in the twentieth century. A huge thing for me was going to the MoMA a few years ago, and they had this Mondrian exhibit. You sort of go through the whole thing and then in the end you come to this glorious conclusion, which is these two late paintings, "Broadway Boogie-Woogie" and "Victory Boogie-Woogie," which is the stuff he made after he came to New York in the early '40s. And it's these amazing paintings, and they're so moving, and they're sentimental. And I realized they have this tremendous amount of energy, they have an energy which you associate with the US and with New York, and I'm sure that it was part of something that reanimated Mondrian at this late stage in his career. But what I think they also are animated by is this sentiment—this love. That stuff is embedded in those paintings, and I think that's an American thing, and it's African, and to the extent that it's an American thing it's also necessarily and deeply an Afro-American thing. Look at American movies. As crappy as American movies can be, the great American movies are sentimental movies, among other things. Like, you know, Ford or Scorsese. To me, John Ford is amazing. And I agree with Stanley Crouch on that one point only! But I love John Ford, and part of what you love it for is his ability to harness, in this totally aesthetically interesting and radical way, sentiment.

AM: Well the blues do that. It was a real revelation when I realized, after all these years of dumbed down Top 40 songs shoved down people's throats, with banal lyrics that spell everything out, if you go to old blues lyrics, especially Delta blues, they contain very ambiguous, haunting, beautiful lyrics. They're poetic in that way of being elusive and mysterious, and these were folk songs, they were popular songs. What happened?

FM: No, it's this amazing reservoir of stuff that, in the full beauty of it, in the full energy of what it can still give us, people are only beginning to tap into. Because you're right. There is this tremendous confluence of sentiment and emotion and content and sound and syntax which is as radical and broken and fragmented and abstract as any of us who love certain kinds of things could hope to get, you know. And I think rap, a lot of good rap stuff is like that too. Some of these guys are like, 18-, 19-year-olds, and they're amazing. They're doing stuff that is just amazing with language. And so much of what's written about it is kind of disappointing, just because I think people haven't given the attention to it that it deserves as art, and paid attention to it as language. But the blues, all that stuff is just waiting for people to look at it.

AM: When I heard Lauryn Hill's album, I was dazzled. There were some passages there that left most poets I know in the dust.

FM: No, it's true. There's a lot of good stuff like that. I mean, it's just so accelerated, 'cause I remember when I started college twenty years ago, it was like Grandmaster Flash, but the juicy stuff now, it's like three hundred years of development happened in twenty years when you listen to, you know, Lauryn Hill or the RZA, you seen that album?

AM: Just how they rhyme . . .

FM: That's the other thing! That they brought rhyme back into the mix in a way that has got to be taken into account. So, there's just a lot of good stuff going on right now. There's enough good stuff so that it's possible just to avoid, not totally, but there's enough good stuff so that you don't have to immerse yourself in bad stuff unless you want to. (*laughs*)

LISA JARNOT INTERVIEWS STAN BRAKHAGE

OCTOBER/NOVEMBER 2000   NO. 181

Avant-garde filmmaker Stan Brakhage met poet Robert Duncan and painter Jess Collins in San Francisco in 1952. In 1953 Duncan and Jess invited the twenty-year-old Brakhage to live in a basement apartment at their house on Baker Street in San Francisco. While there, Brakhage met many of the artists who would influence his work, and he came to recognize Duncan and Jess as mentor figures. Brakhage completed some of his first film projects while living with the couple, including *The Way to Shadow Garden* [1954] and a collaboration with Jess Collins called *In Between* [1955]. The following is an excerpt from an interview I conducted with Brakhage in Boulder, Colorado on December 24, 1998. Brakhage and I had spoken on previous occasions regarding my research toward a biography of Robert Duncan.

LISA JARNOT: You met Helen Adam in San Francisco and I've been trying to find out when Robert Duncan first met her . . . I assume it was with the workshop that he taught during the fall of 1954.

STAN BRAKHAGE: Well I can describe, to my knowledge, the very night that he met her. It was when Ruth Witt-Diamont gave Robert a workshop placement at San Francisco State . . . and one night, very near the beginning of that workshop, if not in fact the very first meeting, Helen Adam came with her sister. And I'll never forget it because everyone took turns reading and when it came to Helen Adam a storm came up and was flashing lightning

outside the window, and it was very spectacular, and she cut loose with one of her witchy poems and she just completely charmed Robert with this, and everyone else—we were flabbergasted with this lightning and poetic display of Helen Adam's. She then came regularly and that workshop went on all across that period. But it was that night—that was the first—she suddenly blew in right before the storm and took us all literally by storm, absolutely. I still have little chills go up and down my back remembering that night. She really made an incantatory scene. I forget which of the poems she read, but it's one of the first two or three poems in her book, one of those long ballads. And for Robert it was also enchanting because he had a sense of ballad—that was something that was missing, someone who could do the ballad. Now Jimmy [James Broughton] of course could do ballads, but really Jimmy's world was something closer to [Christian] Morgenstern, or Lewis Carroll, or someone like that . . . He was involved in his own ways in the same things that Duncan was, and in another way that Helen Adam was, you know—magic. They all kind of flutter in some sense around Robert Graves' world. And that's why Robert went to Mallorca[1], because of Robert Graves with his sense of these magics that were invented, but all the more real for that—leaning on Jung who says the imagination is most real. So that was Duncan—I mean Duncan was also a good Freudian, but he respected that sense of Jung, and he more lived that sense of Jungian psychology— that the imagination was more real than any other form of reality. But then Duncan also had that way, that he would teach you, as he did me, that "real" meant "royal," and reality. It meant the king's way, and so the imagination from a language sense became more real—not more real—but became the mode of being that you could most fully inhabit. I know for example, let me tell you one thing—when I got married . . . I went to Princeton, New Jersey, and I went then on assignment over to Switzerland to attend the Atomic Peace Conference as a professional cinematographer.

LJ: What year was that?

SB: That would be 1959. When I next saw Robert Duncan—which is probably when Jane [Brakhage][2] and I brought him to Boulder to give a program which would be like 1960, or 1961—I told him about this experience of going to the Atomic Peace Conference and I said a man named Peron delivered the opening address and I was in charge of a bank of cameras up in the balcony that were focused on him. And really . . . you don't want to waste a lot of film, but, you know, you turn the cameras on and you get the opening and then you turn them off; you don't record the whole speech. Because it's not like video you know, you're recording film. And suddenly this Peron, who was from France, and was a very highly considered physicist, begins ranting and raving on the stage, "we have the task to warn people against fairy tales, against myth, against so on . . ." and he went on this diatribe against how people's minds are being warped and twisted so that they cannot comprehend the science of the age in which they're living by all these past hocus-pocuses and religion—he included religions. And I thought he'd gone mad. And I went to my cameramen and I said, "Turn on your cameras, turn on your cameras!" I thought that at any minute someone's going to come out on the stage and grab him and remove him. Instead, he finishes his speech and you know, half the audience stands and gives him a standing ovation, throws their papers and their hats into the air and says, "Yeeh!" So I told Robert about this and he was very interested in getting the speech itself . . . You see, what he wanted to do was then turn that back on them. He felt under assault. The moon landing was not a happy event for Robert or Jess. It was like desecrating the moon. And the destruction to the moon as an imagination was so horrible, in relationship to what was gained by landing there. So this very much speaks to his partisanship for the world of the imagination. And Robert was very infatuated with Helen Adam and he saw her as an authentic time traveler—that this was true time travel. This was not someone rewriting the Scottish ballads—this was someone who was imbued with that spirit who had managed to survive into the twentieth century.

LJ: It seems like he was also fascinated with that whole tradition, just being a Duncan. I mean I don't think he knew that much about his real family, but he did consider himself Celtic.

SB: You know until this moment I've never thought of that. He was Scotch, of course! Duncan. How could I, having read *Macbeth*, not think of that! It's amazing I never thought of that. Yeah. And Robert always took things so personally. I mean don't please think for a minute I'm criticizing him for this, but he was very clearly the center of his universe. So if Helen came to him it was for him, touching these roots. You can see this most clearly with H. D. and *The H. D. Book*[3]. He thought of these things as given to him for the furtherance of his, and their, poetic possibilities. Not just him, but them—it was like the magic junction.

LJ: But then that's a different kind of magic than another kind of magic, like Kenneth Anger's[4] magic.

SB: Yeah, he was afraid of black magic, power magic . . . And Jess didn't like people leaving belongings or leaving talismans or leaving anything or sending little balls of hair in the mail, or whatever, you know? (*laughs*) That kind of thing didn't go over at all well. That has a lot to do with their difficult relationship with Jack Spicer. Because Spicer was always being too personal, like they say. He'd leave a trail of cigarette butts or I don't know what, you know, and Jess was always cleaning up after such things. But you know, Jess was very kindly always and he'd serve people tea, but he'd sit back in the corner very quietly . . . The *In Between* movie is half concocted with things that he said, "well let's try this" or "why don't you do that?" It has his input in it. So you get a real sense of that strange spirit of those times . . . Robert was going over to Berkeley and Jess was being a medical assistant in the mornings and he'd come home at noon and make peanut butter bisque soup and he'd read to me for a couple hours and then he'd paint until Robert came home, usually at five or six, and that was a routine day after day, five days a week. And then quite often there'd be some people come over in the evenings; San Francisco was lovely in this way at that time, that people felt free to drop in on each other. And you know so Spicer, or [Robin] Blaser when he was in town, would just drop in. Like I say, Kenneth Anger would just drop in. And Jess would get involved with Kenneth, almost like to wrap him up in a more familial sense, in the family of Robert and Jess. So that in fact there was a film that Kenneth made with my photographing a collage of Jess's that had cutouts of hundreds of male nudes that were from everything from nineteenth-century engraving—they were pin ups. And he cut out all of these and they were wrapped into something—the only thing like it I've seen is Rodin's *The Gates of Hell* in Philadelphia which is such a great experience to be able to go and see. Well this had something of that feeling and Kenneth wanted to photograph it, so he photographed it through lit fires in an ashtray and I photographed through the heat waves in those little matches, and we made a whole hundred feet which someone has; I think Anthology Film Archives has it actually. A collaboration by Kenneth Anger and me. It doesn't have a title because it never got finished. But by that point Kenneth was being involved in Jess's aesthetic. And I think in some curious way Jess gave Kenneth more inspiration than Robert did. The vision of Jess was very intriguing to him because of course it corresponded to Kenneth Anger's grandmother, after whom he has invented his name. Most people think he means "anger," well he also lets that stand, but "D'Anger" is what he really means. That was his grandmother's shop where she made these costumes for Max Reinhardt's *A Midsummer Night's Dream* that Kenneth appeared in. Kenneth's the changeling in it, the little boy. So anyway, Jess with his nineteenth-century infatuations touched, I think, a chord in Kenneth related to his grandmother.

LJ: Right. They had a long correspondence during the 1950s about fairies.

SB: Oh what a wonderful thing. That's lovely. Well, I can well believe it, and Jess believed in fairies, and I'm sure he still does. For that matter so do I, which is regarded as a complete madness in the world I live in. That says a lot. But then you see, for me, before I met Robert and Jess I had some sense of the muse, of god, of angels, of guardian angels, of fairies, of elves, of demons, of daemons. All of these things were running in my bloodstream, but finally Robert and Jess gave me a way to be able to acknowledge that, and to live according to the tenets that these apparitions, or whatever you want to call them, brought to me. They are, to me, as real as you are sitting there. Though I am perfectly content to talk about them as if they were projections of my unconscious or my imagination. It doesn't matter because in either case their effect on my work or my life remains just the same. So I don't need a supportive religion, but I did at some point need some sense that there were other humans that recognized these oddities for which you were ordinarily in the twentieth century regarded as insane. And that really is probably the basic relationship that I had with them—more with Jess in that respect than Robert. I don't know, I really think but for them I might not have made it. I was very fragile when I went to San Francisco. I feel I've been so lucky. I inherited something of their charmed circle, and them really as magic parents for me . . . That's in a way what it was like for me—they were like magic parents. They gave me things that I should have had when I was young but I didn't, and that has been very sustaining. I don't know how to put it. The things you can name are the Oz books and [George] MacDonald⁵ and so on, but it was deeper than that—a sense that this kind of magic could and did live in the world, and could survive.

LJ: What about your work? When Robert saw your work what was he saying about it?

SB: Well, first of all, what Robert saw was *Interim* [1952], which was kind of modeled after Italian neorealism. And then he saw a thing called *Unglassed Windows Cast a Terrible Reflection* [1953], which was a melodrama that I actually used to secure a job to study with Hitchcock. So it was a Hitchcockian melodrama. But both of them shared this quality—they had one solid foot in Symbolism. And I was probably one of the few younger people that Robert met who had read Mallarmé. Mallarmé was not much read in those days if you can believe that. And you know, I had a lot invested in symbolism at this point in my life, and that was very enchanting, I think to both of them, because Jess is very . . . I wouldn't call him a symbolist, but he's always reverberating; his work is reverberating. Like if you hit the side walls three times and hit a ball which hits another ball which hits the symbol and it goes into the pocket. It's that removed—it's very delicate and hovering in there— some invisible stitch—at least I feel.

LJ: Well yeah, I think that's true in Duncan's poems too.

SB: Yes. I'd say so.

LJ: Something happens on the eighth layer down. He's built it into the piece somewhere. But I guess I'm curious about Robert's understanding of your work. It seems like he would be interested in it because there's so much organic field theory in the work. It seems like he would catch onto that.

SB: I don't think he was ever in a way of seeing enough of it for instance, or of that later work where you're seeing that. I don't think he ever saw much beyond my very earliest psychodramas and things of that sort. And he always had the idea that I should really be in Hollywood. And then I heard the nicest thing I ever heard, is that someone told me that when asked about me, that he said, "of those who make that kind of film he's the greatest." I thought jeez I'm not ever going to get better than that. I mean one of my rages finally got to be that for all the poets I knew, the minute you'd mention film they start to talk about John Garfield and *The Maltese Falcon* and things of that sort, and finally Bergman sort of settled that, so that they could settle on Bergman. But I was struggling to rise up out of these Hollywoodisms into an art form . . .

LJ: Yeah, I also think that Robert could locate stories anywhere—even if it was a television sitcom, that he could locate his sense of myth and story within it. He was very democratic in that way.

SB: Yes he was. He's a beautiful American poet. You can say "American" poet with him more than you can with many. Many are yearning to go over to the Orient, but not Robert. He stops right on these shores actually; he also has that sense of Olson of not to take all that bric-a-brac from Europe either. He's remained local in that sense, which to me means most universal. You can't be universal unless you're literally well rooted in where you are. So he was never affected much by things elsewhere. The most that he took from Europe was Gertrude Stein.

LJ: And she grew up in Oakland. (*laughs*)

SB: Yes! And anyway he called them "Stein-like" imitations. I think he's been one of the clearest in that respect. He and Olson. But I must say for Robert I think and for artists in general, and certainly maybe more for poets than anybody, there's such a neglect and it finally gets them—it gets them in some way and makes them cranky in a way that no jury would convict them if it understood fully how they've been neglected. But there have been great times for poetry where a poet was a revered thing to be. But certainly during the time that I'm talking about, when I went to visit them, you would never write as occupation "poet" or "artist" of any kind on the motel entrance form because you'd be asking to be killed in certain places. Can you imagine checking into a hotel anywhere in the west and putting under your occupation that you're a poet? In Central City, Oscar Wilde was run out of town in fear of being tarred and feathered. Really there's a tremendous neglect— you know you have this power, you have one of the greatest powers in the world—you have the power of language. You can make leaps of the imagination, and make music as you talk, and no one's listening. Then it's even more maddening—you get a crowd of people that pretend they're listening. That's what we had in the '60s. Hundreds of people would gather like in Macky Auditorium here [at the University of Colorado Boulder] to listen to whoever you brought. And they're all like meerkats or something, sitting there like that. But you know that wasn't really listening, because where have they all gone? They all disappeared the minute it wasn't fashionable . . . the problem is that with film, people will look at even a nutsy film, but how many people will sit for a poem? I mean, Kenneth Rexroth, I remember him telling me, he said, "Music's doing well because you can put it on in the background, you can do the dishes, you can talk to your mother-in-law on the phone, but a poem you have to sit down and read." Therefore it never rises to a popular mass movement, which is one of its blessings. I mean just think of all the crap we've had to put up with in the film movement of all these people gliding in thinking that the poetic film was a stepping stone to Hollywood. Well you don't get too many people doing that with poetry. (*laughs*) What would it be a stepping stone to?

Notes

1. In 1955, Duncan and Jess moved to the island of Mallorca, off the coast of Spain. They lived there for almost a year.

2. Now Jane Wodening.

3. Robert Duncan's *The H. D. Book* is a two-volume study of poet Hilda Doolittle's work and the Modernist movement as a whole. Published in part in small magazines throughout the 1960s and 1970s, the book as a whole was published by University of California Press in 2012.

4. Filmmaker and magician Kenneth Anger was born in 1930. His first groundbreaking film, *Fireworks*, was completed in 1947.

5. Frank Baum's Oz books served as a creative inspiration to both Robert Duncan and Jess Collins. Their childhood collections of Oz books held an esteemed place in their San Francisco household. Scottish novelist George MacDonald's *Lilith* and *The Princess and Curdie* were favorites in the San Francisco poetry scene during the 1950s.

INTERVIEW WITH CHARLES NORTH
BY ANGE MLINKO

FEBRUARY/MARCH 2001   NO. 183

This winter, Adventures in Poetry will publish Charles North's *The Nearness of the Way You Look Tonight*. It brings full circle a career that began with the 1974 chapbook *Elizabethan & Nova Scotian Music*, from the same publisher. These will probably remain my favorite works from one of my favorite poets, who also happens to be one of the quieter ones. (This is his first interview for a literary audience.) He lives on the Upper West Side, not far from where I recently moved: now that I live there, I don't so much see the neighborhood in his poems as see his poems in the neighborhood, which has become imbued with the light and grace I get from reading his "People and Buildings" or "Building Sixteens." The challenge of writing about the sensual qualities of New York City, which seems so tired, by North's pen becomes transcendent again. And that's only one of the things his poetry accomplishes. He is witty when wit seems all but lost, gorgeous when gorgeousness is supposed to have crawled off to wherever Frank O'Hara's odes came from. *The Nearness of the Way You Look Tonight* is about as flawless a book of poetry as I have come across. This interview took place at 119th & Amsterdam, New York City, on November 12, 2000.

ANGE MLINKO: Can you tell me about your relationship with James Schuyler?
CHARLES NORTH: It wasn't as much of a relationship as I would have liked! Mostly a poetry relationship, though I did see him once in a while and for a couple of years he came regularly to dinner. And of course, we wound up

doing the two *Broadway* anthologies together. When I first began writing poems, it was pretty much worship from afar. After I met Tony Towle, who knew him, I dedicated a poem to him which Tony, to my embarrassment—I was pretty shy—forwarded to him. Months later I got a poem out of the blue ["Light from Canada"] with a note saying, "Let me return the compliment." You can imagine how I felt. I finally met him at a party and was almost literally dumbfounded. I felt that was it, I had blown it! Later, I realized that he had said almost nothing either. Part of my regret is not having known him when he was healthier. I had heard how lively and witty he was. When I knew him, at least at the beginning, he was anything but animated. I used to visit him, at the Allerton Hotel on 8th Ave., one of the most depressing places I've ever set foot in, then at the depressing Lincoln Square Home for Adults uptown—at 50 or so, he was the youngest person there—and finally when he moved into the Chelsea. I envy those friends who lived far enough away to get his fabulous letters. *Broadway* and *Broadway 2* were extensions, sort of, of a one-shot magazine he had done in the late '60s called *49 South* —South Main St., Southampton, where he lived with Fairfield and Anne Porter. We chose the poets and artists together, and boy, could he be tough! I remember him absolutely putting his foot down about certain potential contributors. I also remember him chuckling over the invitation we composed and the pressure it would put on certain people: "Please send us your best poem or drawing."

AM: So he wasn't really a mentor?

CN: Only by example. I never sent him poems to critique. Actually, I've rarely showed unfinished poems to anyone, with one or two exceptions.

AM: In *No Other Way* you argue forcefully against critical frameworks—systems—that approach poetry prescriptively, proscriptively, or on anything other than "its own terms." Interestingly, a hundred years ago William Carlos Williams argued the purpose of art "lies in the resolution of difficulties to its own comprehensive organization of materials." And I'm reminded that Fairfield Porter's criticism is called *Art in Its Own Terms* (Rackstraw

Downes, for one, talks about how Porter's stance contra Clement Greenberg was very helpful to him as an artist just starting out in the stifling critical climate of the '60s). In his inimitable way, Frank O'Hara was doing the same thing with "Personism: A Manifesto" and John Ashbery has always stood up for the autonomy of the artist, which the publication of *Other Traditions* makes abundantly clear. I see a web of associations here: you have written on Porter, Downes, and Ashbery, and *No Other Way* opens with a quote from O'Hara's "The Critic." Since poetics is more fashionable than ever in my "generation" (actually, I hate that concept), I fear that poetry is more in thrall to critical frameworks than ever.

CN: On the one hand, what you're describing is the ongoing battle between the artist and the critic who thinks he/she knows better than the artist, which often results in reactions like de Kooning's and Porter's: if the critic says I can't do this, then that's exactly what I'm going to do! In fact, that sort of rebellion is one of the chief impetuses for new art, isn't it? I know it's been one of mine. In my darker moments, I try to console myself with the thought that whatever the latest prescriptions and proscriptions, they're likely to become the impetus for new rebellions! The other side, I think, is what I railed against in *No Other Way*. Well, I tried hard not to rail, but yes, I do feel strongly about the dangers of not taking art, poetry, etc., on its own terms, however that's to be done. My own feeling, as I think you know, is that *all* good poets elude their critics at least partly. But with some, including some of my favorites like Schuyler, Schubert, O'Hara, the work is like Gore-Tex: the criticism doesn't penetrate. It's hard to imagine the three I just mentioned ever getting their public due.

AM: Scary!

CN: Well, only to a very few, relatively speaking.

AM: You were trained in philosophy, and despite the fact that a lot of poets name-drop philosophers, your work contains constructions (e.g., "while deracination is fast qualifying as essence rather than attribute") and ways of *thinking* which indicate more than a passing acquaintance with the history and methods of traditional philosophy. Is this a temperamental thing? Is it, as I suspect, a deeper rigor? And how does *rigor* figure into poetry? Where is the intersection of poetry and philosophy—beyond the conventional surface interest to each other's rhetorics?

CN: Whew. Actually my "training" in philosophy didn't go very far, though philosophy was my first love. I majored in it as well as English in college and did enroll in a PhD program, but didn't go through with it. Now that Jill, my daughter, is in her third year of graduate school in philosophy, I'm much too aware of how inadequate my training was! Is my interest temperamental? A deeper rigor? I don't know that I'm qualified to say. My guess is that there must be something temperamental about it, though I don't know how to pin it down. Rigor is something I care a lot about when I write critical prose— though I don't know if it shows. (*laughs*) Rigor applied to poetry is much trickier, it seems to me; I'm not positive I know what it means. I'm sure you don't mean form! I hope you don't mean something like "tightness" or "coherence," neither of which I value in and of themselves. I think I remember using the term about Joe Ceravolo's poetry, but I'm pretty sure I hedged there too. Something about no sloppiness, which isn't quite the opposite. My friend Marjorie Welish uses the term "scruple" when she speaks of poets she admires, which I take to be something like artistic integrity. If that's what rigor means, I hope my poems have it! But that's pretty far from whatever rigor means in philosophical matters. Maybe avoiding sloppiness of whatever kind—thought, when that's involved, feeling, diction, line breaks—is meaningful with respect to poetry?

AM: I thought you'd connect rigor and line breaks!

CN: You know what an aficionado of line I am. (*laughs*) But even with lines, if rigor means anything. I don't want it to mean "logical" or "grammatical" or "coherent." As I tried to suggest in the piece on Schuyler's lines, I find mastery of line ineffable, is that the word? You know it when you see it and hear it and feel it, and often it's impossible to do anything other than point to it. And of course not everyone cares about lines or views them in the same way even if they do care. Schuyler appears to break his lines intuitively, even casually—can the term rigor apply? Here again, you have to stretch the meaning. As for the "intersection of poetry and philosophy," that strikes me as even harder to talk about. I'm not sure why I'm revealing this, but in my senior year in college I applied for a fellowship to do work that I hoped would combine my chief interests in school, literature and philosophy. When I went for the final interview—I didn't get the fellowship—I remember being intimidated by more than one member of a committee who sat behind a table and pressed me for better explanations than I was giving about the very intersection you're asking about! I know that doesn't prove anything. Obviously ideas, including philosophical ideas, have made their way into some interesting poetry. On the other hand, the philosophers who have written interesting poetry represent a committee smaller than the one I faced. The two mix, and they don't mix. Actually, even while I was still thinking about graduate school, I felt—though I didn't trust the feeling—that the people who specialized in aesthetics had pat ways of looking, when they *looked*, at novels, poems, sonatas, paintings, etc. They didn't really seem to understand their subject matter, for all the conceptualization they were bringing to it. Actually, this relates to the current focus on poetics and theory at the expense, I would argue, of poetry. Too much talk *about*. It's a big topic and it includes whether or not there's simply too much School for Poets these days, but what appears to be falling by the wayside is the private engagement with the poetry of the past—both before and after *The New American Poetry*. To me, that's dismaying. I really do have to add that the "interest in one another's rhetorics" seems to me perfectly valid. If it seems to you merely conventional, something's gone wrong! Poetry deals in language. I remember Ashbery once saying something about not writing philosophically, but using philosophy in his poems. That seems valid to me. You can use anything if you use it well.

AM: But you used to be a classical musician too. Don't music and philosophy share an analogous rigor, built as they are of structures? I keep thinking it must have had some effect on your poetry.

CN: Some music isn't so rigorous, just as some philosophers don't think as well as they should. I'm sure the music had an effect, but I don't think I'm in the best position to say what it is. Actually, I feel music had an effect on my prose too. Are you sure you're not trying to make me into a philosophical poet? (*laughs*) That's not how I see myself. One thing about music, and not philosophy, is that it can move you to tears, whereas the tears in philosophy come from struggling to make sense, as my daughter has had to do, of philosophers like Wilfrid Sellars!

AM: You've written that before. Is that emblematic to you, is that what the arts do—bring you to tears?

CN: No! Only sometimes. They also make you laugh. And, as I keep trying to tell my poetry students, they make you react in all sorts of unexpected ways, often for mysterious reasons. They stimulate and satisfy, how's that?

AM: You don't seem to publish very much. Do you write slowly? Are your work habits pretty steady, or do you work off and on as the muse strikes? You mention someplace that you drag out poems that are months or years old to revise; do you let things sit awhile before publishing? Do you think publishing is a curse? A distraction?

CN: I don't write slowly, but I *finish* slowly. Too slowly. I don't labor over poems, but I'm always putting things into a drawer and then not liking them enough when I pull them out again. At my worst, it can take years of putting in and taking out! As it did, though I'm sure it doesn't look it, with a short prose poem in my new book, "Landscape and Chardin." I do scribble in notebooks, but only a small portion of the scribbling amounts to anything. As you can see, I don't believe in Ginsberg's "First Thought, Best Thought." (*laughs*) Actually, hearing him say in an interview that he published "about one percent" of what he wrote in his notebooks leads me to believe that he didn't believe in it either! I would like to publish more, and give myself pep talks from time to time on the topic. It's hard not to feel like a failure, at least temporarily, when you're asked for poems and don't have anything to send. Sometimes, I think I'm making progress in this area, other times no. By the way, a secret—formerly secret—reason for titling my first big book *Leap*

Year was learning from Elizabeth Bishop's introduction to her anthology of Brazilian poetry that certain poets in Brazil who produce books rarely are given the name "leap year poets." That, especially in light of Elizabeth Bishop's own small production, gave me courage. As for the way I go about writing, "habits" is probably too strong a term. Sometimes I try to write steadily—especially summers and between semesters—but that's worked, really worked, only occasionally. More often it's when I have some free time or, as you say, the muse strikes, which for me can mean that I'm not as distracted as I usually am. I don't think, though I haven't given it a try, that I'm cut out for Yaddo or MacDowell. Publishing one's work is an interesting topic for other reasons. I know it will sound like *very* sour grapes, but I really do believe that many poets publish too much. I certainly don't advocate my way; but I think there must be a happy medium—even though it may be impossible for any individual poet to discover just what that is for him/herself. (*laughs*) Patience, of the non-pathological kind, is one of the seven literary virtues. Publishing's useful side—it certainly can be a distraction and more, if you let it—apart from fame and fortune, is freeing the poet for new poems. It accomplishes a kind of separation that, at least in my experience, doesn't happen otherwise. The bad side is that publishing gets to be seductive and even addictive: it's very hard to resist the temptation, especially when you're asked for work. My friend Paul Violi and I try to remind each other of those occasions when we succumbed to temptation and rushed things into print—and invariably regretted it. They stay in print! Most of the time I'm pretty good about it—of course, helped along by my private difficulties in finishing things that, in Schuyler's words, I'm "not unproud of." But sometimes the temptation is too strong. The latter happened to me recently, and I can't bear to think about it! It's endlessly embarrassing.

AM: What was the impetus for "Day after Day the Storm Mounted. Then It Dismounted"? It seems to me to be the centerpiece of your new book. What was the seed of it, and how did you proceed with it?

CN: This is the type of question I was dreading. (*laughs*) I don't know if I can say, or actually if I want to say, much about the origins of particular poems. It's not like the origin, say, of Superman, which as a kid I found endlessly intriguing. I always find myself distrusting poets who say a lot about their poems; it's as though they're erecting a podium for what won't quite stand on its own. The "seed"—as in seeding clouds?—was the desire to write a longer poem than I had written to date, to keep a poem going over a period of time. I do recall that I had just reread the *Iliad*. As I look over the poem, it certainly doesn't seem very happy! There's death and darkness all over the place. It took me much longer to write than is apparent, I'm sure—again, not to get down what's there, but to decide that what I had was finished, that it proceeded in a way that seemed to me acceptable. And then when it was printed in *Lingo* I got depressed, because it looked small and squeezed together, when I had meant it to be roomy, have more air than I usually had. Does this illuminate anything? Oh! The title came from a Looney Tunes cartoon on TV, it might have been Woody Woodpecker. But it took me years to decide how and where to use it.

AM: You mentioned your poem "Landscape and Chardin." Have you been a lifelong student of paintings (I know you're married to a painter, Paula North, and have written on art)? What have you learned from painting about poetry? So many of your poems engage in a *plein air* vocabulary—buildings, windows, trees and leaves, kinds of light.

CN: I think it's as much the actual air, trees, and light as it is painting. Both. *Weather* moves me. (*laughs*) So does a Chardin still life. It's true that Paula's painting was, and is, extremely important to me—she began painting just before I started writing poetry—and we went to galleries all the time, read the art magazines, and so on. And when I came on the scene in the late '60s, it seemed like every other poet was writing about art. My own brief career as an art critic began in the middle '70s when Peter Schjeldahl, then Senior Editor—I think—of *Art in America*, invited me to write a piece on Richard Tuttle, who was then having a retrospective at the Whitney. One thing I rapidly discovered was how different the experience of looking at art becomes if you're going to write about it. There's a special focus and intensity that can be present at other times, but isn't always. It's also qualitatively different if you're not forced to look at paintings over other people's shoulders! The experience is quiet and private, as it should be; in the gallery, unlike the grave, one can "embrace" the art. I know I'm going against the grain, but as I said before, I believe a certain privateness is vital for poetry too. Things have gotten *too* public. I'm sure I've learned some things about writing poems from looking at paintings. Saying what they are is, as usual, the hard part. Painting in this century has represented innovation—fresh air—more consistently and dramatically than poetry has, and is therefore a more consistent encourager. To me, the beautiful paintings one keeps going back to are a sort of impossible ideal. You know you can't possibly, but you find yourself trying to do something equally beautiful, or wonderful. That's happened to me with Chardin and Vermeer; it's happened with Rothko and Guston and Johns; it's also happened with Albert York and Richard Tuttle and Wayne Thiebaud and Trevor Winkfield and Paula North and loads of others. But there's Chopin too, and Palladio, and Thelonius Monk.

"SURPRISE EACH OTHER"
ANNE WALDMAN ON COLLABORATION
BY LISA BIRMAN

APRIL/MAY 2001 NO. 184

The following is taken from two interviews conducted on December 4, 1998, and February 23, 1999, in Boulder, Colorado. The interviews are part of an ongoing project investigating the history of collaborations between painters and poets, and will be included in Anne Waldman's forthcoming book, *Vow to Poetry* (Coffee House Press, June 2001).

LISA BIRMAN: When did you start collaborating with artists? Were Joe Brainard and George Schneeman the artists you most often collaborated with in those early years?

ANNE WALDMAN: Well, collaboration was always there as a possibility. I'd already started coediting a magazine, working with others in performance contexts, writing with other writers. Yes, probably I began collaborating in the "art realm" in the late '60s, early '70s after I met Joe Brainard. We did a cartoon entitled "White Noise." And I also began working with George Schneeman around the same time. Collages, cutups (à la Tristan Tzara) with words are a kind of collaboration. There was the Surrealist "exquisite corpse," applied both to words and pictures. The anthology *The Dada Painters and Poets*, edited by Robert Motherwell, published in the fifties was

a major "statement" including various trajectories of collaboration. Of course the lineage and legacy of the New York School poets and painters was exciting, compelling. The poets always had outstanding art covers on their small press pamphlets. Those folks had been having a conversation for years. It's as if they could speak through a contained "field" (the large canvas or sheet) that also came alive in the way poetry does—off the page. Composition by field was an important poetic stance. You also had Gertrude Stein's attention to the methodology of artists, as a writer.

LB: So you knew about a lot of the other collaborations going on?

AW: Somewhat. It was part of the induction into the so-called New York School of poets. And there were lineages to consider. Marcel Duchamp's works, which hover between poetic and plastic and have witty ideas in them. There was Frank O'Hara and Larry Rivers's famous "Stones." Kenneth Koch's collaborations with Larry Rivers which included sets for his plays. Alex Katz liked to have poets pose for him. There was also—on the West Coast—the work of Robert Duncan and Jess. Yet so many of the artists I first encountered personally seem inimically bound up with the praxis and thinking of the so-called New York School poets. They did covers for them, references to them and their work appear in the poems. Barbara Guest seems a particularly painterly poet. James Schuyler as well. Think of O'Hara's ode to Michael Goldberg, his ode to Anthony Machado, his "On Looking at 'La Grande Jatte,' the Czar Wept Anew," his poems for the painter Jane Frei-licher, Larry Rivers, Joseph Cornell. And a landmark poem, "Why I Am Not a Painter," in which he describes the resonant process of Mike Gold-berg's naming his painting "Sardines" and his naming a poem "Oranges." Neither have sardines or oranges of course IN the finished work.

LB: So in the past, collaboration was more connected with a social setting?

AW: I think of most of the collaborations I've been involved with as social occasions. You know something of the artist's work, you may even have a shared sensibility. But you are also willing to "wing it" without any agenda. You aren't thinking about the concept, the finished product, making money.

That was true in the early days. So you surprise each other. During the '60s and '70s collaborations were made possible by a particular bohemian lifestyle. You dropped in on painters at work, they dropped in on you. Donna Dennis was living across the street when she worked on the cover for *Memorial Day*. There was a reading coming up. You needed a flyer. If you were publishing small press editions, as I was, you needed the artists for covers and drawings as well. Joe Brainard had been doing wonderful comics with Kenward Elmslie, O'Hara, Ron Padgett. He did the cover for the first Angel Hair book—Lee Harwood's *The Man with Blue Eyes*. I was posing for him and we'd have an idea about a project. Likewise, George Schneeman. After George moved next door on St. Mark's Place in 1968 he was generous and available to me and others as well. His studio, a small back room on the fourth floor, was filled with cutout images from old magazines. Various crayons, paint, pens, paper. Much like Joe's studio which had a plethora of cut-out images arranged in piles according to color and subject. George was also doing a lot of portraits of poets at that time, covers for mimeograph editions. We would get to work, have a tea break, and then his wife Katie would make a delicious Italian dinner. Afterwards we would swoon and fuss over our brilliant productions. There's a collaboration I did with George in 1971 on the wall here.

LB: Do you remember anything about how this was created?

AW: Well the usual procedure (and I continue to collaborate with George) is having the open sheet—usually a quality Arches-type paper—where George begins to dab a little color on (paint, gauche, crayon, ink), or actually draw an object, sometimes a cutout image. I have a few lines mulling about, sometimes I'll go into a notebook. Or I riff off his shapes, pictures. Recently I worked with him using lines from Italian translations of my poems done by a mutual friend Rita Eposti—we did a series of eight pieces—and then, even more recently, some lines from *Marriage: A Sentence* (we were making a wedding present for friends) played in two other drawings. I call this older piece you see here "Amerigo Vespucci." I think he introduced the tomato first, floating in the space like a planet or star. I then wrote "vegetable love" and "egg love" most likely, and then "I I I I / it's a celestial little BODY." There's a postcard here, looks hand-tinted, possibly from Italy, with children in an ordinary street setting, and underneath George inked "Spoleto: Festival of Two Worlds." He changed "little titties" into "little ties" and I think we both agreed on imbedding "A merry go around" inside "Amerigo Vespucci." You have in the way of readable images: a car mirror, stars, a partial map of America, a zipper and tomato in the sky. Also "the afterlife" "goes on singing" "workers of the world unite." It's a very American work, you could say, about space, aspiration, discovery, and it's a field composition. My handwriting, however, seems very primitive in retrospect.

LB: Did this all happen in one sitting?

AW: Perhaps there were other works from that same day. We often work on a couple of things simultaneously. Knowing George, he probably touched up things a bit.

LB: Did he actually compose any of the words in the collage aside from the changes?

AW: George majored in literature actually, he reads Dante all the time, and I think LIKES to add some of his words (or Dante's) on top of mine. Likewise, I've put a few brushstrokes and images on the "canvas" and the handwriting is very visual. I mean the words register as "art." Then there's the *Homage To Allen G.* project . . .

LB: From what I understand they're tracings of Allen's photos.

AW: Correct. We worked on this within hours of Allen Ginsberg's death in New York, George already had the series of tracings he had made off Allen's photographs which he had planned to have Allen write on. In fact we visited Allen at his loft so that George and he could discuss the project, and although nobody knew—the cancer had not been diagnosed yet—Allen was dying at that point. He lay prostate on a sofa, then got up to cook us lunch. The project took on a different tone after his death—ghostly, haunted you could say. It was consoling to have a place to put the grief which also included the literal traces, as well, of Allen. I stayed up all night sitting in front of George's tracings, and wrote a few lines at a time. The text is quite spare. Both text and tracings: black ink on white.

LB: And then he wrote the words in?

AW: Yes, it's George's handwriting, although I had placed the words in pencil on the xerox copies of the tracings. *Homage* feels more of a piece in that the words seem extensions of the artist's own hand, his own line which in a way continues the line of the photographer's (Allen's) eye. One page I like is a drawing of a mendicant Gregory Corso holding a stick. The lines read "A BOWL"—"A ROD"—"A STAFF"—"Poetry's (large letters) accoutrements" —"stabilize"—"THE VOID." I was thinking perhaps of Gandhi's possessions at the time of his death, as well as Allen's particular modesty. Steve Clay, the mastermind/scholar of small presses behind Granary Books, was interested immediately in publishing the project.

LB: How do you find that the process differs in working, for instance, with Susan Rothenberg or Elizabeth Murray?

AW: Well I know George better personally. And we've worked on many collaborations over the years. The environment of his modest home is less formal. He is also a master collage maker, collage being a medium poets feel at home with. We also go back and forth quite spontaneously with fewer inhibitions. I worked with Susan Rothenberg through the mail and the project—finally entitled *Kin*—was being sponsored and produced by Granary Books as well. We actually started with my manifesto "Kali Yuga Poetics" which Susan couldn't relate with. She wrote to me that she spent a lot of time going out and drawing "animals in the barnyard" (she's on a ranch in New Mexico) and the tone of Kali Yuga was too heavy. That was amusing to me actually, and being an admirer of her work and in particular the mythic quality of her horse paintings, I was comfortable taking her lead. The animals she drew were provocative as "subjects." And I wrote a suite of eight poems I probably would not have written otherwise. I worked off her drawings primarily, but with my own thoughts about animal-realm dualities. I wanted to go along with her sense of a light touch, almost comedic at times. Her charcoal drawings in this project are quite lush. Whether it's two cats, crows, two horses, or a horse and a man in relation, the images have a "talky" presence and I picked up on that. *Kin* is elegantly printed by Philip Gallo—each poem opens out into a triptych with the drawing placed at the center. Here's a little sample of the text which includes the footnote "in winter they gather at night by thousands in communal rooks":

> *peck.*

> *then head. along. home*

> *pecking order*
> *obviates*
> *transmission*
> *or cowpoke*
> *kind of bliss*
> > *flies thru here*
> *to take scraps for supper*
> *hungry*
> *extemporize a 'caw'*

> *transfer of bird*
> . . . .
> > *light*

> *feather-headed*
> *a literal p.o.v.*
> > *for literary manners*

> . . . .

> *doggerel dodges the wind*

The project with Elizabeth Murray began when I visited her studio. I made some notes in a little notebook from seeing some work in progress and must have sent them to her. She had been asked to do a project with Universal Limited Art Editions, or at least they were available for her to work with a poet. So that was the "seed" for "Her Story." She had also given me a couple of "discarded" scraps.

LB: So you'd send her poems and she'd send drawings?

AW: The initial notes lead to the urtext and then it was back and forth a bit and I was decidedly responding to her drawings (she'd sent color xeroxes). At one point I revamped the text entirely, sent it to her, and she responded that she had been counting on the earlier version. In a way I was pleased that she felt strongly about the words and liked them enough and didn't want me to keep messing about. I probably thought I was improving things, but she seemed to have a better grasp on the situation. I remember thinking the text was too simple compared to the complexity of the drawings. Her palate—eleven colors?—is grandiose. The drawings are coils, bursts of energy, fantastically witty, like cartoons gone awry yet made elegant in their transformation. She seems to be located in "things," but what are they?

LB: As you were working on it, did it begin to take shape in a linear sense as a book or were you simply working on the individual pieces?

AW: I read the text as a kind of serial poem. It had a narrative logic. It embeds being female, being pregnant, being in a kind of humorous, hormonal situation vis-à-vis the world, the "male." It's a contest, a struggle. Her drawings suggested a story, not necessarily hers or mine but the story of a state of mind taking shape. In fact her work, generally, is very hieroglyphic from some point of view. In that the "imagery" which is suggestive, not literal, takes place in a kind of zone of subtext, imaginatively wild. The finished product is very atmospheric—you could say it has a strong feminine quality—our signatures are in the watermark of the paper, which adds a kind of authorial depth to the whole creation.

LB: Whom else have you collaborated with?

AW: There's a piece I did with Red Grooms that is a triptych of Madonnas and sons. Jack Kerouac and his mother, William Carlos Williams and his mother, and Marianne Moore and hers. It's quite beautiful. And quite funny.

LB: So with that one did you come up with the concept of the piece first?

AW: Yes, the idea was to depict these writers and their long-suffering mothers as Madonnas, as icons. Red has worked with depictions of artists, heroes, writers for years: Gertrude Stein, Pablo Picasso, Fats Domino. The idea of these particular writers and their mothers was simultaneously amusing and poignant. You had the whole Madonna tradition to play with, and then you had the legendary stories about these odd "couples." William Carlos Williams is wearing glasses and he has a grown head on a baby's body. Stella Kerouac is looking quite weary. I drew on the description in Ann Charters' biography of Kerouac of their drinking and fighting and her doing the laundry in the middle of the night and his pulling out a knife and threatening her. Marianne Moore and her mother are going to the circus. The idea draws on an anecdote Elizabeth Bishop tells somewhere. The triptych is a bit dark perhaps, but the three distinct worlds work together beautifully. It's clearly an homage to the mothers. I used my own language as well in the "tales." Red did the lettering on each panel in gold, in gothic letters. Susan Hall did mysterious fine line drawings for the book *Invention* published by Kulchur Foundation in which we exchanged ideas back and forth quite a bit. Yvonne Jacquette and I worked on a piece for the Poets and Painters Show some years back. I responded to one of her "on the wing" pastels, drawings she does from airplanes, from terrific heights. So the poem, too, is from an aerial perspective. Most recently I collaborated with Richard Tuttle and the Chinese opera director and performer Su Chen on an "object"—a magic box, really, that includes a lantern, text, photographs, and a performance video. Richard had heard me read the poem "Makeup on Empty Space" in New Mexico and he said it stuck in his head and became the basis for making literal "makeup" designs that would adorn the actor Su Chen's face. I also wrote a text "off" the designs Richard had made that he had sent me color xeroxes of. I had been boning up on Chinese opera makeup and these were a distinct departure. We all went to the home of the printer and designer Gunnar Kaldeway in upstate New York and had an entire weekend to create a kind of art-word-performance-theatre piece. An elderly makeup artist from China applied the designs which include, for example, a tiny paper boat as a kind of mustache and what could be almost a traffic sign image—or warning sign—over a sideburn. We also had a video camera crew, a still photographer, Gunnar's wife, who is a composer, others. Quite a production. I took the role of director at one point, while we were filming, giving commands/suggestions to Su Chen who would be up in a tree, or in the pond, or crouching behind a rock. It was filmed entirely outside. It has a wonderful elemental quality. I also took notes during those days and wrote more after the event that is, in part, included in the final adventure. In a way, it is an opera. At one point Su Chen is singing an old Chinese shaman song upside down in the tree.

LB: Collaboration seems to have entered into your poetics in various ways—with other poets, visually, and maybe most often with performance. Could you comment on the different types of collaborations, how they interest you and ways in which they are similar or different?

AW: Certainly the Poetry Project and the Jack Kerouac School of Disembodied Poetics at Naropa have been huge collaborations. I always work with the people around me including the person I'm living with. It's a way to be in the world together and to make something that has intrinsic value because it is a statement of connection, of camaraderie, and it also goes beyond particular relationship or duet and becomes what William Burroughs has called "the third mind." So something new, or "other," emerges from the combination that would not have come about with a solo act. The collaborations from the earlier days, with a whole range of poets, including Ted Berrigan (*Memorial Day*), Bernadette Mayer (*Rattle Up a Deer*), Eileen Myles (*Polar Ode*), were necessary as a way of manifesting our "poetics" which includes a sense of community and collaboration. These writings weren't being sponsored or produced the way some of the later art projects are. We were "going on our nerve," getting inside each other's heads. We were working to surprise ourselves, each other, sometimes to show off and get closer to one another, like birds in an elaborate mating ritual. Editing magazines or books involves compromise, give and take, and it's going to provide, usually, a broader range, a more interesting mix. Working with a fine letterpress printer is also an opportunity to slow down, to appreciate the work and its presentation— letter by letter. When Reed Bye and I worked with choreographer Douglas Dunn and his dancers on *Secret of the Waterfall*, which was a live show as well as a video (directed by Charles Atlas), we tried to see the parallels that exist or come about spontaneously between gesture and word that aren't literal, that again create a third possibility. That may also incorporate an almost mystic sense of the "other." Musicians are often solipsistic, set in their ways. You need to get them to hear the words, respect the words. I've been fortunate in being able to work with Steven Taylor, for example, a classically trained musician, a punk rocker, a fiddler, also a poet, and who is willing to make things up on the spot. Or Claud Brown with whom I've collaborated on the John Cage performances, also a fine musician and a Cage aficionado. Or Steve Lacy, master composer/sax musician and Irene Aebi, chanteuse and vocal interpreter extraordinaire. So often there's no time to rehearse and you are about to get up on that stage in front of hundreds of people (in a stadium in Italy or wherever) and you have to trust the other person to be as vulnerable yet as fully prepared and as capable as you feel you are. Sense of humor and the beauty of mishap help. Fundamentally, collaboration is a calling to work with and for others, in the service of something that transcends individual artistic ego and as such has to do with love, survival, generosity, and a conversation in which the terms of "language" are multidimensional.

INTERVIEW WITH ALEX KATZ
BY VINCENT KATZ

APRIL/MAY 2001   NO. 184

Alex Katz met Frank O'Hara in 1954 when the poet and critic came to his studio to pre-
view the work for his upcoming exhibition at Roko Gallery. O'Hara wrote about Katz's show
in *Art News*: "Color is used sparingly and tellingly in a structural way, though the represen-
tation of the subject is not neglected. Refinement and an almost Oriental quiet in the per-
ception are the predominant qualities." Thus began Katz's personal involvement with
contemporary poets.

Known for his portraits of friends—artists, dancers, critics, and poets—Katz in the 1950s
and '60s painted those people who made up his segment of an intimate coterie. His cutout
portrait of O'Hara (oil on wood, 1959–60) was seen recently in the exhibition *In Memory of
My Feelings: Frank O'Hara and American Art*. He has also done portraits of John Ashbery,
Edwin Denby, Kenneth Koch, and James Schuyler. Throughout the '60s and '70s, he consis-
tently came back to poets as subjects for his work, portraying Ted Berrigan, Bill Berkson, Joe
Brainard, Jim Carroll, Kenward Elmslie, Larry Fagin, John Godfrey, Dick Gallup, Ann Lauter-
bach, Michael Lally, Frank Lima, Gerard Malanga, Alice Notley, Ron Padgett, Anne Wald-
man, and Lewis Warsh, among others. Katz has also collaborated extensively with poets,
doing books with Ashbery, Robert Creeley, Koch, Harry Mathews, Padgett, and Carter
Ratcliff. I wanted to know what attracted him to contemporary poets and why he felt com-
pelled to paint them and collaborate with them. This interview took place at his studio on
January 17, 2001.

VINCENT KATZ: When did you first collaborate with a poet and what made you want to do that?

ALEX KATZ: I had a show of painted cutouts at the Tanager Gallery in 1962, and Kenneth Koch approached me. He asked me to do cutouts for his play *George Washington Crossing the Delaware*. I read the script, and I liked it a lot. It seemed two-dimensional, so I said, "Let's make a stage that's only three feet deep and do the whole thing flat." Kenneth thought it was a great idea, but when I got to the theater I found the director was a conventional director, so we were in 3-D.

VK: Later, you and Kenneth did the book *Interlocking Lives* [Kulchur Press, 1970].

AK: Yes. Kenneth came over one afternoon and said, "Let's make something." So he started doing the stuff he does with Larry [Rivers]—you know, I draw and he writes on it. And I thought, "I'm not going to have some poet mess up my drawings!" but I said, "Wait a minute, Kenneth. This isn't working. Let me think about it." A little later, I sent him these cartoons with empty balloons and said, "You fill in the balloons." It took him a couple of years, and he came back with the idea of leaving the balloons empty and distorting their meaning by repeating the same images with different texts on the facing pages. His solution was brilliant. It was a real deconstruction.

VK: This is an approach you've consistently taken to books, in which you have a limited number of images that you repeat over and over.

AK: Well, Kenneth repeated them. I just had a set of 21 drawings, and it was his idea to use them five times in different sequences. It is a deconstruction because each time the image means a different thing. And finally the image means nothing.

VK: You also repeated images in your collaboration with Harry Mathews, *Selected Declarations of Dependence* [Z Press, 1977, reprinted by Sun & Moon Press, 1996].

AK: Harry repeated nursery rhymes and proverbs in variations. The work was based on repetition, so I thought it would be appropriate to use the same illustration in recurring patterns in three different tones. I knew his text was mathematical, so I gave him the artworks and said, "You put them in. You sequence them any way you want." He sequenced them, and I was very pleased with the result.

VK: How did *Fragment* [Black Sparrow, 1969], your collaboration with John Ashbery, come about?

AK: I thought John's poetry was fabulous! He has lots of different visual images that just flash, and there's no narration to them. That meant I could make images whose relationship was indeterminate. In fact, I didn't even have to put them into sequence. I took a lot of images I'd already done as oil paintings and reduced them to a simple form so they would work as illustrations. I did them very roughly from photos in gouache or tempera, and then I did them over much more accurately. I gave them to John, and he took a martini and sequenced them.

VK: I've noticed that you like to do things that are extreme on occasion.

AK: You don't want to be passive in a collaboration. You really have to come up and out at it. I spoke to Rauschenberg, and we thought the same way. When you do stage sets, you make that set so if that dance isn't real good, you're going to kill it. If the dance *is* real good, it's going to be unreal. You don't want to be a mere decorator.

VK: How would that attitude apply when collaborating on a book?

AK: I don't want to explain the writing. I want to do something that has as much juice as the writing, that isn't a passive illustration.

VK: A lot of the second generation New York School poets were involved with publishing books and magazines, and they would often ask you to do covers. How did you get the idea for the cover of Kenward Elmslie's *Motor Disturbance* [Columbia University Press, 1971]?

AK: From the title. A bunch of cows just seemed like the craziest thing you could put with it. I ran out to a field and drew a lot of cows. A bunch of cows seemed perfect for *Motor Disturbance* and Ken Elmslie! I did a cover for Kenneth once for his book *The Pleasures of Peace* [Grove Press, 1969].

That's an early one. I also did the original cover for Jimmy for *Freely Espousing* [Doubleday and Co./Paris Review Editions, 1969], based on a collage.

VK: How did you decide on the image of the flag for *The Pleasures of Peace*?

AK: The first image I came up with the publisher wouldn't use. It was much too minimal for them. It was just a line that made a curve, like the earth. It was pale green, and the title was on the bottom. A salesman said, "They'll never see it on the rack. It won't sell." Which to me seemed so insane I couldn't believe it! A poetry book, for Christ's sake! It isn't going to sell in a drugstore. So I had to come up with a different idea, and I got the idea of the flag, since it's heraldic.

VK: I like those punchy colors.

AK: These are the second colors. The first colors I chose were very fugitive. People would call them "gay" colors. Violet and pink. I think the salesman was homophobic. Then I just threw up my hands and said, "Make it yellow, orange, white, and black." I got away with using orange.

VK: Let's talk about some of the projects you've initiated. What motivated you to do suites of prints in collaboration with poets?

AK: I always wanted to get away from the European model of beautiful things that end up on shelves. Any time I did a portfolio of prints with poetry, I also wanted to make a catalogue so that it would be affordable. The first one was *Face of the Poet* [fourteen aquatints with fourteen poems in an edition of 25, published by Brooke Alexander and Marlborough Graphics, 1978]. I chose the poets and asked each to contribute a poem. We made a portfolio of prints and poems. I thought I could make cutout prints that wouldn't have a rectangular border around them. The border would follow the contour of the poet's head. That would make it less materialistic, less like an old print. So we selected the poems, and Prawat Laucheron printed it. It was a modern looking book. Then I spoke to Brooke Alexander, and we made a catalogue with all the images and poems in it. That turned out real nice. We didn't have access to any distribution, though.

VK: In the '80s, you did *Give Me Tomorrow* with Carter Ratcliff and *Light as Air* with Ron Padgett. For *Give Me Tomorrow* [thirteen soft-ground etching and aquatint prints with texts by Carter Ratcliff in an edition of forty, published by Alex Katz and Marlborough Gallery, 1983], you did have a book version of the print portfolio, published by Vehicle Editions. How did that project come about?

AK: I like Carter's poetry, and I liked that suite, those gangster-type poems. It was out of the movies, a Humphrey Bogart thing. It seemed arch, so I thought I'd make up people who looked like they could come out of a movie, glamorous people. We did the aquatints with Aldo Crommelynck in Paris. The kind of printing we were doing no one had done before. They don't look like typical etchings. The next project I did with Aldo was a suite of soft ground etchings, where we made it look like charcoal. That was *Light as Air* [twelve aquatints with texts by Ron Padgett in an edition of thirty, published by Aldo Crommelynck, 1987]. I made all these drawings and handed them to Ron. He had to write something to go with them, and he was really ingenious. He wrote in the person of a girl. What he did was sensational. You give him a problem when you hand him a bunch of drawings and say, "Write some poems!"

VK: Especially when they're all portraits of your wife!

AK: Every one was a portrait of my wife with her hands in different gestures! It really puts him in a box! But when you're given a restrictive problem, you have to work, and you can arrive at something with some energy. It pushes you around.

VK: Your most recent collaboration is *Edges* [a book containing thirteen etchings and a poem by Robert Creeley in an edition of thirty copies, published by Peter Blum Edition, 1997]. How did you get to know Creeley and decide to do something together?

AK: Raymond Foye told me to look him up in Maine, because he lives about an hour from us. I've always liked his poetry, and we got along real well, so we decided to do a collaboration. This time, I wanted to make something that was the equivalent of one of those great European portfolios. Really simple and tough like the books Miró and Picasso did. Super elegant and really materialistic. But I wanted it to be tough. I didn't want it to be soft. When you look at it, it's like there's nothing there. You don't have any gushy tones. You don't have any color. It's just black line on white. The etchings were based on drawings.

VK: Did you choose that stark, black-and-white line approach because of Creeley's poetry?

AK: It seems appropriate. His poetry has a restrained elegance. I must have been influenced by his poetry to come up with those techniques. The drawings are severe. I don't think they are seductive or charming.

VK: I know Frank O'Hara's poetry has been important to you, and I'm interested in the idea of the interaction between poets and visual artists . . .

AK: Frank's temperament was completely different from mine, and he was almost in a different time period. He had a problem with God, and he liked the older painters more than I did, and in a different way. Pollock, de Kooning, Kline. I liked them a lot, but the difference is he could adore them whole-heartedly, whereas I wanted to get rid of them.

VK: But that's because you're a painter!

AK: Yeah, I'm a painter!

VK: It's easier to think they're great if you don't have to compete with them!

AK: If you're a painter, you say, "I want to dump you." That puts me in another time period.

VK: What is your total assessment of O'Hara, from your first meeting with him until his death? What would you say was his impact on the art world?

AK: He had an involvement with so many people, trying to help them with their art. And his sense of style was the strongest thing around, period.

VK: In his poetry or in his opinions?

AK: His poetry comes from a philosophic base about art. You want to make something that has some real life to it, so therefore someone like Tennessee Williams is okay. It's got life to it. That's the first thing, and then you try to go over that. There's a certain amount of style, a certain amount of risk a person has to take to get into that. O'Hara's sense of style in terms of art was really strong. He exerted a lot of influence on everybody.

VK: When you talk about his style, it sounds like you're talking mainly about his own poetry.

AK: It went into painting, too. He told me once at four in the morning which way I should be painting. He was a real pain in the ass! I was ready to throw him out of the studio. He thought my painting *The Red Smile* [now in the collection of the Whitney Museum] was great, and he thought these wet-on-wet studies I was doing in Madison Square Park were "Chelsea," and I should stop them. Actually, I could never get those studies to work big, but I developed a technique from them. I liked *The Red Smile*—that was where I was going—but you can't repeat it. He didn't want me to become a Chelsea realistic painter.

VK: It's unusual for someone to be so involved in what you're doing.

AK: It's a big risk to the friendship to tell somebody something like that. But he did that to all the poets—all his contemporaries and all the younger poets. He had a strict sense of what's right and wrong. He was basically a Catholic who got turned around somehow. He was a real moralist.

VK: What about Edwin Denby's criticism?

AK: Edwin's writing relates to Frank's in that it comes from a position in esthetics, and you don't have to be interested in the dance to get something out of the writing. It's like Eisenstein on movies. That's terrifically useful for a young painter or anyone in thinking about what art should be. Edwin is one of the strongest estheticians of his time. He was a classicist—and by classicism, he meant de Kooning—but he was very involved with the avant-garde at the same time.

VK: How does one reconcile those two things?

AK: The classicism he was talking about wasn't like Winckelmann. It was like de Kooning, who had an open linear style. Denby was unsympathetic towards Clyfford Still, Rothko, things that were more aggressive, but he

could take the avant-garde, because the avant-garde of Cage and Cunning-
ham was like the old-fashioned European avant-garde. Edwin could relate
to that, because he grew up in that. Frank's writing has the sense of what art
should be, and it's more open than Edwin's.

VK: Do you feel there's an esthetic counterpart to your clean, hard-edged style
of the 1960s—in which you portrayed Ted Berrigan, Dick Gallup, Ron Pad-
gett, and others—in the poetry of those writers?

AK: I suppose the plainness and the use of the vernacular, and vernacular
images, are similar. Those poets somehow seem to come from France and
Oklahoma, whereas the previous generation of poets came from France and
England and the United States. The dropping out of English poetry gave
the younger poets' poetry a new look. With Ron Padgett, there's no English
poetry in his work. The words are more American than English. With Frank,
there's a lot of French Surrealism, but basically it always seems like the roots
are in Elizabethan English. The energy of it always seems Elizabethan to me.
It's frothy and verbal. It hasn't got that tightness of a French language or the
plainness of American images.

VK: And you sense that more in the second generation New York School poets?

AK: Yeah. I think Ted Berrigan's language is amazing. It was so new.

VK: Does it still seem new?

AK: Yes. If something has a style edge, it never loses it.

VK: Why is that?

AK: It's a kind of energy. If you look at a Rubens, it still looks like a jazzy
object. I always said a Rubens looks like a 1965 Cadillac. It's the newest,
flashiest thing in the world. And I think Ted's language, although pills
are gone and all, was an adventure into language that was really quite
sensational.

VK: Does all art have personality?

AK: I think so. Every artist has his temperament. That's the personality of the
artist. The thing is to make your temperament fit. When I was starting to
paint, everyone was Dionysian. All these macho guys around. It was really

alien to me, all that excessiveness. There was no way I could function like that. I had to function as me. You like people because they have a personality different from you in some ways and in some ways similar.

VK: What would you say is the role of the person in art, keeping in mind O'Hara's essay "Personism," in which he wrote that he could as easily make a telephone call as write a poem to someone?

AK: He was connected with the French avant-garde. I'm quite some distance from that. I think a painting's a painting, and at its best it's a high art object. The telephone is like a malted. Holy malted, holy chair, where art is life, and everything's art. I don't feel it. I feel a painting can be a unique art object.

VK: Do you think there's a difference between visual art and poetry? Poetry doesn't have a physical object in the same way.

AK: It has a similar effect. A work of poetry is a unique experience. A work of literature is something you never forget. It's not like a sunset. A sunset is beautiful, but you can't remember one from another. After a while, they disappear. But the poetry that's really affected you is a unique experience. That's one of the qualities of poetry, literature, music, painting and sculpture.

VK: The weight toward evidence of a specific life or lives, as opposed to the literary, is present in O'Hara's work, but in your work too, which uses subject matter from daily life.

AK: There are different forces of energy trying to determine what you're going to do.

VK: Which forces?

AK: The forces of "great art." "Great art" shouldn't be personal; it should be impersonal. When I was a kid, the line was, "Art should be abstract; it's modern." I always felt, "Who the hell are you to tell me what to do?" The self has to do with instinct. You like something and you do it. It's not a strategy. You adapt your instincts to the world, and you try to make something that has some relationship to what other people are thinking and what other people are doing and what other people are sick and tired of. I've always had a sense of getting sick and tired of conventional Modernism. Early on, I said, "I know one thing, I'm not one of those conventional Modernists, and that might be good, and it might be bad." It's like the way you dress.

VK: Would you say a young person has a duty to be aware, as much as is possible, of what's going on in all the arts?

AK: No. I don't feel that. Whatever interests you, you follow. Things interest you, and you follow them. I was with Paul Taylor in Paris, and Bob Rauschenberg was there with some young dancer, and the dancer said, "Paul has sold out and gone Broadway," and I said, "He may very well have, but I hear bells, and when you hear bells, you just follow them." And Bob agreed. That's what it is. You hear bells, and you say, "Hey! Let's go!"

ADVENTURES IN POETRY
AN INTERVIEW WITH LARRY FAGIN
BY DANIEL KANE

APRIL/MAY 2001   NO. 185

After a long hiatus, the legendary mimeo magazine *Adventures in Poetry* is being reincarnated as an imprint under its original editor, Larry Fagin, and the Boston publisher Chris Mattison. The 2001 author lineup includes John Ashbery, Clark Coolidge, Charles North, David Perry, and Jacqueline Waters. Daniel Kane interviewed Larry Fagin last December and January at two apartments on East 12th Street. Comments in brackets are Daniel Kane's.

LARRY FAGIN: ... so no matter what, you come off [in an interview] sounding either brittle or glib. Though Charles [North] managed to avoid both in the February/March issue of the *Newsletter*.

DANIEL KANE: Well, let's give it the old college try.

LF: Rah rah.

DK: *Adventures in Poetry* began in 1968 as a mimeographed magazine, 8½ by 11 inches, stapled—right?

LF: Let me get my catalog ... it says here the first number is from March 1968. And the pamphlets begin in 1970.

DK: The pamphlets were booklets in the same format?

LF: Yes, from two to four dozen pages, depending on whether text appears on

both sides or just one. The first was Tom Veitch's *My Father's Golden Eye*, about thirty pages. 400 copies were made and 26 of those were signed. Speed was the key. The idea was to get them out fast.

DK: You say speed was the key. I have this vision of Benzedrine speeding or feeding this process. Is that true, or am I just being corny and romantic?

LF: There was some amphetamine going around—"black beauties." And, of course, major weed and acid were everywhere. But I don't think drugs were the main source of inspiration. That came from all the good work being done in the same place at the same time. People were writing and publishing almost simultaneously. There was that '60s concept of "nowness." So it's amazing that the quality was that high. It would have seemed absurd to wait for six or eight months to see something set in stone. On a typical evening, the last of the magazine would be run off on the Gestetner [mimeograph machine] in the Project office, followed by a collating, stapling, and distribution session in the Parish Hall that lasted well into the night. Then we'd find ourselves at four in the morning eating dinner at Ratner's, a few blocks down Second Avenue.

DK: Why did you start *Adventures* in the first place?

LF: There was plenty of incentive—the writing, of course, and some good magazines [that had recently folded] to serve as models: Ted Berrigan's *C*, Aram Saroyan's *Lines*, and Tom Clark's *Once* series, to name a few. Actually, the first mimeographed magazine I ever saw was Spicer's *J*. But, for me, the most important example would've been *Open Space*, edited by Stan Persky in 1964 in San Francisco.

DK: But it was the *Once* series that provided you with a link to New York.

LF: I guess so. I was curious about the New York scene, and had lived here in the winter of 1963–64, but hadn't had much contact with the poets and writers. Jamie MacInnis and I found a nice, big apartment on 8th Street at Avenue C for about $75 a month. We attended readings at Le Metro and the Five Spot, where we heard Louis Zukofsky read his versions of Catullus. And we hung around the jazz scene a lot. One day, I went to a Kenneth

Koch reading at NYU. There were these three smart alecks in the audience, whispering and giggling, who were obviously "insiders." It was Ted Berrigan, Ron Padgett, and Dick Gallup. I sort of "knew" them without knowing them. Later, I met Ted at the Berkeley Poetry Conference [1965], where he read his sonnets. That was a turn on for some of the San Francisco poets. But, yeah, I didn't really know that much about the work of the younger poets in New York until Tom Clark began to publish them in *Once, Twice, Thrice, Frice, Vice, Slice, Spice, Ice,* and *Nice.* Wow.

DK: That magazine came out of England [1966–67], where you had gone to live, after your years in San Francisco.

LF: Right. Tom was studying and teaching in Essex, where he ran off the series. He would come down to London and we'd hang out on the music and poetry scenes.

DK: London in 1966 must have been incredible.

LF: Yes, but I don't remember.

DK: Let's go back a few years to San Francisco, where you were among the poets gathered around Jack Spicer.

LF: Yeah, other than that brief stay in New York I spent most of those years [1962–65] in Gino & Carlo's Bar on Green Street, trying to write a poem that Jack would like.

DK: Any luck?

LF: No luck. Well, actually, I wrote some science fiction poems that he liked, but they were so imitative of his style, I eventually threw them out.

DK: After Spicer's death, you left for London.

LF: A lot of those people had scattered by the end of 1965. I went to visit my parents, who were living outside of London, and wound up staying for a couple of years.

DK: Other than your discovery of the young New York poets, what made you come back to the US?

LF: It was just time to go. Also, Lewis Warsh, whom I had met in San Francisco, and Anne Waldman showed up in London and convinced me that it was "all happening in New York." So I returned in the fall of 1967 and gave my first New York reading in the Parish Hall of St. Mark's.

DK: How did that scene differ from San Francisco?

LF: It was happy and stoned, not neurotic and drunk. And it was somehow familiar. I felt I should've been here all along. A little later, I got this rent-controlled apartment. And that's the story of my life.

DK: You've said that starting *Adventures in Poetry* was a way for you to gain control of people's minds.

LF: I never said that! I said it was a way to pass myself off as an arbiter of taste, and to gain acceptance—to click with the scene. I didn't realize that I'd been accepted from the start; I was still paranoid—a hangover from the Spicer days. But I had enough nerve to persuade people to give me their best new work for my magazine.

DK: What with the demise of *C*, *Lines*, and the others you mentioned, the main competition for *Adventures* must have been *The World*, which I remember you once compared to a game of pickup basketball.

LF: Intramural sports. Anne Waldman, the most spontaneous person in America, was the editor, so *The World* had this fly-by-the-seat-of-your-pants quality. Like most magazines, it would publish one or two poems each by thirty or more contributors. What I tried to do with *Adventures* was present big chunks by fewer people—something Ted had done with *C*. The first issue began with eleven poems by Joe Ceravolo. *Adventures* #3 had just three authors. So I was going for more depth, trying to be serious. But playful, too.

DK: Speaking of playful, what about all that goofy, collaborative stuff you guys used to do? When you open early issues of *The World*, you see single poems that were written by three to seven people.

LF: Oh yeah, well, that was one aspect of the scene: community effort. Someone would come into your apartment and type something on your typewriter, and someone else would add a line, then you added one, yourself. That happened all the time. It was a stoned thing. But Ashbery, Koch, Schuyler, and O'Hara had already done it, and so had the French Surrealists. An issue of

Locus Solus was devoted to collaborations. I did my share of it; I still do, with Clark Coolidge. But I didn't publish much of it in *Adventures*—a few things by Ted and Ron. There's hardly been any collaborative writing since those days.

DK: *Adventures* #10 was entirely anonymous—no table of contents, no authors' names appear anywhere. Even the name of the magazine is missing. The covers are pornographic cartoons.

LF: I like that issue very much. It's interesting how anonymous writing alters the way one reads and understands. Something funny happens between the reader and the text. The reader is made uneasy by a strange presence— absence, really—and spends time trying to figure out who it is. It's hard to free yourself of all that baggage—history, culture, identity, and "team" mentality. (Yes, I realize that I'm retailing Foucault.) It can be intimidating, but it creates the possibility of an unbiased reading of the poem, without a whole set of those associations.

DK: So if, say, O'Hara is on your "team," you'll read his poem with a positive mind-set. And maybe Stanley Kunitz is on the other side, so his poem might not get a fair hearing.

LF: Yes. The Kunitz poem doesn't add anything to your intellectual property because it comes from the "wrong" team. Is this the end of the information part of the interview and the start of the metaphysical/political section?

DK: The end of the brittle and the beginning of the glib.

LF: God, I hope not.

DK: To continue, I suppose the idea of quality becomes a lot wobblier when you don't know who the author is.

LF: Your whole critical apparatus gets turned on its ear. Readers are used to judging a priori by brand name alone. Maybe I should have done the whole run like #10. But I doubt if anyone would've read it. They certainly wouldn't sit still for it now.

DK: I can't imagine anyone consuming something without a label/author. The cult of personality is too powerful.

LF: I don't think they have the curiosity, let alone the stamina.

DK: What else has changed?

LF: I don't know, maybe everything. Recently, Godard said about young people: "They have no doubt." That sounds true. And sad.

*

DK: Looking through the list of poets you published in *Adventures*, it seems pretty apparent you wanted to focus on the New York School.

LF: Well, I was here, wasn't I? It was one point of view. But, Daniel—New York School? I guess it'll never die. People still get so earnest around that idea. They think it's an entity that actually existed. Anyway, if you look again, you'll find plenty of work in *Adventures* by Wieners, McClure, Whalen, Borregaard, Bruce Boyd, Helen Adam, Meltzer, Spicer, Ginsberg, Corso, and even Stanley Kunitz, for cryin' out loud!

DK: I sit corrected. You were also extending what *C* did in featuring translations of earlier French poets, such as Apollinaire, Picabia, Cendrars, and Valery Larbaud.

LF: Robert Motherwell's book *The Dada Painters and Poets* [first published in 1951] had a lasting effect on New York artists and writers of the '50s and '60s. Certain French and Russian poets were important influences on the first generation. And later, Ron Padgett and others did some brilliant translations.

DK: Let's talk about the new *Adventures in Poetry*, the series of books that you're starting to publish.

LF: No, first let's talk about my new magazine, *Sal Mimeo*, which is more like the original *Adventures*.

DK: Yes, the name alone says a lot. It duplicates the old magazine's modest format—8½ by 11, stapled, etc. And you're still publishing generous amounts of work by fewer poets per issue.

LF: And providing space for neglected poets like Merrill Gilfillan, George Stanley, and Carol Szamatowicz—people who don't exactly fit into easy categories.

DK: But you're also introducing some younger writers as well.

LF: Yeah, interesting, peculiar writers—young or otherwise: Fran Carlen, Jacqueline Waters, Geoff Bouvier, Ron Horning, David Perry, Rick Stull, etc. The current issue begins with fourteen jittery, spidery, rueful lyrics by John Godfrey, a poet who deserves a big trust fund.

DK: And it ends with translations of some of the earliest prose poems.

LF: Yes. Aloysius Bertrand, from the generation just before Baudelaire.

DK: Now, what about this new press?

LF: Several years ago, I asked John Ashbery if he'd be interested in republishing his funny "poem," "100 Multiple-Choice Questions," which had originally appeared in *Adventures* #5. John liked the idea, but for one reason or another, it was put on hold. Then I met Chris Mattison, a publisher in the Boston area. He proposed that we start a small press. We agreed to launch it with John's booklet and a selection of Charles North's recent poems, *The Nearness of the Way You Look Tonight*. Three other books are due out later in the year: David Perry's *Range Finder*, Jacqueline Waters' *A Minute Without Danger*, and a gang of Hopalong Cassidy poems by Clark Coolidge, *Far Out West*.

DK: So you're reaching back to North, Ashbery, and Coolidge to echo what the old *Adventures* did, and you're taking us on new adventures with Perry and Waters.

LF: You could say that.

DK: Some of you old fogies continue to grouse about current poetry.

LF: And we will until we die. Unless it changes.

DK: Can you specify any of your complaints?

LF: Well, let's see . . . The obsession with the recent past seems shallow at best. The way some poets try to extract the ironic tone of '60s poetry—all the faux Frank O'Hara stuff—comes off like lame stand-up comedy—lots of name-dropping and product placement. And the timing is way off.

DK: It sounds like you've been attending poetry readings lately!

LF: Some. There's so much playing to the crowd, which is a way to connect with one another, I guess. Conversely, there's a good deal of fractiousness and paranoia. So, who knows if there's a real community to speak of? Younger writers don't seem to have that much in common, except a desire for self-expression and the fact that they have to work like stevedores to meet their absurdly high overheads. So they can't be serious. And they're no fun.

DK: Is the nervous tittering you mention really nervousness or in-crowd clubbiness?

LF: I dunno, maybe it's the anxiety of wanting to belong. Plus ambition, which is silly because there's so little at stake. A young friend of mine calls it "The Regarding Pole"—people trying to get on top of other people. It sounds like fucking, which might be more productive than writing at this point. In fact, it would be fine with me if everyone were to stop writing for, say, five years.

DK: Do you and poets of your generation feel marginalized in light of the current "scene?"

LF: On the contrary, I think that many of us are doing some of our best work now, though we do occasionally refer to ourselves as "fellow strugglers in the desert."

DK: Why do you think the younger poets can't pull it off without sounding stilted, derivative, or worse?

LF: Maybe fear of disclosure. Trying too hard to avoid sentimentality. Of course, the apparent ease, the irreverent worldliness that we associate with O'Hara, Schuyler, Koch, and Ashbery comes from a time when people had more control over their diction and destiny. They were able to develop a large, sophisticated frame of reference. It was practically a birthright of the late Victorian age.

DK: Which ended when?

LF: In the spring of 1975, when real estate took over the world.

DK: I've been doing some research, and I find that you are one of the very few poets of your generation who continue to work as an editor of a little magazine—that being an activity that characterized the scene in the '60s and was a way for "beginning" poets to establish themselves in the universe.

LF: And not in the university, which still kills poetry in spite of providing work for poets.

DK: You're a wonderful person.

LF: So are you.

DK: So, back then you guys didn't have to work all day like we do?

LF: No, we just got stoned and wrote.

DK: When there's so little at stake, in terms of rewards for your work, authorship or personality becomes your commodity. I mean, no one really reads contemporary poetry outside of a tiny group. The level of visibility is so low that the sense of ego is conversely elevated.

LF: Way up there.

DK: One only has to leave a poetic community to realize that, I suppose.

LF: Or just ignore it.

DK: Should I move to Turkey for a year, you think?

LF: Sure, be an archaeologist.

A complete run of *Adventures in Poetry* may be seen in the Berg Collection at the New York Public Library.

TINA DARRAGH INTERVIEWED BY MARCELLA DURAND

OCTOBER/NOVEMBER 2001   NO. 186

Tina Darragh's books include *on the corner to off the corner* (Sun & Moon, 1981), *Striking Resemblance* (Burning Deck, 1989), *a(gain)2st the odds* (Potes and Poets, 1989), *adv. fans - the 1968 series* (Leave Books, 1992), and *dream rim instructions* (Drogue Press, 1999). Darragh is employed as a reference librarian at the bioethics library at Georgetown University. She lives in Greenbelt, Maryland, with her husband P. Inman and their son, Jack, and has been active in the Washington, DC poetry scene since the early '70s.

MARCELLA DURAND: I'm very intrigued by your idea—and practice—of linguistic/poetic "investigations." In particular, I'm interested in how you recast a poem outside its initial medium. You frequently "illustrate" your own work, with the illustration containing all sorts of doorways and loops, through which language appears. It's like you're investigating how your own writing can be reinterpreted and reformed beyond the limits of typed text laid out in lines on a page.

TINA DARRAGH: Well, the first investigations, really, involved looking words up in a dictionary! I was working as an editorial assistant at a legal publishing company, and I wanted to have an office "writing" life the way Stevie Smith had one (writing her *Novel on Yellow Paper* at odd times at work). So if I wanted to write a poem about someone, I would look up that person

in the dictionary using an "off" association instead of a proper name and then transcribe that part of the dictionary page. Sometimes dictionary illustrations became part of the transcription as simple things that I could draw on the page, like an arc. Using the _____s on the page where I'd find them was the most fun, actually, and made reading the poems aloud interesting since I'm hammy and would move my head instead of making sounds. Then with the transcriptions for each letter of the alphabet that became *on the corner to off the corner*, I started drawing on the page in a way suggested by the first/last words for that page. For the ambiguous figures project, I "built" the figures using photocopies of parts of dictionary pages, and with the bunch-ups, I'd cut out the bunched-up part from the window blind drawings and paste them over photocopies of random dictionary pages. I could "follow" words around like Francis Ponge followed soap around in his poems. I felt that I was taking myself out of the poem and letting the words relate to one another, the image replacing/critiquing the "author."

MD: Do you know Ponge's *The Making of the Pré*, where he writes and rewrites a piece over and over again? I found his book a really interesting way to break down the boundaries of the discrete text. You have an epitaph in *a(gain)2st the odds*—is he an important poetic figure for you?

TD: I spent a day at the Library of Congress once looking for that quote, getting all the Ponge books I could to see if I could find it. At one point in the late '70s when Jack was a toddler, I worked part time as a "deck attendant" at the Library of Congress—shelving books in the stacks—and I looked briefly through a Ponge book as I reshelved it and saw a quote about figures of speech. Then, years later, I was in one of my "what is this writing _____" phases that I get in, and I remembered seeing that Ponge quote on the fly but couldn't remember much else about it. So I took a whole Saturday to go to the Library of Congress to see if I could dig it up—it was such an extraordinary event, timewise. P. took care of Jack for the whole day instead of us splitting it, and I spent the whole time just looking at things. So it started me on to a new project. I'm going to try to get *The Making of the Pré* out of the library tomorrow so that we can talk about it, since you love his work, too.

MD: I think when I read *The Making of the Pré* (which was a while ago), Ponge was someone I was very much looking for: a poet involved with "matter." I had been getting involved with deep ecology, where you try to move away from human-centered (anthropocentric) stuff and into equality of all beings. I wanted not so much the fox to represent the poet's deep dark interiors, as to be a fox in and of itself, and Ponge was very exciting to me in that search into the existence of "things" and processes.

TD: I never thought about Ponge vis-à-vis deep ecology, but you are so right about that. Reading your observation took my breath away, because I've been taking notes on a deep ecology book I came across at work—*Contesting Earth's Future* by Michael Zimmerman—but haven't done anything with them. It would be interesting to line them up beside *The Making of the Pré* and see what would happen. Maybe we could both do something like that re: Ponge as a collab. I think any interview is really a collaboration, and it would be good (if this is all right with you) to have a collab develop out of our exchange.

MD: Michael Zimmerman was my teacher in college and the one who got me turned on to deep ecology in the first place! He was wonderful. I didn't know he had a book out—I will have to go find it immediately. A collaboration sounds great. Also, I'm interested in hearing more about how work and poetry intersect for you.

TD: Sometimes the effect of working in a library on my writing is the equivalent of not wanting to eat donuts because you work in a bakery—I can't look at another book. Other times it is very calming to be surrounded by books when I'm trying to sort things out. When I worked at the Epilepsy Foundation library in the late '80s/early '90s, it was amazing to read about the history of the treatments, the stigma, the sterilizations, and the different cultural explanations for the epilepsies—even to know that it was not plain "epilepsy" but many epilepsies. Also, there were some researchers at the time using chaos theory to try to figure out new combinations of drug therapy for those with intractable seizures, so chaos theory seemed to have a "practical" problem-solving side to it, not just a trendy side! I really miss doing reference work for people with epilepsy. Of course, the epilepsy library was a room in an office building, and now I work in a "real" library with stacks, etc. In terms of my writing, a difference here is my coworkers' response to my writing. It used to be that when it became known at work that I wrote poetry (usually when I had to go somewhere for a reading), coworkers would ask to read my work. I'd make sure to let them know that it was more than okay for them not to like it. It would be funny because people would insist, "Oh, you are being too modest—I know I'm just going to love it." And then after they'd read it, they'd say, "You are right, I don't like it!" Here at the bioethics library, with a big collection of Nazi medicine literature, the response was, "Well, *I* would not like work like this, but at least you are a postmodernist with a sense of humor." So there is a way in which a major part of the library collection is a critique of my work, portraying postmodernism as a philo-sophical approach advocating erasure of history and the subject—post-modernism as veiled Nazi collaboration. Of course, there are books like Zimmerman's that address issues such as Heidegger's collaboration with National Socialism while seeking to retain the "best parts" of postmod-ernism and link them up with civil rights and radical ecologies. As you can imagine, it was a real relief to find his book!

MD: Speaking of science (and epilepsy), I'm also quite interested in how you integrate that into your work. You mention popular science and how much you enjoy popular science books, and how you felt when someone dismissed those.

TD: Well, growing up, "science" was all about "fear"—not just because the nuns who taught the science courses were tougher than the others, but also because of that '50s mix that brought us the dive-under-your-desk nuclear attack drills. Once we were on the moon, I think science got a lot friendlier, but by then I was a total phobe. My high school guidance counselor told me that I would flunk out of college because I wouldn't be able to do the science (or math either)—that I should go to a community college, but even that might be too hard for me. I finally told a friend of mine from high school that story about a year ago, and she clued me in that the guidance counselor said that to everyone! Maybe it was the nun's habit she wore—one of the real uncomfortable ones that made her look as if her face had been caught in a bus door. Anyway, by college there was a science subculture mix of cultural revolution (erase the distinctions between the intellectuals and the technicians), advanced Cold War (if we don't do science, commie science will do us), and self-help (let's eat a bunch of things we can't pronounce to keep fit). I know that most of this mix ended up as New Age day-glo products, but the questioning of scientific certainty going on in the background gives us real permission to challenge our deferment to "rigor" so we can "experiment" with materials from lots of different sources. Having said that, I don't think we are caught in the circular argument of "well, you can't prove something with certainty, so why should we _____ (stop burning fossil fuels or stripping forests, etc.)." We can still do ranges! And the fact that we can include various kinds of information in calculating the ranges (since we're not bound at the hip to "rigor") may mean we'll come up with interim solutions that would never surface if we relied on strict data.

MD: I'd like to hear about your current project.

TD: My current piece started out as a tribute to the Sea Turtle Restoration Project demonstrators at the Seattle anti-WTO march back in December, 1999, and by default the blue-green coalition getting going (the Teamsters just LOVE the turtles!) Now it is looking at language and animal rights. Traditionally, humans are responsible for protecting animals because we have language and they have pain. I don't like that dualism as a basis for fighting for rights, either for human animals or other animals. I've been rereading the Zimmerman book since this question cuts across both the deep ecology and social ecology arguments. Very tentative, but of course I've been saying that for a couple of years now! Did I mention how important it was for me to read an essay by Bernadette Mayer in a magazine in the mid-'70s where she says something like "poets never admit how long it really takes them to write something." I can picture where I was sitting at the time (waiting for a bus at Porter and Connecticut Avenues). Maybe it will help other writers to mention that again here—it certainly continues to help me. Have I said thanks? Starting our Zimmerman/Ponge collab has been such a help. Thanks again.

Zimmerman/Ponge/Durand/Darragh collab (a beginning)

Deep eco pre 1

8/11/01

DEEP ECO PRE - conceived as a collaboration via the Internet, this summer, not far from such places as the green belt around the co-operative where I live with P. and Jack, and the best harbor in the world.

We, e,e, we

From (deep) ecology from (social) ecology from ecofeminism, the pre as eco, eco as a pre. Great _____ delle LAY brugge 1300 poems.

Mixed extension (from the point where we were, the spot where we happen to be, from where we overlook the scene, where we thought of it, first time, as a pre), we were among bucklings, common colors, popular scrubs, ant-wide wypoutes.

And right below us ran shape betrays, some relation Outl before Listener laws end chemicals.

Between the two, deep eco pre. A summer camp class picking up trash from their playground.

We reflected, then, on nature without homage to origin. A trans-what-is-morph-isis of natter, we said to ourselves, linked with the Internet, that is, with lines that are sometimes up and sometimes down, small fragments reduced to letters, seconds— and layers, questions round. That nonetheless remain sound, wagging.

LEWIS WARSH INTERVIEWED BY PETER BUSHYEAGER

DECEMBER/JANUARY 2001   NO. 187

Lewis Warsh has written poetry and fiction for decades. He has continually reinvented his work and remained prolific, which has been dramatically demonstrated in recent months: between May and the end of the year, four new Warsh books will appear. Three of the publications—*Touch of the Whip*, *The Origin of the World*, and *Debtor's Prison* (a collaboration with video artist Julie Harrison)—offer new fiction and poetry. His long-standing reputation as a laser-eyed editor is documented in *The Angel Hair Anthology* published by Granary Books. The *Anthology*'s some six hundred pages offer a generous sampling of work he and Anne Waldman published during their legendary 1966–1975 stint as coeditors of *Angel Hair Magazine* and Angel Hair Books. The publication also includes a detailed bibliography, vintage photos, and memoirs from many of the writers included in the collection. During a mild July afternoon at the Orlin Café on St. Mark's Place, we talked about two of the new publications: *The Origin of the World*, a collection of jump-cut collage poems published by Creative Arts Book Company, and *Touch of the Whip* from Singing Horse Press, which features poems and short fiction.

PETER BUSHYEAGER: Let's talk first about *The Origin of the World*, a suite of seventeen poems with a very particular structure: prose-like segments strung together in a nonlinear way to create energy-charged mosaics. This is different from your earlier work. When did you start working with this structure?

LEWIS WARSH: In 1990. The first poem I wrote using this method was "Travelogue," which appears in *Avenue of Escape* but not in *The Origin of the World*.

PB: What's the genesis of this style?

LW: I had all these interesting lines in my notebook and it occurred to me that I could work with them in a way that would engage both my fiction-writer and poet sensibilities. And that's how the poems work. The individual sections are made up of sentences, so they're prose. But they're also lines of poetry. You can have it both ways.

PB: How do you write these poems?

LW: I wait until I have around 150 or so lines. Then I stand back and take a look at them and begin creating a structure, which is similar to what I do when I write fiction. I usually end up discarding around fifty of the lines, but I hold onto them for future use. I'm a recycler, constantly going over old discarded work to see if there's something that makes sense.

PB: I would think that assemblage/collage engages a very different part of the brain.

LW: It's a different way of working that comes from a different place than "regular" writing. It's extremely liberating and, in fact, has influenced me outside the realm of poetry. In the mid-'90s, after I'd been making this kind of poem for awhile, I began creating collage artworks, which is something I'd never done before. Now I do them all the time. Not too long ago, I made a series of 24 small collages and titled each one after a John Donne poem. They appeared in a limited-edition artist's book and the original collages are now in the collection at the University of California at San Diego.

PB: One of your collages appears on the cover of *The Origin of the World*.

LW: Yes. The cover is a kind of mirror for what I was doing in the book.

PB: *The Origin of the World* has a relentless quality, along with a somewhat disaffected, flat tone. That's a curious combination.

LW: I'm in a totally cool state when I'm ordering one of these poems. I'm aiming for a fragmented narrative and I use different voices to create dialogue. In other words, when you read "I," it's not necessarily Lewis Warsh speaking.

PB: There are different dictions, too.

LW: I don't want to create a "whole." The excitement for me is that I can include anything without thinking too hard about how it's going to all add up. I want to learn how to put each poem together as I'm doing it. I'm not a handy person in real life, so this is my way of building a kind of house. The lines are a lot like bricks, one on top of the other. The world is fragmented, history in general is fragmented, my personal history is fragmented. A lot of the lines relate to memories from different periods in my life. I don't know what's happening from line to line when I'm putting together one of these works. In a way, these poems are similar to what I did in an earlier book, *Methods of Birth Control*, which involved ordering "found" material.

PB: For me, *The Origin of the World* is monolithic. It's like the mysterious plinth that appears in the movie *2001*, dark, monumental, and impenetrable.

LW: I like impenetrability. Past a certain point, this book simply exists. What more can you say about it?

PB: Well, it's important to note that the poems are very fresh, but they're also part of a tradition.

LW: Yes, there are a number of precedents: Ezra Pound's *Cantos*, which linked disparate lines and cultures, and encoded numerous historical threads, and Ted Berrigan's *Sonnets*, which worked with a variety of material including "found" text. I don't mean to imply a lineage, but both these works are inspiring sources. There's also a connection with Pascal's work, and Wittgenstein's, the way they build a philosophical essay from numbered statements. I consciously kept them in mind—and Edmond Jabès as well—as possible models.

PB: Did you try for a certain flow when you were deciding about the order in which the poems appear? That could be a challenge with this type of work.

LW: For the most part, the poems appear in chronological order. But there's one exception. I wanted to end with "The Secret Police," which is different from the other poems because it goes back and forth between several distinct narratives. The final section of the poem has a nostalgic feel that's created through the oceanic imagery. I was thinking about looking out at the ocean during the time I lived in Bolinas, California, during the late 1960s. Also, the final line is a good way of ending the book: "This is the time I like best, late evening, when the sun disappears, & there are no secrets."

PB: Do you plan to continue creating poems in this mode?

LW: I don't like repeating myself—but I still think there's something new inside this structure that can keep me interested. I currently have several hundred lines, but I haven't assembled them yet. Of course, I'm also writing other poems too—poems that aren't built on this structure.

PB: Let's talk about *Touch of the Whip*. It's a good companion to *The Origin of the World*. Both books explore some of the same themes—particularly dislocation—but they feel quite different from each other. *Origin* is concentrated and intense. *Touch of the Whip*'s combination of poetry and short fiction is more expansive and welcoming in its approach.

LW: That may be because of the prose. When you're presenting fictional characters with specifics attached to them, people who have some resemblance to "real" people, you create a different context than the one you find in poetry. You're dealing with a kind of reality that is hopefully available to everyone. Fictional characters help you meet the reader halfway.

PB: I thought the blend of prose and poetry worked very well. Did you set out to make a book mixing the two?

LW: I have to thank Gil Ott, the publisher and editor of Singing Horse Press, for shaping the book's final form. We began corresponding after the publication of my book of short stories, *Money Under the Table*. Gil liked that book and said he wanted to publish new work. So I sent him a short-fiction manuscript modeled after *Money Under the Table*. After he read the manuscript he called me and made a radical request. He asked that I take out the longest story and substitute other work that would make the manuscript more diverse. I breathed deeply, decided to take his suggestion, and began to make a different kind of book.

PB: Was it difficult to accept his feedback?

LW: Only for a minute. Gil is a dedicated, experienced editor and I trusted him. He wasn't suggesting I rewrite any of the work, just restructure the book. In the long run, his comments gave me permission to break the mold—I was trying to write a sequel which maybe wasn't a very interesting idea—and create something new. That's what good editors do.

PB: The book begins with "G & A," a fictionalized account of the Georgia O'Keeffe/Alfred Stieglitz relationship that reads like biography. Why did you write about them?

LW: I'd seen Stieglitz's nude photos of O'Keeffe, which communicate both Georgia's vulnerability and incredibly focused strength. I was interested in the great age difference between Georgia and Alfred, and about Paul Strand and Leah Harris, who also loved O'Keeffe. I wanted to write a story about people making choices and the transactional aspects of relationships. The moment when the photos were taken is the focal point for all of this.

PB: It's interesting that you mention "transactions." *Touch of the Whip* often portrays relationships as transactions. People make deals with each other in order to connect in some way, but the connections don't seem to change them. By starting with a piece that could easily be considered non-fiction, you give the whole book a particular edge—as if it's a collection of true, amazing stories. Be honest. Aren't at least some of the prose pieces transcriptions from your life?

LW: I'm a fiction writer and that involves taking bits of my life as jumping-off points for the narrative. But there's a lot of embroidering, expanding, a lot of fictionalizing, if that's a word. So the stories aren't directly based on real experiences, although I hope they have the ring of truth. The one exception is "The Line Up." I was mugged on the streets of Boulder, Colorado in the late 1950s, and the story hinges on my memories of all that.

PB: *Touch of the Whip* has two family-themed stories that appear back to back: "Family Romance" and "Anonymous Donor."

LW: Everyone has family fantasies—this is Freud's idea—because many people are dissatisfied with their real parents and need to transform them into different people. He called this the "family romance." Families are either too mundane, too conventional, too inattentive, too smothering. In these two stories I created some family fantasies. But not a word is true.

PB: Too bad! I wanted to hear more about your grandfather, his prison term, and his relationships with much younger women.

LW: Sorry to disappoint you!

PB: The book's title work, the poem "Touch of the Whip," is one of my favorites. I have a distinct memory of hearing you read it and being impressed by its power.

LW: I was fascinated with the story, in the early 1990s, of the couple who kidnapped the Exxon executive and buried him in a box in New Jersey. That was the starting point. The poem is built around a collage—a layering—of longer diverse pieces of writing. Even the title is a kind of alchemical mix of other book titles: Philip Lamantia's *Touch of the Marvelous* and Robert Creeley's *The Whip*. For some reason these titles were echoing in my head when I was writing.

PB: You're good at closing your books with the perfect piece. *Touch of the Whip* ends with the story "She Was Working." The main character, a young woman working a minimal sort of job, is bored and restless in a passive way.

LW: I'm talking about the standard job situation in this story, office jobs where people spend hours repressing themselves and their sexuality in the interest of being responsible. I dealt with the same idea in my story "Crack," the opening story in *Money Under the Table*. How do people spend these hours? What are they thinking when they're there? How do they break out of this world?

PB: The character certainly finds a way to break out, although it's a bit appalling. Her decision seems effortless, pragmatic, and completely logical, which makes it all that more disturbing. But I won't give the ending away for the *Newsletter* readers. This interview has focused on the present—specifically, your brand-new books. But sometimes history becomes part of the present, as it has with the publication of *The Angel Hair Anthology*. Is your history a burden? How do you feel about the past?

LW: Well, the impulse is to close the door on it all and embrace it at the same time. There are all these voices in your head, all these feelings for people who are no longer a part of your immediate present, all these places where you used to live. They keep coming back and doing battle with the adamant present. So you're living a kind of double life and it's a constant struggle, but there's a lot of positive energy generated from the tension. *The Angel Hair Anthology* brings together various communities of writers from the late '60s and '70s when Anne Waldman and I were editing the magazine and books. It's a testament to all the interrelated friendships from that time when most of the contributors were fairly young. The book includes the early works of a lot of people who are still going strong. Steve Clay, the publisher of Granary, is the person responsible for initiating this project. He has a beautiful feel for making sense of literary history in our own time, and that's what the anthology is about.

JACK COLLOM TALKS SPANDRELS, FOXES, AND RECEDING PATHS WITH MARCELLA DURAND

OCTOBER/NOVEMBER 2003   NO. 196

In 2001, the publication of *Red Car Goes By*, a compendium of Jack Collom's work from 1955 to 2000, selected by a group of poetic heavy hitters, including Reed Bye, Clark Coolidge, Larry Fagin, Merrill Gilfillan, Lyn Hejinian, and Collom himself, was the first step in remedying what, for many, was the unacceptable neglect of a poet essential to any innovative "canon." Exploring the environs of language and world, undistracted by trends, schools, or cliques, Collom has created his own place in poetry. As Ron Silliman has written on *Red Car Goes By*, "Part of what is so very interesting reading these earliest poems by Jack Collom is that he seems to have already figured out what it seems to have taken so many other poets another twenty years to get straight—it's not a zero-sum competition. Liking the New York School need not preclude an interest in the Beats, the Projectivists, nor anything else for that matter. In that sense, Collom is writing—these poems date from 1955 to 1964—very much like a poet of the 1980s. The man was literally a quarter century ahead of his time." Born in Chicago on November 8, 1931, Collom grew up in Western Springs, Illinois, and moved to Colorado at age 15. He worked at factories for twenty years and now teaches part-time and freelance, mostly at Poets-in-the-Schools and at Naropa University, including courses on Ecology and Literature. He has published seventeen books of poetry with small presses and two CDs and has twice received a National Endowment for the Arts Fellowship.

MARCELLA DURAND: Some of your poems are formal, like the sonnets, and then others have their own individual form—do you invent it for them, or do they invent the form for themselves?

JACK COLLOM: If you're asking how I come to this unusual variety, I'm surprised that everybody isn't as varied. Part of it has been through working with kids, developing an assortment of approaches. Also, I feel validated in "trying anything" by my sense of biology. I have a sentence here from Darwin that I find a real poetics root-statement: "The truth of the principle that the greatest amount of life can be supported by *great diversification of structure* [emphasis **JC**'s] is seen under many natural circumstances." He goes on to say that a three- by four-foot patch of turf he had studied had twenty species of plants that belonged to eighteen genera and eight different orders, and all of this was just by chance: it was the best and most workable thing, as opposed to a monoculture-type situation. To me, the sense of poets finding their "voice" in poems is artificial and overpsychologized. But maybe it's right for a lot of folks. How would we define somebody like Robert Creeley? Or Alexander Pope? They have very distinctly limited voices, but within that limitation, universes take place.

MD: You've said that you're interested in writing "what's in front of you."

JC: That's an old remark that I think I got from William Burroughs. It's a little odd that Burroughs would say that, when you think of some of the scenes in *Naked Lunch* . . . I suppose one can nudge the concept so that something happening in front of you in your imagination is eligible. Then at least it's not concocted out of a series of intellectual steps. For me, it's a corrective to the idea I originally had as a very young fellow trying to be a poet—that the poem was some wrestling of the universe into callow generalities.

MD: Could it also have to do with your interest in processes and systems— concepts of the natural world?

JC: Yeah. When I was a little kid, I was taken for walks in the woods by my father. I fell in love with nature and became a passionate birdwatcher at age 11. I guess what happened to me—I'm sure this happens to a degree with a lot of people—was that I became somewhat alienated from the human world. I felt that the adults that I saw were engaged in a deceptive series of conversations. I didn't have the maturity to realize that this is simply the grease the world needs to whirl on its axis.

MD: What did you love about nature?

JC: I loved the variability and the spaciousness. I was out with Jenny [Heath] recently and we looked into the woods and saw the darkening series of recessions that one sees. It reminded me that the image of a path disappearing into the woods or just a sense of a way going into the woods was stunningly attractive for me as a kid.

MD: It's on the cover of your book [*Red Car Goes By*].

JC: Yes, snapped by my son Nat. That's, oddly, within the NYC city limits. And there's having a secret place of one's own. Then of course the animals, and this was partly through readings that I did when I was very small. Thornton W. Burgess wrote these little books about humanized animals wearing little jackets. *The Adventures of Reddy Fox*, *Old Mother West Wind*, etc. Later, Ernest Thompson Seton's books.

MD: So many have that hope of communicating with animals . . .

JC: Oh, I had that so strongly. It was the hardest thing—I can still feel the pain of withdrawing from that belief that we could talk with animals. Of course, nowadays, the scientific evidence is piling back in that the communication of animals is much more evident, intricate, and complex than some of the behaviorists and other sort of cynical scientists have wanted to say. Nature as machine. When I was a kid, my favorite animal was the fox. I identified with the fox and his sneaking around the woods. But also with the gawky blue heron, just standing there.

MD: What about that mouse you've written about so much?

JC: That came later and was more of a deliberate choice, based on the desire to write effectively about nature and thereby choosing the despised little mouse, which, as my sister Jane says, might be called "mammalian popcorn." I thought if I could write a series of poems, if I could demonstrate that the mouse is a glorious complex of endless applications and glittering life, if I could hint at that by writing about the mouse in a variety of strange forms, then this would perform a service perhaps.

MD: Do you have hopes that poetry can shift perceptions?

JC: Yes, it always has. Probably most when it isn't attempted. There's that thought of poetry becoming preachy propaganda and of course ruining itself. Sometime in the late '80s, I was over 50 already and had been writing poetry for a long time, being a nature boy for a long time, and keeping the two more or less apart. Of course, nature entered my poetry, birds and whatnot, but I resisted any temptation to become a "nature poet" for the reasons given. You don't want to sound like Chief Seattle in a school play. But I was convinced by Jennifer and my paleontologist son Chris to give it a try. I thought, well, if I just try to write a "hip" poem as poem—the word "hip" is kind of silly, I don't feel like a hip person at all—but hip in the sense it's active in all details, if that's what hip could possibly mean. Even if *the* or *of* or *in* has to turn into a little jumping frog. If I do get something going, qua poem, then I can say, "Save a leaf!" (and blow the poem, Larry Fagin might say). Hence *Arguing with Something Plato Said*.

MD: What were you arguing with?

JC: With Plato's famous remarks about the cave, that all of the variety of actual physical life on earth is as ephemeral and unimportant as the flickering shadows on a cave wall. I doubt if Plato could light a bonfire; it's not inductive enough. By the way, I had been calling that manuscript "Around Here," which Anne Waldman, the publisher, thought kind of drab. Ron Padgett has termed it, "Arguing with Some Potato Salad."

MD: Some of your poems strike me as philosophical. Yesterday you were throwing Kant's name around . . .

JC: I threw it around twice, I think. But I don't know anything about Kant. I've never studied philosophy, but I am very drawn to it, as many people who haven't studied it are. I particularly like phenomenology and Husserl.

The emphasis that our perceptions are very much shaped by physical distortion, bias, and limitation, which becomes glorious.

MD: I'm interested in how you work out scientific concepts in poetry.

JC: I think I have a tiny, amateur feedback loop with my science readings, which are not in any way professional. It's just that I like to read people like Stephen Jay Gould. He, for example, has this concept of "spandrels." Spandrels are little architectural spaces in an arch. The arch is affecting a curve at its top and in older constructions of the arch—this had to be done in a series of little zigzags. You couldn't just bend an arch, you had to step an arch. So these little "steps" had little triangles of space in them. If you go by 90-degree increments when you're trying to arc over a space, then you have these space triangles—those are spandrels. Gould uses the idea of spandrels for all "stuff" that doesn't perform an exact function. It's just the fluff, the effluvia of a natural process. This little extra space that's repeated is a byproduct. It's not anything in itself. It's a leftover of achieving something in a not-quite-direct way. And nature's *absolutely full* of this type of thing. When you look closely, everything real is spandrelized.

MD: Including poetry!

JC: Including poetry! You can see poetry as more central if you don't overemphasize the blunt logic of natural selection. People have this idea of natural selection as this series of very blunt logical happenstances. Nature's not a 12-step program. It's 90 percent spandrels and secondary uses. The human tongue was not created for yodeling. (*Voice from the kitchen, "Amen."*)

MD: Could this be seen as flexibility? A multiuse organ lends advantage?

about

on a that blue onto for the an
where tan when what why whiles
is of although through crimson
could are purple were till why

as was under white while to be
yellow throughout which in was
unto among chartreuse has have
thru gold out and but this tho
when magenta should is could o
wasn't until pink will neither
not or into brown can and over
without with do teal do either
ochre nor would upon the isn't
this which etc. in still there
there's aquamarine been hasn't
of especially greens that that
off-white those what won't hey
away inner these gray although
to turquoise who black them at
she it scarlet him their among
up before down after it beige-
rust outer them his but and/or
this upon under unto red in be
up through ivory her when then
uh to shouldn't will be orange
a over why battleship gray the

JC: Yes, and all of this is utterly parallel with poetry. It's just a percentage of randomness. If you're writing a poem and you feel strongly about this biological bubbling complexity that I'm trying to express a little about, then you're open to what happens to language in the same way. The language is bubbling along just like the gene pool. Each idea's a mutation. So I do feel encouraged by that kind of biological understanding to open up more in poetry, to subvert the intentional fallacy more, to just try things out and experiment, because nature is one big experiment.

MD: And you think this idea has developed over your poetic career?

JC: Yes, I do. Because at first one feels intimidated. The only freshness is ignorance. The first day I ever wrote poems, on the shores of Tripoli, Libya, I thought you had to rhyme. I was 23.

MD: How did you come to write poetry in the first place?

JC: My little story—I say "my little story" because one tells oneself stories and they become a little too pat, perhaps—is that I went to college in Colorado and studied wildlife management and forestry, following out my slightly misanthropic, throw-self-in-nature mode, then I got interested in culture suddenly and didn't want to sit in a swamp and count ducks the rest of my life. When I finished college, it was Korean War time. I joined the Air Force to beat the draft and met some artist friends in South Carolina where I was stationed and became very interested in being an artist. I'd always loved the quirks and humors of language, but had never thought to write before. Aside from essays and exercises, it wasn't encouraged in schools during the '30s and '40s. So I just started writing, wanting to be my own boss.

MD: Poetry as opposed to fiction?

JC: I started with stories and wrote a few horrible, self-absorbed, exceedingly romantic stories and then turned to poetry one day and found that, I don't know, maybe I have a musical sense. Or my brain is fragmented. I found a home in poetry. Poetry was a discovery process. In a story, you're carrying a burden of some kind of mostly predetermined logical development. Or so I felt.

MD: How did you find the courage to break away from your initial view of poetry?

JC: It was sucking other people's courage for a long time, whose examples I would follow, or just by getting deeper into the poetry that was available to me. I was pretty isolated. I did live in New York City for a couple of years ('56 to '57), but I didn't know any other poets. Then I went to Germany, then to a Connecticut factory town. I worked in factories for twenty years. I wasn't really in the soup of other poets as many people are, I fancy, in New

York and San Francisco. Little by little, I would get examples of things. Donald Allen's anthology, *The New American Poetry*, was sent to me in 1960 by Stan Brakhage, who had married my sister. After an initial negative response to that book, which lasted about five minutes, I really came to love it. I still think of it as the great upheaval in my own personal poetry. Before that, I had been stuck with Louis Untermeyer's *Golden Treasury of English-American Upchuck* as a set of models. But even the more conservative great poets that one finds in such an anthology—you get into them. The conservative aspect just crumbles away and you find the genuinely exciting poet within. I was (am) certainly in love with Gerard Manley Hopkins, a dynamo of innovation. Even reading the Brownings, or Lascelles Abercrombie, at first you're struck by the conventional thing, but as you become more deeply acquainted with the poetry, your appreciation of it falls into insane grottoes of who knows what.

MD: But you started corresponding with some of the poets in Allen's anthology?

JC: I sent Diane di Prima a Bertolt Brecht translation that she printed in *Floating Bear*. Then she came to Boulder and I set up a reading for her. She very generously gave me a huge address list of "alternative" poets. I was in touch by mail for a few years with Gary Snyder, Ted Berrigan, and others, then Naropa came to Boulder in '74.

MD: What was that like?

JC: At first, it was like Gulliver's Isle of Laputa, the island in the sky that rules various domains below and plops down upon them when it needs to exert its authority. There had been a lovely little mini-renaissance in Boulder just prior to Naropa's plopping in. People like Reed Bye were involved and some of the poets resented the oblivious incursion of the hotshot bicoastals. It's true that many of them were not very curious about this Colorado hick town they'd splashed into. I was a bit of a liaison there, because I was the one who happened to know these poets, at least by mail, and very soon, resentments dissolved away. Naropa was of course a great boon to Boulder, especially poetically. It's been a tremendous piece of luck to anyone living here to have the access to poets, in the summer writing program especially.

MD: I wanted to ask you about your collaborative poems. You're known for whipping out that paper and pen . . .

JC: It's a great love of mine. It was the '50s when I first got into that. I was living with some artist friends in New York City and they had a party game of making a collaborative poem. What you got was instant disjuncture and that pleased me so much. I've always had such a great love for absurdism. Part of my fox-child image. The adults are talking a certain way and it seems pretentious and false to me, and I constantly want to break it up with absurdism. I absolutely loved Spike Jones—Clark Coolidge did too, by the way. Just a real breakup of the established modes with the most ridiculous, absurd goofery. Anything that broke up conventions was totally refreshing to me. Much harder, then, to break up my own conventions.

MD: Would you say you never really know a poet until you've written a collaborative poem with him or her?

JC: It's a great way to converse.

MD: Who have been some of your most successful collaborators?

JC: My own children. Reed Bye, Lyn Hejinian, Larry Fagin, classrooms of kids, many more. A buddy of mine here named Dan Hankin, who's not a poet, but a musician. He and I write collaborations all the time. All of this symbiosis resembles, uh, symbiosis, which is the hot revelation in biology. Lynn Margulis, a very precise relativist, Gaia proponent, champion of the mitochondria (the original "poets in the schools") is leading the way.

MD: So what have you been writing lately? What projects are you working on?

JC: Well, I'm cleaning my room and have been for weeks and I found this huge envelope containing a lot of very short poems. For years, off and on, I've enjoyed writing shorties, haiku, lunes, little senryu, teeny-weenies of all kinds, usually three-liners. Some have been published, but I have a vast collection. Part of it too was Ken and Ann Mikolowski's postcard project, which I did 600 cards for a few years back.

MD: 600?

JC: That's what they did. They would send you 600. Alice Notley did it twice,

I believe. So that activity involved marshalling a lot of short works into examination. Then I stuck it away and that was years ago. I do have a habit of being organized, to an extent, of sticking things into big brown envelopes with the words "Short Pieces" on them in big marker. I get into these jags of concentrated hacking away at something and that's what I've been doing, trying to mark the ones that might be possible now. I'm 71 years old and I say that because I think I'm coming to an ability to work with my own writings, better than I ever have before. Just a slight maturing of my editorial eye. In the mornings, I don't jump up and go out to work in the factory anymore, so I've been taking advantage of the ability to lie in bed and think about things and thinking about poems. I find it a wonderful place to just come to a very nuanced feeling about what you're going to do with the poem once you do get out of bed. So I'm really enjoying that and am able perhaps to make good decisions with pages and pages and pages of poems. Within the last two days I typed up fifty pages of short poems and then went through and chopped out some. So now of course, it's got to sit there. And brew. I think I've finally learned to shut up in my poems. On the other hand, of course . . .

ANNE WALDMAN TALKS POETRY INFRASTRUCTURE, SAFE "ZONES," AND OTHER VERSIONS OF THE WORLD

WITH MARCELLA DURAND

DECEMBER/JANUARY 2004   NO. 197

It's easy to think in times like these how much Anne Waldman is needed, particularly here in New York City, where the anxious and beleaguered poetic community has had to make do for the last several years with only occasional restorative visits. But our times are selfish—Waldman's work is too restless, inquisitive, and expansive to be confined to the frettings of one temporal moment. Yet how glad we are in New York to have her back with us—her untiring efforts to push language past the boundaries of oppression recenter us, erasing our doubts and hesitations, reminding us just how very much there is to do and that poetry is alive with the lights of possibility. *In the Room of Never Grieve: New and Selected Poems 1985–2003*, a massively gorgeous selection just out from Coffee House Press, includes new work from Waldman's ongoing epic, *Iovis*, which investigates the tropes of masculinity and war. She has also recently published *Dark Arcana/Afterimage or Glow*, a meditation on the aftereffects of the Vietnam War. Some of her current projects, that is, in addition to reinvigorating us worn-out New Yorkers, include coediting with Lisa Birman an anthology of poetics and activism, titled *Civil Disobediences*, and, with Ed Bowes, a collaborative film, *The Menage*, in honor of Carl Rakosi's 100th birthday. In early 2003, she cofounded the Poetry Is News Coalition with Ammiel Alcalay and was part of the Not In Our Name/ Poems Not Fit for the White House event at Lincoln Center, New York.

MARCELLA DURAND: You've been a major figure at The Poetry Project and a mentor to many poets at Naropa University. Now you're back in New York City, making a new life. How does it feel?

ANNE WALDMAN: It feels comfortable in many ways. But edgy too. New York is definitely the political and artistic "charnel ground" it always has been. Last fall and spring, I was caught up with a lot of political activity—as many of us were—that still permeates everything. It was like the '60s in some ways. Recently I sang my piece "Rogue State" at an anti-Ashcroft rally on Wall Street, SWAT team looking on. (Ashcroft was well hidden in the neighborhood on his Patriot Act promotional tour.) And certainly I have been following the work of younger writers for decades and many of the current "new"—aged 30-plus-some—generation have either gone through Naropa University or have been frequent teaching guests there—Brenda Coultas, Rachel Levitsky, yourself, Renee Gladman, Kristin Prevallet, Alan Gilbert, Anselm Berrigan, Lisa Jarnot, Elizabeth Willis, Bhanu Kapil Rider, Thalia Field, Akilah Oliver, Laird Hunt, and Eleni Sikelianos now of Boulder, kari edwards in San Francisco. These writers and others are all in the mental spectrum. But New York demands thinking about the way writers live here and the "culture" they make, and how they intersect with one another and the larger world and interact with other artistic and divergent communities. Do we want our poetry cultures locked in academies and universities? In MLA conventions and primarily white literary conferences? In safe havens alone? Granted, these institutions are supportive of writers, but there's a self-reflective solipsistic risk involved. I'm interested in writers outside the mainstream, meaning those who work beyond careerism and who have also been active as cultural workers—as journalists, editors, translators, performers, curators, or "infrastructure" poets, people who work in and for the community. Infrastructure could be interpreted as a pejorative term, but here it's used to describe the person who sees a need for structures and zones, "temporary autonomous zones," where folk have an opportunity to gather and create some kind of oppositional or counter-poetics community. That was the original vision for The Poetry Project and its "projective" space, which in the early days was working side by side with the Young Lords, the Black Panthers, the Motherfuckers, the Trotskyites. Nobody had any money to rent space and people "tithed" their time to benefit the groups they were affiliated with. The rent at St. Mark's is over the top now. Economics are harder now, but one can still tithe time. Ammiel Alcalay has suggested a Free University that maybe we can work on together, inviting scholars and writers and artists to teach short stints for free. And of course there's the community vision of the Summer Writing Program Kerouac School at Naropa, which co-administrative directors Lisa Birman, Max Regan, and assistant David Gardner—all wonderful writers and graduates of the MFA—are continuing to navigate. We create a unique poetics zone every summer. The transmission of infrastructure certainly exists at Naropa even though it costs real money to study there. The Wednesday night readings at St. Mark's are really about the work. There's not a lot of excess production involved. I appreciate that kind of austerity around the writing. I remember Edwin Denby saying that St. Mark's cultivated an exquisite ear for poetry. People learned how to LISTEN there. I went to a recent reading at the Tribeca Grand Hotel and here you are in this very chichi place, very modern, with this awful music wafting from the lobby. The wine is $14 a glass and not very good, and it's an insult in a way, although it's great to see friends and the work is solid. But it's as if the work is being co-opted—that it's just an accessory to the space.

MD: I'm interested in your idea of "zones" for poetry. Is there a way for New York to expand these zones?

AW: Probably. There are a lot of hidden (and possibly problematic) zones of course, which include homeless shelters, prisons, schools, outdoor spaces, community centers, or out-of-the-way libraries. There are a lot of writers working in those spaces already. Maybe the forms have to change a bit, go beyond the solo promotional reading. The modest bookstores or bars— the Zinc Bar (which also has expensive drinks!) or that lounge near the East River.

MD: The Parkside Lounge, where you read *Iovis*. Now, that was creating a very interesting zone—you had musicians performing in different places around the room.

AW: It felt both vast and intimate in sound and scope. Sam Hillmer was the musician/composer in charge. A Cage-like strategy allowed for improvisation—some of the musicians recited words and made sounds from live instruments and computers. Other readers included Elizabeth Reddin, the director of the series, my husband Ed Bowes, and Akilah Oliver. Grazia Della Terza danced during several sections. We only had time for one walkthrough prior to the performance. It took eight hours and we didn't even get through Book I of the poem. We created an ambient sound at times, but then distinct instruments would be programmed in, or certain decisions were made about holding back during particular sections of the poem. The art gallery scene should be totally liberated by poets. The current disjunct between the art scene and the poetry scene amazes me. In the past, there was more of a connection, more collaboration. It would have to come from the artists themselves, not the galleries. In terms of cultural activism, the galleries don't seem to be part of the same world. I'm talking mainly about upscale galleries with their "product," which can be deadly.

MD: I would suspect that things used to be different . . .

AW: The Paula Cooper Gallery used to do readings—the Stein and Cage readings. And to Paula's credit, Vincent Katz hosted a political event last spring there with Creeley, Ann Lauterbach, Michael Lally, and Ramsey Clark. But where is the ongoing commitment? Ted Greenwald did a terrific series at Holly Solomon years ago. I remember giving an early diaristic performance there with slides of South America. And there was Bernadette's celebrated *Memory* installation there, too. There was a sense of giving poets a kind of venue they don't normally have because they have nothing to sell. The new Cue Foundation/Gallery in Chelsea that has Bill Corbett on its board is planning some readings—that's a promising start. Ed [Bowes] teaches video and film at the School of Visual Arts, so I've been going to shows by his students, who are often very accomplished moviemakers. But where do you see this work outside its own circle? It's not necessarily scheduled as part of a film festival somewhere. There should be more arenas where you can look at something, have a discussion, include a literary reading or performance, like the salon Stan Brakhage used to host in Boulder. So, coming back to New York, and being an infrastructure poet for thirty-odd years, I naturally think about this stuff. Before Ammiel and I organized the Poetry Is News event [at The Poetry Project, February 1, 2003] and before the US invasion of Iraq, when we went to readings it was as if we were in a space that was not acknowledging what was going on "over there." People were too depressed or scared. Or there was compartmentalization at work—now we'll do our "antiwar" reading, next week it'll be something else. There was a serious disjunct. But that really changed very quickly. Somehow reclaiming the Parish Hall for that event felt very much like the times during the Viet Nam war when poets were speaking out, hosting major benefits, bringing information and news from the fronts. It was in the air as the war began, very palpably— the urgency of our human condition. It's not to say that the work was necessarily about the war—it was more the alertness, the concern, the urgency, and the attention to the details and exigencies of lives happening everywhere, the interconnectedness of it all. There's also New York City's rawness and vulnerability and its position as an international city—a people's city. That there could be a blackout that people survived and somewhat bonded during is heartening. You feel that this place has been tested and people have come through extraordinary trials and tribulations (even with all the corruption and police brutality). New York City is always able to transcend the catastrophic. It's a "holy city."

MD: I think of your work as creating a verbal space around you, a physical effort that pushes the boundaries between poetry and other mediums. So it's interesting to hear you talk about zones, spaces, and the political body. I wonder how that relates to the individual poet?

AW: Well, by claiming the space as an extension of your body, you're inviting the public into that sphere where you extend voice and body and mind. It's extremely physical and participatory. While performance may be somewhat exhibitionistic, it can also be generous, cathartic, and empowering; it's a transmission that goes both ways. The ground where you take your stand, the ground that you're on, I often invoke as "charnel ground," which I mentioned earlier. This is a Buddhist term that refers to the place where energies meet—life and death, moment to moment—and choices and risk. It's best for me when it's not all figured out or scripted, but the text, the words feel strong. So, more dependent upon where I am psychically and psychologically and physiologically in the moment, counting a lot on body and voice, mind's attention to the work and what the work is calling out of me—rage, gentleness, grief, love, wit, other states of mind, other voices. How it demands to be presented or heard. I use the term "modal structures" for what I do in performance. Sometimes it's sung, sometimes it's *sprechstimme* (spoken/sung), sometimes whispered. Maybe I have to lie or crouch down or move in circles. And then it's exciting to invite in some music or dance. I recently did a collaboration at the Omega Institute with musician Steve Gorn and dancer Douglas Dunn. I read from my book *Dark Arcana / Afterimage or Glow* at one point, which is writing from a trip to North Vietnam, but I was also "intervening" with it, expanding and recombining bits of things. Douglas had created a huge mortarboard hat out of cardboard that he could turn over and stick his face in. He played with that most elegantly and then he put a bandanna over his eyes and "conjured" a hostage, a victim, or soldier, as I knelt down close to his body, reading. While my writing has these voices and dynamics and thematic situations, it also in this context invites intervention. There's no one strategy that dominates the trajectory. When performing solo, I like to stretch my voice so it goes operatic on one end and then down to a low deep male bass—it just happens organically. I don't even know where it's going much of the time.

MD: Have you ever scored your voice?

AW: A couple of people have tried to score texts based on listening to tapes, but there seem to be too many variables in the way the work is presented. I like the musical arrangement, the soundscape. My son Ambrose Bye composed for the CD that accompanies my new book, *In the Room of Never Grieve*. He plays keyboard, but there are many other embellishments that he created to weave around my vocals. I would like the documentation to exist. It's also useful for the musicians I work with. Bethany Spiers now plays the mandolin for me on occasion and we are thinking about a CD project.

MD: I think you're one of the few poets who reaches out to non-Western traditions. We've lost touch with Asian cultures . . .

AW: And it's showing in this terrible rift with the Asian Muslim world, Indonesia being just one example. People forget that Indonesia is 90 percent Muslim. People do not know the difference between Hinduism, Islam and its diverse traditions, or the various kinds of Buddhism, not to mention Shinto, Jain, Newari, or Hinduism Bali-style. Indonesia is huge. India is huge and multicultural. We have ambassadors residing in other parts of the world who have no connection to the culture, who never even think of studying the language or reading a book about where they are or how to dress, how to conduct themselves. Do our ambassadors and attachés to France even speak French? I once went to a reception at the US ambassador to Nepal's residence. He was a Nixon appointee and liked to trek; that was about it. He had a very superior racist attitude concerning the beggars at his gate—no compassion. There's a pressure that the world be dominated by American culture, which includes, in the current myopia, American greed, paternalism, certain religious values. When Muslim practitioners are held captive here, there's incredible insult to their praxis, around dietary restrictions. The literary canon is heavily European dominated and so invested in a colonial view—the great Anglophone Empire. And the commentary from France—brilliant, elucidating, but what about the incredible subtleties of nonlinear form? The cosmological complexities of gamelan? I was always drawn to Asia, and I wanted to study with Buddhist teachers at the source. I also had such a strong fascination with ritual, shamanism, oral traditions. What is scary is the great capitalistic maw and the sense that other cultures will all be ultimately subsumed in it. Marxism is troubled in Asia and elsewhere. Late capitalism? Little hope there for respect for the "other."

MD: When I taught at Brooklyn College, I found that most of the students wanted to fit in. They wanted to read American texts, to be "American."

AW: My own name was originally Waldemann. I grew up in this neighborhood in [Greenwich] Village with Portuguese and Italian friends and they would be embarrassed about their names. But to go back to your question [about Asian culture], I'm preparing for the Lorine Niedecker conference [held in Milwaukee and Fort Atkinson, Wisconsin, on October 8th to 12th] and want to take my comments elsewhere, talk about the orality of her work, and the silence—that contradiction and irony—bring in some of Thoreau's and Cage's ideas. And also her deep sense of *pratitya-samutpada* (Sanskrit for interconnectedness) as an "ecologically" alert human being. What is the link between these more Buddhistic notions and this rational Objectivist (although that's disputed with her early and late work)? There's something attractive about the Spartan sincerity of the Objectivists—the "no frills" approach, the intellectual rigor forged from a deep commitment to socially progressive values. That has some resonance with Zen. But there's also something about Niedecker being "silenced" and repressed by Zukofsky— the fact that she had to destroy the whole correspondence from the '30s because of their romantic relationship, their entanglement. Again, the positioning of the woman versus the man. But then she's able to move into this spiritually "bigger mind" that holds contradictions and a magnificent sound in her later work. So look at the literal "gaps" there, the manuscripts that were lost, the letters that were destroyed, the editing, the serious elision in that relationship, which was the principal one, you could say. And there's a lot of sound at the same time in that absence, sound that plays in the poetry. She mentions her favorite texts: Marcus Aurelius, a book of Japanese haiku, and Thoreau. She works with the "heaven/earth/man" principle of haiku and I find also sympathy with the *ti bot* of Thai/Asian poetics, the striking of the gong or the word. The poems are runes that have to be activated. Koans you have to crack. They have to be unleashed, in a way, opened up by the imagination, whether you're reading them out loud or silently (her preference). So many have this erroneous idea of a passivity coming from the East, yet Eastern philosophy examines the minutiae of sense perception and mind to an extraordinary degree and describes these insights with clarity and depth, which is in itself, for me, a kind of poetics of engagement, activity, and liberation.

MD: Tell me about your new project.

AW: It's a long serial poem entitled "Structure of the World Compared to a Bubble," which is the title of a particular Buddhist sutra (or religious text). It started out from a pilgrimage I made in '96 to a specific site, the Borobudur stupa in Java, Indonesia. The stupa had been buried for hundreds of years under dense vegetation, although its fame existed in lore and legend. (It's now claimed as a national treasure.) As you climb the stupa, you circumambulate circular passageways that are carved with panels telling various stories and sutras. One is the Jakata Tales, which describes the former lives of the Buddha when he manifested in various animal guises. And there's another sutra where a pilgrim journeys into the phenomenal world and has a host of encounters with mythical creatures, with a rabbit, with a goddess of the night, with empty space, with a rock—where everything is a teacher. I love that idea of the picaresque voyage and the view that anything in your experience, wherever you are—here in 2003, New York City, MacDougal Street—is vibrant. The poem is a walking meditation on the phenomenal world. You move towards the top of the stupa and things become more abstract. You move into this realm of the boddhisattva path and then everything becomes even more vibrant. You ponder the Six Realms of Existence, the darkness of the Hell realm, the paranoia of the animal realm, and the sex and desire of the god realm. In Dante's *Paradiso*, somehow he's able to pull off through language an experience, a very abstract experience of light and love towards the top of the mount. There's the aspiration for some sort of parallel in language to the strong experience I had being there. Then, of course, the meditation is all over the map, so to speak, the references to the mundane, to my own reality, to the intersecting circles and cycles of history and mental discourse. It's very exploratory that way. We'll see. It's mostly in place, but still needs dramatic intervention. I also want to get the gamelan sounds, which were such an important aural landscape to my stays in Indonesia and part of my study there, into the poem. I attempt here, as elsewhere, to resist dominant forms, resist my own Western grasping and didacticism. I'm very grateful for the opportunities that I've had to travel to Asian *fellaheen* lands. Did you see the First Cities show at the Met? [*Art of the First Cities* at The Metropolitan Museum of Art through August 17, 2003] The translation of the legend of "Enmerkar and The Lord of Aratta" on a cuneiform tablet is interesting. It describes the rivalry between the cities Uruk and Aratta, which are both vying for the attentions of the goddess Inanna. The focus of the text, however, is the "cultural superiority of Sumerian civilization over the lands that provided its luxury goods by means of tribute and trade." The poem begins with a hymn to the city of Uruk, then quickly zeroes into the battle of wits between the cities' respective rulers.

This speech was long and difficult to
understand;
The messenger's mouth was too heavy
and he could not repeat it
because the messenger's mouth was too heavy
and he could not repeat it
The king of Kulaba formed some clay and
put words on it as if on a tablet.
Before that time the inscribing of words
on clay (tablets) did not exist;
But now, in the sun of that day, it was

indeed so established)—

the king of Kulaba had inscribed words as

if on a tablet, it was indeed so established)

The king of Aratta set a clay lamp

before the messenger

(in its light) the king of Aratta looked at

the clay (tablet)

the spoken words were but nails, and his

brow darkened

the king of Aratta kept staring into the

clay lump.

The rivalry between these cities is settled not by force, but by wit! At that time "the inscribing of words onto tablets did not exist . . . The spoken words were but nails." This is a great story! The beginning of written language! If we could only fight our battles with wits and wills—create a new language and write some lasting treaties!

MD: This is good to hear—I had been a little bit depressed after that show, seeing all the warlike images. I thought, all humanity does is fight!

AW: I love the staring into a lump of clay. It's a little bit like how we were made.

MD: Having language pressed into you. Speaking of language and experience, you've been part of many different literary movements . . .

AW: I did want to say something first about how *Dark Arcana* was also a pilgrimage, and a way to look at that war that was so much a part of our history [the Vietnam War]. But there was also a sense of going in obeisance. A sense of homage, of bowing, of trying to transform the horrible suffering—or acknowledge its gravity as an American. I didn't even think of it as a poem at the time, it was a list of questions. Now it's part of *The Eternal War*, the last book of *Iovis*.

MD: There were some things in there that really struck me, like that [the Vietnam War] was not called a "war." Like that the "war" in Iraq has been declared over.

AW: Oh, the euphemisms ... We're not in The War now, but we're in the middle of what is in a way the REAL war—the war of psyches—and it's a guerilla war.

MD: In *Dark Arcana*, you write that we hadn't protested "enough." Today it seems like the '60s were the ultimate protest. And my generation maybe feels, well, look how much you did, and it still wasn't enough ...

AW: In a way it's never enough, but you have to keep the struggle going. I wonder about the staying power of the young people now involved, spearheading the environmental and antiwar movements. There are still some veterans, but there's a gap. It's as if some people were sleepwalking through a generation and got lost—where are they? It's interesting to go over [to Vietnam] to see these elderly survivors—they didn't fight because they were parents and grandparents. So many millions of people died who would be my age now ... You really notice that because you see very old people and very young people. And then thinking, you're a psychological survivor of that war in a way.

MD: The Vietnam War wasn't the first time a war was protested, nor the last. Supposedly, the protests stopped because there was no longer a war. But it doesn't matter what they call it.

AW: There's a lot going on, everywhere I travel. Your question about what more could we have done—it had to do with being less naive at that time and being able to really see back in time—cause and effect—and see larger forces and scenarios at work. What's really behind all our sword rattling now? Isn't China the real perceived enemy to US hegemony? So all the moves being made now are related to that bigger picture.

MD: While reading *In the Room of Never Grieve*, I saw various influences during different periods of your work. Are there any particular "tools" you've made your own?

AW: Some of the performative strategies, the look and feel of the *Iovis* sections, the play with gender, genre, other voices, story, the sentence (particularly in *Marriage: A Sentence*), rhizomic moves of all kinds, documentary and investigative poetics based on personal research, travel. Asia, Buddhism, Tantrism, shamanism. Feminist praxis, political concerns. Self-imposed experiments and attention to the smallest increments of speech, breaking it down, but with a lot of emotion. I've always been interested in the relationships in gender dynamics, the tensions there.

MD: Speaking of interviewing people on the "other side," *Iovis* really delves into this territory that is so forbidden to women . . .

AW: I had to look at my own energy, which corresponds to the karma family energy in Buddhism that craves leadership, wants to monitor the battalions, lead the troops. There is something in my specific conglomeration of tendencies that needs to be engaged with "skillful means" or *upaya*. Be on the move, make things happen. Go to battle for the imagination. Transmute the war energy into something equally as powerful—compassion? I was insulted that the epic is primarily seen as a male form. There are female epics, H. D.'s *Trilogy*, or Alice Notley's *The Descent of Alette*. Ambrose made a comment [about *Iovis III*], saying, what, another book called *Iovis*? Can't you think of another title? So it's subtitled *The Eternal War*. Ambrose is the secret Virgil of the poem and if he's not going to be a part of it, I'm lost. I need to have a young male voice countering the hag. There's so much of this dual-gender energy in it. The events of all our consociational time are in there, organically, atmospherically. I can't give up this investigation just yet.

MD: That question is so unexplored—why do we go to war? It's such a norm.

AW: Why? It's the fallacy of our mental projection. Suicidal death wish? We are actually killing ourselves in this current mess. We think we have to kill the "other" to be who we are, to have power. And we are killing so much else—the planet, its other nonhuman denizens. An empire wanting to shape the world in its own image. I couldn't believe that Wesley Clark, in a recent *New York Review of Books*, gave an assessment using all this strategic language of why the war failed. The whole premise should be questioned from the start! Who is doing that? Where are the wise leaders? And, of course, as Patti Smith aptly sings, "people have the power." The vitality of the "warring god realm" has very much to do with paranoia and incredible aggressive intelligence, an intelligence that *needs* somewhere else to go. It's not only about gender—war has some interesting passive support from women. What is going on? We're under a blinding habitual pattern of destiny that we just cannot see our way out of. It's just one fucking version of the world. It does *not* have to be this version.

EDWIN TORRES TALKS INTERACTIVE ECLECTICISM, BANANA PEELS, AND WALKING IN YOUR CALLING

WITH MARCELLA DURAND

FEBRUARY/MARCH 2004   NO. 198

Out of the mists of confusion, nonsense, and non sequiturs, comes the figure of the Poet, i.e., as in Interactive Eclecticism, Edwin Torres. Gargoylesque, in that he hurls nonsense back at nonsense in order to make sense, he talks into himself the multiplicity of words, activating each one before he delivers them back to us, creating buzzing wires of interaction and possibility. Torres is one of the most challenging poet-performers around, always inspiring in his unwillingness to rest with the "given." He is also one of the very few poets who moves across the various cliques, factions, and schools of the NYC poetry scene—from the Nuyorican Poets Café, where he "began" as one of their top Slam Poets, to the Poetry Project, to Roof Books, he transverses false boundaries to offer something new to everyone, while remaining himself in full veracity and integrity. He is the author of *Fractured Humorous* (Subpress); *Onomalingua: noise songs & poetry*; and *The All-Union Day of the Shock Worker* (Roof Books) as well as the CDs *Holy Kid*, which was part of the Whitney Museum's exhibit, *The American Century Pt. II*; *Please* (Faux Press); and *Novo* (Oozebap Records). This year through Composer's Collaborative, he worked with composer Akemi Naito on "The Liminal Skin," a suite of poems with music by The Nurse Kaya String Quartet. The same text was used by sculptor Nancy Cohen in their collaboration, *Mute Thunder*, for an exhibition at The Hunterdon Museum of Art.

MARCELLA DURAND: The School of Yelling?

EDWIN TORRES: The School of Yelling. There's this French theater director, Enrique Pardo, who teaches a workshop on choreographic theater. In one of his workshops he says, "Then there's also this manner, what is ugly," where as a performer you have to know there are all these things that are not schooled, that have this feral kind of energy. That's ugly sometimes and that's where the School of Yelling comes in. What are the highs and lows of the possibilities? How far can I go with this? You need an audience for that.

MD: To tell you when you've gone too far?

ET: In the good old days of Bauhaus, it was "Shut up! Get off!" Now people are too kind.

MD: You're one of the rare figures at the Poetry Project who also participated in Poetry Slams at the Nuyorican Poets Café . . .

ET: It's kind of a dubious distinction, like, "Oh yeah, you used to be a Slam Poet." People are quick to place you in a certain setting. And then there's my last name. The last year or so, I've had to come to grips with what my last name has made me become as a writer. My heritage is not really what I write about, but it does enter my writing in obvious ways, so I've been feeling a little more responsible. I need to address that I represent a certain kind of people.

MD: Who are you representing to?

ET: I wrote a long time ago that "my people roam the open field," and that hasn't changed. I write for people who are open to experience and different ways of perceiving things. That's why I gravitate towards the experimental. I feel a need to address—as opposed to "my people," who might be Puerto Rican people or Spanish people—the "other," the sense of not fitting in, which I can hold onto a little better, because it speaks to more people. It speaks to me.

MD: You have that one poem about how you don't quite fit in, "I Wanted To Say Hello To The Salseros But My Hair Was A Mess."

ET: I've always felt that somewhat, not fitting in. I think every poet feels that—

we all have "messy hair." The poem is about going to a Spanish festival in Columbus, Ohio. The next morning I shared a van with a salsa band back to the airport. [They were] these older men wearing typical macho jewelry and clothing and wisecracking jokes. I just felt so out of place. I wanted to be there, but I was embarrassed for being who I was. I didn't fit in, but I liked these people. They're full of life and so am I. It's just a different perception of what life is.

MD: I'm intrigued with how you got into the Slam scene, then became interested in the Russian Futurists, then performed at the Kitchen, these other worlds. How you made these jumps, found these doors . . .

ET: Well, there are so many avenues in New York City, so many places to try stuff out. I got into performance first at Dixon Place in '88. I was fed up with monologues and performance art at the time and I thought, oh, I can do that too. Plus I lived in squalor. I lived in a little studio apartment and I didn't throw anything away for years. I was one of those people. My floor was a few feet off the ground.

MD: What did you collect?

ET: Newspapers, clothing. I did throw food away, although a year before I left, Liz [Elizabeth Castagna] found a banana peel. I lived in this situation that was totally claustrophobic and it was like a womb. Everything I wanted was there. It was my playground. It was the world that I was in. In hindsight, I realize it fueled a lot of my writing. That the sense of holding onto things and the tangents I love so much in poetry come from this idea of collecting and holding on and seeing if it will work. This hodgepodge mentality.

MD: I can see that—your work is very unpredictable, like, where did he just find that word?

ET: When I was an amoeba, I saved every little molecule and it became me. *I am my own me.* So I'm living in this squalor and conquering the world with graphic design. I would cut type apart, make it do weird shapes—playing with the page was really satisfying to me. I would write little notes and over time the notes became kind of poems—I didn't call them poems, they were just word-things. So then fast-forward a few years . . . I invented an art movement called Interactive Eclecticism, or I.E. This was before interactive was a catchphrase. I did these I.E. shows for about a year. They became popular, had music and involved the audience. I.E. needed a mantra and the mantra was the audience. There was this one I.E. ritual where one side of the audience got one tape recorder and the other got another. One tape had snoring and the other had Gregorian chanting. One is sleeping and one is revelatory. I was mocking religion left and right. I realize now that it came out of a search for belief, to realize what it is we all believe in. There's this courtship that happens with God and religion that's fascinating to me, this need for us to believe in something outside of ourselves. Plus my family is fundamentalist Pentecostal.

MD: Were you raised Pentecostal?

ET: No, Catholic. They converted about twenty years ago.

MD: What a mix!

ET: *Guilt.* A Pentecostal pastor doesn't wear a robe like I was used to, he wears a normal suit. It's more direct and honest to me. It's clear. Nothing gets in the way. It's just *the book* and the people. And I respect that—I have problems with it, I couldn't live by just one book, but I can respect their dedication. I.E. came about through this search, although I never considered it as religion. It was only years later when I realized the rebellion that fueled this idea of the shaman, of what words can do. I felt very gratified being up on stage with people watching me, my congregation. I have all this writing that I did before writing poetry. It's innocent, bad writing, but it was rooted in sincerity. It dealt with the theater as a body and that both of us are in this body together. I had these profound things and didn't quite have the language for it. So then this one woman came to me, after I was having a modicum of success downtown, her last name was Torres. She said, "I've been looking for you. You know, you have a responsibility." I was like, "Oh yeah?" I was pleasing her, just listening to her. What's the phrase? Appeasing her.

MD: Playing along.

ET: Yeah, playing along. She said, "People are coming to you, you should do something for *your* people." I was like, whoa! Heavy. I don't want to hear that. Get out of here! So of course that stuck. I was doing this I.E. thing from a place of process. When you do something without an end in mind, there are mostly questions. At the same time, you've got to have some kind of solution, some sort of end in mind, even if that ending is to continue. I'm not interested in telling you what the answer is, because you'll have a different one anyway, which will change my perception. And that's partly a Gemini thing, where I don't want to tell you everything because I want to see the options. There's a certain diplomacy there that I embrace and is part of what I'm about. So then a week or so after meeting with the female Torres, I noticed there was a reading by three poets from the Nuyorican Poets Café put on by Poets House: Miguel Algarín, Bimbo Rivas and Jorge Brandon. Jorge Brandon was this 90-year-old poet who invented, if not perfected, decimas, which are 10-line poems with a certain rhyme scheme. I went to this reading, not knowing what to expect. What's this poetry stuff, you know? Jorge Brandon is this frail old man, huge bowler hat on, orange duct tape taped around him. Miguel is on one side and Bimbo's on the other— they're joking and carrying around like it's the funniest thing in the world. Miguel and Bimbo go into this song, "We got into the cab and Jorge found this tape on the street from a construction site and he just put it on himself and here he is." And I'm like, man, this is nuts. This is poetry? Miguel reads his great words with this beautiful voice and Bimbo was all heart. And Jorge, this frail little guy, had this incredibly deep, sonorous voice. He'd been doing this all his life and you could tell. Right there I got a lineage. I got a sense of place and history. So I went to the open mic at the Café a week later and it began from there.

MD: Had you read or written poetry seriously before then?

ET: Just my text-things for I.E. performances. Very first thing ever. So I went to the open mic, I was on the verge of a relationship—I just met the girl but already there were problems. So I wrote about her. All this love poetry came out. After a few years, I broke up with her—there are a lot of poems that came from that confusion.

MD: This was right off the bat? You're introduced to poetry and—

ET: We had three breakups and this was right when I was doing I.E. and performing. I would use some of the ideas in performance. She said, you don't always have to use me in your performances. As she's pouring her heart out, I'm writing it down . . .

MD: A true writer.

ET: A true writer and a real idiot. The breakup guy who just writes everything down and makes it into performance. So going back, my interaction with the audience stemmed from I.E. and what it meant that there's a performer on stage and people are listening. It's about the ego, you know, but it's something else too. Why get up there and be heard? My older sister put it beautifully: "Edwin, you're walking in your calling," which may come from Pentecostal ideology, but it's true. I realized that we, as poets, are part of this path. Otherwise, we'd keep our words in our journals. What is it that wants to be heard? What's important enough to share with the world? It's a huge responsibility, but it's also dangerous, because you can get carried away with that kind of power. That self-belief can negate the world around you.

MD: I've seen you do performances where you completely negate that presence. One time at Tonic, I knew you were performing but only heard a disembodied voice. It took me twenty minutes to find you, crouching in a corner, whispering into a microphone.

ET: For about thirteen years, I've been collaborating with this amazing drummer, Sean G. Meehan. As an improviser he becomes invisible to his instrument. Approaching sound as if you're a vessel, channeling what's happening around you through your instrument, you know? In the last few years, he's been working with a snare drum—as opposed to the full drum kit—which is incredibly restrictive, but it's opened up other avenues for him, where he's being incredibly creative with just the snare. It becomes as much an orchestra as a full drum kit. With that in mind, I thought, what can I do where it's not always Edwin?

MD: You seemed deliberately to decenter yourself.

ET: Do you know Stuart Sherman? He does these performances where he has a suitcase with all these props in it. In one hour, he'll do twenty different things. Rarely talks. He takes out Kraft cheese slices and a hole puncher, punches holes in them until he's got ten slices punched, puts a lid on them, reaches in and pulls out a little suit jacket made of Kraft cheese slices with holes in it. And that's it, that's his joke. Then he puts it away and prepares for the next one, so performer becomes stagehand. I loved that because what that did was give the audience some breathing room. As an audience, I can now not watch you as a performer, but watch you prepare for the next thing. It's a Cage thing, where you present your work, then let it go, unfinished, and the audience receives it. In the performance at Tonic, I wanted to let the sounds grow on their own, so I crouched down and that's when you walked in. The scenario dictates what happens. In "Ball," which was a fuller theatrical production [at the Kitchen], there's still a sense of disappearing there, but definitely a sense of being in the center of everything. That's a theatrical dynamic. How do you take this spatial dimension and bring it into poetry? How do you expand the words, the page into this other realm?

MD: Well, "Gecko Suite" [at the Kitchen] was about disruption. In these huge spaces, you'd be reading and then Gina Bonati singing.

ET: There's a huge amount of space at the Kitchen, almost too much space. We felt like a little league team playing in Yankee Stadium. By not presenting something totally polished, the audience tends to jump in and complete it. But it's raw. And in that rawness is where dialogue happens. The audience has to figure things out. It's chancy to do that—people say, well, if you added this and this and this, it would've been more finished. People will always put in what they need. But the staging was also dictated by the text. It may be nonlinear, but I see a flow, a story being told. What happens with color, with lighting, with space that can help the dramatic situation evolve?

And then this year, I did these two collaborations using the same text, which was another way to decentralize. I worked with a composer, Akemi Naito, and wrote a suite of poems based on her music. She then wrote new music for the poems to be played by a string quartet [The Nurse Kaya String Quartet]. Then the sculptor Nancy Cohen, with whom I'd collaborated before, wanted to work on a new collaboration at around the same time. I thought it'd be interesting to see how this same text would evolve when used in another medium, so that's what I sent her. She created four arches, fitting into the poem's compass-point sections.

MD: Tell me about how you put together your book, *The All-Union Day of the Shock Worker* (Roof, 2001).

ET: Well, I chose poems meant to be read out loud, with Roof in mind. I knew there was something worthwhile in the work, although I hadn't put it on the page properly, and now I had this chance. I had been impressed by a book of László Moholy-Nagy's, an oversized chapbook limited-edition thing, letterpress, with these graphics designed into the words. It was Dutch translated into German, so I couldn't understand it, but it was beautifully designed, using simple type cases, little symbols mixed in with words, restraint and space on each page. The book read like a musical score and I wanted to design these new poems that way. I kept myself to circles and triangles, keeping in mind the idea of an old metal foundry, which dealt with size and indents as much as with text and form. The design's restriction was what opened my brain.

MD: So, just to get a little more biographical background, you curated the Monday Night Series at the Poetry Project . . .

ET: In 1991, Wanda Phipps was curating the series and she saw me at the Knitting Factory, so she asked me to do a Monday Night. I remember what a great night it was for me: I did a film projection, worked with two musicians. I also had three tape recorders telling an I.E. joke at the same time, I'm there behind them drinking water. Every once in a while I say the punchline and keep drinking water. A year after that, Ed Friedman asked me to teach a workshop, I said no thanks. Then a year later, he asked again. He wanted something that wasn't the normal Poetry Project thing in there. So I took a chance. I had one person sign up that first year.

MD: Harsh.

ET: About two weeks before the class, no one else had signed up. I said, Ed, we can just cancel it. He said, no, no, no. So, thank you Ed Friedman. For ten weeks, I figured out different assignments. We did a great year-end Poetry-Kabuki performance at Thread Waxing Space. Ed asked me to come back the next year and I had ten people, the year after I had more. Through Frank, my one student, the transition into teaching was seamless. With one person I felt I could take my time and make mistakes. Frank would be at one end of the room, I'd be at the other, each of us with tape recorders. I'd say, GO, and we would walk towards each other while talking into them. Then we'd rewind and play the tape at the same time and write what we thought we heard.

MD: Do you keep in touch?

ET: No. I think a few years afterwards I saw him and he was wearing a top hat and a cape, coming from a magic show. At the workshop reading, he said, I don't want to do poetry, I want to do a magic show. Not sure if my class pushed him in that direction, but born of the seed of the Poetry Project is magic!

MD: So who are some poets you go back to time and time again?

ET: Khlebnikov, for sure. Paul Celan is a real influence. Creeley. Octavio Paz is a big one. But I have a very porous brain and what I call a convenient lack of memory, which means I can keep doing something over and over and forget that I've done it. You stay young forever that way.

MD: How about bilingualism?

ET: Bilingualismo.

MD: I think a lot about scansion and how speaking another language affects that.

ET: Growing up in a bilingual family you definitely pay more attention to sound and the moment between words and what their meaning is supposed to be, how something is said, why it means that and not this. More cultures get fused into more poetries as the world gets smaller. But then culture becomes homogenized. It's interesting this idea of what your culture is supposed to represent. We all are who we are, and we're made of what made us here.

MD: You mentioned sincerity way back, and I'd like to talk about that a little more. In your work there's a kind of urgency, a sense that we're not just playing games for the sake of games.

ET: When I would travel with a group and perform my complicated language stuff, and other poets would perform their more accessible stuff, people would bypass me and go to the other performers. In the beginning, I was like, oh damn, why don't you come to me. But I realized it wasn't meant to be for everybody. You have to believe what you're saying, because you're presenting this world that's different. If you believe in it, somebody out there will believe it with you, and that's where the sincerity comes from.

MD: Is that how you see poetry as revolutionary?

ET: There's an economy of language in poetry that allows interpretation. We're being told something, but we're given the respect, the chance, and the trust to interpret it in our own ways. The poet knows that what they're sharing is for us to consume, for us to make what we want of it—our stories grow that much bigger. I did a reading with Yusef Komunyakaa at a university in São Paolo this October. Someone asked us, how does it feel coming to South America, representing America? So we answered that the poet is a citizen of the world—our nationality is poetry. Poets from all over the world are one. That's a very spiritual thing, but what do you do with it? As a poet, what do you do with this incredible honor you've been given?

MD: It's rather embarrassing to talk about spirituality . . .

ET: In poetry especially, the idea of poetry as a religion. The converts show up to hear the speaker [and] there are social implications in this. It's very heavy to get into and I don't have an answer, but it's an interesting layer—the audience gathered to hear *the word*. Although *spirituality* is a different spectrum than religion. The aura that you project is you. Then there's a God somewhere and is that God shining through you or not?

MD: Experimental poetry is so much about mystery and what's more mysterious than the divine?

ET: What's more experimental than the divine?

MD: Experimental poetry!

ET: At St. Mark's Church!

HARRY MATHEWS REVEALS THE <u>INSIDE STORY</u>
TO MARCELLA DURAND

APRIL/MAY 2004   NO. 199

It has been known to be said a few times in the dark corners of the literary world that writers of fiction and writers of poetry don't always see eye to eye. While we're not sure if these differences have ever driven the two to *West Side Story*–like rumbles, the chasm between them has only been crossed by a few singular writers. One such intrepid soul is Harry Mathews, whom, if every poet has not read, then every poet should read immediately after reading this interview. In his utterly un-put-downable books, a single word may appear to carry the entire intricate weight of the novel (think of the word "Tlooth" in *Tlooth*) and below the ostensible "plot" are a thousand other plots, moving through chapters like underground rivers filled with ornate stalagmites and secret veins of ores. In Mathews's works the pleasure of wondering what it all means is infinitely more pleasurable than actually knowing what it all means. Mathews, the sole American member of Oulipo (the *Ouvroir de Littérature POtentielle*/Workshop for Potential Literature), has recently published a book of essays, *The Case of the Persevering Maltese*, and a book of stories, *The Human Country: New and Collected Stories* (both from Dalkey Archive). His novels include *Tlooth*, *The Conversions*, *Cigarettes*, and *The Journalist*, while his books of poetry include *Armenian Papers: Poems 1954–1984* and *Selected Declarations of Dependence*.

HARRY MATHEWS: I have to tell you that I'm very skeptical about the value of writers talking about writing.

MARCELLA DURAND: Why?

HM: I've listened to so many who would've done better staying home and writing. Including me.

MD: One thing that's interesting about interviews with writers is hearing what they're reading, since most read independent of schools or assignments . . .

HM: True enough. Obviously some interviews are worthwhile. It's panel discussions that really get me down.

MD: You've said that the *Locus Solus* group was one of the most important literary environments in your early history.

HM: Absolutely. In the late '50s I was an innocent—I knew practically no one who was an active writer and my own age. At the age of 23 I'd started writing poetry again (my passion all through adolescence, but it had died at college), thanks to my wife Niki de Saint Phalle, who'd just given up an acting career for painting. Her example inspired me, and I never looked back. But only after I met John Ashbery in Paris in 1956 did I feel connected. John had a fantastic effect on me—not only through his work, but through his attitude towards writing, one that I'd never imagined.

MD: How did you meet him?

HM: Through a mutual friend, Walter Auerbach, whom we'd met in Mallorca. He'd known John and his friends in New York. In the spring of '56 John was in France on a Fulbright, and one afternoon at a café on the Luxembourg Gardens, Walter arranged a meeting. Friendship ensued at once.

MD: Did John ever give you specific advice about writing poetry?

HM: You know how he is—he never talks seriously about poetry. He'd rather be allusive and elusive and witty about it. When we met, he told me about French poets that I might be interested in reading.

MD: Who were some of those poets?

HM: Wait. What's more interesting is that I didn't read them right away (I have read them all since). Just by telling me about them, John somehow managed to cut me loose. Before that, my knowledge of contemporary poetry was very much what I read in *Poetry* magazine.

MD: Dreadful.

HM: No, not dreadful. The '50s were the time of rather precious, well-fashioned personal lyrics. I thought that was the way poetry was supposed to be. My only other inspirations were Pound and Eliot (I didn't much take to Auden or, for some reason, Wallace Stevens). I had discovered Laura Riding—in Mallorca I'd become friends with Robert Graves and gotten interested in his life. However, even reading Laura Riding hadn't lifted me out of my self-imposed rut. I realized in talking to John—I don't know how he communicated it to me, but he did: there's no rule about the way poetry should be. He never *said* that, but he let me know I could do anything I wanted. Three weeks after I first met him, I gave him a new poem of mine, he liked it, and he said, I see you've been reading the French poets we talked about, but I hadn't. It was enough for him to tell me about them to somehow have their influence exercise itself on me. It was as though I'd been invited to join a new family, one where I belonged. I do believe that you can be influenced by writers without reading them.

MD: How?

HM: I've always felt Hawthorne's *Twice-Told Tales* influenced me and I've never read one of them. I think that when you're told what a writer is doing, you think, well, that sounds good, maybe I can try that, and then you do something not unlike that author.

MD: Who are some other authors whom you've never read and whom you're influenced by?

HM: Borges, certainly, before I read him. I heard about him while I was writing my first novel, *The Conversions*. I carefully avoided reading him then because what he'd done sounded similar to what I was trying to do and, if he was as good as people said, reading him might stop me doing what I wanted to do.

MD: I haven't seen Borges mentioned in any of your previous interviews.

HM: After I'd read him he didn't influence me at all, although I became an avid fan. It was also reassuring to know that someone was working in a genre of fiction so different from what I'd known. The *New Yorker* was held up as a model of fiction then—I'd tried that way of writing and just couldn't do it.

MD: The first time I discovered your work was *Selected Declarations of Dependence*, so I initially thought of you as a poet. You've talked about how you composed *Tlooth* and it seemed to me the way someone would talk about composing a poem.

HM: You're right. I've always thought of myself as a poet and my ambition in fiction was to write fiction that was organized the way poetry is. Not to write poetic prose or a novel with a poetic texture, but work where fiction doesn't originate in the illusion that we're reproducing some other reality.

MD: Do you feel more comfortable with a project, such as the perverbs?

HM: It certainly makes it easier to produce a work of some length, although in the case of *Armenian Papers*, there wasn't a structure at all. (It started as poetry-poems and not prose-poems. Later on I rearranged the lines into paragraphs.) I'd decided to do what Browning did—write a poem a day, and for about ten days I kept that up. The first poem appeared out of nowhere and I found myself inside another civilization. There was no formal prescription, other than keeping each item to about the same length. With the story in *Declarations*, I limited myself to the vocabulary of the 44 proverbs on which the book is based: a daunting constraint. I had to try putting the words together in different ways, and a love story emerged.

MD: Do you revise your poetry?

HM: I do lots of rewriting in prose, much less in poetry. I suppose I'm scared of destroying the element of surprise—that is to say, what surprised me in writing the poetry. In prose I at least think I know the effect I want to get. I'm much more of a pro in prose than in poetry. I tell myself I write poetry for fun. Often I don't know whether a poem is good or not, but I don't want to screw up the life in it by trying to make it better.

MD: What surprises you in a poem?

HM: It seems to me that in poetry the paradoxical relationship of written language to what it is claiming to say becomes very intense. Even the relations between words themselves achieve a level of dislocation, of disjunction which prose can only equal at exceptional moments. One poem I wrote is called "Condo Auction," a long, seemingly obscure poem. I thought, OK, this is the way it is and who knows? With time it may achieve some kind of coherence, and I think it ultimately did. Similarly, there's a group of stories I wrote about the same time (published as *The American Experience*) which were generated by a "poetic" procedure of alternating different rhetorical tropes, always with a particular object in mind but without much concern for their immediate coherence. In my recent collection of stories I called them "Stories To Be Read Out Loud" because most readers seemed unable to get these stories—except when I read them in public. At readings, nobody has any problems with them. When they're read silently—we all tend to read too fast—confusion apparently sets in.

MD: In your essay, "To Prizewinners," you take a section of Kafka's story on Don Quixote, and you rewrite it using the same rhythms and sentence constructions. It seems that there is some essence that has to do with sound . . .

HM: It's not exactly sound. In that essay, I call it "syntax," extending the meaning of the word beyond the relationship between words in a sentence to the relationship between sentences in a paragraph or between paragraphs in a chapter. I claim syntax is where the meaning of a written work essentially lies. In other words, you can write about one thing and mean something else. Rewriting the Kafka piece was intended to demonstrate that meaning and nominal subject matter are not one and the same. In this sense, poetry and the kind of prose that Kafka writes are not that far apart. That's the sort of prose I've always aspired to.

MD: Could you explain "syntax" a little more?

HM: In poetry we're often moved or interested by what isn't there, what we're not told about. I think that is true in fiction, too, but less obviously than in poetry. An example I often give is the Blake poem that begins "O Rose thou art sick!" There have been many interpretations of it, and none of them suffice. The poem grips us and we don't know what it's about. Clearly something is happening, and it affects us in spite of the ignorance we're left in.

MD: What if you end up with too little? What if there's not enough material for the reader to assemble?

HM: I don't think it's a question of the material. The sound or rather the musical elements are what matter. The syntax of the famous Tyger poem for instance is concentrated in its tightly written quatrains and very bright rhymes; that's what makes it work. A prose paraphrase would not work at all—it would literally leave out the meaning. That's why I'm fascinated by Mallarmé. If you haven't read Mallarmé in French, find an edition of his poems in French with plain, literal prose translations. That's what you want. They'll provide a solid point of departure. They certainly won't make the poems any clearer to you—they're not meant to be clear. Mallarmé would start with a scene, a woman stretched out on a sofa in front of a fire, let's say. Then in successive versions he leaves the scene farther and farther behind until he reaches a point where the poem is so removed from the original image that it's impossible to reconstruct it. Nevertheless, it's still there, operating, even though we don't know it's there, or we can't explain that it's there, or how it's there. Whatever element of non-literary reality the poem began with has been put through a series of distillations to produce an elixir that is in itself delicious and evocative and can suggest many more things than what gave the poem its start, just the way Blake's poems do. Such poetry aspires to the abstraction that music has.

MD: One school of poetry seems to be trying to corral words into a representation of reality—as a stand-in. Then the other school has the unexpected happening even within a supposed narrative. At some point, the language or mystery takes over. Surprise!

HM: Maybe it's surprise, but not only that—let me read you something, something I quote on every possible occasion. It's from an essay by Robert Louis Stevenson called "A Humble Remonstrance." In it he says: "The novel, which is a work of art, exists, not by its resemblances to life, which are forced and material, as a shoe must still consist of leather, but by its immeasurable difference from life, which is designed and significant, and is both the method and the meaning of the work." He was saying that about fiction, but it's certainly true about poetry. People can't accept this; they want literature to be about something other than itself. And people will go on trying to prove that it is, until the last mad cow has come home.

MD: How do you feel about readers?

HM: That's what I am. As Laura Riding says, "Writing reading isn't all that different from reading writing." In that essay you mentioned, I say the responsibility of the writer is to make the reader the creator by providing the materials and impulse for creation. Some people find this simplistic, but I think that even if it's not the only thing that can be said to happen, it's certainly part of what happens, because who else is present but the reader when reading takes place? The reader's voice is the only living voice around.

MD: They're responsible for the final version anyway.

HM: *Their* final version, at any rate. If the reader can be involved by the poem so that he is actually right there, word after word after word, it's almost as though he were making it up himself. Once you give up the traditional scheme of the poem as having to begin someplace and end someplace else, your interpretation of the poem will become one where the meaning is to be found at every point in every line as you move through it.

MD: One thing about fiction, say, Jane Austen—here's the plot, the riddle, and it's what you follow through everything.

HM: To me, *Persuasion* is the epitome of that. You know from the first page what's going to happen, but you nevertheless get incredibly excited and anxious for this virtually stated conclusion to be worked out.

MD: Did you see the film?

HM: I *never* watch movies of books I like. I'd have to give up being a creator-reader. When you read a book, even the most realistic one, there's a limited amount of detail that can be provided. In Jane Austen's work, there's very little detail, which means that sentence after sentence you are creating the furniture in the room, the clothes people are wearing, the way they talk, the way they look. When you see a movie, all that has been done for you.

MD: I hear you have a new book in the works, something about the CIA. I was told to ask you if you were in the CIA.

HM: You have to read the book to find out. It's called *My Life in CIA: A Chronicle of 1973* [forthcoming from Dalkey Archive Press, May 2005]. Every American male abroad at that time was thought to be a CIA agent and my own reputation got consolidated by my being on a list compiled by French counterintelligence. The book is about my response to this.

MD: Did you find out why your name was on that list?

HM: Yes, I did.

MD: And . . . ?

HM: You have to have some reason for reading the book.

MD: How much did you research the CIA?

HM: I did, lots. If you're at all interested, there's an absolutely fabulous book . . .

MD: I am. The Poetry Project community is fascinated by the CIA.

HM: It came out last year. It's by Milt Bearden and James Risen, *The Main Enemy: The Inside Story of the CIA's Final Showdown with the KGB*. Risen reports on intelligence and counterintelligence for the *New York Times*, Bearden was high up in the CIA. An ideal collaboration and a very informative read.

MD: How would you characterize your reading now? Do you vacillate between high and low reading?

HM: Mainly, I have to read books of writer friends—no, I take that back. It's very irregular. The lowest reading I manage is Patrick O'Brian, whom I admire as well as thrill to.

MD: I guess you didn't see *Master and Commander*.

HM: I wouldn't think of it. Most of the fiction I've been reading is fairly recent and that's not just because I know the authors. Do you want to hear what I read in 2003?

MD: Sure.

HM: A couple of books by Sybil Bedford, one of the best writers of the twentieth century. I think she's still alive, drinking away happily somewhere in southern England. A biography of Jacques Tati, by David Bellos, the man who wrote the biography of Georges Perec. A couple of books by Robert Coover, *The Grand Hotels (of Joseph Cornell)* and *The Adventures of Lucky Pierre*. Ben Marcus's second novel, *Notable American Women* (terrific). I read a very interesting book (edited by Laurie Bauer and Peter Trudgill) called *Language Myths*. A gigantic tome devoted to *Some Like It Hot*, with the complete screenplay, corrected typescript, lots of anecdotes and so forth. My wife put me onto an excellent autobiographical book by Gertrude Stein, *Wars I Have Seen*. Jean Echenoz's latest novel, *Au piano*; he's one of my favorite writers. Robert Glück's glorious novel, *Margery Kempe*. *Gazelle*, my favorite book of all by Rikki Ducornet. I finally finished reading Madame de Sévigné's voluminous correspondence. A book on American English by Allen Walker Read, a famous philologist who among other things discovered the origin of "OK." John Ashbery's *Chinese Whispers*. *Embers*, by Sándor Márai, which I didn't think was quite as great as some. *Darling* by Honor Moore. Ron Padgett's wonderful biography of his father, *Oklahoma Tough*. Anne Hollander's fascinating *Fabric of Vision: Dress and Drapery in Painting*. The third book of Viktor Shklovsky's trilogy, *Third Factory*. *Breezeless Harbor* by Patrick O'Brian. A book called *The Poet's Calendar* by a fellow Oulipian, Michelle Grangaud. Alison Fell's nifty novel, *Tricks of the Light*. An enthralling autobiographical work by Keith Waldrop, *Light While There Is Light*. Ben Jonson's *Epicene, or the Silent Woman*. Alice Massat's brilliant and funny new novel, *Le Code civil*. Then two books by Richard Holmes, the literary historian, *Dr. Johnson & Mr. Savage*, about Dr. Johnson's first strange friendship when he came to London, and *Sidetracks: Explorations of a Romantic Biographer* (second time). *Found in the Park* by

Barbara Henning, which I liked a lot. An installment in Jacques Roubaud's series of autobiographical writings. F. T. Prince, *The Doors of Stone*. A collection of George Perec's interviews and lectures. A first-rate Hungarian novel called *The Door* (or perhaps *The Gate*—I read it in French) by Magda Szabó. Albert Camus's last book, a most compelling one, *Le premier homme*. Dallas Wiebe's latest, *The Vox Populi Stories*. A second reading of *Splendide-Hôtel* by Gilbert Sorrentino. William Gaddis's essays and occasional writings. Another book—I look at the title and don't remember reading it at all. This is terrible.

MD: Do you keep a journal of what you read?

HM: Why yes, I wouldn't remember them otherwise. Then Laird Hunt, *The Impossibly*. A book by Colette about changing apartments in Paris, quite wonderful. Gilbert Sorrentino's collected stories, *The Moon in Its Flight*. Carmen Firan, a Romanian writer, mainly a poet. She's very good. I discovered her hearing her read at the Brooklyn Library a couple of years ago. This is a book about life in Romania just before the "revolution"—*The Farce. On and Off the Avenue* by Eileen Hennessy. A play by a French friend, *Richard Morgiève*. And, last but not least, an extraordinary book by someone named Sarah McPhee. I was alone in New York for while a year and a half ago, and I'd often have dinner at the bar of Gotham on 12th Street. One evening a nice couple came in and we started chatting. She was a teacher of art history. I said, what's your specialty? She said seventeenth-century Italian architecture. And I, asked, oh, have you published anything? And she said yes, it's about Bernini's bell towers for St. Peter's. And I stopped and thought and finally said, but there are no bell towers on St. Peter's. She said, that's what the book's about. I ordered it and couldn't put it down. It's technical and scholarly, as scholarly as you can get in a book called *Bernini and the Bell Towers: Architecture and Politics at the Vatican*, and enthralling. It's pricey, though—maybe you could put it on a credit card and then change your address.

MD: Maybe they have it at the Strand.

HM: Lots of pictures, too. So that's it, honey, the reading list for 2003. I just finished *Nine Stories* by Robert Walser. He's probably one of John's and my favorite writers.

MD: He's someone whose work you've been following for years.

HM: I've always hoped he would influence me, but I'm afraid that's too much to hope. It's very hard to pin down what he does. He's completely unlike anybody, including Kafka. I had the loveliest "real life" experience, thanks to him. I love hiking, and hiking in Europe is great because you go out and walk all day long in any direction and you're always assured of finding a nice restaurant at the end of the trail. A man called Carl Seelig published a collection of conversations with Robert Walser. Seelig used to visit him on Sundays in the asylum in Herisau where Walser had had himself confined, and they would go off on a walk, no matter what the weather was. They would explore different areas of this part of Switzerland—the part where women only got the vote a couple of years ago by federal decree. Totally reactionary, I guess, nevertheless a pocket of wonders. Around Appenzell. That's where I went. Every day I would go on one of their walks, then I'd come home at night and read about what had happened to them when they'd gone over the same terrain. So one day I set out on a road up a mountainside, and after a couple of hours, about ten in the morning, I came to a village. I had a piece of bread and a glass of white wine and then went the rest of the way up this mountain. I must have gotten up there around noon, then I walked down on the other side of the mountain to a town on the Austrian border called Altstätten. I misjudged my timing and arrived there at ten past two. I went into a restaurant and said I was famished, could I have lunch? They said, the kitchen's closed, you can only have a cold lunch. I said, I really feel like something hot. So I walked a little farther and went into another restaurant. Same story, only cold food. I asked them, is there no place in town I can get a hot meal? They said, yes, there's a hotel on the square at the bottom of the hill. One of the big squares in town, you can't miss it. Just walk down the street you're on and you'll get to the Drei Kronigen, something like that. I went in and had this lovely lunch. That evening after dinner I went to my room and read about what Walser and Seelig had done. They had started up the same path I had taken, and at ten they got to the same village as I and had some bread and white wine, and then they had gone on to the top of the mountain. They'd gone down the other side, they'd gotten to Altstätten at ten past two, they went into one restaurant and were only offered cold food, then went to the second restaurant where there was only cold food, and then they went down to the Drei Kronigen (if that is indeed its name) where they had their lunch, just like me. I felt as though an angel had reached down and patted me on the head. It was like a recognition of this intimacy I had always felt with him. The restaurateurs of Altstätten were following the same pattern . . .

MD: They never learned that hikers would like a hot lunch! Who besides John are some poets you correspond with?

HM: Bill Berkson. Ron Padgett to some extent. In France, mainly people in the Oulipo: Jacques Roubaud, Ian Monk, Jacques Jouet. Most of my other poet friends are dead, alas. André du Bouchet in France. Kenneth [Koch], Jimmy [Schuyler], Jimmy Merrill. I mustn't leave out Gilbert Sorrentino. I didn't know he'd ever written a poem until he gave me a slim volume and I was, as they used to say, blown away. I've only met him twice, but we exchange letters monthly and have been doing so for ten years or more.

MD: Are there younger poets or prose writers with whom you correspond?

HM: Well, Ben Marcus. Lynne Tillman. A Canadian called André Alexis, whom I admire enormously. Barbara Henning. Dawn-Michelle Baude and I used to be in touch. Mark Ford. Vincent Katz. Tom Mandel, a very good poet, a philosophical poet, a rare breed on our shores. Albert Mobilio. Lynn Crawford. She's a great friend and a most original talent. Lytle Shaw. Mark Swartz, who wrote a very funny first novel [*Instant Karma*] about a man who plans to burn down the town library. Also Doug Nufer, Alan Wearne in Australia, Cydney Chadwick, Richard Beard, Honor Moore, Raphael Rubinstein, Schuldt—the word "younger" is giving me trouble. At this point, practically *everybody* is younger.

BRENDA COULTAS TELLS THE TRUTH TO MARCELLA DURAND

OCTOBER/NOVEMBER 2004   NO. 200

When the news hit the city that Brenda Coultas's book, *A Handmade Museum* (Coffee House Press, 2003), had been selected by Lyn Hejinian for the Norma Farber First Book Award from the Poetry Society of America, there was all-night jubilation and dancing in the streets. Well, not exactly, but among poets there was the rare feeling that once in a great while all goes right in the world and that awards are given to the writers who most deserve them. Coultas is a poet of origins and a remarkably original poet: she starts with matter most overlooked by us preoccupied, overloaded souls, finds the right, new, fresh language for it, and then moves on to find the language for us preoccupied, overloaded souls who are ourselves overlooked. A contemporary transcendentalist, a non-judgmental "transparent eyeball," and a democrat as generous in her spirit as in her writing, Coultas finds an abandoned beanie baby as deserving of attention as the almost unbearably "poignant formation" (as Hejinian writes in her note for the award) of people writing their wishes down on small pieces of paper on the soon-to-be-"developed" (or ruined) Bowery. In writing and in life, Coultas has a resume few can match, and has worked as a farmer, a carny, a taffy maker, a park ranger, and as the second woman welder in Firestone Steel's history. Her previous publications include *A Summer Newsreel*, *Early Films*, and *Boy Eye*.

MARCELLA DURAND: When did you start writing?

BRENDA COULTAS: I tried to write when I first started reading at age six or so. I read all the time, I was totally in love, I read under the covers. I think that

when I was around ten or twelve, sixth grade or so, I tried to write a novel, but then I never got past the first page.

MD: A one-page novel?

BC: It wasn't intentional. I didn't know about white space. I didn't know you could use paragraphs to move things along. I recorded everything. *And then Marcella adjusted her glasses, and then she smiled and thought to herself, Oh, I've got a live one here.* Like I couldn't figure out that I could have a blank space. It drove me crazy. I couldn't do it because I was going nuts. I was trying to describe everything, the green grass and the color of the formica table. Then I had these little projects, like I'm going to read every book in the library. I'm going to read all the plays written this year. I could never quite fulfill those goals.

MD: What sorts of things did you describe?

BC: Daily life. I remember being really angry at the way country people were portrayed, so I thought I would write about them in a way that they aren't just rednecks or fools. I thought I'd write about Spencer County. I remember wanting even as a very young person to write about the Midwest and rural life where the characters were not stereotypes. Something that showed the complexities.

MD: But you're an urban poet, too. How do the two come together?

BC: Bowery is Dutch for "farm." When you're in the East Village, you think of Peter Stuyvesant or Peter Stuyvesant's farm—at least, I am. People who pass by Peter Stuyvesant's statue every day, like we do, probably think more about it just because they're on his burial grounds and his farms, walking on his farm.

MD: So in a way, New York is part of the country.

BC: I've been in NYC almost ten years now, so I pay attention to what's going on around me, or at least I try to. The corny thing I always tell you, you know, about writing from the heart, usually means pretty schmaltzy, schlocky work. But I think you have to have a gentleness toward people, even if you're pissed off or ranting. I think the job of a poet is to uplift and to criticize. Certainly, we need lots of criticism right now. Maybe the people don't so much, but the government does.

MD: Not the poets!

BC: Not the poets, for god's sake. But poets can uplift people. People turn towards poetry in times of sorrow. Funerals, particularly, a time of very deep sorrow, many people turn to poetry. I had a conversation with Jo Ann [Wasserman] and David [Cameron] and Eleni [Sikelianos] and David was asking us, well, which poet did you turn to during 9/11? All of us thought of Whitman. He was a poet of Brooklyn, lower Manhattan, that particular area, the older part of the city. He was a democratic poet, which I love about him. His inclusiveness and his openness, his candor. It's the nineteenth century and he's writing about getting naked and sleeping with young men.

MD: Do you try to be candid in your work? I think of your work as particularly truthful. It's interesting that you said you tried to describe everything. I still see that.

BC: In some ways. Obviously, you learn not to tell on yourself. You have to be protective of your own self. I was way too candid in my twenties before I became a writer. Just in my personal life. Too much information. I've learned to withhold, or at least not to say. Just to be more private. I realized why people change their names, so that they can write candidly. I should have changed my name so I would be able to write candidly about my family. Since I didn't, I have to think. Invading my own privacy is one thing, but if I talk about my brothers and my sisters, I have to think about them. It's not just me. Did you change your name?

MD: No. Kristin [Prevallet] says it has to be close to your own name. Like mine would be "Cella And." Yours could be "Enda Oultas."

BC: That's horrible! Usually you take the maiden name of your mother. It's too late for me. What am I going to write about my family now?

MD: Tell me about your family.

BC: Well, in Spencer County [in southern Indiana], my family had a small

political dynasty going, a hillbilly dynasty. My uncle was the mayor of
the county seat for 22 years, before he went to jail for buying votes. I think
they'd give you a bottle of whisky, or a goat, or a chicken with your vote.
It was the old days.

MD: When were the old days?

BC: My grandfather was a local politician after the Great Depression and then
my uncle, his namesake, became a politician. They were all Republicans.

MD: Are they all Republicans today?

BC: It's like they were born Republicans and therefore they are Republicans.
There's no questioning. It's not about philosophy. It's more like, it's my
team. Obviously, many people are like that.

MD: Do you think that can change?

BC: Not all of my siblings are Republicans. My brother who was a Republican
joined the Union and is now—probably an Independent or a Democrat, but
mostly a cynic. One of my sisters is a Democrat.

MD: Do you have a vision of America?

BC: I have a transcendentalist or utopian impulse. I'm very attracted toward
ideas of community. I guess I'm idealistic—the world could be a better place.
People could be more generous with each other. Governments could be more
responsible. A lot of the work I'm doing now is going back to the nineteenth
century, looking at Abraham Lincoln. I grew up ten miles from the Lincoln
homestead, so he was always a large figure in my life. I didn't realize until
now that I'm 45 that this was so. Recently, I've been thinking about what
difference he might have made in how I think, as opposed to other Midwest-
erners. I was reading a book about abolitionists living on the Ohio River and
this town Ripley, Ohio, and the problems they had with slave masters. Slave
hunters would cross the river into free territory and look for runaway slaves.
They (the Kentuckians) tried to enact laws to punish the Ohio abolitionists.
It was insane, these horrible slave masters. They were running the country.
Imagine knowing that one fourth of the population across the river from
you were enslaved, and that anyone who interfered was at risk of being

arrested or murdered by a mob. I plan to visit the National Underground Railroad Freedom Center that opened in Cincinnati this summer.

MD: This idea of America being on one side of the river and watching this horror unfold on the other side of the river is riveting.

BC: I was reading through the Naropa University Summer Writing Program catalogue and the first week was about borders. I started thinking "borders." This border I grew up on was still very vivid to me, but I hadn't explored it. It was still part of who I was, living on the free side and crossing this border every day as an ordinary act, which 139 years ago would have been going into another country, the Confederacy. I started to think about the differences between people raised on the free side and people raised on the slavery side and to explore what sort of difficulties people (free or enslaved) were faced with during that time. In winter slaves froze or drowned while trying to walk over [the Ohio River] in the middle of the night. Steamboats came through that the slave traders would stop and get on board trying to find runaways. It was horrible, horrible . . . If you go down to Spencer County, there's a plaque that shows where Lincoln took off on his flatboat trip to New Orleans where he first saw slavery and he said, I'm going to end this. He swore that he would destroy slavery. I guess maybe in some sense it gives me some hope that someone like Lincoln would come out of this country.

MD: He wrote poetry, too.

BC: And he was a poet! He was pretty amazing. He was big and strong, but melancholy, very thoughtful.

MD: I just can't dispose of America altogether. There are such beautiful things and then such awful things.

BC: It's like anything else. You have to be able to reconcile the contradictions. What is it when you can hold two opposing Americas in your mind?

MD: Paradoxical?

BC: They're both the same country.

MD: How does this connect to your work on ghosts?

BC: A lot of it has to do with my childhood. Ghost stories that I heard growing up. I had cousins who saw monsters.

MD: Were these local monsters?

BC: Yes, there was the Spotsville monster, the Silverdale Road monster. Teenagers especially would see monsters.

MD: So there were haunted areas?

BC: Border areas particularly. In thickets or woods, people would see Sasquatch-type monsters. The weird thing is that Evansville, Indiana, is a hotbed for UFO sightings. I don't know why, but southern Indiana is where a lot of UFOs are seen. Maybe it's culturally isolated, or maybe there really are UFOs. I knew a guy who said he got abducted. He told me his abduction occurred when he and a friend were relic hunting and they came across an open grave.

MD: What do you mean by relic hunting?

BC: Looking for Native American relics. There are a lot of relic hunters in southern Indiana because in that area along the Ohio were Mississippian cultures. Mound Builders.

MD: Are they related to the Hopewell mounds in Ohio?

BC: Could be. I'm talking about Angel Mounds in Evansville, Indiana, which flourished from 1100–1450 AD. There are a lot of mounds and a lot of burial grounds and archaeological sites in that part of the country. Some are documented and some are not. Usually when they build a highway they come across something and they're required to have an archaeologist look at it. It's dense with Native American presence.

MD: How do you deal with skeptics?

BC: It's part of the human experience. Whether it's physically true or not is irrelevant, but more that it's emotionally and psychologically true. People want to see or do experience—they actually are having experiences—but whether they are hallucinations or what we call reality is not proven. I'm interested in both. Are they really real? It's part of what makes things more interesting. I want there to be something more, even though it's really scary.

MD: How do you investigate this in poetry?

BC: A lot of it through reading UFO literature and Web sites. Then talking to people who have seen them. Quite a few people have seen UFOs or experienced UFOs, or some sort of paranormal incident. The only kind of criteria I have is that the person believes it to be true. They may be found wrong later, but this is something they believe to be true. It's an eyewitness account, or even a secondhand account of an experience. I think it's fascinating whatever it is. It's part of the great mysteries: is there other life out there? Is there life after death? Does personality continue or do you join a collective consciousness or do you just become food for worms?

MD: Do you follow standard investigatory procedures? Do you use Ed Sanders's techniques?

BC: I was a student of Ed's and his teaching assistant at Naropa. I investigated a murder. A friend of mine's mother had been on a jury. The murder took place 75 miles from me, and I had never heard of it. A guy had kidnapped two women. One of them was killed and one of them escaped and that's how he got found out. I talked to my friend's mother. I think he got the death penalty, but for whatever reason they haven't carried it out. After class with Ed, I was very inspired, so I went to Terre Haute. I took pictures, I walked around the neighborhood, I found the house where things had occurred. I realized I couldn't do it. I couldn't write about someone else's pain. It would have been completely exploitative. It was not for me to write about. The amount of time you would have to live in that world was too much—it was too dark. I realized I couldn't do that kind of writing. It was too negative and too exploitative. I've gotten away from true crime. True crime is out the window.

MD: But you seem to approach investigative projects with this kind of creativity where you're giving something back to people. Like when you filmed people writing their wishes. You brought them something where they could express themselves.

BC: I was also very interested in performance art and guerilla theater, street performance. I guess I think of them as very democratic forms of art, being able to participate without an MFA from here or there. Just go out and do it, be a citizen. Part of it goes back too to trying to have a heart, to be gentle. Have kindness towards humans. Treat other people decently and with dignity. I think you have to start with the heart and beauty and then the other things can follow, at least for me. Part of it, as a learner, I have to be physical. I have to feel things, touch them. I'm too concrete, too grounded, too earthy. Even though I have abstract ideas, I have to have this very physical foundation—it might be a Midwest thing. Maybe being raised on a farm, working as a carny, making a home in every little hotel you're in.

MD: How did you end up at Naropa?

BC: I was 31 years old when I went to get my MFA. The first year I applied to graduate schools, I got rejected by pretty well all of them. I almost went to Gainesville where Harry Crews was, but my GPA was too low. The second year I applied again but to different schools. Someone saw the group picture of the students at Naropa and said you should apply here! Then I did. At the same time I got accepted there, I had been about to go into the Peace Corps, but I had a physical. I had checked [a box] that I had seen a psychologist and that I had depression at one time, so they kept treating me like I was a mental patient. They thought I was crazy. They said, we don't send people with a history of depression to Eastern European countries.

MD: You think you're depressed now!

BC: I met some of those Peace Corps people—they're *really* crazy!

MD: Did you feel like you found a community?

BC: I didn't know anybody. When I went there, Anne Waldman picked me up in her orange Volvo. The first student I met was Eleni Sikelianos. Then I met Bobbie Hawkins. I was like, these people want me to come here—they're so nice! It was perfect.

MD: What were you like before and what were you like after?

BC: I was an activist before I went there. My roommate and I led a protest against George Bush [Senior]. He came to University of Southern Indiana to do a campaign fundraiser. He hadn't counted on me and my roommate and twenty other people having a counterdemonstration. We had signs about the environment, signs about Iran–Contra. There were two ropes and we were supposed to stay behind the one rope. Well, I got very excited when the motorcade pulled up and Bush came out and walked toward the auditorium. So I ran to the second rope and I was looking at the president, he was pretty far away. At that time, everyone behind me saw the sharpshooters turn their weapons towards me. My friends all thought I was going to be killed. I had no idea. I stayed behind the second rope. He gave us the finger. Bush gave us the finger.

MD: Wow.

BC: So there was a group of activists in Evansville who protested against the war, industrial pollution. In any community, you're going to find people like this and this gives me hope. You'll find thoughtful, intelligent people who are trying to find a way to live peacefully and trying to create social justice. They really are out there in these little communities, everywhere.

MD: You've said that lately you've been working on how to write political poetry.

BC: That's been tough.

MD: Why?

BC: My political poems are more like rants. There are people who do it really well, like Ginsberg. Anne Waldman is really great at doing curses. But mine are like, "Bush is bad. Bush sucks." I haven't found an interesting or beautiful way to say, "Bush sucks." I like Kristin Prevallet's political poems, particularly. She's always finding a new way to say it.

MD: Do you think poetry can create political change?

BC: Yes, I do think so. I'm a sucker. I am one of those people who still thinks one person can change the world. I do believe that poetry can change the world—hopefully for the better.

MD: You know about this new NEA project, Operation Homecoming . . . ?

BC: As soon as those soldiers come back and tell the truth, [that project] will be out the window. It's not going to be rah-rah, it's going to be my leg got blown off for Bush's fantasy. I think it's a brilliant project because those soldiers are going to come back and they're going to tell the truth and they're going to be shut up as soon as they do.

MD: After Naropa, did you come straight to the Poetry Project?

BC: No, I was in a car wreck and I broke my neck. I went home to recover. Then I came to New York City to work for the Poetry Project.

MD: Now, why did you do a thing like that?

BC: I wasn't ready to be in the farmhouse forever! It was a great opportunity to really be involved in a poetry community. I think that writers should live in New York City for some period of time in their lives.

MD: Why?

BC: I think it's the most American city. It's the melting pot. You lose your provincialism. It's the only way you can get a bigger picture. It challenges you. It can destroy you too, but you can't be afraid of it. It's where so many American writers have passed through, like Whitman. If you're studying New York School and Beat poets, you have to come to New York. It gives you an edge. Your anger or your frustration can help you create. It can motivate you to write really powerful work. Where else are you going to be exposed to so many different kinds of people? I walk down the street and almost every day I see a poet. Some of them are strangers, but I know their faces. That's just amazing.

MD: Do you say you're from New York now when people ask?

BC: Usually, because it's easier than explaining. I guess because Atticus [Fierman] is from here and my in-laws live here, but I still love Indiana. It's so beautiful. I know people won't believe this, but tolerance is a very high virtue in Indiana. There's a great degree of tolerance. Maybe it was just my parents, but people of color would come to our house, it was not a big deal. I wasn't raised to have any sort of prejudice.

MD: Do you think you hold a unique place, as someone who comes from rural Indiana and yet someone who writes in the NYC hothouse poetry scene?

BC: There are a lot of transplants from the Midwest to NYC, if they want to plug into that. It's also like, who are you? Maybe that's a part of your essence, maybe not. I was there until I was 31. Many people leave when they're 18 or 19. The thing that unites poets is an interest in language. I mean, that's your tool. Language should come first and attention to language, and then content. That's the way I define poetry as opposed to prose.

MD: Do you think of yourself as a prose writer or as a poet?

BC: As a poet, because my first interest is language. But when my first concern is getting the story, then the language, I think of myself as a prose writer.

MD: I know for a while you were exploring narrative . . .

BC: I'm one of those hybrids, like Renee Gladman or Dodie Bellamy. A lot of poets are using prose lines, too. Why not? Why shouldn't we?

MD: Why not? We're experimental poets. We can do whatever we want.

BC: We can experiment. That's what I like about poetry. I don't have to think about conflict, a climax, a resolution. Not that I ever thought about those things when I was writing prose. I got bypassed on the character train.

MD: How would you say you organize a poem? There's so much in your poems, yet it all works . . .

BC: Every word has to count, every word has to be essential. But it's hard because you're in a particular mood when a certain kind of music sounds good to you, or a certain rhythm, and then you come back to it cold and you're like, this doesn't work. It's clunk, clunk. Mostly it's an interior cadence, an interior language. Or maybe sometimes it's just fun to talk about. But mostly it's process. I write on paper usually, taking notes, and then I start to type things up. I find a memory or an object. It's going back to that physicality. I don't know if that's so natural to be so physical. I think sometimes it's a learning disability. That's why there's so many objects in the poems, because I'm so physical and touching things, feeling their weight. I wish I wasn't so earthy sometimes.

MD: One of my pet peeves is driving in a car with poets and they never look out the window . . .

BC: Maybe if they were driving in the car alone they would look out of the window. I do think theory is good. It gives you a vocabulary and a context. I do think some good things can come out of it. I think we should use it all.

AKILAH OLIVER TALKS TO RACHEL LEVITSKY

DECEMBER/JANUARY 2005   NO. 201

Between poet and audience lies a vast reservoir of space and air. Some poets push through it, striving to achieve some sort of liftoff between paper and ear. Akilah Oliver reaches fearlessly into and through this mutable medium, engaging body, sound, and breath in her conjoining of the physical activity of writing and performing with the ideals of justice, peace, and compassion. Oliver is the teacher of "Flesh Memory" workshops, which facilitate a multi-disciplinary approach to activating and connecting with the writing process, and the founder of LINKS Community Network, a Boulder-based group dedicated to creating action for positive change in the healthcare industry and honoring her son Oluchi McDonald, who died tragically and unnecessarily in a Los Angeles hospital in 2003. She is the author of the *she said dialogues: flesh memory* (Smokeproof/Erudite Fangs, 1999), as well as a new chapbook/CD, *An Arriving Guard of Angels, Thusly Coming to Greet* (Farfalla Press, 2004). She currently teaches at Naropa University in Boulder.

On Friday, July 25, 2003, Rachel Levitsky spoke with Akilah Oliver about her evolving work/performance/opus, *An Arriving Guard of Angels, Thusly Coming to Greet*, written and performed by Oliver in collaboration with LaTasha N. Nevada Diggs (voice, chaos pad), Fanny Ferreira (voice), Bethany Spiers (guitar), and Rasul Siddik (trumpet), which was performed afterward in Brooklyn.

RACHEL LEVITSKY: I'm interested in how performance and poetry interweave and separate.

AKILAH OLIVER: In my mind they are always separate and I'm surprised that people think of me as a performative-type poet because that's seldom my intent. I'd envisioned *An Arriving Guard of Angels, Thusly Coming to Greet* as a text piece that incorporated sketches and graffiti art, some documented from photographs and others from my son's sketchbooks, and that I would write a text that would weave in these visuals. The piece changed very quickly, and the next element that came out of it was a collaboration with musicians: electronic music, jazz trumpet, and electric guitar, morphing it into an oral piece. So for me that was a surprising intersection. It hadn't necessarily been the intent of the piece, to become a collaborative performance with musicians.

RL: Tell me about the visual versus the oral, and the history of visual elements in your work. Where does the visual exist for you? It sounds like you were very specifically thinking about image in this piece.

AO: In most of my performance work, the visual existed in the living body. The body was the central visual element—the body nude, the body semi-clothed, the body interacting with other bodies—so it was a living kind of visual that depended on subjectivity and the gaze. That is, those performances depended on how the audience viewed the body and how I contextualized it in a given text and all the elements in a stage play—lights, space, props, and so on. *An Arriving Guard of Angels, Thusly Coming to Greet* is a very different piece performance-wise for me. I'm very much influenced by graffiti because my son was a graffiti artist and this piece came out of his death. By graffiti, I mean large-scale murals of names, tags, and graphics, which are very beautiful, but they are temporary in the sense that they're placed in public spaces. They interrupt the discourse because the public discourse is reserved for advertising. Large billboards are in the realm of paid advertising, so these what I call phantom bodies—in other words, graffiti artists—put up a piece on a train, or on the side of a wall, and there is a certain lifespan for that piece. I don't know how long that lifespan could be, but it's not going to be years, we know that much. Sooner or later that disruptive image has to be eliminated. I'm fascinated with graffiti, how these bodies, these people who create graffiti challenge the discourse around the death of the author, blah blah blah, in that postmodern bullshit discourse. Graffiti was postmodern before the postmodern ever was. Graffiti questions who owns the material, who can even "read" the text, the notion of accessibility. I mean we look at graffiti and we're engaged, whether we're revolted, attracted, or dismissive, or even if we think it's pretty or ugly—it forces an engagement. Often the nonconsensual viewing public can't read that script, those letters, literally. I don't know what it means and even if I can make out all the letters, I can't necessarily ascribe meaning to it. Part of that has to do with the anonymity of the author and the codes of the text and the lack of accessibility. So, the sense of these invisible, phantom bodies creating visual text, beautiful large-scale visual disruptive text in public space, is, to me, fascinating.

RL: And they are very often literally "moving" pieces as well, whether in a style that mimics movement or they are literally on a train, or that you are on a train moving and a piece is in the station, so again it has the phantom sense you speak of—it goes by really quickly.

AO: It's fleeting. It's nomadic in that way. It has an unstable quality, but is weirdly fixed in urban landscapes and not-so-urban landscapes, in little alcoves all over the country, like Boulder.

RL: And the world.

AO: And around the world, absolutely. I have about three pages of photographic documentation of graffiti in four different cities in South Africa. Beautiful stuff, you know, in terms of the lettering, styles that are so incredibly different, gorgeous fonts. Graffiti artists have an entire glossary and vocabulary that they use to critique and to read their own work.

RL: In advertising language they call it branding, and in graffiti, it's called tagging. The graffiti artist is certainly aware of it as advertising space, in terms of tactics. What do you see as the difference between tagging and branding and how do they inform each other?

AO: There's definitely a sense of informing back and forth, an existing dialogue. I think graffiti writers are aware of their position as insurgent authors. Even the word "tagging" has a sense of usurping. I'm going to tag, hit split. (*laughter*) Even "the tagging" has the sense of an active moniker, it's an action. Time informs how the work goes up—do I have a lot of time, a set number of hours, do I have a few minutes to get this up? So there is always this interloper sense. As for "branding," I think even the term itself has a more proprietary sense. I can brand this space. I can own this space, name it, and claim it as mine. Architecture and public space act like bodies. The buildings are these bodies that hold up the culture.

RL: Competing forces of how space is used, whether it's moved through or colonized . . .

AO: . . . has to do with power relating to empire, on one level. There is a certain amount of disregard and co-opting, which is nothing new. But a lot of graffiti artists work in advertising, in graphic arts, in all kinds of surface, legit jobs. Just like what any of us do for money.

RL: The visual has moved in your work from being a moving, living body to a more phantom graffiti artist. Where do they intersect?

AO: What I'm saying about graffiti is that it's an aesthetic informing a text that is a collaboration between musicians and poets, and poets are voices. There won't be anything, when people come at this stage of the show, that will be visibly graffiti. We don't have artwork as part of the show, so it's interesting that the absent body, the phantom body, the graffiti artist, the producer, is feeding this piece, is part of the aesthetic of it, but isn't obtrusively anywhere in it. Rather, I'm pulling on the energy of the absent visible, this idea of how bodies mark time, name, and disappear. What does inform this piece in terms of the phantom body is ritual around death and spirit and the dead. A lot of this piece is about naming the dead. In many cultures there's a belief that "the dead are not under the earth." That the dead are with us in spirit, that death is a complicated thing and bodies don't necessarily just give up attachment to the earth. So there's this sense of the present phantom body as always being present in this piece. It is about the process of how we honor the transition of bodies into spirit. For me, it is the absent visible, phantom body again. I keep using those four words interchangeably: absent, visible, phantom, body.

RL: Absent and visible, that's nice.

AO: Just like in a graffiti piece, I see the piece and know that some energy, some labor, people, or a person went and created that and made that happen, and I can feel the presence of people when I look at graffiti, very, very strongly. This same sense of feeling the presence of the absent body is what *An Arriving Guard of Angels, Thusly Coming to Greet* tries to achieve. I want to create a space where the absent body is very much visible and a part of our aesthetic and a part of our struggle and a part of how we construct ideas about what it means to live.

RL: We're speaking around words, how the visual becomes musical, becomes electronic, and the boundaries that do or don't exist between the dead and the living. Words seem to be very amorphous and mutable. Music is another one, amorphous like words.

AO: Maybe somewhere down the line I'd like to do a performance with visuals, but I'm not very interested right now because I feel like we're making tags hit in space orally with the text and especially with electronic [sounds]. I haven't considered electronic devices as instruments before, as serious instruments. Before working with LaTasha Diggs, I thought of electronic instruments as something to play with for feedback, reverb, and echo. But collaborating with her has opened up the possibility of electronic music, in particular the chaos pad as a serious instrument. I'm fascinated by its range—[you can] hit, tag, reverb, sing, echo something, then it disappears and the next minute something thoroughly different happens. It's a way of creating text with the nomadic sense of tagging, hitting, and it hits in different spaces, then withdraws, or it can keep repeating and looping or doing something. It's almost like the aesthetic that I've created around graffiti art (I admit not all graffiti artists share this aesthetic) and my sense of the absent phantom body. The nomadic guerilla writing of graffiti art has fed the composition of this performance piece, which is exciting.

RL: I'm thinking about the connection between the Anglo-European capitalism that colonizes spaces as land that one possesses and puts borders around, and burial that is a dead person under the ground and the notion of nomadism—a different use of space as well as a different understanding of death. How in this moment in NYC and in the United States, which is a colonial venture into a nomadic culture, do these ideas coexist? Is there room for a nondominant idea of nomadism? Maybe it is one of our classic American paradoxes, these two ideas coexisting?

AO: New York is a very nomadic culture and city. There's always some displacement, replacement, some motion happening with bodies constantly throughout the city [such as] subterranean trains always moving. But there's also a level of immigration that shapes and changes the character of entire boroughs such as Queens, Brooklyn, and Manhattan—changes the faces and face of the city. It seems very much the center point, the epicenter. And it's the most capitalist place in the world at this point. It's one of the centers for markets and for tracking market investments. It makes sense that it's the place of confluence. Like in ancient Arabic cultures, centers of capital were also the places of cultural confluence.

RL: Though dominance repeatedly fails, it's necessarily the impulse of the power, the erasing of graffiti, the cleanups in Queens, the battles against the return of graffiti as reported in the New York Times.

AO: Capital has to keep up the gesture that sustains itself, that sense of dominance, of erasure, the guise that it's never-ending. It's limited, but it must keep up the gesture or how else could it maintain the illusion of dominance? And if we can't erase you, what else can we do? Metaphorically, erasure is a gesture of death. We will just erase you—in Queens, in Iraq, we'll shoot you. In public hospitals, like the one my son Oluchi was in, they'll let you die.[1] There are all kinds of ways that bodies are erased in capital culture. I'm saying capital culture instead of capitalist culture because I think capitalism is something that happened already. We're talking now about a different kind of market and the way capital is distributed and maintained and manipulated. In my mind, it's beyond postindustrial capitalism, via globalization.

RL: Another reason why I asked you about the conflict between the erasers or the dominators.

AO: I like calling them erasers. Have you ever seen Gumby cartoons? There were Gumby erasers to put on the end of your pencil.

RL: Since Oluchi died, in what to me was an obviously wrongful death, you've talked a lot about activism and connecting with activists and fighting and making this not silent—what are the (confines) and where is the fight?

AO: There are several ways to think about bringing performance to specific communities, or inviting those communities to spaces where performance is. It becomes difficult to use performance as political conduit when there's a lot of grassroots work to be done in specific communities, a lot of organizing, but the idea is to make the work available to multiple specific audiences, to pinpoint those audiences, then fund it. And where are those audiences? We can't expect huge diverse audiences to come to my two performances, one in Williamsburg and one in the Lower East Side, and I don't live in New York and I don't have those grassroots connections, even though I desire to build that into this piece. There's a way to do that and I know how to do it. But the whole funding process is exhausting. Grief is so private in this culture and by that I mean across cultures in America. It is proscribed and limited to certain realms—we have funerals, we do whatever we do, and then we go back to work, we get a few days or weeks off, just like giving birth—but since communities are strangulated by grief in private spaces, the work I'm doing, creating a public space for transformative mourning, challenges my sense of who the audience potentially can be and the strategies I need to use to connect to those audiences. Back to capital, it even influences the culture that we're permitted to develop around grief. You get your pills, and you're back into the medical capital system, the pharmaceutical companies. The cycle continues. Death has even entered the market economy—Costco now sells coffins. One of the things I attempt to do with this performance is explore the question of why six months after Oluchi's death are we still talking about this? Why are we still grieving? And I feel that it's because the phantom absent body/visible absent body/the dead are not dead, they're always with us. Why would we not be talking about them? Why wouldn't we be naming them?

RL: Like the Sweet Honey in the Rock song.

AO: "The dead are not under the earth, they are in the whimpering of the rocks . . ." That comes from a poem by a Senegalese author named Birago Diop. It's a beautiful, absolutely gorgeous song. I share the worldview that the dead are not under the earth, and I make that central to this piece and central to the dialogue with the audience. It is an important thing for me to keep doing. And it's not timely. We didn't do this a week or month after my son's death. If we do it three years from now, it's right on time. To make a public space is to make a political space, in the old sense of the word political.

RL: The town square.

AO: Here we are creating in the town square.

RL: It's also a secular space . . .

AO: Taking it out of the temple, out of the obscure, and putting the temple into secular space. And when that happens, something happens in the secular space as well. I often use the term "ritual" to talk about this performance. And at the Williamsburg performance, we are for the first time going to set an altar up and have people place things on the altar. The candles might face the wrong way. Gods might get upset, but we're going to throw up a pagan altar, so be it. There's a separation between ritual and religion. Oluchi's death started this process for me, but so did your councilman[2], Bethany Spier's 20-year-old friend who just died of a heart murmur, the wife and son of Yusef Komunyakaa, my cousin Sherman last week, Nina Simone, Celia Cruz last week . . . The constant cycle of transition is the continuation of this piece.

RL: Idi Amin on his deathbed.

AO: Let him die. We're not helping him out in this performance.

RL: It brings up a moralistic idea of only the good dying.

AO: Reagan never dies. We keep certain of them around for counterpoetic reasons. The lucky ones, bad, good, indifferent, they get to die. And lucky us, we get to live. I'm being facetious. It's not like that. Oh luck! We're lucky we get to die, we're lucky we get to live . . . We're bodies and all are going to transpire, transform. There is constant, constant energy around us, so I turn to public space, to create just a little space to embrace this constant energy. We're all dying all the time. Not to be judgmental, but I think that some of us have brought a conscious grace to our time on earth, the planet, and some haven't necessarily done such a great job of it. One of the refrains we use in this piece is: "How ya livin', How ya livin'." It's almost biblical.

RL: Like Ecclesiastes, which is sort of secular too, more open as a question. Whatever god is, we're living together now, in the public square. How we are to each other determines the space.

AO: There's something important about being a good friend while we're here. I don't think that Idi Amin was a good friend. Lives are qualitatively different, so I guess that the experience of death is qualitatively different for all of us.

RL: I've not asked you much about the transgender work you've done before. Transforming gender has resonance with the transformation from life to death, a death of the female, birth of the male.

AO: That's a hard one to answer because I'm not a transgender person. In my experience, witnessing people who have actively transitioned from one gender to another has been unlike my witness of death.

RL: Yet there's a grieving . . .

AO: . . . that is very similar, the grieving for the lost body that we've identified as the person.

RL: I was thinking about how much one performs when they're public—as I'm public with you right now. I imagine the dead aren't different for themselves and for the group.

AO: That's the odd thing about people dying. Somebody who didn't know Oluchi, to whom I showed a picture of Oluchi a few weeks ago, asked how old he was. I was really thrown off. I was like . . . he'll always be 20. No, first he asked, "What was his name and how old was he?" And that threw me off for a minute; I got really disoriented. I felt his name was Oluchi and he'll always be 20. The panic that arises in me sometimes is that of course his name is probably not Oluchi anymore and he's probably not 20 anymore and in my knowing of him he'll always be 20, he'll always be Oluchi, and will he remember me? There's a terror sometimes in that question, will he remember me? As he's becoming . . . it is kind of like transqueer dialogue where we don't even have pronouns. How shall I receive him? What do I call him? What form is he in? What form? There is that panic that some have when people change genders, over losing the familiar markers.

RL: I had a vision of him as Oluchi. I think his name's Oluchi.

AO: I think so, too.

Notes

1. Oluchi McDonald died at Martin Luther King Hospital, a.k.a. King/Drew Medical Center, in Los Angeles, CA, on March 13, 2003, from a surgically correctible condition. He went untreated and undiagnosed for over thirty hours. He had been transferred to King/Drew from a private hospital because he lacked medical insurance. Oluchi, twenty years old at the time of his death, was, in his own words, a "scholar and graff vandal."

2. On July 23, 2003, Brooklyn Councilman James Davis was shot and killed at City Hall by political rival Othniel Askew.

WILL ALEXANDER
A PROFOUND INVESTIGATION
WITH MARCELLA DURAND

FEBRUARY/MARCH 2005   NO. 202

Will Alexander brings the ancient concept of Renaissance person (which actually predates the Renaissance by quite a bit) to twenty-first-century life: not only is Will Alexander a poet, painter, essayist, philosopher, and playwright, but he embodies the "original current" of Renaissance thought, the indestructible creative energy that has continued through centuries and continents of multitraditional artistic and scientific innovation, an essential counter to the destructive energies of the fragmenting corporate, military, and fundamentalist mind-set that seeks to limit, abolish, forbid, or annihilate. Through his mental travels, projecting his "carbon" self into the personae of Tibetan monks, les Morts of Haiti, the Japanese Crested Ibis, or vertiginous lumen, he reaches spaces—or more literally, space—that he transfigures into language that is like no other poetry: an irresistible spiral of word and energy that shifts paradigms. His amazing journeys are chronicled in *Asia & Haiti*, *Above the Human Nerve Domain*, *The Stratospheric Canticles*, an essay collection, *Towards the Primeval Lightning Field*, and forthcoming works *Compression & Purity*, *The Sri Lankan Loxodrome*, *Sunrise in Armageddon*, and *Exobiology as Goddess*.

MARCELLA DURAND: It's funny—I was looking for your phone number, and then you called me. I thought, how fitting for Will Alexander.

WILL ALEXANDER: It's interesting. [Clairvoyance] works out of almost a blind state in terms of the rational context, or a conscious perspective. It doesn't seem to have a clue, and then all of a sudden it arrives on the conscious plane.

MD: How much does clairvoyance figure into your writing?

WA: I'd say a lot because I tend to pick up energy and areas of knowledge that I did not know much about consciously. When I go back and check them out, it's absolutely accurate. I read and I look at the synecdoche. The yogi Swami Vivekananda[1] pointed out that he'll go through a book like that and get the very essence of it. It is not an excuse, but it is a way of working with the text that is supposedly unconventional. It's something that Edward de Bono talks about repeatedly in his book *Lateral Thinking*, that there are different approaches to the mind, rather than this knowledge adds up to this knowledge adds up to this knowledge. There are other ways of approaching reality.

MD: You've described the I as a bit of "carbon"[2] released outward into experience. Is that what you're talking about as a process of knowledge? Releasing an identity that can be anything?

WA: It's true. This piece of carbon can be an eye, a human being, a leopard, or a remora—there are many ways of speaking through animals. In my latest group of poems, there is one with a voice whose energy is water, but water on another planet. It's called "Water on New Mars" and the water on New Mars is the water of a parallel Mars.

MD: Where is the parallel Mars?

WA: It's in trans-vicinity. Over and beyond vicinity. I'm actually locating and exploring this water in this zone of trans-vicinity. I do mention specific locales on Mars, and they become proto-locales and supra-locales sometimes, but they are locales in themselves, like the Olympus Mons.[3]

MD: So it's a combination of physical locales and the realm of the mind?

WA: Intersecting, because that goes back to the triple mind, the supra-conscious, the conscious, and the subconscious. In other words, this spills out into all of reality, probably into every zone of the universe that one can find, although we don't really know the mysteriousness of the universe.

There may be areas that don't even have carbon-based life. But for this particular level of exploration, the carbon particle is quite apt.

MD: You've said you don't travel much physically, but you're a great mental traveler.

WA: The imagination has to ignite the process, wherever the base is. That said, I find that because the mind goes at such a rate, I can almost—as the old metaphysicians talked about—go directly to Mauritania or to Haiti, or Canada, or Detroit, or wherever I've been to and then relate it to the idea of the supra-plane and the physical plane. All of those levels partake of one single substance. The interesting part comes when divisions take place, and separate cuisines, separate psychologies, separate environments come into play—turmoil, political situations, such as in Sri Lanka or Madagascar. I can go there instantaneously. [Gilles] Deleuze talks about that—traveling from your chair. And it works because if I had to travel as fast as my mind was working, I couldn't do it.

MD: Right, and it saves on plane tickets.

WA: Right! I mean, that's the way I work. I know William Vollman talks about having to write his books in the next few years because he won't be able to physically take himself to all these environments that he goes to.

MD: It's not so much that you're using mimetic language—that you go somewhere and try to reflect it in words—rather, you're creating something as you perceive it. I wanted to ask you how you research . . .

WA: Again, by synecdoche and by predilection and going through a book almost as Tristan Tzara would open up a dictionary. I can read four or five passages out of a book and begin to explore in my mind. Of course, the accuracy of the vocabulary and the accuracy of what I'm talking about have to be explored, too. I'm not going to just say anything. I want to be very site-specific if it's something on Mars or on another planet. I will read in the particular area I need to read on as early as I can and get the logistics, then let the imagination explore and create, as though that part of the universe reflected the whole of the universe with the motion of living that had gone into creating that part of the universe, then manifest it in language. So in that sense I'm joining the creation of the universe, but in my own particular way, which is opening and opening and opening and opening, which is not a literal reality, but an experiential reality. It remains fresh and it remains fresh and it remains fresh. When I've explored it, I've gone through it, I'm finished with it, it's published and put in the world, and it remains in that state of motion.

MD: How do you revise?

WA: I re-hear something maybe once or twice, mostly just once. I handwrite everything and then I get on the typewriter or computer, and I hear other levels and that's my finished product.

MD: In your interview with Harryette Mullen[4] you say Rimbaud was an early influence. When did you decide to be a poet?

WA: When I saw that it was the only thing I could really do in this life—like Bud Powell, playing the piano. What he wanted to do and what he could organically do were inextricably linked. I had lived an intense emotional life up to that point and the mediums out of which that emotion could express itself had been inadequate. Around that period, I found this little book on Rimbaud and I read it and I felt it was me. I was able to begin to explore a medium that hitherto was unknown to me. At that point, I felt it more than knew it. I felt poetry. I literally felt it. I had felt poetry when listening to the great jazz musicians, really deeply. When I heard John Coltrane play, I couldn't believe it. It was that good.

MD: I've often thought if I could sit George Bush down and make him listen to *A Love Supreme*, his mind would be opened . . .

WA: Those types are very resistant to reality. They are trees in a hurricane. Since they don't bend, they ultimately break. They don't have any flexibility. When I listen to this music, there's this incredible flexibility. A combination of flexibility and formal sophistication, emotional and technical accuracy. I remember as a child I saw an American doctor's wife on the evening news in attendance at a Haitian voodoo ceremony. They showed her swaying—

she had to walk out because she said it was taking her over. Breton had that same sense of the ceremonies, in the 1940s. There's an imaginal power that comes from all over the world, but particularly from the former colonies in the Southern Hemisphere, energy that started the knowledges in the world, which is basically a right-brain knowledge. In the early kingdoms, the right brain was the dominant factor. I'm thinking specifically of Egypt, but it did not preclude profound investigation of the arts, of the sciences, of mathematics. There's a great writer on that area, Beatrice Lumpkin.[5] Cheikh Anta Diop[6] talks about this area, as well. I'm coming from an energy and experience that predates the Western idea of reality that has been discredited in the past 500 years or so.

MD: You write quite a bit about Kemet.[7] Could you talk a little more about what that pre-Greek idea of reality was?

WA: Kemet actually means "black soil." For me the "black soil" relates to both the physical climate, as well as the climate of the mind. [In ancient Kemet] if you were studying geology, astronomy, poetry, you got into the whole activity of the cosmos as a whole rather than a part. Knowledge had its own dynamic. Say I was studying the activity, the motion of the land in geology, I would understand it not as a secular or separable activity. Another analogy is to look at how an orchestra is set up—the oboes, the flutes, the piccolos. In some pieces, certain instruments dominate, but the flow of the whole orchestra propels that particular domination at that moment.

MD: When you write, do you feel it adds an essential movement to the symphony, even if it's not read by everyone?

WA: Absolutely. If you move something on Earth, it affects something else in the cosmos. These knowledges that I'm talking about are echoed through different times in different individuals. We're not born to set up an artificial division between what happens in the West and what happens in the southern climes, although there are essential differences. You have people like Roger Bacon[8] or Robert Grosseteste,[9] Bacon's teacher, who talked about light and elemental conjunctions of reality, which is pre-Leonardo. Roger

Bacon was the first person in the West to talk about a flying machine, not Leonardo.

MD: Leonardo wrote quite a bit on light in his notebooks.

WA: Grosseteste preceded that by a couple of hundred years. They were persecuted by the church because the church is based on a separable condition. Basically [Grosseteste and Bacon] were coming out of Moorish culture.

MD: Oh yes, you've talked about the Moors and how as scientists they had discovered things very early.

WA: They actually created the Renaissance in Europe, but they're never given credit because of their religion and their color. They held the Iberian Peninsula for 500 years. It was the only place where there was an organization of knowledge at that time. After the Roman Empire fell, there was a dispersion, a tremendous dispersion. Texts were held in monasteries, but never was there a concordance of sustained exploration for centuries. This was pointed out in an astronomy seminar I used to go to many ages ago. I'd go on these retreats with Dr. E. C. Krupp who runs the planetarium[10] here. One day we talked about the Crab Nebula and why it hadn't been recorded in Europe, but was recorded by the Chinese and the Moors [in 1054]. One of the astronomers there said, and I'm paraphrasing, "Well, maybe there was a fog over Europe and they couldn't see it." In other words, you have to have a system of organization to create knowledge. You have to have some sort of consistency with reality in order to organize and understand, say, water systems or water tables. There were hundreds of bookstores in Cordoba, and the seeds for the modern university were sown there. Jewish scholars, Christian scholars, Islamic scholars—it was one of our last hopes, because the three religions [pursued] knowledge in a way that was harmonious without losing their individuality. After the fall of the Moors, Christians began to dismantle the bathhouses, to disrupt and persecute and destroy. It coincides with the mounting fervor of the Inquisition and the beginning of the slave trade. Hermeticism seemed to be lost in Europe. It went underground and went underground and went underground.

MD: Why do you think these things happened at the same time, the Inquisition and the slave trade?

WA: I don't want to give some kind of answer to that. Things coalesce in history and there seems to be some sort of a tie that takes place. You have an idea that other people who are Asian or peoples of color, or people of other psychological persuasions, like Bacon, were no longer necessary. The internal state was superseded by external reasoning and definition began to accrue in terms of outer form. Exterior perfection was exalted, inner form dissolved, or was reduced to a minor rhetoric. Malraux points out the difference between the image of a ninth-century Christ and one of a fifteenth-century Christ. The former is less technical, but charged with interior feeling, the latter is commanding by means of its painterly virtuosity. The inner reverberation is replaced by technical expertise.

MD: What do you think about the shutdown of the Hubble Space Telescope?

WA: I think it's a disaster. [The Hubble] was an opportunity to explore things that really and truly are unknown. We don't even know about everything on this planet. We don't even know about ourselves. [The Hubble] was a gift. The problem is that we don't have a sustained society, but a truncated one, that moves from fragment to fragment.

MD: Do you see the poet as having a mission to discover wholeness again?

WA: I wouldn't just say the poet, but also the mathematician and the scientist. I think mathematics and science in the created sense come out of the same spirit. We've gotten to this extreme level of separation where we have to have conflict. Once in a while, a few conjunctions appear.

MD: I think astronomy is one way to restore people to their proper sizes.

WA: Astronomy does, because it is so strange. We've come to this point that when you look at astronomy, it explodes completely into another zone. None of our ideas of God—how can I put it?—none of our ideas about religion are capable of understanding it. The shadow system that they're exploring now—dark matter, what put that there? Stellar nurseries in Serpens with cloud towers six million trillion miles long. Yet the movement of life found there is the same energy that's populating this zone.

MD: Have you heard this theory that the chemical involved in the Big Bang is the same as when people fall in love?

WA: Basically what love is, is conjunction. What I think plagues the West is this whole idea of separation. Lots of beings, lots of objects. It's why the ecological situation is such a disaster. I've thought many times about how we can run an economic system without a stable weather system. You can't. Whether you call it global warming or climate change, it will destroy the economic base. A perspicacious 10-year-old can figure that out. I've talked to children and they understand it.

MD: It's not really about money. It doesn't make monetary sense.

WA: It's an ideology. There are other knowledges being explored that are not on the level of the strictly visible. There have been writers in the West who have actively sought this, most notably René Daumal. People like him keep this underground current that goes back to Bacon alive. It's everywhere. Octavio Paz said this current will always be here no matter what name we call it. It will never go away, no matter what the dominant ideology that seeks to prevent its praxis is.

MD: What other poets are you inspired or influenced by? You've mentioned the Surrealists . . .

WA: Oh, there's been so many. Basically, they come from obscure areas. People like Robert Marteau and Dino Campana, Fernando Pessoa's heteronyms. Of course. The Mexican poet Gorostiza, for topical relevance. For the impact he had on the modern world of poetry, Ramón López Velarde. Edgar Rincón Luna from Juarez, Mexico, for his dialogue across borders. Martín Camps. Gaspar Orozco, who translated my poetry into Spanish. Julian Semilian. César Vallejo's poems are incredibly exciting and powerful. Also early Williams.

MD: Not later Williams?

WA: Not the *Paterson* Williams but Hart Crane. Philip Lamantia. Bob—I've been in his presence. ·

MD: Bob Kaufman?

WA: Yes. We were in the same house together, although Bob was sitting in another room. It was myself, Philip Lamantia, and Neeli Cherkovski looking at the original typescript of *The Ancient Rain*; I saw the original form and the original type.

MD: Are you in contact with Philip Lamantia still?

WA: I just called him yesterday. I had finished an incredible experience with the Alice Farley Dance Theater. It was amazing—we had dancers, forms, all the incredible costumes she makes, we read the poems to the poet Laurence Weisberg. It was the most unconventional reading because we choreographed it like theatre, music, sound, poetry, dance. It was fortuitous energy. It was recorded and filmed, so we have the document.

MD: I wanted to ask you about your essays. Do you work out philosophical concepts in them that you use later in poetry?

WA: Certain energies come out as poetry, while certain ideas come out as essays. They form into this or that configuration. For me, my initial idea in writing essays is something I came to not right away, but I just found that I needed another way to express myself. I got the idea from photography. When a photographer is out shooting things, he or she finds things that impress him or her instantaneously. For me, an essay is like that—I find something interesting and write about it.

MD: I was particularly intrigued by your essay on Azarian Mathematics.[11]

WA: Oh, yeah. That was *completely* something I created. I would like to get enough knowledge at one point to actually study the symbols of higher mathematics and visualize Azarian Mathematics—mathematics simultaneously strengthened by a powerful visual stimulus. Mathematics and poetry are very, very close in the sense that a theorem or an equation functions as a penetrant calligraphy. Here's a quote from an essay called "Beauty of Mathematics: A Review"[12] on British mathematician Godfrey Harold Hardy:

"Everyone knows that mathematicians sometimes speak of perfectly formulated equations as 'beautiful' and are excited by them as the connoisseur is excited by works of art. The present volume will be of greatest interest and value to 'aestheticians' since it is here for the first time that the 'beauty' of mathematics has been discussed by a mathematician. Professor Hardy's analysis of this beauty is penetrating and illuminating, and in welcome contrast to the vagueness that is so characteristic of most modern writings on the criteria of beauty in other kinds of art." Here's another quote: "A mathematician like a painter or a poet, is a maker of patterns . . . The mathematician's patterns like the painter's or the poet's, must be 'beautiful'; the ideas, like the colors or the words, must fit together in a harmonious way. Beauty is the first test: there is no permanent place in the world for ugly mathematics." This is the way I look at it because as I see it, poetry has to be this beautiful and this accurate.

MD: It reminds me of the golden mean.[13] So many painters used it in their work. And what about your artwork, which has patterning in it reminiscent of astronomical or biological patterns?

WA: That realia of drawing came to me before my first recognizable poems evinced. I had been studying so much of Miró's work that I began to draw a figure in pencil one day and it worked—I've been working that way ever since. Federico García Lorca's drawings gave me the initial impetus to go forward in this direction, simply working with intuition. I've never taken an art class in my life. I've never had a tutor. I'm seriously involved right now in finishing a volume of drawings.

MD: Who is your writing community? Do you have a community in LA?

WA: There is a community, people that I know in different parts of the country—yourself, Andrew Joron, Nathaniel Mackey, Philip Lamantia. There's so many of them, I can't tell you. Listen, I'll leave people out, but I know they're there, and they know they're there. And there are some who are not in print, and people reading this interview will have never heard of them. For instance, Jim Henderson. The lifelong conversation I had with him was spectacular. We discussed an integral metaphysics combining the whole of life, sparked by our mutual understanding of Sri Aurobindo. He's passed on now, but he was very vital to me. People like that have been important to me.

MD: Do you correspond with writers in the Caribbean or Tibet?

WA: At this point, I don't. I quite, quite strenuously tried to contact Aimé Césaire. Last spring, I organized a national Surrealist conference, "The Imaginal Present And Future," cosponsored by the French Consulate. I posted contact with Césaire, which they transmitted. We did not get any response. This is unfortunate—I know there may be a language barrier, but that's not insurmountable. I'm thinking about going to Martinique in the not too distant future.

MD: People have compared you quite a bit to Césaire—Do you feel that's accurate?

WA: Well, in a spiritual sense, yes. What he was doing, and continues to do—there's nothing like it. He'll come up with a phrase and it's like a beautiful breath of oxygen. He was speaking in his "Letter to Maurice Thorez" about the particulars of the Southern Hemisphere and people of color and the way he put it together was quite extraordinary. There's just nothing like it, the power in the poetry and his *Discourse on Colonialism*. I call it the "big book." It is some 75 pages, but it seems as though one had gone through 300 pages of insight. So, it does feel accurate in that sense, but not in terms of my experience—I'm coming out of another world.

MD: He's very involved with his locale.

WA: Well, I grew up in an urban society. I don't want to make this a pat answer, but I've had to have a big city in order to do the kind of work I do. You need a lot of resources.

MD: Like libraries?

WA: Libraries.

MD: And universities?

WA: Universities. I need to travel across an eclectic range. Libraries, bookstores, cinemas, all kinds of metaphysical societies—I've been going to lectures for years. I have an incredible conduit, a man named Roger Weir. He continues to educate with insight after insight as if a current were running through you. Lectures on China, quantum physics, exobiology, Jung. He's given me a lot of information that I've been able to work with over the years. His lectures should be transcribed and published. He has volumes and volumes; you could fill a library with these lectures. People like that, you wouldn't find in many parts of the world. There's so much out here, so much to work with. You work with what you can and you work at your capacity. I understand I have limitations and I have to understand those limitations in order to continue to evolve.

MD: You grew up in LA.

WA: Yes, yet I've never looked at LA as a provincial enclave. There are some poets who defend the region against other regions. There's no need to do that. In fact, that's something I've never adhered to. It's antipoetic in the sense that they immure themselves in a desolate topography. I find this to be incredibly limiting. But the western coast has its own particulars. Many years ago, Jack Wise, the Canadian painter said, and again I'm paraphrasing, "We are looking out at China on the West Coast." In the east you're looking at Europe, we're looking at China. The Asiatic influence is incredible. I do customer service for this company, and I've been writing these names down. Incredible long, long, long names. Indian long, Laotian long. Long, long names. I mean, it's unbelievable. My next experience, because I'm gathering all this, is I want to write a novel from the Saxon perspective concerning the reencroachment of peoples of color overrunning the West. The encroachment of the other.

MD: How are you doing that?

WA: It's very complex. I've done some twenty books and I am at this point where—whoa—I have got to assess some of what I've written. I need to work on getting my trilogy of novels out into the world. Spuyten Duyvil is going to put them out late next year under one cover. And then there's another handwritten novel in a duffel bag, called *Diary as Sin*. Douglas

Messerli has a novella called *Alien Weaving*. So the Saxon novel would be my fourth attempt, but I'm going to take my time with it because I have other things to do and a lot of things I have to work with. As I said earlier on, I'm going to be working on researching and basically being a visual artist for a number of months.

Notes

1. Sage, prophet, and wandering monk Swami Vivekananda (1863–1902) was founder of the Ramakrishna Math and Mission.

2. ". . . the moon of each of the bodies' vibrations is understood as the flower of spontaneous carbon embodied in the impelling elusives of pure experience itself." "Isolation and Gold," *Towards the Primeval Lightning Field*, O Books, 1998.

3. The largest mountain in the solar system, over three times the size of Mount Everest.

4. "Hauling Up Gold from the Abyss: An Interview with Will Alexander," *Callaloo*, Spring 1999.

5. Author of *Math: A Rich Heritage* and *African and African-American Contributions to Mathematics*.

6. Senegalese scientist and historian, author of many books, including *The African Origin of Civilization: Myth or Reality*.

7. An ancient name for Egypt.

8. An early (1214–1294) English philosopher, also known as Doctor Mirabilis, considered one of the first advocates of modern scientific methods.

9. Early (1175–1253) English statesman, theologian, mathematician, and physicist.

10. The Griffith Observatory in Los Angeles, CA.

11. "Isolation and Gold."

12. Ananda K Coomaraswamy, "Beauty of Mathematics: A Review," *Art Bulletin*, Vol. XXIII, New York, 1941.

13. A number, represented by the Greek letter "phi" and also known as the "divine proportion" or the "magic ratio," in which the smaller dimension is to the greater as the greater is to the whole. It is found throughout the natural world.

RON PADGETT LIFTS OFF
WITH EDMUND BERRIGAN

APRIL/MAY 2005   NO. 203

From Tulsa teenager publishing the likes of Jack Kerouac, Allen Ginsberg, Robert Creeley, and others in his *White Dove Review*, to close collaborator with Joe Brainard, Ted Berrigan, and Dick Gallup, Ron Padgett has cut a swathe across the floor (or ceiling, depending on where you stand) of contemporary poetry. At first read, Padgett's poetry might seem cutup, but the lines leap from shining bar to shining bar, setting themselves ablaze and then landing (maybe) at their starting point, blinking at you while animated characters point and chuckle in the background. Other poems are not so comic, as some leaps defy imagination for unsettling conflicts of memory and mortality. Recent years have seen Padgett venture into the past with prose recollections of Berrigan (*Ted*, The Figures, 1993); a biography of his father, Wayne Padgett, a well-known bootlegger in Tulsa (*Oklahoma Tough: My Father, King of the Tulsa Bootleggers*, U. of Oklahoma, 2003); and, most recently, his memoir of longtime friend and artist Joe Brainard (*Joe: A Memoir of Joe Brainard*, Coffee House Press, 2004). Padgett's other books include *You Never Know* (poetry, Coffee House Press, 2002) and *Complete Poems of Blaise Cendrars* (translations, U. of California, 1993). I caught up with Ron Padgett this winter at his East Village apartment, where we discussed, among other things, these recent forays into history and memory.

EDMUND BERRIGAN: I've been thinking about four of your books: *Joe, Oklahoma Tough, Ted*, and *Albanian Diary*. They're all memoir or biography to

some degree. What is it about prose that appeals to you when you deal with something like a memoir? For example, why didn't you write *Joe* as a long poem?

RON PADGETT: I'm fairly traditional: most memoirs or biographies are written in prose. Not all, but most. Ed Sanders wrote a long poem that is a biography of Allen Ginsberg. Writing *Joe* in prose gave me more room to make the kind of structures that I thought would be too hard to do in a poetic form. Also I didn't see the point in having line breaks in what I wanted to say. The language in *Joe* doesn't dance, because I didn't want it to. I wanted to make boxes.

EB: *Ted* lends itself to that kind of dancing.

RP: A bit, yes, but only insofar as the sequence of the little boxes in *Ted* could be rearranged, which is not true of a chronological book such as *Joe*.

EB: Did your structural decision for *Joe* consciously come out of writing *Ted*?

RP: No. Both are memoirs about close friends of mine, but I think the resemblance ends there. Writing the book about Ted probably gave me courage for the more extended and complicated book that *Joe* is. But at the outset any decision I might have made was an unconscious one. When I first started writing the book about Joe, I didn't know that it was going to be a book about Joe. I intended to write down, as clearly as I could, salient moments that came towards me from my memory—somewhat the way Joe wrote his "I remember" entries. I vaguely expected the piece to run to fifty, sixty, seventy pages. Later I felt that I needed some biographical glue for these fragments that were accumulating, so I made a timeline and started researching, and then the whole thing took off. I had a tiger by the tail.

EB: It does seem to be a cross between a memoir and a biography.

RP: That's exactly what it is, which might trouble people who like to classify things neatly, because it is neither a full biography nor a memoir. I don't mind. Besides, I was writing from both those points of view.

EB: *Oklahoma Tough*, on the other hand, functions a lot more as a biography. Do you think the writing of that influenced the impulse to make *Joe* more biographical?

RP: Probably. Writing the book about my father required a lot of research—mostly interviewing people in Tulsa—to discover things that otherwise I wouldn't have known. I enjoy research. It's intellectual detective work. It was a lot of fun and a lot of hard work, with some emotional ups and downs. Eventually it became somewhat exhausting, so although I was enormously happy with having finished such a demanding project, I didn't think I would have enough energy to write another book like that. In both books the moral responsibility weighed on me, because I was not only expressing my view of things, I was also making a representation of the world, saying, in effect, "This is the way it was." Of course everyone could write his or her own book and come out with a different picture, but since there was no other book about Joe's whole life, I felt that I was the only game in town at the moment. I tried to make it as accurate and true and honest as I could, because that's what he would have done.

EB: I suppose the research for the two books was quite different. Did you have to go back to Tulsa for any special research for *Joe*?

RP: Very little, because I knew Joe's friends a lot better than I knew my father's friends. To put it more generally, I had a far better feel for the personal universe of Joe than I did for the personal universe of my father. And I had immediate access to Joe's letters and other documentary material. A lot of the research I did on my dad involved official archives: court documents, the Tulsa newspapers' dead files, and FBI files.

EB: Did you encounter much resistance from the FBI?

RP: They were very resistant. Under President Reagan the revisions to the Freedom of Information Act made it possible for the FBI to withhold more information than in the past. After a year and half the FBI sent me 1300 pages on my father, 99 percent of it blacked out with a magic marker. It looked like a Fluxus book, almost every word marked out! For example, one sentence began "Wayne Padgett's mother is named—" and the rest was deleted. In other words, they were withholding from me my own grandmother's name! There were a number of such instances. A civil liberties lawyer told me I had grounds for an appeal, because the FBI had exercised "excessive zeal in the lack of disclosure." To my surprise, the FBI granted my appeal, and after another year the 1300 pages came through again, this time with only 80 percent marked out. But the new 19 percent was illuminating, and this time they accidentally left in some things they were supposed to have deleted.

EB: How did you move from being the son of a bootlegger to being a poet?

RP: It's not as much of a jump as it might seem. In the Oklahoma milieu I grew up during the 1940s and 1950s, being a poet was considered very unusual, something that people didn't do in that society. That is, poet equaled outsider. That's what my bootlegging father was, an outsider. He did pretty much what he wanted to do his entire life, even when it meant going against the grain of society. I suppose I had a similar willfulness, and I must have felt entitled to be rebellious, like him. The difference is that I was bookish and intellectual, and had the advantage of an education at an Ivy League college. But in high school I'd already decided to be a poet. If my father were alive and in this room today, you would see resemblances between us. The bootlegger vs. poet dichotomy would seem less compelling, because there's a lot more to a person than whether he or she is a poet or a bootlegger.

EB: Is poetry still exciting and outlawish for you now?

RP: No, I don't think of poetry as being outlawish at all. Not in the least.

EB: Really? Don't people still look at you strangely sometimes when you tell them you're a poet?

RP: Not so much, because I'm older now and I look serious. I'm not a skinny teenager that people think they can push around. I'm bald and gray and 62—that is, I can look "mature." People ask, "Have you published any books?" And I say ten or twelve or whatever, and they act impressed. Then I look for the nearest exit. But poetry doesn't seem outlawish at all to me, because vast numbers of people from every culture have done it throughout history. I happen to be one of those people. It's a big deal only if you buy into the cliché of poet as oddball.

EB: When did you start to read poetry?

RP: More or less simultaneously I discovered two books, *Howl* and *Leaves of Grass*. I had read a poem of Whitman's in school, "O Captain, My Captain," one of his worst poems, which made no impression on me. But when I found *Leaves of Grass* and read "Song of Myself," wow! Very quickly after that I discovered the Beat poets and the Black Mountain poets, and some New York School poets. One day the owner of the best bookstore in town said to my buddy Dick Gallup and me, after we bought a book by Camus, "Have you guys read Kerouac?" I thought he was speaking in tongues: "Kerouac" was like a mysterious phoneme to me. The owner recommended *The Subterraneans*. Soon afterward Dick and I read *On the Road*, *The Dharma Bums*, and *Dr. Sax*. I immediately ordered the City Lights books—Corso, Ferlinghetti, Marie Ponsot, Jacques Prévert's *Paroles*—anything they published I would buy.

EB: So this would be '59?

RP: About '58. The bookseller also recommended e. e. cummings and T. S. Eliot. Anyway, the floodgates were opened, and I found *Evergreen Review* and devoured it, and I pored over the ads in the back for small presses, I subscribed to magazines such as LeRoi Jones's *Yugen*, and I discovered New Directions—Pound, Williams, Lorca, Kenneth Patchen, and Rimbaud, among others. So my literary reading outside of school was City Lights, New Directions, and Grove Press books, with some Modern Library, Doubleday Anchor, and Meridian thrown in.

EB: What kind of influence did Kerouac have on your writing?

RP: He showed me, I think more than any writer I'd ever read, even more than Allen [Ginsberg] and Whitman, that writing can be exhilarating. The pleasure of that rush of linguistic energy was like driving for the first time in a really fast convertible with the top down. For a while I imitated his style, which was fun. I had been a maudlin, introspective, quiet writer. I'd always think about what I had to say, and then bear down on it. At its best my writing was sensitive, at its worst it was sodden and self-important. But I was just a kid, what the hell. When Kerouac showed up it unscrewed the car doors at 120 miles per hour.

EB: I wanted to ask you about individual poems in *You Never Know*. "Not Partic-

ularly" struck me because the first line, "Out of the quarrel with life,"
reminds me of my dad's poem "Tambourine Life," which has the lines
"Rhetoric / is what we make / out of our quarrels / with others // out of /
our quarrels with ourselves / we make poetry."

RP: By the way, I wrote some of the lines in "Tambourine Life." But in the case
you mention, my line wasn't based consciously on Ted's. Sometimes I will
have a phrase in my head, with no idea where it came from. Sometimes it'll
be from a poem I read and forgot, or sometimes from a poem of my own.
Or from anywhere. It is a line or phrase that the poem will generate itself out
of. Then years later I'll be reading John Ashbery or Andrew Marvell, and,
O no! There's that line! I see my using it as an unconscious form of respect
to the original source.

EB: What I liked was that whereas Ted says, "Out of our quarrel with ourselves
we make poetry," you said "Out of the quarrel with life / we are a whirlwind
of invisible whirs that / go around a statue by Giacometti." I thought that
was a great substitute for "make poetry." It just was poetry!

RP: I like that poem. It's not really a poem by me, and I like that.

EB: How's that?

RP: I mean it doesn't sound like me.

EB: This first poem, "Morning"—

RP: That's not by me, either.

EB: Really? Who wrote all these poems?

RP: I did.

EB: I found the poem kind of spooky. Was it launched out of memory, or a
feeling?

RP: Yes, it's about my parents.

EB: And this strange wooden Indian that gets set ablaze.

RP: Isn't that weird? I remember writing this. It was morning, I was in my lit-
tle room in Vermont. Sitting there, I sensed a presence in the room. I don't
mean to sound mystical, but occasionally you look around and someone is
standing in the doorway, or the dog is there. The feeling wasn't scary or

spooky, just a slight intuition. I started the poem, "Who is here with me?" Then, somehow, I don't know how, the answer was "My mother and an Indian man." The third line is "(I'm writing this in the past.)". The use of the anachronistic word *Indian* suggested that the setting is anterior to that of the moment of composition. But it turned out that this Indian is not a man but a statue, apparently a cigar store Indian, a thing that used to be fairly common. The statue brings with it the association of wood and smoke, and then the scene is discovered to be prenatal. "Morning" was an interesting poem for me to write because I didn't give in to my penchant for humor. There are several spots in this poem where I came to a fork in the road: I could have gone down Comedy Court or Straight Arrow Lane. Something made me avoid Comedy Court.

EB: "Album" also struck me. It ends: "They betray us, those molecules, we who have loved them. They treat us like dirt."

RP: There is some humor there, but not much.

EB: How did you decide to avoid the comedic route?

RP: First, I tend to be wary of doing the "Ron Padgett thing." Not being mercurial or witty was one of the main things I could do to avoid writing a "Ron Padgett" poem. It's like, okay, you've got a curveball, a slider, and a changeup. But do you have a fastball? And can you throw it right down the middle of the plate at 95 miles per hour? If you are as multifaceted as you always claim you are, why aren't you showing that in your work? What is the reflex that tends to shunt you into the comfort zones of the comic imagination? So I try to write—at least sometimes—against my own grain. Second, things that seemed funny when I was young aren't as funny now. *You Never Know* has an elegiac tone, but it has funny things in it too. How about this: try writing a comic elegy. In the years just before the poems in this book, both of my parents had died, as well as a number of friends. When my parents died I spent a lot of time looking at family photographs, which, by the way, can be good for writing because they have details in them, and when you look at them with a magnifying glass you sometimes see things that you never noticed. Also, photographs are so evocative of a moment, and if you can project yourself into the scene, like having been there when the picture was taken—even if it was before you were born—it's wonderful. Hence the title "Album."

EB: On a different note, I've read that you've had an interest in Woody Guthrie. Was that because he was from Oklahoma?

RP: Partly for that reason. His hometown, Okemah, isn't far from Tulsa. He was about ten years older than my parents, and he wrote songs about things that my grandparents experienced. "Tom Joad," for instance, could almost have been written about my relatives, but, unlike Steinbeck's characters in *The Grapes of Wrath*, my people stayed in Depression Oklahoma. I felt a close sympathy for the people in his songs, the poor, the uneducated, the powerless, the underdogs, because most of my relatives were like that. I loved Guthrie's children's songs, too. Also, he could be very wry and ironic, even in his political songs. When I was 16 or 17, for me the two poles of folk music were Woody Guthrie and Lead Belly.

EB: What about Lead Belly appealed to you?

RP: His sheer amazing natural force. What an unstoppable driving energy, with that twelve-string guitar and the occasionally complicated fingerings. Talk about a wall of sound! In those last sessions that Alan Lomax recorded, Lead Belly casually tears through his vast repertory, song after song: from "Alabama Bound" to "Goodnight, Irene" to "Hitler Blues," with its staggering first line, "We're gonna tear Hitler down," as if Hitler was a building! I loved Lead Belly's voice. The accent, the rhythm, the intonations were very similar to those of my relatives from Arkansas. This is going to sound weird, but he felt like a relative. Around the same time, I discovered modern jazz— Miles Davis, John Coltrane, Dave Brubeck, Gerry Mulligan, Monk. I more or less happened onto classical music when Dick Gallup joined a mail-order classical music club. The first time we listened to the *Brandenburg Concertos*, I fell on the floor laughing. Bach seemed incredibly far out. But before all that I was surrounded by the cowboy swing and big band music my mother

loved, and of course early rock 'n' roll and rhythm 'n' blues: Jerry Lee
Lewis, Little Richard, Gene Vincent, Chuck Berry, Fats Domino, Bill Haley
and the Comets, Little Willie John, just tons of people, followed by Light-
nin' Hopkins, Blind Lemon Jefferson, Big Bill Broonzy, and Muddy Waters.
You get the picture.

EB: It's been a crazy millennium, politics-wise, especially here in New York.
Have you written about that at all?

RP: Yes, I have, but with little success. Over the years I've marched against
the bomb, the Vietnam War, and other things, but I assumed that I did not
have to immerse myself totally in politics or social issues because there were
enough people who were going to set things right in this country. They were
burningly interested in doing so. I was burningly interested in writing poetry.
The country would go off course, and then the people I admired would put it
somewhat back on course. But in recent years, the country is not being put
back on course. As part of the generation that has allowed this to happen,
I feel responsible, hence angry with myself and guilty. I've always had an
enormous problem with writing a decent political poem. In the last couple of
years I've had the feeling that I must try to do this difficult thing. One recent
poem, of seven or eight pages, contains overtly political statements. Not just
about politics, in the narrow sense of the word—let's call it world manage-
ment. To say that I'm dismayed by the recent history of our country is a radi-
cal understatement. If I weren't able to practice a certain kind of daily focus,
I'd be seriously depressed. Giving money to Howard Dean and the Demo-
cratic Party, signing petitions, marching at the UN are not enough. Most of
my life I've been congenitally optimistic, but the scales have tipped now. Of
course our country isn't the only problem, but I don't see any national lead-
ers in the world addressing the situation in a meaningful way. Periodically I
go off to Vermont for months and live without a TV or a newspaper, to keep
myself from going completely bonkers thinking about the world mess. Okay,
there *are* other reasons for going there. My hope is that the mental state I
maintain myself in will allow me to do something helpful. Of course there's

more than a little vanity in such a notion. Anyway, I'm going to do what I can—in politics and in writing—but who knows what that might be? Things have become more than a little spooky here. You have to wonder, who are all these barbarians who are running the country, and why are so many people panting and drooling along behind them?

EB: Some of them have been there for years, like Cheney. But media manipulation is an unquestionably negative influence, because people don't get all the facts, or much analysis of the things these people say.

RP: Another remove from that is that even when people *are* given facts, if they can't think, the facts have no effect whatsoever. I have a relative who's a knee-jerk conservative. He believes in the abolition of gun control; he thinks the invasion of Iraq was great. When presented with facts, his mind takes them, puts them to one side, and goes right around them. He can't understand what the facts are telling him, he can understand only what he *wants* the facts to tell him. And if the facts don't tell him that, he gets some other data—any bric-a-brac that sustains his point of view. You can't reason with someone who can't think straight.

EB: How long did it take you to translate *Complete Poems* by Blaise Cendrars?

RP: I'm glad you changed the subject. The Cendrars work stretched over decades, because it was never a concerted effort. The first time I translated his poems was in the spring of 1966 in Paris. The Paris editors of the *Paris Review* were going to publish an interview with Cendrars, and they wanted to include some poems alongside it, so they invited me to translate some. I said, "I don't know his work that well." They said, "Go out and buy his *Poésies complètes* and see. And send us the bill." Oh goody! I found that some of the poems were both cute and translatable. That got me interested in Cendrars. Over the years I would wander back to his poems and translate some, such as his long poem, "The Prose of the Trans-Siberian," which already existed in a number of English versions. One of the best was by John Dos Passos, but its 1920s diction had gotten a little stale and it had a couple of bad spots. Then I translated a group of poems called *Kodak (Documen-*

taries), composed entirely of found poems. I wish I could have located all of his sources, but I could find only some of them.

EB: It's fascinating to think of translating what someone found, rather than what they wrote.

RP: The things he found were mostly from French sources, although at one point he quotes from Captain Cook's journal. Cendrars wrote it all in French, but if I'm translating I should really go back and find the original English he's quoting from and just use that. Such literary research can get pretty heavy. It was because someone else had done the legwork that I then took on a very challenging book of Cendrars's called *19 Elastic Poems*, a collection of "cubist" poems. Fortunately a scholar named Jean-Pierre Goldenstein found out just about everything about these poems, which made it much easier for me to understand how to translate them. Then an editor at the University of California Press asked me if I would like to translate all of Cendrars's poems, something I had never intended to do. But there I was, having done 80 percent of them, so I set about translating the other 20 percent and going back and reworking some of the 80 percent. During this period I got to know some terrific scholars in the Blaise Cendrars International Society and I went to Switzerland and France to work on the translations with Cendrars's daughter, as well as with others. I really got into it, and we produced a book that I like.

EB: Is translating like writing, does it have those kinds of discoveries?

RP: For me translating is like revising. You change the original creation, and then you go back and change *that*. In the initial translating phase, yes, sometimes there's a bit of the liftoff that occurs in spontaneous original composition. Often when I'm reading a piece in French, I just read the French. Other times, I'll read it and ask myself, "What would that be in English?" Then other times it just flies off the page into English by itself. That's the liftoff.

WAYNE KOESTENBAUM AND
MAGGIE NELSON IN CONVERSATION

APRIL/MAY 2006   NO. 207

WAYNE KOESTENBAUM: When asked to think about poetry, I can only think about prose, or Déodat de Séverac, or *Pet Sounds*.

MAGGIE NELSON: That seems right and just. It reminds me of the opening of Anne Carson's *Economy of the Unlost*, where she talks about having to write on Celan and Simonides at the same time, because if she picked just one, she'd end up "settling": the worst thing. Or bored: equally bad.

WK: Now I'm writing an essay about artist Amy Sillman and using this assignment to think about why poetic lines often feel claustrophobic to me. Odd, that while writing an essay I'm more inventive with "poetic lines" than when I'm writing a poem . . .

MN: I've been reading Schopenhauer, who is completely hilarious and, for some reason, more heartening to me than anybody even vaguely uplifting. He postulates suffering as one surefire way to avoid boredom. Unless suffering gets boring—then I guess you're sunk.

WK: Can't believe you're actually reading Schopenhauer. I've never cracked the spine of that one. Today I threw out an old unread Aristophanes paperback.

MN: The Schopenhauer is all aphorisms—not very hard to crack. That's about the only kind of philosophy I can read, anyway.

WK: Joseph Joubert never actually wrote a book, only aphorisms and fragments, warm up for a book he never arrived at . . .

MN: Lately I've been trying to stay focused on this prose "sequel" to *Jane*, which I've modeled (loosely) on Peter Handke's *A Sorrow Beyond Dreams*. Although whereas his language is flat, exacting, and excruciating, I worry that mine's just flat.

WK: I never dug Handke's *Sorrow*. Maybe I wasn't sorrowful enough when I read it. I'm finding it hard to finish my Sillman essay, mostly because, I realize, I'm APPROVAL ADDICTED. (A self-help book I saw advertised on the F train: *Approval Addiction*—and how to get over it.)

MN: This AA seems a group I could really dig.

WK: How's your shoulder? Mine hurts. Say something about how writing damages the body. (Somehow Plath's "the blood jet is poetry" fits in here.)

MN: Thanks for asking—mine hurts too. I've just moved to CA, where they're much more concerned with bodily well-being than in NYC, and the computer keyboard that CalArts has bought me has a sticker that reads: NOTE: SOME EXPERTS BELIEVE THAT THE USE OF ANY KEYBOARD MAY CAUSE SERIOUS INJURY. As if the keyboard were a rock of crack instead of a keyboard. Poetry has never injured me, bodily, but prose has. My process of writing poems has much more BODY in it: I write on napkins, in notepads, on receipts, etc., and then put it all down in one place and tote the pages with me to different locales. But prose makes me feel like my ass is waxed to the chair. Instead of marking time, prose makes it disappear. Whole days, lost to the wormhole of work. Perhaps you and I have this in common: rhetorically we privilege indolence, but we both really like to work.

WK: We're both weirdly giddy. Nervous, afraid to offend, jumpy, a combination of focused and scattered . . . I'm fascinated by what you said long ago about the poetics of fast-talking. Do you speak more quickly than I? I've slowed down with age, I used to be a mile-a-minute guy . . . When very young, I stuttered; I still tend to hesitate. Self-interruption is why I love Robert Walser. His voice—at once grandiose and shattered, nervously observing itself crawl through syntax—helped me write *Moira Orfei in Aigues-Mortes.*

MN: The necessary & sheer rush of energy I get from talking to you has much to do with our mutual speediness. It's a drug, really—sometimes I can get to talking so fast with you that I feel like I'm about to skid off the planet. I probably do talk faster than you, but only because I've yet to master the art of talking very fast while always remaining understandable. You pause for effect, you enunciate clearly.

WK: If I pause, as you say, for effect, that's a teacherly affectation, or fatigue, or a consciousness that what I'm about to say might be offensive—a wish to gain mileage from indecision. Plus I love commas, colons, paragraph breaks, line breaks, any chance to halt *in medias res.*

MN: You and I have never talked about our mutual history in speech therapy.

WK: I remember going into some trailer? I've "blocked" the memory (how melodramatic!). My first-grade teacher told me I stuttered. I remember being caught inside the stutter; it seemed not a stigma but a decorative peculiarity, an embroidery.

MN: I'm now remembering that great part of your essay on James Schuyler where you compare the stutter in his untitled villanelle with Bishop's stutter in the final line of "One Art," and talk about them as "two great postmodern statements of the poetics of the closet." Coming out/staying in: seems like we both have the desire to offend while also being afraid of offending *fatally*, as it were: a recipe for shame if I ever heard one! I too have "blocked" speech therapy. What I haven't blocked is the metal device once affixed to the roof of my mouth with a little spike on it which pricked me every time I tried to put my tongue against my front teeth to make a lispy "s." My speech took on a totally weird rhythm: "s," then "ouch."

WK: Recently in a fit of closure I gave my friend Matthew Stadler my *Hotel*

Theory manuscript (at the moment it's in two columns: a nonfiction meditation in the left column, a novel in the right column). *Hotel Theory*'s not poetry (maybe it isn't even literature, just turd-arranging), but the fact that it runs in twin skinny columns helps me see it as poetry. Or at least vertical language. Is it too late to be "experimental"? Now I'm reading Joan Retallack and thinking, "Can I play, too?"

MN: Weirdly, part of the experiment of *Jane* was to let some poems fall flat, which felt sinful: can I really publish a poem this "bad"? But the project wasn't about delivering lyric flourish at every turn. It had other goals.

WK: Your avoidance of embroidery is refreshing. I love Marie Redonnet's novels because they, too, renounce "lyric flourish." Someone once called my poems "flat," and the adjective hurt. I'm reminded of the time some psycho girlfriend of mine (decades ago) answered a long rhapsodic letter I'd written her with this terse, humiliating rebuff: "Next time, write to me." One command, on a tiny slip of paper, tucked into an envelope. Derrida hadn't yet written *The Post Card*, so I had no context for my failure as a letter writer, as a sociable being.

MN: It's so unspeakably painful to feel the thrill of thinking you've found someone who might want to house or hear the excitation, and send back his/her own "toomuchness," & then to receive any rebuff which leaves you suddenly alone with your own reams of rhetorical flourish. Maybe that's why the drug-addled dialogue—or monologue—between Warhol's "A" and the "B" on the other end of the phone line feels more reassuring—"A" may eventually have to hang up, but it isn't punitive.

WK: Your *Jane* gloriously refuses to package itself as poem, novel, or memoir. I respect its unwillingness to dress up grief or placelessness; its ruminations and circlings have a sustaining austerity. A memoirist's or poet's vulnerability, as you've suggested, can be a form of packaging, a hard sell.

MN: And what a perverse form of the "hard sell" it is, in a country meanly obsessed with "protecting itself," from terrorists, from identity theft, from whatever. True bravery, which, I think, involves failure, and loneliness, is harder to come by. Fanny Howe says that she avoids titling her poems because titles "put a lid on the loneliness." I think that's brave.

WK: Antipackaging stance number one: I'm trying to move away from writing that too clearly aims at a reader. Reader-friendly = reader-molesting. Give the reader some privacy! Claudia Rankine's newest book, which I admire, is *Don't Let Me Be Lonely*, but I'm equally drawn to Schoenberg's insistence (in his essay "How One Becomes Lonely") on becoming-lonely (like becoming-animal!) as interminable and desirable. Certain reading experiences are touchstones of this loneliness: Benjamin's *The Arcades Project*, Stein's *A Novel of Thank You*, or Sade's *The 120 Days of Sodom*. As Artaud put it, "But at any given moment, I can do nothing without this culture of the void inside me."

MN: I wonder if the market panic that someone won't pick up a book & read it without knowing what it is has something to do with the culture's panic about loneliness: God forbid we're left alone with something, especially ourselves. Recently I was in an airport bookstore and saw a bestseller with the title *Never Eat Alone*. I didn't know, before being interpellated by this book (a self-help guide to becoming a better "networker"), that eating alone was something one was supposed to avoid. In what I've been working on lately I've felt—or it's felt—voiceless. It's been very painful to *not* know what I sound like for the first time in my life, although, I suppose, important— a reversal along the lines of what psychologists like Adam Phillips are always harping on about psychoanalysis: that its point is to become a stranger to oneself, not to bask in some golden halo of "self-knowledge."

WK: The quest to "become a stranger to oneself": that's the "hit" (as Avital Ronell would put it) of writing: seeing a strange face in the mirror, hearing one's voice as strange, like the strange face that psychologist Silvan Tomkins suggests inspires shame in the child—you turn to seek the parent and instead see a strange unloving face. One of my first memories is of my mother's face seeming a stranger's: I wondered, who is that stranger hanging out in my backyard? Too often in my work I give place to the familiar rather than to the strange—I tend to cut odd passages and retain comprehensible ones.

MN: Me too. Partly because to go headlong into the "strange" can court breakdown. Since working on this "sequel," which literally "returns to the scene of the crime," has occasioned, or at least come on the heels of, some form of nervous breakdown, many friends have sagely counseled me to leave it alone, or to come back to it when I feel stronger. All I can say is that I wouldn't be doing it if it didn't feel like something I have to do. I admit this may be a little childish—petulance, or masochism, masquerading as adult inquiry.

WK: I doubt I've ever had a proper "nervous breakdown," though I'm often in the midst of a slow-motion, barely detectable dissolution of the threads of sociability and normalcy, a process of becoming-strange to friends, becoming-strange to my own language. A migration in my reading life—toward writers who violate the pact of sociability (Blanchot, Bernhard, Genet, Jelinek, Lezama Lima, Sarduy, Ponge, Huidobro, Celan, Guyotat)—comes from a wish not to repair the slow-motion breakdown but to nourish it, find a mirror for it in equivalently difficult literature, even as my own writing seems, sometimes, so woefully transparent and legible.

MN: I don't know if the term "breakdown" applies unless you're chasing after a rock of crack in the carpet of a hotel room or being involuntarily shipped off to Bellevue, but perhaps there are gradations, and if so, I think it fair to call them breakdowns. The reopening of my aunt's case was contemporaneous with a terrible accident suffered by a dear friend of mine, and tending to her near-fatal injuries while being reimmersed (by the state, by the media, by my own compulsions) in my aunt's fatal injuries has sometimes not felt psychically tolerable. Judith Butler's *Precarious Life* has helped: "To be injured means that one has the chance to reflect upon injury, to find out the mechanisms of its distribution, to find out who else suffers from permeable borders, unexpected violence, dispossession, fear, and in what ways." A useful project, especially during this horrible and pointless war.

WK: Talking with you gives me so much energy! I want to belong to the School of Maggie, to reinsert myself (post facto) into whatever tradition or ecosystem you're participating in, even if I don't belong . . .

MN: Wayne, you have to be kidding. The School of Maggie? There is no such thing!

WK: And yet I'm inspired by your statement, "I write on napkins, in notepads, on receipts, etc., and then put it all down in one place and tote the pages with me to different locales . . ." I want to be in those different locales! I want those napkins, those receipts! I want your speed and mobility and flexibility! I deplore my dependence on filters (as in mentholated cigarettes): genre is a filter, publication is a filter, the "poetic line" is a filter, plot is a filter, fact is a filter, "I" is a filter, rhetoric is a filter . . .

MN: If it makes you feel any better, I seem to have lost the "different locales" School of Writing for the moment—I've been doing all my writing in my office at CalArts, a round, navy-blue asylum, CA '70s motel-style, which, as David Antin notes, has no windows, so a huge storm could be raging outside and you'd never know it. Often I emerge to find huge strips of eucalyptus flying through the air like clubs.

WK: A dear friend recently expressed surprise when I told him that I considered myself indebted to the so-called New York School of poetry. Are the traces of my indebtedness so difficult to parse? I don't demand that New York school(s) be cohesive—on this subject I've learned much from your forthcoming book on women and abstraction in the New York School—and yet appearing in The Poetry Project's pages feels like homecoming. Maybe poetic identification should remain fugitive or exiled—but without the foster-parentage of Schuyler, O'Hara, Brainard, Ashbery, Cage, Feldman, Ginsberg, Myles, Notley, and Warhol, I'd be voiceless. This NYS affiliation means more to me than the old-school "gay" badge.

MN: Yes—whatever the "NYS" was or is, I think of it as a rubric, a practice, a place, in which aesthetics can occupy the foreground rather than gay identity politics, but without the customary downgrading or erasure of being queer which that preeminence usually (unnecessarily, homophobically) entails.

WK: I love the picture of you chasing after a "rock of crack in the carpet of a hotel room"—like a photo of Liza Minnelli (by Chris Makos?) . . . I'm enamored of the phrase "rock of crack," like Artaud's "claque-dents" (which Anne Carson borrows for "TV Men: Artaud"). Do we call the phrase ("rock of crack," "claque-dents") a fricative? If only you could have recited to your speech therapist Artaud's last words (as translated by Clayton Eshleman and Bernard Bador):

> *And they have pushed me over*
> *into death,*
> *where I ceaselessly eat*
> *cock*
> *anus*
> *and caca*
> *at all my meals,*
> *all those of THE CROSS.*

Say after me: caca. I believe in spells. And so, I think, do you: I turn to your first book, *Shiner*, and find "Ka-boom, ka-boom," I find "chunky snow," I find "Well I want jack pie," not to mention "pet rock" and "The plung- / ing wall"—signs of the claque-dent aesthetic. We needn't have undergone electroshock to understand that when we write we sometimes reapply the voltage we once passively accepted. In "The Bum" (from *Jane*) you address this hyperaesthesia: "As a child I had so much energy I'd lie awake and feel my organs smolder." This smoldering is inspiration, but it's also the death-sentence shock of overexcitation.

MN: I don't know if I love the image of myself chasing after a rock of crack in a hotel room carpet. But "when we write we sometimes reapply the voltage we once passively accepted"—this I love. Maybe it's precisely here that writing becomes cruel—not cruel as in sadistic, but cruel as in Artaud's "theater of cruelty": the manifestation of an implacable, irreversible intent, a kind of wild spitting back at the world that begot you without your choosing to be begotten into it. You can hear this spit and crackle, this rock of crack, in Artaud's voice on those final recordings. The earth moves.

WK: In those recordings, Artaud sometimes sounds like Shirley Temple.

MN: Amen.

WK: Being-about-to-burst: my primal scene of writing: sixth grade: teacher gave us fifteen minutes to write a story: the noon lunch bell rang: I hadn't finished my story: that sensation of wanting to crowd everything at the last minute into my story (not enough time!) has never left me.

MN: That's how I feel almost every day in my writing life. I don't think it's necessarily a "healthy" way to write, or to live—a poetics of the rush may be interesting, but is a poetics of the cram? But when the blood-jet is on, that's how it feels. I don't know if I would get anything done otherwise, though I am realizing that always writing and/or living with an undercurrent of desperation can be exhausting. So maybe I'm moving away from "The Burn"—first toward the controlled burn, then I don't know where. It would be good to stay alive.

KNOWING ISN'T ENOUGH
A CONVERSATION WITH JOHN TRUDELL
BY BRENDAN LORBER

APRIL/MAY 2007   NO. 211

> *"He is extremely eloquent, therefore extremely dangerous."*
> —from John Trudell's 17,000-page FBI file

More than mere activist or poet, John Trudell is adept at living beyond specific identities. His reinventions emerge not despite but because his humanitarianism renders any one allegiance artificially confining. As a poet he's discovered a means of maintaining authentic presence, of connecting perceptual, physical, & spiritual reality that incorporates & builds on a life of struggling against economic & cultural deprivation. Trudell, the son of a Santee Sioux father and a Mexican mother, became involved in Native American activism after returning from the Vietnam War. He was the spokesman for the All Tribes occupation of Alcatraz Island and was later chair of the American Indian Movement, amassing the largest FBI file in the agency's history. In 1979 Trudell burned an American flag outside FBI headquarters on the grounds that the flag had already been desecrated by race & class injustice. Twelve hours later, his mother-in-law, pregnant wife, and three children were killed in a suspicious fire at Trudell's home on the Shoshone-Paiute reservation in Nevada. After that, he began writing "hanging on lines," his poetry. Since that time he's recorded about a dozen albums, often with traditional music, and has remained an outspoken philosopher whose power transcends hemmed-in notions of what activism can accomplish.

BRENDAN LORBER: You've said you felt you were knocked unconscious when you were born and have spent your entire life trying to come to. What techniques have you called upon to become more aware?

JOHN TRUDELL: I never thought in terms of technique. There are some things I can't explain. I went through my life experiences and at a young age things just didn't seem right to me. I was always influenced by that and as different things have happened in my life I thought about them a lot, maybe out of necessity. It's apparent to me that the reality that's being imposed upon us, something's not right about it. It's almost like this is not real, what reality's supposed to be all about. My mind goes off with these kind of things but I've never thought in terms of any technique. I just do what I do.

BL: Everyone from the FBI to Kris Kristofferson says you are dangerous—who are you dangerous to and why?

JT: (*laughs*) I'm not dangerous. But when Kris says it and the FBI says it they're saying it in two different contexts. In the FBI's context . . . well I don't think I'm dangerous to anybody or anything. It's just that I see reality as I see it, I think the way that I think and I speak the way that I speak. If there's anything in this area that's dangerous—which I truly don't understand—it's got to be about perceptions of reality. I'll put it like this: I have my moments of coherence, I can be very coherent at times, this isn't a full-time thing, but I can be very coherent at times. I think that's what's being perceived as dangerous, because the system itself, not just the FBI, they don't want people using their intelligence clearly and coherently and really thinking about things. They want people to just believe what they're told because if people are busy believing then they're obviously not thinking. It's about perceptions of reality.

BL: My next question touches on those perceptions of reality. What are you able to achieve as a poet and musician that you were not able to achieve as an activist? That is, how do the goals of being an activist differ from those of being an artist—and how are they the same?

JT: When I was an activist, when that was my identity, it wasn't a goal. It was just something I felt I had to do. It seemed that the only realistic thing for me to do at that time was to be involved in the activism. But when that changed and I became involved in the writing and the performance and what is called the artist thing, one of the main things I noticed in the transition is that I was more free. That's because the political activism thing is a very limited way to view reality. When I had the activist identity, I was perceiving reality as a political activist. That's a limiter, it was putting blinders on. I could only see what was going on based upon my political activism and when you get right down into the reality of politics, and what it really is all about, politics is very territorial, very competitive, very aggressive. It's based upon beliefs and party lines. It has its own extremism. No matter how good or righteous the cause is, whether from the Left to the Right, or the Indians to the whites, it doesn't matter. Politics is aggressive in nature and competitive. It's non-cooperative. So when I had a political identity, I was limiting my ability to see what was really going on in a larger context. When I looked at us as native people, this political activism served a useful function. But in the long run it wasn't our politics. And if it's not our politics then how can we use it to speak our truths and our realities? We can blurt out a lot of repressed emotional frustration but venting repressed emotional frustration has absolutely nothing to do with coherence. So when the change went over and I started writing I realized I could express my truths the way I want to. And that's what's needed now. It gave me peripheral vision that I didn't have.

BL: That notion of identity leads into the next thing I wanted to touch on. You've said, "Some people call me a poet. Others say I'm an activist. Some say my poetry and music is political. Others say it's about the spirit of my people. I don't buy into any of those labels. I may be a little bit of all those things, but I'm more than any of them. We all are. That's what makes us human." How do people get pushed into those specific limiting identities?

JT: It starts at birth, the programming. We are human beings. That is who we are. That is our identity, each and every one of us. That is our identity. We may be female or male or we may be one race or another but we're human beings. That is our identity. Everything else is how we're dressed up. But from the time we're born, we're programmed to not perceive reality as human beings. We're programmed to perceive reality by race, gender, religion, guilt. The purpose of that programming is to create chaos in our thought process. It's to confuse our real identity. As long as that chaos and confusion exists then we can be manipulated. Our anarchy can be manipulated to serve someone else's purpose.

BL: Continuing with that, the Civil Rights and American Indian Movements were viewed as threats by the US government in part because they were bridging communities that had been kept apart for a long time. Your work as an activist and a writer connects the fight against racism, sexism, and classism, yet many activists and writers view each as a separate battle. Why do so many people want to divide the issues into smaller parcels?

JT: We are programmed to do that. We're addicted to that energy pattern.

BL: You've said, "Most people are trying to find solutions to the problem within the confined abstractions of democracy and if they're not willing to think objectively about responsibility to our descendants then they will come up with no solutions—they will only perpetuate the enslavement and feed it." How can a person break out of their programming, out of that cycle?

JT: We need to respect the value and power of our intelligence. We need to use our intelligence to think. We need to think clearly and coherently. We need to activate and understand the power of our intelligence and if we would use our intelligence clearly and coherently we will break out of that. But as a society we're not using our intelligence clearly and coherently. We use our intelligence to be fearful, to be insecure, to believe. We *believe*, we don't think. We've been programmed to believe so the effectiveness of our intelligence has been neutered. Instead of us using the power of clear and coherent thinking we've been neutered down to where we just use our intelligence to believe what we're told to believe. You can't really think and believe at the same time—it's one or the other, because if you just believe you're pretending to think. When you're just believing, your pretend-thinking is limited by the definitions of your belief. The power of our intelligence, the energy of our intelligence, the power that it represents, it needs to flow. We need to understand the value and power of our intelligence and use it clearly and coherently. An example of the power of our intelligence is if you've ever had the experience of feeling powerless, overwhelmed, and depressed. How bad can you make yourself feel when you're feeling that way? How does it affect the people around you? The irony there is you're feeling powerless but in reality that *is* power. The worse you can make yourself feel—that's power, that's your power. And how it affects the people around you is the physical side of how your power spreads. We really need to come to grips with reality. What I'm getting at is, if we understand and respect the power of our intelligence and use it clearly and coherently then that power that we use to make ourselves feel bad, that power can be used to create coherence. In dealing with beliefs—and I'm not saying that to have beliefs is bad—but what I am saying is to use the word believe and use it all the time is a negative because it stifles our thinking. The people, whoever they believe their creator is, whether it's God or Yahweh or Mohammed or Allah or The Great Spirit, whoever people relate to as a creator, we need to show respect to that creator. We can make all the rah rah words about a spiritual this or whatever we can rah rah ourselves all we want but the reality is, if we truly respect our creator, we would respect the gift of intelligence that our creator gave us and use that gift appropriately. Clearly and coherently. It's in our best interests to reach that realization. We've been so confused, disoriented, and disconnected, we're not showing our creator respect no matter how much we rah rah. We can drop on our knees and pray at the drop of a hat, we can rah rah everything. But if we're not using the gift of our intelligence clearly and coherently we're not fulfilling our responsibility to the life that our creator gave us. It comes down to this: recognizing who we are and what our own power is. I don't have a manual or a step-by-step process on how one goes about this. But l think the first step in going about it is for us to make a decision within our own selves, "I'm going to use the power of my intelligence to be as clear and coherent as I possibly can. I'm going to think. I choose thinking over believing," and head in that direction, because it'll activate.

BL: In some ways the US government has been acting more overtly, as though they're making it easy to use our intelligence to see the economic injustice and military oppression around the world.

JT: People aren't using their intelligence to do that. They're seeing it, but if people were truly using their intelligence they would deal with it. We have to watch out for the slight of mind. I don't think the US government is more overtly doing it now. From how I view reality, they've been very overt the whole time, it's just that people don't want to see it. What's happening here and why I'm saying it like this is that we're not activating our intelligence clearly and coherently by what we're seeing. We're emotionally reacting to what we believe. But we're not thinking in ways to create solutions. Let's say, using your terminology, they may be more overt in what they're doing. The people who are for it react out of their beliefs and they support it however they support it. The people who are against it emotionally react out of their beliefs. We go through these motions to act out our emotional reactions, but if you look at it, historically speaking, we haven't produced any results. We haven't settled the issues. The missing thing here is using our intelligence clearly and coherently in facing reality. We're still within the limits of the abstractions of democracy. Either we're going to serve humanity, either we're going to be respectful to our creator and create a more balanced reality, or we're going to be loyal to some dark age belief system that was imposed upon us. We need to think beyond the way we've been programmed to believe because the way reality stands right now, you can't save democracy and save humanity. You can't do it. If you look at it, practically speaking, why would you want to save democracy? Democracy in reality means the right of the entitled to rule. But who decides who's entitled? In an ownership-of-property world, the entitled will always be the ones who own the property. That's just reality. I'm not advocating this—the only thing I'm advocating is that we use the power of our intelligence to really look at reality very clearly if we want to produce coherent solutions. When I look at where the situation stands now, and I came through the 60's, I'm talking about *how come nothing's changed?* How come the beast is worse now than when we started out? Our intentions were good, so what's missing? I think the missing link is we didn't really think—we reacted. And that's the shift that has to be made now. We'll see . . .

BL: That programming goes back a long way. Back when colonial leaders first showed up here—

JT: It goes back to the fucking Romans, to the pharaohs, man. It goes way, way back.

BL: But the techniques have been similar all along, of pitting different groups against each other.

JT: Yes.

BL: Like a few hundred years ago it was African slaves versus white indentured servants versus Native Americans so none of them would band together against the ruling class. The same strategy more recently in Vietnam and Iraq where soldiers have more shared interests with the people they're shooting than with the people who sent them over. But it's very difficult to overcome the misplaced allegiance and manufactured, artificial fear that's placed in people.

JT: It's difficult to overcome it, but the way it gets done is one individual at a time makes up their mind, "I'm going to be as coherent as I possibly can." And we'll get there, because the change we're looking at has to happen in an evolutionary context, not a revolutionary context. There is no revolutionary solution. Revolution just means you spin back to your starting point. Oppressor/oppressed. A revolution always goes back to its starting point but evolution is more linear. It continues on its own circular manner so to speak, or maybe it's all about spirals. *(laughs)* Evolution continues on and we are a part of evolutionary reality. If we make decisions that we are going to be as clear and coherent as we can, we'll see where we're at in a couple of years.

The power of depression can affect the people around you. Well the power of coherence can also affect the people around you. We'll just replace the power of depression with the reality of coherence one individual at a time and power will spread.

BL: One way is through the use of language. Corporations and governments have always recognized the power of language to control people. They've used it to separate populations from the accurate perception of their surroundings. For example, by making corporations rather than humans the subject of terms like health, growth, and efficiency, they have masked what would more accurately be described as profit, hegemony, and exploitation. It becomes difficult to even conceptualize a world in which the well-being of people is the priority. Resisting that corruption of language and reconnecting it to its human and environmental origins—has that been in your mind as you've gone forward as a writer?

JT: No. *(laughs)* Not really. I'm not surprised by anything that they do. They're doing nothing new. Historically speaking they're doing what they've always done. To have a small minority ruling class feed off the larger mass. There's nothing new going on here. The technology, the terminology. and the generations change but the system remains the same. So I'm not surprised by anything that they're doing. I just started writing because it happened. There was no thought where, "I see things more clearly." There was no thought of nothing. I started writing because it happened and I just follow it. I can't take any credit. I just went where my life took me, all right. In that attempt to become conscious I just followed where life took me. That's exactly in the end what happened.

BL: That's the way interesting things happen. Rather than coming to some conclusion beforehand and making it fit. Just allowing it to emerge.

JT: One of the things I learned out of it though, that I think is a step in the direction is: *knowing isn't enough.* Knowing isn't enough. It's understanding what we know. That's the piece that seems to be missing. We were programmed in school to memorize and to know how to be able to come up with the right answer. Whether we understood or not, that wasn't important to them. The only thing that was important to them was that we understood to go along with the program. It was actually important to them that we *didn't* understand what the program really was. So whatever's going on here, knowing isn't enough. Understanding what we know is very important but we can only reach that understanding through clear and coherent use of our intelligence.

BL: What poets, artists, activists, or other people continue to inspire you and lead you in new directions?

JT: Well, that's a hard one to answer because I don't want to say names and leave out names. Willie Nelson is one. He's a big influence.

BL: How does he inspire you?

JT: He—and Kris Kristofferson's another one, and Jackson Browne—because they see reality. They understand what's going on. Things like that, I like. There's a lot of stuff I listen to that I maybe don't remember the name. I wouldn't say I'm hearing a lot, but I'm hearing more and more by different artists that's heading in the right direction. But I'd say Willie because I just like his style.

AN INTERVIEW WITH TED GREENWALD
BY ARLO QUINT

DECEMBER/JANUARY 2008   NO. 213

I got together with Ted Greenwald in September for lunch and an interview. I was particularly interested in talking to Ted about his poems, his methods of writing, and the New York City poetry scene. Ted did not disappoint. What follows is a series of excerpts, loosely arranged by topic, from the much longer complete transcription.

The Poetry Project & the NYC Poetry Scene

ARLO QUINT: Since this is for *The Poetry Project Newsletter*, and you've been associated with the Project for such a long time, I want to ask you about how your relationship with this place started.

TED GREENWALD: I've been around here basically from the beginning. When I was going to school at Queens College, Lorenzo Thomas and I used to come in and read at the Metro, and that's how we met Ted, Ron, Joe, and Dick, and it was sort of on from there . . . basically, there was a scene. In terms of the Project it basically drifted into the scene. Anne Waldman and some other people were running it early on. First it was Paul Blackburn, and I knew him. It was all a part of that Lyndon Johnson stuff—the Great Society or something like that. It was a place to read, and a lot of really good poets were hanging out.

TG: You have to make the scene. It's the energy of the people involved and the quality of what they're doing. Early on at the Project, if you weren't any fucking good, and you didn't have the goods, and you got up here and read then you were gone and that was it. For life. Finished! . . . I'm not kidding you. And that was why everyone was getting pissed off about the Project. That was the edge.

*

TG: Look. In this age of the Internet which is one of the great levelers of all time . . . it's basically this piece of hardware that makes everyone think they're an artist. It's only doing now what video did in the '70s, and everyone thought it was this great thing, but it's just a piece of hardware. It's a hammer. I believe that there should be a democracy of access, but there's not a democracy of skill. Some people are better at things than others. Period. Some people figure it out differently. Some people figure out how to do it for ten, fifteen or twenty years at a high level, but then there are people . . . it's like watching a guy play saxophone on a beer commercial . . . maybe that's what he does for his whole life, you know? He plays those six notes and makes a living. The main thing is bringing the edge back in, making this the place to be. Making this the place young poets can get published. *The World* was important for that. You had *Mother* magazine with Peter Schjeldahl, you had *C* magazine. There were all these fast come-and-go magazines—Johnny Stanton's *Siamese Banana*. There was always stuff coming out. Plus you had the people that we didn't hang out with. The Judson Church people who were putting out a million magazines . . . sort of like the anthropology type. Jerry Rothenberg, David Antin . . . those guys were doing something really different. It's really a question of giving people access to publication. It doesn't matter, they don't have to have . . . I'm not going to identify people but there's a whole generation of poets that have now reached a certain age where they waited to have $2000 books, and they blew it because that's not the point. You showed me your books, and they're side-stapled books. That's all you need. I did a book with my daughter, a collaboration, a number of years ago. We did the drawings and I took 'em across the street to the copy shop. The books were made and that was it. Speed. Get in and out fast. Get the people wanting to be in things. What we used to have when the magazines were being published . . . you would have a collating party. There would be like twenty people there, and when you were done you'd be left with the book. It was a scene. You had the poetry aspect of it, and then it sort of drifted off into the social aspect . . . people who were living on the lower east side . . . people who were hanging out with Ted [Berrigan]. Ted was a great poet. Ted was a literary man . . . he required a certain level of attention. And then there was that whole other scene . . . quality became social. Shit, I didn't live in the neighborhood so, you know . . .

AQ: And now all the poets live in Brooklyn.

TG: There's no scene in Manhattan at this point. The worst thing that ever happened to the United States was making Manhattan real estate expensive because you can't get young people here. So now it's gonna be someplace else, and it's like a great deal of other things in this country—it's just not good for the overall culture.

*

TG: The art world, through the '80s, started to become very expensive. It started to become very expensive just to hang out. It wasn't cheap to be on the scene, and all of a sudden it costs a lot of money just to have a drink. A lot of these chic places you're paying twelve, fifteen dollars for a fucking ridiculous martini! All that is ridiculous. I don't drink anymore but, let me tell you, I've had my fair share over the years of lots of things and there's no way I would pay twelve dollars for a martini. I'm not cheap either. It costs a lot of money just to walk down the street here. I'd hate to be young and coming up here now. I think that you'd have to be very cunning nowadays to figure out where a margin is to operate on and make a living. The margin is just not so visible. And to do it legitimately without selling drugs or some other crap like that.

Poetry & Competition

TG: The key is, you know, how ambitious are people? Do you all think that you're the most important poets who are alive at the moment? Now, if you feel that way, then you're gonna have a scene. If you don't feel that way, if you assume you're just another poet, then you might as well hang up your cleats right there.

AQ: I think that feeling might be missing now.

TG: That's because a lot of people discourage competition. Sometimes competition is not a half bad thing where you sort of, somewhere in your head, compete with someone who you think writes really well and you would like to write as well as them. Shakespeare or Frank O'Hara . . .

AQ: O'Hara thought he was writing the best poems around.

TG: And generally he was . . . other people around him were writing pretty interesting stuff but not quite as good as him.

AQ: Who were you in competition with?

TG: It's all long past . . . and as I've gotten older I've learned to be extremely diplomatic. (*laughs*) But what I'm really talking about is people whose work you like. You read a nice piece, and you go home, and you've gotta write a piece. That's the competition.

AQ: I think poets now tend to imagine themselves in competition with the people whose work they don't like—an "opposing camp" or something like that.

TG: No, No—you've gotta respect the competition. Why would you wanna compete with someone you feel is an inferior? . . . Unless you're into "non-hierarchical thinking" which is another layer of bullshit in the culture now.

AQ: One type of competition in poetry you have now is, you know, competition for jobs and that sort of thing.

TG: In that case you're not gonna be . . . well you might be some sort of a superstar with your "great poems" published on the front page of the *New York Times*, or maybe you'll have academic credentials with a PhD and articles published in critical journals . . . but your poems are gonna be worth shit. You're not going to be interested in your poems. You'll only be interested in them insofar as they add up to "fame and glory" in the academic world. Who cares? I mean . . . an MFA? Look, I did graduate-level work. I'm sort of an ABT, but when I did my paper for my master's degree I had a guy who said, "you gotta rewrite it," and I didn't want to rewrite it, so I never got my master's but I did all this fucking work, and I passed all the exams. I actually wrote the thing. I even wrote 25 pages of a doctoral dissertation, and I had set up a theory that I was going to operate from. Then I said to myself, "Geez, why am I wasting my time doing this? I might as well take all this secret knowledge that I'm coming up with and just write some great work." That's sort of the way I was thinking.

*

TG: If you go back to the '60s there was only one MFA program in the country and now there's zillions of them. And the academy has so tremendously usurped . . . has placed itself as the mediator of taste in the art . . . and it's just horseshit. It's utter horseshit. The standard is that poems have passed through the hands of a PhD somewhere or something resembling that.

Early Publications, Collaborators, & Editors

AQ: Can you tell me about your first book, *Lapstrake*?

TG: I just knew Aram (Saroyan) from around. I sent him work for *Lines* magazine, and then when I moved into the city after I graduated from Queens, I was living uptown. I was going to graduate school up at City College, and one day I came home and there was a postcard from Aram, and he said, "I'd like to do a book of yours." So I quickly put together the book, and it's called *Lapstrake*, and he published it very quickly. Then, shortly thereafter, he did a book by John Perreault and one by Clark (Coolidge), and he might have done one by Dick Kolmar. I'm not sure. And we were friendly for a while. I haven't seen him in a number of years . . . he moved to the coast and drifted away. He's a terrific poet. His new collected book is very nice. So that's how I got the first one. I got on the scoreboard very fast.

AQ; How old were you?

TG: I was 21 or 22 or something like that. It meant that I could sort of relax a little bit so the next book that came out, *Short Sleeves*, was a little letterpress book that, my then wife, Joan Simon printed. She was learning printing up at Cornell when I said, "Well, here's a book—do a real book," and so she did it. I had another one intervening around that time called *No Eating*. That was put out by *Blue Pig*. George Tysh and David Ball had this terrific magazine in Paris, and I went there in '68 and lived there for about six months. I met George and David there through Michael Brownstein who was there on a Fulbright. Michael is old friends with some very old friends of mine from Queens—guys named Jerry Hiler and Nathaniel Dorsky— they're filmmakers and they live in San Francisco—legendary people! They're really old friends.

AQ: That was around the time you did *Somewhere in Ho*, right? The collabo- ration with Ed Baynard.

TG: It's amazing if you even found a copy of that!

AQ: I've got a photocopy.

TG: Ed was a friend of mine, and around 1969 I was spending a lot of time down in Soho. I would go up to Cornell to see my first wife at school; she had met Gordon Matta-Clark up there, and Gordon and I were friends, and then he moved down to New York before Joan graduated. I worked with him on some pieces, and then an old friend of mine, Manfred Hecht, worked with him on a lot of pieces. Manfred was basically a mechanic, so he worked with him on *Splitting* and some of these other things. We all hung out together and at that time Gordon did a construction job at 98 Greene St. which was being put together by Holly Solomon . . . it was really the first alternative space down in Soho. The second one was 112 and the first one was 98. It was through her that I started running poetry readings, and I got interested in doing art shows, and that's sort of how I got into that world. Through Holly Soloman. Ed Baynard was a friend of Holly's, and we all became friends and hung out together, and then Ed and I got together and did the collaboration one day. It was around the time we were reading that stupid book on . . . *Subliminal Seduction* it was called. It's a book on advertising . . . how in strange ways advertisers write sex into everything.

*

TG: *Short Sleeves* is only like twelve, thirteen poems. This is where I think people get it wrong when they say they're waiting for some bigger thing. Take what you have and say that it's an important work. I don't make any distinction between chapbooks and big books because, to me, when I have twelve pages I make a book of twelve pages. Basically I'm modeling it after an LP record—there's twelve cuts. It's a real book. Everything should be a real book if you're gonna do it at that level. It shouldn't just be a throwaway where you waste time and energy and money . . . everything should be worth something. If you yourself don't think it's good, how the fuck are other people gonna think it's any good?

*

TG: This book (*Common Sense*), the only way I could get that manuscript— it was edited by Curtis Faville. I tried that manuscript a hundred times and couldn't get it and Curtis did it. Curtis really did an absolutely great job. He really . . . I could not have done it if he hadn't done it, I'm telling you that flat out. He said he was interested in doing something—he had L Press at the time—and he gave me a page limit. I sent him a bunch of things, and then he sent me a letter where he said, "Now listen, I want you to send me all the work," because I was holding back work or not thinking of work that he was aware of. So that's what I did and we ended up doing it bigger.

*

TG: I've been lucky. My first wife was an editor. I had Curtis. I did *Making A Living* with Larry Fagin who's a terrific editor. Bill Berkson is another one. I've been lucky that, in the course of putting together books, I've worked with good editors. I was able to get good things out of the work, and it wasn't me—it was them. I mean, I produced the work but they sort of . . . until you get yourself to the point where you can be really hard on yourself and less self-indulgent you need a good editor. And sometimes it's important just to get the work away from yourself and have someone else look at it. I mean somebody who knows what they're doing, not just someone who happens to be there and wants to be involved. I'm talking about someone with real skill in editing whose judgment you respect. And have a few of them. I've been lucky to have a few people that have been helpful that way.

*

TG: The only person who knows if you're full of shit is yourself. It may look great to everybody else, but you will know you're full of shit on some level because you know what's wrong with it. Everybody says, "This is fabulous," and you go, "Oh yeah, right—little do you know!" It's like being a magician to some degree—you don't want to give away the trick.

Methods & Forms

AQ: You've been writing for a long time and have published a lot of work with a huge formal range . . . the really short lyrics in *Short Sleeves*, narrative work like *Smile*, and eventually the really long poems like *Word of Mouth* . . .

TG: First of all, I didn't want to be limited. Sometimes a piece came out as a prose piece. I've been doing it for 45 years; that's why there's a lot of it. The other thing is, after I published *Lapstrake* and the work in *Lines*, I sort of set up . . . I had started around 1964 writing the first of *The Licorice Chronicles*. Basically the way I laid them out for myself, in some sort of half-assed way, was that each piece was gonna be as much as I knew about poetry at the time (I didn't know enough about poetry). Each one of the sections I figured, at that date, that was what I knew, and I wasn't writing stuff in between. And it went on until 1969, and when I did the last one that was it. And that led me to the first work where I figured something out. The big work in one sitting. The first work of that type was *Makes Sense* and then I did others like that ... *You Bet*.

AQ: *You Bet* is one sitting?

TG: Yeah, I did it in one day—one shot. Then *Word of Mouth* is approximately the same thing every day at the same time for about a month ... under the influence of the same drug. It was like a fall poem ... it was written in October. I like the idea of writing in one sitting or the illusion of one sitting. I let my mind do the organizing, you know, use my mind like a hammer. In other words, not put a structure over it but let the structure just sort of arrive. And it will. Your mind will organize it for you, and it saves a hell of a lot of time and sweat.

AQ: So you set up something like a loose compositional method ...

TG: I work a lot. I work every day. Like, right now I've been working on something for about three years, and I don't quite know what I have. I haven't got to the point where I'm going to edit it or put it into a bigger form. I gotta see if that works. Some things are sort of worked up to like *The Up and Up* ... that was sort of worked up to in a certain way. I found one thing at a certain point when I started doing those repeated lines. They started with a book called *Exit the Face*, and then there's a book that's never been published called *Going Into School That Day* along that continuum, and then there's a work called *In Your Dreams* which has never been published. What I was basically saying to myself is, "What's the difference between poetry and prose?" Generally poetry organizes itself line by line and generally prose organizes itself by paragraph. So, let me just go line by line. What that does is ... you don't get into the issue of how to turn the line, so then you get a whole different other kind of shape happening. Every poet in the world, once you get to that turn, then it turns prose-like in the second line. That first line is poetry, the second line is always prose if you continue that particular thought. If you stop the thought and let that thought go out that way and do another line, another thought or something . . . whole other thoughts, whole other lines, and you move along that way and see where that goes.

AQ: What do you think about the prose poem as a separate form?

TG: Well, you know, it's applicable. Historically, it refers to something French. It's cool. But, you know, generally what makes poetry poetry is line by line. Even if it happens to be by paragraph it still should be line by line. Once I stopped writing without caps on the left flush line—that wall to work from— as soon as you don't use those caps you don't have a beginning, you're just dealing with a bunch of words floating all over the place, and it's very amorphous and very confusing. I just found it was very helpful for me to shove the whole poem flush left because then I didn't have the excuse of using the location on the page as a way of saving a bad line. You know, when you get involved in projective verse which is basically a theory of how you write poetry on a typewriter . . . which is pretty much what it is . . . I handwrite so, you know, as soon as you get flush left you can see when the line sucks. There's a lot of things that show up when you're flush left that you can't get away with. And when I edit, I edit with a dark black pen so I can never see that line again. I don't want it saved . . . it's over. Once it's gone, it's gone. Let the poem go through it.

*

TG: I tend to read a lot, and writing is the flip side of reading. Really, if you read a lot you should write a lot. I also steal a lot—the things that catch my eye or catch my ear. The way I work through a poem is with my ear. When I type it up I use my ear and my eye. Generally, if it doesn't look right, it's not right but . . . how does it sound? The one reason that I'm not particularly a Language poet is very simply that I'm more interested in spoken sources and spoken material than I am in written material. I read a lot, but if I'm going to mine things that I'm reading I'm going to look for things that are "spoken nuggets" as it were. I think that the most interesting thing in the language is the noise. You can't have any communication without it. In any communication channel you have to have a minimax of noise, and what interests me is the noise. If you can't communicate without it—you gotta have it—you might as well see what it does. I like things that would be noise or something that you wouldn't even notice. I sometimes say to people that I know the poem is really good if you dream about it.

The Poetry Reading

TG: You have to have a sense of delivering the work in public. A competitive sense. You don't have Ethan Hawke to do your fucking poems in public . . . or Madonna. How do *you* deliver the work in public? And despite all their fantasies about it, rock-and-roll singers are not poets by any stretch of the imagination. The day Bob Dylan does anything very good without a band is the day that hell freezes over. He can't do anything without a band, and he sometimes barely gets slightly close, but it's all still just four four four four. If you put it on a page, it's ridiculous.

AQ: I love Bob Dylan!

TG: I like him too. He's a wonderful songwriter; he's not a poet. I've said this a million times to the point at which I bore myself when I say it: poetry is the only thing which hasn't been called poetic. You're sort of functioning in public. Part of the competition or part of the tradition is, over the years, the tradition of programming competitively. You would get the people that hate each other and put them on the same program and see what happens. Or you get two people who like each other, but they're competitive. A great case in point once was Ted Berrigan and Dick Gallup reading. Ted read for what must have been an hour and a half and then there was a break and poor Dick had to follow that. Ted was very good at that kind of crap! (*laughs*) That's the kind of thing you know—you have to take care of some of your business in public. You're gonna read with somebody, you know? A lot of times I don't like to read the same thing twice, and so I go ahead and write new stuff for the reading . . . try it out in public, give it a test run, see what it sounds like. The situation has to be available to that. You can't throw in people that have been doing stuff for forty years with people who have been doing stuff for two years. A lot of times that's not gonna work. The other thing is that as people get older, they have a tendency to want to introduce their own work, which I find tedious. I don't think that work should be introduced. Tom Raworth, who's an old friend, and I are of the school that you get up, you do your shit, and you go home. That's it! You lay it out. I don't want to discuss how I wrote this. I don't want to give these little historical notes. Just let the work have its own air! But I also have never been a teacher. A lot of people have made their living in the academy, so they end up learning how to deliver their work in front of a class.

Last Five Minutes

AQ: Do you consider yourself a mystic?

TG: No, but there are ideas in the poems that appear to be mystical. I think that poetry is special. I don't want to turn it into some variety of religious experience. There are moments when things are going really well when you're channeling something else. But, you know, it's just that you're really into it. And, finally, it's not a question of mysticism but it's, "Where do you put the work?" It's only in the sixteenth and seventeenth centuries that you had biographies of artists that were very well known, or a circumstance where a lot of that kind of information about somebody's life was desired. It seems to me that the ideal situation is Shakespeare's, where all you have is half of a document and a name, and that's it. The rest is make believe. It's impossible in the twentieth and twenty-first centuries for that to be the case because there's all sorts of residual information—there's all sorts of other crap around—there's interest in ephemeral documents, so that's never gonna be the case anymore. But it seems to me that you want the work out in front. The work should be what people look at.

AN INTERVIEW WITH EILEEN MYLES
BY GREG FUCHS

APRIL/MAY 2009   NO. 219

Eileen Myles has been writing for forty years. She began while attending the newly formed, nontraditional, and urban UMass (Boston), in her hometown, at the end of the 1960s. Yet, Myles really hit her stride when she entered the legendary scene of the inchoate Poetry Project of the early 1970s. In these four decades she has achieved a distinct style, so eco-nomical as to be almost invisible, that has verisimilitude yet is able to destroy our socially constructed realities, giving a reader ample opportunity to reevaluate his assumptions of life. Myles has reached deftness in poetry, fiction, criticism, journalism, drama, even libretti. This eclecticism reveals her bravery, born of curiosity and necessity, to regularly risk the unfamiliar. Myles and I arranged to meet to discuss her life and work at Veselka, the popu-lar Ukrainian restaurant on 9th Street and Second Avenue. She is a writer that I have long admired. I've been lucky enough to perform and casually talk with her, but this was a very special meeting for me. The opportunity to interview someone for whom I have great respect and admiration was thrilling. I was a little nervous because the more I prepared, the more I realized how little we really know about anyone.

GREG FUCHS: Thank you for being tolerant of my wealth of correspondence and false starts leading up to this interview during the past month.

EILEEN MYLES: First can I tell you what I did today? Moved the car. Rode my bike to the Cooper Square post office. I sent books to people. I met Peggy

Ahwesh. She's a filmmaker. We're doing a talk next week at CUNY. I visited Joe Westmoreland. You know him? He's a great writer. He wrote *Tramps Like Us*. He was my campaign secretary. His partner is Charlie Atlas. In fact, I am Joe's literary executor. You should always have a healthy executor. Maggie Nelson is my executor. Went home to write recommendations. Got back on my bike and rode to Veselka. Hi Greg.

GF: When did you first know you were a writer?

EM: I suppose in college when I got a certain response from professors. I realized that something that seemed easy to me was actually a skill. I kept a journal of responses to things we were writing. Hawthorne was really moving to me when I was 18. Thoreau. I went to UMass (Boston), not Amherst. The Boston campus was new. The school was built for the Boston kids. Some of the teachers were working-class lefties. Idealistic. Others were sometimes too excited about teaching "less educated" students like us. A teacher there inspired my novel, *Inferno*.

GF: What did you write?

EM: Mostly poems, and I guess a lot of a kind of imaginary journalism pieces. I always wanted to be a journalist. Going to the Saint Patrick's Day parade in Southie [a nickname for the Irish section of South Boston] during busing. Seeing the strange, intense responses people were having towards their local politicians. I always loved the city. The city, Boston being the first one, made me want to write.

GF: In *The Importance of Being Iceland* you mention how you really need an assignment to write prose. How were you able to write these imaginary journalism pieces?

EM: They were never finished—notebooks, beginnings. The unspoken thing is that the poetry comes from somewhere else. It's as if I am commanded to write the poetry.

GF: When did you come to New York? Why?

EM: It felt great here. It always did. The place flowed. It was full of millions of different kinds of people. It seemed anonymous and personal at once. You could get lost here, be excited. It was so full and fast.

GF: How did you get to the Poetry Project? When?

EM: Initially I came because I was a grad student at Queens College, and a professor was doing a study of the East Village in 1910. I was his research assistant, and the Church was on the map, so I went in. Later, I met Paul Violi at a reading at Veselka, and he told me he was doing a workshop. I had gone to someone's for about a second the year before, but I totally didn't get it. I couldn't figure out what this place was. It seemed cavernous and cultish. I dropped out of grad school. I didn't want to be out in Queens. New York was like a big school, a laboratory. Amazing performances right on street corners. Patti Smith was performing poetry.

GF: Did you feel immediately welcomed into the Poetry Project?

EM: Sure. I was living in SoHo and did a magazine called *dodgems*, which were like bumper cars. Aesthetics as bumper cars, all different styles bumping into one another. I was reading quantum mechanics. Trying to understand randomness to figure out the avant-garde.

GF: How and when did you become Artistic Director of the Poetry Project? For how long?

EM: 1984. Two years, close to three. After I left the Poetry Project I stopped living in poetry, the poetry world, for a while. The Project had been my home. When I left I started performing, writing plays.

GF: Describe the milieu of the Project at the time.

EM: I'd rather talk about when I just hung out here in the '70s. It was a mess. It was so great. You could smoke and stomp your cigarettes out on the floor. It felt like our institution. But there were big readings then too. Lowell and Ginsberg. History. Robert Duncan. Denise Levertov. When I worked at the Project my first reading was—well it was Alice [Notley] and Dennis Cooper. The second season was Audre Lorde and Diane di Prima. The third was David Rattray, George-Therese Dickenson, and John Wieners. I initially ran it with Patricia Spears Jones. We were two firsts. The place really opened up I think. Funding was getting cut. The NEA was downsizing, but we had an art auction. Maybe, no definitely, we expanded the notion of who read at the

church. Not so straight, not so white. People were mad. I think it was a
generation shift at the Poetry Project, which was long overdue. It was fun.
I loved being able to think about a whole institution. Maybe I wasn't so in
love with the culture of poverty that attaches itself to poetry so easily. The
neighborhood was full of excitement at that time, and we were part of it.

GF: How does it compare and contrast to the current scene?

EM: We were breaking out of something entrenched, and the place is just less
entrenched now. But it's hard maybe not to have something to break out
of. I wonder how people feel. We should ask people how it really feels in
the current scene. I think everyone is haunted by institutions, the academy,
these days. It's harder to be outside—if there even is such a thing. It seems
like combinations; what's next to what has replaced the idea of an inside or
an outside.

GF: How did you come to work for James Schuyler? What can young poets
today learn from Schuyler?

EM: Oh they should just read him.

GF: Describe becoming friends with Ted Berrigan.

EM: I loved Ted and Jimmy, but I'm way too alive to want to spend this con-
versation talking about them.

GF: What is your definition of New York School?

EM: Wayne Koestenbaum was teaching a class on it and he asked me that
question. I wrote this in my notebook:

They are poets
involved in
the history
of the present
the school is still open.

GF: What do you think about being described as the last New York School
poet?

EM: Generally, and I'm excepting you from this, when someone wants to talk

about me as a New York School poet it means he considers himself a LAN-
GUAGE poet and that's how he gets to say it. People really don't like to say
they are this or that. They like to say what you are, though. I'm a literalist.
I truly did grow to be a poet and an intellectual here. I feel largely created by
the city of New York and the institution of the Poetry Project, at least for the
first ten years I lived here. But that demolishes the fact that I'm really from
Boston. There was a cool book that came out about ten or twelve years ago
from the ICA [the Institute of Contemporary Art] in Boston called *Boston
School*. In the nineteenth century, the Boston School was a bunch of painters
who did realist work. In the twentieth century it was largely photographers
—Nan Goldin, Jack Pierson. A kind of romantic, punk, realist approach,
a kind of using everything sensationally, large, then maybe close and inti-
mately. It was about a very contemporary kind of scale. Pictures. Cameras.
There's so many more things to say about any of us than schools of poetry.
I mean now it seems that if you aren't mainstream you're a LANGUAGE poet.
Even John Ashbery gets called one. That mainly means that LANGUAGE
poets got a foothold in the academy like no other experimental school of
poetics has yet. Sometimes the work is not that different from other work.
Except that there's a very obvious commitment to identifying with each
other in that endeavor. They recommend each other. I recommend my
friends too, but still, as a gay poet it was always something else. There was
a really interesting transition that happened in the '80s when a lot of poets
started writing prose. New Narrative is that. It's the same people who didn't
become LANGUAGE poets but really wanted to talk about sex. And lan-
guage. I mean Kathy Acker's that. Bob Glück. Dennis Cooper. I did start
writing prose too, but part of it was being a poet writing around people writ-
ing fiction, non-fiction. People writing about art. *L=A=N=G=U=A=G=E*
magazine never had any pictures. It was a little stern. I always had a cool
photo on the cover of *dodgems*. Who doesn't like pictures? I only did a cou-
ple of issues. I was broke. *Little Caesar* [Dennis Cooper's] was a much more
interesting magazine—so permissive, filled with pictures. For a while there

was an interesting social flow between all the various groups. I like to say I'm not not a LANGUAGE poet. But AIDS changed everything.

So there was a whole scene of poets from the '70s and '80s, some stopped writing poems, some kept going, but there was a feeling that there might be more space in prose. More room to do things. To make an interior model of a culture. So I think the poetry school thing really misses the point of movements that are both bigger and smaller than the groups we either assign ourselves to, or get described into. The New York School or the Boston School, or the School of Fish, are about a way of being in reality, using technology, desiring things, people, having a body. No school.

GF: Respond to being described as a rock star of modern poetry, the first punk rock poet and cult figure to a generation of post-punk females forming their own literary avant-garde.

EM: Now you're talking about the tyranny of the web. A little bit of information becomes unstoppable. I had some nice things said about me in the *New York Times* in 2000 when *Cool For You* came out, and I put it into my bio on my website. Then, when I published my next book of poems, I got these reviewer guys saying Myles is a punk poet. She's from the slam scene. Blah blah blah. Everything goes on for years now. What sounds nice once sounds really horrible nine years later. I have to change my website.

GF: What is the difference between poetry and prose?

EM: Prose gives you a chance to describe a culture. I've written a novel about everything I'm saying. There's no better way to say how the worlds move than in prose. I love poetry because it's naturally incomplete. Historically, it sometimes feels like LANGUAGE poets love poetry. I don't love poetry. I want to destroy poetry, writing. Destroy it with glee. Smash it, take it all the way out, push it as far as possible until it is unrecognizable then bring it back. Destroy the frames. At the very least make it kind of invisible, that it's art. To me that seems like a challenge. When I say destroy I might mean barely doing it at all. Hardly art. I mean because I use language in the service of other kinds of vision, looking for connections.

GF: You've written poetry, fiction, libretti, journalism, blogs; why do you like to write in so many genres?

EM: I'm a Sagittarius. I don't belong anywhere. Every form takes you somewhere else. Writing a libretto made me understand something that theater never did. A libretto is like an allegory, in the way animation is. The music makes the words move, and you see them in a whole other kind of possibility. It's like the words' second life. I usually feel burned out by whatever I just did. I know one should do this towering, phallic thing in their career, but I like having a wide, dilettantish, female career. Poetry's like the root, like a cutting. Also, I thought that's what writers did. You write reviews, essays, plays. You try it all.

GF: When did you meet Jim Brodey?

EM: Jim Brodey is who you got to hang out with in 1978. He published my first book. He had no electricity or even water. He was kind of like this weird star. He had sex with everyone.

GF: I want to edit a book of Jim Brodey's rock-n-roll writing for Subpress, like Greil Marcus's Lester Bangs book, *Psychotic Reactions and Carburetor Dung*. Do you think that's an interesting idea in 2009?

EM: Well anything is.

GF: How did you become such good friends with Tom Carey?

EM: It was a largely straight scene. I mean this neighborhood exactly. We were both middle children. We sort of got each other immediately. I went to a reading and there was this guy in a coat and tie playing guitar and singing. He was with Neil Hackman. I wanted to be friends with Tom. He was gay. Also, he knew Brodey from California. Later he became a Franciscan, which has fostered a way for me to be near and around religion, always a moving danger. I went with Tom to George Schneeman's funeral, which was a Catholic mass. Very moving. I took communion. My mother would not be happy; she is a strict Catholic.

GF: I always take communion. I believe I did enough time in Catholic school.

Anyway, there is a moment in the mass when you ask God for forgiveness, which is technically all you have to do to receive communion.

EM: My mother wouldn't buy it.

GF: As a former presidential candidate, what are your predictions for President Obama?

EM: I hate his economic team. That's all I can say. He feels great. I love more than anything his daughter taking pictures at the inauguration. That was stunning.

GF: Talk about feminism. Where do you situate yourself in the history of feminist discourse?

EM: I don't know what that means. I'm biologically female, but I've often felt like a man. But when you think about the place of rape in the history of the world, of the kind of mundane enslavement of women that's part of the history of the world ... I have no idea what feminism means. It feels too small for responding to that large an offense. I mean that in the average woman's gene code there's a story of being taken from your home and brought to another land repeatedly for hundreds and thousands of years. Hey buddy. Goin' somewhere? Bring some women! It's hard to really think about what it means to be female in the history of the world. Slavery is our history. All I can ever imagine doing is describing with my male-female eyes what it's like to move with this body and these ideas in this life.

GF: Why do you write about art?

EM: I made art as a kid. All kids make art. At one point when I was no longer sad that I didn't make art I could really let it in how wonderful the things people are making are. It moves your mind around. When you learn to read your brain actually changes. I think all art, really interesting, good art, and who knows what that is, it just picks up everything you know and throws it.

GF: How did you get to the University of California, San Diego?

EM: They offered me a lot of money.

GF: Why did you leave?

EM: They couldn't offer me enough. I wasn't bred by that institution. You're in a constant power struggle with people who don't really understand what you do. I think artists really need a new kind of institution to give teaching the dignity it deserves. I love to teach, but I think I should be able to get health insurance from it, and a stipend, and an opportunity to plug into art and teaching institutions all over the world. The academy is pretty good for academics but kind of stifling for artists. I was lucky to get in and get out. I created the MFA program. I did everything but start it. I guess I wrote it. The building itself now is actually making people sick. It's in the news.

GF: West Coast versus East Coast?

EM: I love the West Coast. Great for writing. Giant. Tons of waiting in cars. San Diego was a small town like Boston so in some ways I was a little too comfortable. LA's great. Good art, wonderful neon, and you get to live in a house. But I grew alienated very easily. I like getting slammed by encounters the way New York City operates. I would like to live maybe in Europe or South America for a while.

GF: Why is it so hard for some to write for a living and seemingly so easy for others? Is it a class issue?

EM: Which people do you mean? I think anyone can write for a living. It's which living, though, that is the question.

GF: How do class issues come to the surface in a classless society?

EM: Is that like a zen question? We're like the alcoholic, classless society. What elephant? I don't see any elephant. Everything's class. Sex is class. Gender's class. I think one is supposed to assimilate. And anything other than that is considered sentimental or masochistic. So you'll have someone like Philip Levine or Charles Bukowski considered working-class writers because of content. But not say Ron Silliman or Rae Armantrout or Amiri Baraka. One could be called a political writer or a feminist writer but not an upper-class writer. Most of us have really complex class relations.

GF: Do you have any advice for writers?

EM: Yeah, have an interesting life. When I was a kid my mom would give me a nickel to put in the collection plate at church. One Sunday upon returning home from mass I reached into my pocket. The nickel was still there. I wanted to give it back to my mother, so I threw it up the stairs toward her bedroom. The nickel went up through the spindles of the banister, landed on her nightstand, on its edge, flickering. It's actually been interesting ever since. That's the thing I'm interested in, the thing that's teetering. What will it become?

GF: What are you reading this week?

EM: *Marco Polo: From Venice to Xanadu*. Robert Walser's *Jakob von Gunten*. CAConrad's Frank poems.

GF: Do you read the newspaper?

EM: The *New York Times*. A lot.

GF: Watch television?

EM: Not at all.

GF: Listen to the radio?

EM: If I'm driving. NPR usually. I hate it.

GF: What do you think about a poet having a day job?

EM: What's a day?

GF: Can you describe the 'zine *Caveman*?

EM: It was based in laughter. We would have these small private ideas of strikes we could make on the poetry community. You know, like two or three people would come up with something that all three would laugh at. We'd either write fake missives from people, lists of who someone would like to have sex with, or had. Then a few real documents would be dropped into the mess. It was like a private joke gone social. They're very odd-sized. Hard to know where to put a caveman, ever.

GF: I simply loved reading *The Importance of Being Iceland*. Can you describe the process of getting that book deal with Semiotext(e)/MIT? The editing process? What was your selection process?

EM: I've had such a book in the works for a long time. They asked for it and suggested I get one of those Warhol grants, and I suggested they do it for me.

And I got it, strangely. I think I shouldn't be allowed to write my own grants. It's been hard. You know, somewhere in your fiftieth year you hit this archival moment where everything seems to make you reach deep into your file cabinets. It's like a root canal. It's like being dead. So, though I dredged all this stuff, mostly only the art things are in it now. Some talks, some essays. It's murder once you start assembling stuff because immediately there's too much, and you have to make criteria for what's in and what's out. I decided it was two books, and that's helpful, but it's really three, so they are wanting the book to be shorter, and I can't let go of this or that at this point. It's been murder, but I'll be happy to see it out and in the world.

GF: I've read many of your poems, your prose, fiction. I admire you and your work. I loved your opera, *Hell*. Thanks for being terrific. You are inspiring. What does anyone know about a writer? Why do we look to others for inspiration?

EM: I think we just don't know how to start, and someone puts something together that's recognizable, but not how you ever imagined anything happening.

GF: What writers do you admire?

EM: God so many. Bob Glück and Dodie [Bellamy]. Jimmy [Schuyler]. Renee Gladman. Ariana Reines. Her play is astonishing. Gail Scott. Juliana Spahr. Rae Armantrout. Steve Benson. Susie Timmons. Tisa Bryant. Trace Peterson. Kim Lyons. Joanna Fuhrman. Roberto Bolaño. CAConrad. Chris Kraus. Fanny Howe. Halldór Laxness. He's the greatest. Always John Wieners. Always Christopher Isherwood. Jonathan Lethem. Chip Delany. Can Xue. Pasternak. Alice Notley. Reb Anderson. Žižek. Bruce Chatwin. Kerouac. Henry Miller. Violette Leduc. Yes, I love Henry Miller. Rosebud. You know the story of Rosebud? Rosebud Pettet. She was friends with Allen Ginsberg. She wrote an account of Allen's death, when everyone was in his loft right before he died. I tried to get it published in *Harper's*. They were seriously considering it, then rejected it by telling me we don't do biography. I loved that categorical denial. Rosebud's piece was brilliant, like an Isherwood piece. She happened onto this intense scene, and her eyes opened like a camera.

GF: Describe your experience working with magazines. Why *Vice*?

EM: The magazine world is contiguous with ours. People work in one place, and you have a relationship and they go someplace else, so then you go there too. My friends at *Vice* used to be at *Index*. Magazines are fun because you kind of have to be shameless. If you want something you have to hound them, and you have to keep doing it in a non-angry way. It's sort of a good practice. Anything I can be that way about I have to keep doing.

GF: Do you think regular people can get ahead in life without being jerks?

EM: No, but you can go someplace else. In the '70s it was possible to break out beyond the poetry community, and I mean that in a good way. I mean you didn't think you were writing for just us. I think all of the writers around thought they could do what Michael Ondaatje or Lydia Davis did. I mean even get rewarded for being weird. No, but I'm saying something larger than that—that we ought to write for openings that aren't there. That we change the manner of our reception by writing for how we receive the worlds we cross to know ourselves. People's careers are as differently shaped as they are. The question remains, do you have the courage to have the career that you want, which is generally the one you already have? It's not so horrible to be here.

GF: Maybe you should write a self-help book.

EM: I'd like to. I've had the idea to do so.

GF: What is your Lower East Side?

EM: A place of deep convenience and old history.

10 QUESTIONS FOR BRUCE ANDREWS & SALLY SILVERS
BY ERICA KAUFMAN

DECEMBER/JANUARY 2010   NO. 221

Q1: When did you first begin collaborating? How did that come about? What was your first collaboration?

SALLY SILVERS: It depends on what you mean by collaboration. For instance, in 1982 at Danspace, in a piece called "Lack of Entrepreneurial Thrift," which was my first piece where I used other dancers and worked with live music, Bruce was one of the five dancers and I don't think he would call that a collaboration exactly, but he followed the movement instructions that I gave him. Then in October of 1982 we started doing BARKING, which was our performance project, and that was a direct collaboration because we put together different scenarios per written section, and the titles were things like "Voodoo for Anti-Communist Tourists," "Sharp Executive Retard," "Make Your Customers Wear Uniforms," and "While the People Slept." They were thematic written texts (three to five minutes) that we combined with music, dance, and events. For example, in one I had an elastic around my neck and I stuffed glossy advertisement pages, as many as I could get around my neck, and that took up one text. Bruce moved, Tom Cora (who was an improvising cellist) moved and read text, and I did too and I played the blender, as well as

spun the dial on a little old radio. So, I would say that was our first collaboration. But then, gradually more texts began coming into my own dance performances.

BRUCE ANDREWS: Well, here's some chronology. We met at the very end of 1978 and became a couple, that was the end of the first year that Charles [Bernstein] and I did *L=A=N=G=U=A=G=E* magazine. Sally did her first concert, her first choreography as a soloist, two years later, the very end of 1980. I took the money at the door, and that was the extent of my collaboration for that first piece. So, during those first two years, we were both devotees of things going on in the experimental music scene, experimental film scene, experimental theater scene, and whatever there was around in dance that was interesting. I think our wanting to collaborate had to do with our involvement in these other scenes and avid spectatorship in those other scenes. When Sally started making work she was the first person to use the free-improvisation musicians that we were starting to hang out with (Eugene Chadbourne, John Zorn, Polly Bradfield, and other people). We became very close with Tom Cora, who was very involved in that scene; he played cello and was a good friend of some painter friends of ours from Virginia. Sally was writing at this point, so she used text in her pieces years before I did any text work for her, she was reading poems of hers or texts of hers before the concerts as part of the piece, but I don't know that she integrated it into the pieces. She used these improvising musicians as part of her first concert, first group concert and I danced with her in that; we did a couple of duets where I was dancing that she choreographed that had texts of mine. So in the early '80s Sally started using musicians, maybe she was using text in her work, I was dancing. Then I started making music, somewhere in 1982–83, I started making tape collages, so I could perform in these ensembles that Sally was putting together because I just wanted to be more involved in the middle of her work. In the same period we started BARKING, this theater project which started as a trio, with the two of us, and Tom Cora. Tom did the music and

I did the texts, Sally choreographed all of us, Tom and I both danced along with Sally, and we had props, sort of theater events with props and gestural stuff that Sally pretty much choreographed. The thing that was the basis in the beginning of our collaboration was me doing the music, so I gradually went from performing in these ensembles to making up scores for the improvisers, which were mostly based on timing, organizing a two-minute duet here, two-minute trio trades here, one-minute solo here—I would have a stopwatch and I would be with these great musicians doing live tape mixing of these tape collages that I started to make. That music also went into BARKING, and then BARKING started to do big projects. We did one large thing in San Francisco where Henry Kaiser did the music, and then we did these two giant theater projects at PS122 in 1985 and 1987 with fifty or sixty people onstage. I organized the band and did the score for the music and the text. I think I directed the actors mostly.

SS: I put some sections from some of my dance pieces in and had improvising choreographers.

BA: We had people doing live instruction onstage, people doing all sorts of things, it was sort of like a three-ring circus.

SS: We had a woman demonstrating how to do Kabuki makeup.

BA: We had someone doing nineteenth century ballroom dancing, we had people sketching, we had people filming, we had people painting during the projects, and we had people drawing on the sides.

SS: It was like a happening but maybe with a little more structure.

BA: Those were probably the most intense collaborative things we did—those BARKING projects. The first big event that we did was about gender damage; we did a version of a Kabuki piece (that was in '85) and the second one about American imperialism in Central America and that was based on the story of William Walker, the soldier of fortune who took over Nicaragua in 1855, and we had him as a megalomaniac narcissist deciding to be the star of Shakespeare's *Coriolanus*, so he invited down the first all-black minstrel troop in the United States (which was formed in 1855) to bring them down to Nicaragua so they could star in his production. So we staged all that with about sixty people, in '87. This was a few years before the movie about William Walker came out. That was right around the time (about twenty years ago now) that I think I officially became her music director. So from that point on I would be centrally involved in picking the performers that would be in the band, coming up with a score, going through the rehearsal tapes, and talking with Sally about the structure of the pieces to figure out what kinds of sections the music would have and what kinds of sound we wanted, but not too much text. The only time we were using text was when we were doing BARKING.

SS: But that has changed now. Probably in the past five to ten years. I'd say that the text integration into my own dance performance works has only been in the last five years.

BA: We slowly began to integrate text, but before then it was pretty much me doing the music and Sally choreographing. By that point I'd had a couple of residencies where I got access to engineers who worked with me doing electronic processing of texts which I didn't have the skills to do myself. That material I integrated into the music I was making—the music was a collage of me improvising on various instruments and editing them and playing the tapes live; I never played any instruments live, but I would basically do tapes that were collages of my own playing on thirty different instruments. So I started to integrate some of that text material that was processed into the sound scores at that point also. Another thing that happened during this time (once we stopped doing BARKING) was that Sally, in addition to her main concerts, would also do a lot of improvising situations, so she would improvise in performance and shorter pieces, and I started at some point (I guess it was fifteen to twenty years ago) doing something comparable to Sally's live choreography. I started doing live editing on stage. I would basically take the editing process that I normally work with at home, taking cards, small pieces of paper, a couple words or phrases on them, and collaging them and making texts out of them. I started doing that live in the same room in the same moment as Sally was improvising her movement and also with musicians, so I did some things with musicians along, where I was doing this live editing and then I did some things with Sally where I was doing this live editing. That was another place where texts came into our collaborations. But that was apart from her big choreographing concerts.

02: What do you mean by electronically processing texts?

BA: Digitizing them and then running them through harmonizers, processors, sound effects, various programs which I am just starting to learn a bit about now so I am able to do them myself. But this was working with electronic composers and studio engineers. In a way, to transform the material similarly to the way I had written it—change the speed, change the texture, chop it up, various spatial and temporal delays and looping and jumps and cuts and textural transforms.

03: Can you talk a bit about your individual processes and how they change when you collaborate, if they change?

SS: Well my process changes from piece to piece. Primarily how I start is myself improvising in front of a video camera, looking back through those tapes, choosing movements, and then writing those movements (as Bruce does) on separate pieces of paper and then organizing them either into different pieces or different sections of one piece. When dancers come to rehearsal, they learn those movements from video. That is sort of a basic thing I've been doing since I got a video camera. When I didn't have a video camera, I would improvise and write things down on a piece of paper and try to describe what it was that I had done. I work similarly, in the sense that I choose from small units of information to make larger phrases. It is different if I am doing partnering work with dancers (which I do a lot of)—then I find I have to make up the material directly on the dancers when they are here and I often have to say I am you now and do something before I know what it is that I want. And then lately I have been also trying to open that up a little more by coming up with ideas that I can allow the dancers to translate into what's going to be performed. Sometimes that gets more set and sometimes I leave it open so there is more improvisation in the performances. I just started putting that in. That might be partially to do with my own body aging—I can't do all the movements I want anymore, I can't give them all to everybody, I need to figure out other ways of generating movement in order to continue to be a choreographer. So, I am starting to open up my process to those kinds of ideas and I am sure other things will happen too, but at least that is a starting point for me, getting older. And it also varies whether I am doing a more thematically based piece, or something based on a film; or this last piece from spring '09, *Yessified!*, was based on race and whiteness, but a lot of my pieces are not theme-centered, so it really varies depending on the kind of information I am trying to present.

BA: The theme-specific pieces that Sally did in the very beginning were BARK-ING pieces; that really was a political project, whereas her straight dance projects tended to be less thematically organized or more abstract maybe . . . And that changed when we stopped doing BARKING, some of that desire to do something that had a thematic focus which might affect the music, might affect the sound, affect whether she wanted text with it . . . [the desire] got channeled into her regular dance projects.

SS: I think the politics in my dance projects at the beginning was more about trying to call attention to the body as a social presence and that was really my project for the first ten to fifteen years of making work. I really wanted to get away from standardized dance vocabularies and try to pull into place an image of a person moving with movement that you wouldn't see every day, but something that would point to the fact that the person was a social body doing it. I was really interested in taking a stance on movement vocabularies and that occupied me for quite a long time and that settled and I came to just realize that it was the basis of everything that I did and I didn't have to focus on it. I could take it and utilize it in other ways while still maintaining it so it became more interesting to me to take on themes.

BA: And that affected the music too, the soundscapes that she wanted for all of the early concerts (leaving the BARKING aside) were free improvisers without any relationship to theme or any kind of obvious vernacular style of music— it was beyond genre in that sense.

SS: When I started becoming more interested in theme-centered pieces I wanted the music organized.

BA: She also wanted other types of sounds, so that in the beginning I was part of these ensembles contributing extended technique—weird noise-based free-improvisation sounds, which was one of our favorite types of music at the time. Then I started to use what we called "cultural material," either processing it, collaging it, layering it, editing it, modular bits of things that I hadn't created—things from an obsessively large record collection came into play at that point instead of just me banging around the kitchen and recording myself or borrowing instruments from school and trying to learn how to play the trombone so I could get eight minutes of trombone edits. For me, when it comes to individual processes, the thing that made it possible for me to make this music for Sally was that I already had a way of working with language that I could in a sense just transfer as an aesthetic or a methodology into sound. So I was already working with these small modular bits ... So, that was how I started working in music and then that changed once Sally wanted different kinds of focus. She did a piece on the twenties and I had period music for that. We did a piece on dreams and I had things related to that. When I started using text in the pieces, that was pretty much done the way I also write. When I did this live editing, that was just taking my living-room sofa onstage in a sense and spreading out fifty cards and being able to make phrases and putting things in the middle of phrases, and come up with what is there.

SS: How do you generate your writing, for instance?

BA: The raw materials? I am jotting things down, I am walking around ... I write in a movie, I write at a lecture, I write in the street, I write on the subway, I write when I am reading, I am just generating raw material so I don't do any of that onstage, I do editing, so that is what I think of as writing. If I am doing that onstage, live. I guess I really haven't had to change that methodology for Sally when she wanted text. I would select things sometimes based on themes, and certainly that was true of BARKING; we did a piece on consumerism, we did a piece on various kinds of oppression and injustice—I would basically pick out material that resonated with that and organize it in the way that I normally would.

04: So, on the cards, is it words, phrases, or does it vary?

BA: Usually two to four words, sometimes single words, very rarely anything longer than a sentence or a phrase.

05: Which comes first—the words or the movement?

BA: The movement always comes first, but I am just thinking of my role as music director. Sally always composes in silence or with something else on the record player. I would get rehearsal tapes that I would meticulously time and figure out sequencing. I would have an idea of what I think the piece would look like. And I would assemble raw materials, and I always do some live mixing—I never made fixed music for Sally that would just be able to be played. I would always have to be there with three or four tape players and a mixing board, doing a live mix to get the timing right and the layering right, but I would always do that afterwards. So, in other words, I am not a composer, I am a sort of a sound designer and also live performer, so I would never compose a piece of music and have Sally perform to it. And, I don't know that we have ever done that with text either. To have a piece of text and you choreograph to a text?

SS: We often do that with improvising. The text is of course there first. We've done a piece called "Snow Pony" at The Poetry Project's New Year's, and in that case I helped edit the material. I chose from writing already done. I also did that with *Yessified!*

BA: The performance of some of the texts that had been previously written that she was going to improvise with, Sally would intervene and have a lot to say about how it was presented.

SS: We did *Yessified!* with your "White Dialect" piece. Often Bruce's poetry functions for me as a mover as sound, but often I can use snippets of imagery that I get from it besides the rhythm and the sound of it I can gesturalize from the meaning there—it is a constant back and forth of listening, interpreting, and decision making.

BA: Well *Yessified!*, not the dialect piece, but the rest of the text, had an interesting history because that came from a text that I generated live in concert with a racial tone to it because we did it at the Vision Festival, which is basically devoted to the radical heritages of the Black Arts Movement and black culture. So we did a couple nights of that where I am editing live composing material with the legendary bassist Henry Grimes and Julie Patton doing vocals and a little bit of text and a little bit of movement. What I like about these live editing situations is that I end up with a text, which I then type up. So then I have some product, something that is done that I can make use of. We did seven nights of that and I generated a fair amount of text that had an A, B, C structure, like a lot of my work has thematically as an organizing hook—so I took those texts, I think it was mostly the B and C material that Sally selected from when she did this solo "Yellin' Gravy" at La MaMa and Joyce Soho.

SS: I was starting to work on a piece about race and the format that it took was a solo for myself and I used the text from Bruce's improvisation at the Vision Festival and edited it down to about a fourth of its size and then . . .

BA: . . . proposed some cuts to me and then we worked it out so it was about the right length and in the right sections and I presented that live to accompany her solo, with music that Sally had selected. So the backdrop, the music for that, which was Booker T. & the MG's, and a few other cult classics of black music that we love, was on in the background mixed in with me doing the text live.

SS: It was on a minute basis. I have composed in minutes for a while. So there's a minute where there's text and a minute where there's not text and something else is going on. And so I chose within a ten-minute solo where the text was going to be and what the nature of the text was, and chose the music for the other sections and I performed that in *Yessified!* in two sections.

BA: We took that and broke it into two parts and that was part of the big *Yessified!* piece. So that was an example of where Sally's editing me. I never get to do the other.

SS: He'll look at something and say, "I don't like that movement." And sometimes I listen . . .

BA: I think it was because it was thematic, so she got more involved in thinking about the text. Normally it would be a bit more abstract in relationship to the movements, and I would just take charge of it because it would be based on my sense of what works as writing.

06: Is there ever a time when you are both doing live improvisation, or are there always some elements of the collaboration that are at least planned ahead of time?

BA: Well, when Sally's improvising and I'm doing live editing of text. Have you improvised with someone else while I am doing live editing?

SS: Musicians.

BA: Musicians, I think maybe not other dancers. We've done this thing at the Vision Festival a couple of times where we had a few musicians and me just doing text, not doing music at all; I guess I've largely stopped doing live mixing of sound with other free-improvising musicians. I don't really perform as a musician anymore like I used to. In the '80s and into the '90s I was a little more directly in the free-improv scene—I would get asked to play gigs by some of my heroes, you know, just as a musician, so that was pretty cool.

07: I was lucky enough to see *Yessified!*, a truly fantastic performance. Can you each speak a bit to the process behind that show? How did the choreography evolve? The music? How much of any given performance or collaboration is improvised?

ss: We talked about my solo part in there already. My process for that was reading like crazy about how different bodies were described in different literatures and when African Americans talk about dance and how they fit into modern dance, what languages do they use, how do they describe it, and then trying . . . —it is very hard to bring out a sense of whiteness because it is like asking someone to describe patriarchy—it is the whole system that you are talking about and the only way to really talk about it is to talk about what is not in it. So it was trying to create some sort of hybrid, to call attention to race but to try to include some aspect of what whiteness could mean physically. It was really hard and hard not to do it in a way that creates further stereotyping, or negativities, so I tried to come down more on the positive side of hybridization and say that you don't draw lines; we are made up of each other in very basic senses, in the way we move, the influence is there, the way we speak, the way we describe ourselves, and the reasons for moving. So it was a tricky balance to maintain and I had to come up with metaphors for things. Like in one section that was more improvisatory, I had two people try to move without either of them leading or following, so how do you take initiative together. Another description was someone gets to a spot first and the other two dancers have to fight over that spot, so there were metaphors about needing mutual support, who is giving support, who is taking it, who is losing it. I had a whole outline of ideas like that and then the rehearsal comes and you start to set things and try to stay with the idea of all of that. It was really stringing together a whole lot of metaphors for interdependency.

BA: So for that piece, for *Yessified!*, I had three chunks of text, two of which were mixed with the music that Sally had picked out earlier for "Yellin' Gravy" (the solo version), which were racially resonant material that we had from these live editing and improvisations that we did as part of the Vision Festival, so that was more or less taking something we had already done and putting it in the middle of a group piece of hers, and we opened the evening with a chunk from this white-dialect poetry project of mine, the title of which is "Success without Goals," and that was just a kind of bravura live-sound poetry performance piece of mine in a sense that I'd ended many poetry readings with parts of (little five to seven minute parts). I started that project out with rustic midwestern dialect material and had just gotten to this Appalachian part of that project so I used just about four minutes of that, which was done live in concert and a lot of people didn't even realize that because I am up in the dark in the back, so that was the text for that.

SS: And that was personal for me because I am from that region, Appalachia, so I preferred that to the midwestern piece. Somehow it had more significance for me moving to it. That was the moment in the piece when I was completely improvising. Trying to channel the sound of the dialect that was personal for me in the sense that it had personal resonance because of my background and trying to translate that background into something that possibly I am still made up of without knowing it.

BA: Both the improvised text material and that project in a sense came out of a couple-year research project, reading project on race, which had a musical component based on an obsession I developed with the Harlem Renaissance in the twenties and then with '60s soul music centered around Memphis where we took a trip the previous year. So the music for that I knew was going to involve this twenties Harlem Renaissance material as well as this soul-music material, none of which was of course mine, so I am just collaging and editing that and trying to fit it into the rehearsal tapes that I am looking at. The music was the most elaborate collaboration I've ever done with Michael Schumacher, the composer who I am very good friends with now, and have worked with ... For the music for that, I was playing very short excerpts of '60s soul music mixed in with material that I had processed collaboratively with Michael of my text material, some of which I had used in some previous concerts of Sally, and some material from this really odd project where Michael gave me six or seven hundred short sound files of him recording various things, people singing, people playing instruments, people making sounds, and then I imitated all six or seven hundred sounds vocally and gave him those recordings and then he made this elaborate sixteen-speaker collage of that, so I had some of that material that I mixed in. Then I gave Michael this whole bank of several hundred of my favorite five-, ten-, twenty-second snippets of material from the twenties (blues, gospel, jazz) and he did just some unbelievable electronic processing of that material . . . I think that was the most complicated musical endeavor I've had with Sally.

SS: I remember that it was one of the hardest pieces I have ever tried to put together. I had all these sections and then I had all these different people and then trying to get the transitions to happen and trying to figure out the order so that just the right amount of that person came in at just the right amount of time and place and creating some sort of symmetry between part A and part B and figuring out how to make it move through what it was supposed to do. I struggled and struggled with the order and keeping up with all the sections and figuring out where the thing could go both logistically and for significant reasons. It was really tough.

08: So how do you decide when you want to do something like that; or does it all depend on the larger choreographic scope of the piece?

BA: Yeah, in this case it had to do with some sort of resonance on the topic.

SS: Yeah, it had to do with some sort of atmosphere that was created that wasn't music.

09: Is there a modern dance equivalent to Language poetry? Is there a Language poetry dance?

SS: What we've been talking about, coming out of the Judson Church theater experimentations, that I think I do come out of, that legacy of experimentation; and I think what I am trying to maybe add to it is some sort of sense of the social body more. They were very interested in that with pedestrian movement and collaging and bringing things in from source materials. Being interested in the movement itself—maybe not at its most pedestrian—is somewhat equivalent to Language poetry as well as the social modernist aspect of it.

BA: I remember when Sally started choreographing, she didn't like the word "dance." She wanted to think of herself as a movement choreographer. It is the same sort of sense that dance was a genre, and that the material you were working with was movement, and that was similar to the kind of music we were interested in, whether it was coming out of Cage and using noise without having it be musical, harmonized sound; or whether it was the free-improvisation scene, which was not jazz, not classical, postgenre, nonvernacular, in that way; so when the so-called Language writers started in the '70s, some of us didn't think of what we were doing as poetry. We thought of it as maybe a new genre. Some way of dealing with language in the same way that Sally was dealing with movement and people that we knew were dealing with sound . . . Leaving someone like Stein aside—who never was considered a poet by the establishment—pretty much all the radical literary writing we were most compelled by was all called poetry in the same way that Sally was compellingly interested by things in the dance heritage; and finding that, however radical her movement explorations were as a choreographer, there was no place for it other than the dance floor; so she ended up as a prominent experimental dance choreographer in the same way that the Language writers ended up being prominent experimental poets, which wasn't what either one of us necessarily wanted. But the Language writers had a group and there was a group of us here in NY and group in SF and scattered, a few others . . . but Sally didn't have that so she was operating really even more on the fringe when she started in the '80s of the dance world than we were in the poetry world, because at least we had a group, we had a community, we had some other people to talk to; she was out on a limb—the people that would have really hooked up with what she was doing were the legatees of Judson, and a lot of that had been domesticated or disappeared and many people had stopped working or were doing much more conservative work . . . The other thing that she was saying about the social body interest, the sociopolitical commitment, I think that was, coming to New York, and starting to write in the late '60s, early '70s; there was this tremendous heritage of experimental writing . . . a lot of it coming out of Cage, of people like Jackson Mac Low, a lot of it coming out of concrete poetry, sound poetry, a lot of it coming out of the European Dada heritage and that was a huge influence on my early work and the early work of my peers in the early to mid-'70s, and that started to change when I got to New York ('75), and heightened being with Sally in the '80s . . . so we moved away from this seemingly more abstract material of a Mac Low or a Clark Coolidge in the '60s and towards material that had more of this social charge to it; this became more phrase-based, it had a little more relationship to speech, it had a little more relationship to a nonliterary vocabulary that had some political implications, and that was really a shift across the board in the so-called Language-writing community in the late '70s. A lot of people's work changed in that way, on both coasts. Like if you look at say, Silliman's work, from the early influences of Grenier from these microscopic bits of language, Grenier and Eigner, then shifting into the New Sentence. I think the interest out West in sentences and that kind of phrase structure had something to do with that. A lot of it had to do with giving poetry readings, which I had never done before coming to New York, being in an urban environment was related to it . . . When you are in the urban environment, then you start thinking with more socially charged phrase-based material. There was just something familiar about that, so we did move away from the somewhat more abstract, nonpersonal material of the '60s predecessors.

10: What's next? What are you each working on?

BA: I am continuing work on this white-dialect poetry project and I've gotten again obsessively involved with developing an aesthetic theory that can be applied to the judgments that the public makes about national security based on Kant's third critique, the Critique of Judgment. I am using my outline for this major essay project as a grid for organizing a giant box of cards from a couple of years ago to make a giant poem that is thematically organized around this aesthetic judgment project. The big change for Sally is working with Yvonne Rainer. That's the first time she's danced for anyone else since she first started doing her own work in 1980. But Yvonne was always a hero of hers so she couldn't turn it down when Yvonne wanted to put a group together. For her to go back to choreographing (which Yvonne mentions in her memoir) is partly based on Sally's intervention in the early '90s, wanting to learn a piece of Yvonne's just from the text that was in her Nova Scotia book.

SS: We're going to be performing in November here. One of the things that Yvonne's work has really opened up in me is a sort of acting. Because she doesn't make movement anymore so we really learn off of either videos of other people doing things—the last piece, I had to learn the antics of Robin Williams, trying to duplicate those comic moments of his, and in the new piece, "Steve Martin and Sarah Bernhardt"—and soccer, we have to imitate soccer moves when you don't have the ball, what you do when you don't have the ball, and pictures from magazines. So there is a certain element of acting that I never did in my own work, taking on somebody else, gesture by gesture, that is very difficult and very fascinating to do. So I am putting a little bit more of that in my work now too I think.

BA: That is something that Sally didn't used to do, which would now be considered a kind of appropriation. All of the choreography that she used to do was based on video, viewing herself dancing solo or with someone else in her studio. It usually started out on her body, or modified from other sources. And that is true of me—a lot of work of mine that might sound like I am walking down the street copying things down that I hear is really just me thinking something else, related to something that I hear or see. So it is not really the mechanical kind of appropriation that has gotten so popular now as a way of othering.

AUTHOR BIOS

WILL ALEXANDER is a poet, novelist, essayist, aphorist, visual artist, and pianist. He is a Whiting Fellow and California Arts Council Fellow, as well as a PEN Oakland and American Book Award winner. He is approaching 30 titles completed.

SHEILA ALSON was the founder of the women's multicultural poets' theater group Cayenne. She wrote plays and short stories, as well as five books of poetry, including *Nation of Separation* and *Fertility in the Desert*, and was an editor for the magazine *A Gathering of the Tribes*. She spent the last several years of her life as a New Orleans–based painter. When she died in 2002, she had been completing work on her first novel, *The Gold Ring*.

BRUCE ANDREWS is an experimental poet, sound designer, & recently retired (after 38 years) left-wing political science professor. As Musical Director for Sally Silvers & Dancers, he has created compositions, collages & performance mixes of music & texts for more than two decades. A founding co-editor of the journal *L=A=N=G=U=A=G=E*, he is the author of over 30 books of poetry and a collection of innovative critical essays. (http://www.fordhamenglish.com/bruce-andrews)

ANSELM BERRIGAN is the author of seven books of poetry, including *Come In Alone* (Wave Books, 2016) and *Primitive State* (Edge, 2015). He is co-author of two collaborative books: *Loading*, with Jonathan Allen (Brooklyn Arts Press, 2013), and *Skasers*, with John Coletti (Flowers & Cream, 2012). He is the current poetry editor for *The Brooklyn Rail* and Co-Chair, Writing at the Milton Avery Graduate School of the Arts interdisciplinary MFA program.

EDMUND BERRIGAN is the author of three books of poetry: *Disarming Matter* (Owl Press, 1999), *Glad Stone Children* (Farfalla, 2008), and *Can It!* (Letter Machine Editions, 2013). A chapbook, *We'll All Go Together*, was published by Fewer and Further press in 2016. He is editor of *The Selected Poems of Steve Carey* (Subpress, 2009) and co-editor with Anselm Berrigan and Alice Notley of *The Collected Poems of Ted Berrigan* (University of California, 2005) and *The Selected Poems of Ted Berrigan* (University of California, 2010). He has been an editor for poetry magazines *Brawling Pigeon*, *Log*, *Lungfull!*, and *Vlak*.

LISA BIRMAN's debut novel, *How To Walk Away*, was awarded the 2016 Colorado Book Award in Literary Fiction. She is the author of *For That Return Passage—A Valentine for the United States of America*; editor of *Dearest Annie, You Wanted a Report on Berkson's Class: Letters from Frances LeFevre to Anne Waldman*; and co-editor of the anthology *Civil Disobediences: Poetics and Politics in Action*.

STAN BRAKHAGE (1933–2003) was a leading figure in twentieth-century avant-garde film as well as an educator and author, teaching at both the Art Institute of Chicago and the University of Colorado at Boulder. He frequently referred to his films as "visual music," or as documents of "moving visual thinking," completing over three hundred works between 1952 and 2003.

PETER BUSHYEAGER's poetry collections include *Citadel Luncheonette* and *In the Green Oval*. Recent poems appear in *Live Mag!* and *From Somewhere to Nowhere*, the forthcoming *Unbearables* anthology. His reviews and articles have appeared in *Talisman, Rain Taxi, The Poetry Project Newsletter, The World in Time and Space* anthology, and *The Encyclopedia of American Poetry: Twentieth Century*.

JACK COLLOM is a poet and essayist who earned a BA in forestry and English and a MA in English literature from the University of Colorado. He has published over 25 books, including *Red Car Goes By* (2001), *Situations, Sings* with Lyn Hejinian (2008), and *Second Nature* (2012), which won a Colorado Book Award. He is the recipient of a Foundation for Contemporary Arts grant, as well as two fellowships from the National Endowment for the Arts. He currently teaches at Naropa University.

BRENDA COULTAS is the author of *The Tatters*, a collection of poetry, published by Wesleyan University Press. Her other books include *The Marvelous Bones of Time* (2008) and *A Handmade Museum* (2003) from Coffee House Press. Her chapbook, *A Journal of Places*, can be read at www.metambesen.org.

TINA DARRAGH started writing poetry in college and upon graduation became part of the Mass Transit open reading series at Washington, DC's Community Book Store from 1972–1974. Darragh was included in many of the *L=A=N=G=U=A=G=E* poetry journals and anthologies and has continued to approach writing as a collaborative process with other poets and with the reader.

SAMUEL R. DELANY is a writer who lives in Philadelphia. His books include his collected journals, 1955–1968, *In Search of Silence*, *Times Square Red, Times Square Blue*, the graphic novella *Bread & Wine*, his autobiography *The Motion of Light in Water*, and the novels *Dark Reflections*, *Through the Valley of the Nest of Spiders*, *Dhalgren*, *Nova*, *Trouble on Triton*, and his fantasy series *Return to Neveryon*, along with a dozen books of criticism.

TIM DLUGOS (1950–1990), was a member of the Christian Brothers, a Catholic religious order, from 1968 to 1971. He quit the order and moved to DC, where he became involved with the Mass Transit poets and worked for Ralph Nader's Public Citizen. He moved to New York City in the late 1970s, editing and contributing to *Christopher Street*, *New York Native*, and *The Poetry Project Newsletter*. After his HIV positive diagnosis, Dlugos returned to priesthood study at Yale School of Divinity, but was unable to complete his degree, dying of AIDS-related complications at age 40. Dlugos published five books of poems in his lifetime and three posthumously.

MARCELLA DURAND's books include *Deep Eco Pré*, a collaboration with Tina Darragh (Little Red Leaves, 2009); *AREA* (Belladonna*, 2008); and *Traffic & Weather*, a site-specific poem written during a residency at the Lower Manhattan Cultural Council in downtown Manhattan (Futurepoem, 2008). She is currently working on a collection of alexandrines titled *Rays of the Shadow*.

LARRY FAGIN is a poet, editor, and teacher in New York City. His books include *I'll Be Seeing You*, *Rhymes of a Jerk*, *Dig & Delve*, and *Complete Fragments*. He is the founder and editor of *Adventures in Poetry* magazine and books. He also was the founder and artistic director of Danspace, the dance program at St. Mark's Church-in-the-Bowery.

GREG FUCHS teaches Bronx students with disabilities to trust themselves and question everything. Fuchs has written many poems, published books, and photographed a lot of things. He has a master of arts yet still believes in its ability to transform humanity. Fuchs survives beneath the underground but occasionally surfaces with his fabulous artist wife, Alison Collins, and their magical son, Lucas.

ALLEN GINSBERG's signal poem "Howl" overcame censorship in 1957 to become one of the most widely read poems of the century. While his poems "America" and "Supermarket in California" are some of the most anthologized of modern poetry, "Kaddish" is considered to be his finest poem. Co-founder of the Jack Kerouac School at Naropa University, he was Distinguished Professor at Brooklyn College from 1986 until his death in 1997.

RENEE GLADMAN is the author of ten published works, including a cycle of novels about the city-state Ravicka and its inhabitants, the Ravickians, and *Calamities*, a collection of linked essays on writing and experience. Her first monograph of drawings, *Prose Architectures*, is forthcoming from Wave Books in 2017. She lives in New England with poet-ceremonialist Danielle Vogel.

JOHN GODFREY is the author of 14 collections of poetry, including *The City Keeps: Selected and New Poems 1966–2014* (Wave Books, 2016). He has received fellowships from the General Electric Foundation and the Foundation for Contemporary Arts. A graduate of Princeton University and Columbia University's School of Nursing, Godfrey retired in 2011 after 17 years as a nurse clinician in HIV/AIDS. He currently lives in Manhattan's East Village.

JUDITH GOLDMAN is author of *Vocoder* (Roof), *DeathStar/Richo-chet* (O Books), *l.b.; or, catenaries* (Krupskaya), and *agon* (The Operating System, forthcoming). She teaches in the Poetics Program at SUNY Buffalo and is currently at work on _____ *Mt. [blank mount]*, a project that writes through Shelley's "Mont Blanc" in the context of climate change and environmental disaster.

TED GREENWALD was born in Brooklyn in 1942. Raised in Queens, he always lived in New York, where he died in 2016. Ted published extensively for over 50 years and was the author of over 30 books, including *Licorice Chronicles*, *Word of Mouth*, *Jumping the Line*, *In Your Dreams*, *3*, *Clearview/LIE*, *Own Church*, *Common Sense*, and *The Age of Reasons*.

RED GROOMS is an artist known for collage sculptures of both fictional and observed scenes. He studied at the Art Institute of Chicago before permanently moving to New York in 1956. His work can be found in the Museum of Modern Art in New York, the Art Institute of Chicago, and the Carnegie Museum of Art, and has been featured in many solo exhibitions across the United States. He is the recipient of numerous artist awards, including a Lifetime Achievement Award from the National Academy of Design.

DAVID HENDERSON was a founding member of the Umbra poets, a group connected to the Black Arts Movement. His books include *De Mayor of Harlem* (1970), *Neo-California* (1998), the widely acclaimed biography *'Scuse Me While I Kiss the Sky: Jimi Hendrix: Voodoo Child* (1978), and the poetry ebook, *Obama, Obama* (2012). He is the recipient of a Foundation for Contemporary Performance Arts grant, as well as a New York Foundation for the Arts Poetry grant.

BARBARA HENNING is the author of three novels and eleven collections of poetry. Her most recent books are *A Day Like Today* (Negative Capability Press, 2015) and *A Swift Passage* (Quale Press, 2013). She teaches at Long Island University in Brooklyn.

VICTOR HERNÁNDEZ CRUZ was born in Puerto Rico and moved to the United States in 1954. He is a member of the Nuyorican movement of writers based in the Bay Area. Hernández Cruz has published numerous poetry collections, including *In the Shadow of Al-Andalus*, *The Mountain in the Sea*, and *Maraca: New and Selected Poems 1965–2000*, which was short-listed for the International Griffin Poetry Prize. He has received fellowships from the Guggenheim Foundation and the National Endowment for the Arts.

LISA JARNOT is the author of several books of poetry and a biography of Robert Duncan. She lives in Jackson Heights, New York, with her husband and daughter.

KEN JORDAN is the founder and Chief Content Officer of *Evolver* and the Executive Editor of *Reality Sandwich*. He held the community representative seat on the Poetry Project board in the 1990s.

DANIEL KANE is Reader in English and American Literature at the University of Sussex in Brighton, England. His publications include *All Poets Welcome: The Lower East Side Poetry Scene in the 1960s* and *We Saw the Light: Conversations between the New American Cinema and Poetry*. His book *Kill Those Bastards the New York School: Poetry and Punk Rock in New York City* is forthcoming in spring 2017.

ALEX KATZ was born in Brooklyn and raised in St. Albans, Queens, by his Russian parents. His mother had been an actress and possessed a deep interest in poetry, and his father, a businessman, also had an interest in the arts. Katz attended Woodrow Wilson High School in order to devote his afternoons to drawing. In 1946, Katz entered The Cooper Union Art School in Manhattan. In the 1950s, Katz met figurative painters Larry Rivers and Fairfield Porter, photographer Rudolph Burckhardt, and poets John Ashbery, Edwin Denby, Kenneth Koch, Frank O'Hara, and James Schuyler. Katz became increasingly interested in portraiture and painted his friends and his wife, Ada. He embraced monochrome backgrounds, which would become a defining characteristic of his style, anticipating Pop Art and separating him from gestural figure painters and the New Perceptual Realism. In 1959, Katz made his first cutout, which would grow into a series of flat sculptures—freestanding or relief portraits that exist in actual space. In the early 1960s, influenced by films, television, and billboard advertising, Katz began painting large-scale paintings, often with dramatically cropped faces. He would continue painting these complex groups into the 1970s, portraying the social world of painters, poets, critics, and other colleagues that surrounded him. Works by Alex Katz can be found in public collections worldwide. In 1968, Katz moved to an artists' cooperative building in SoHo, New York, where he has lived and worked ever since. He spends his summers in Lincolnville, Maine.

VINCENT KATZ is a poet, translator, and critic. He is the author of the books of poems *Southness* (Lunar Chandelier Press) and *Swimming Home* (Nightboat Books) and the book of translations *The Complete Elegies of Sextus Propertius* (Princeton University Press). He is the editor of *Black Mountain College: Experiment in Art* (MIT Press). He curates the Readings in Contemporary Poetry series at Dia Chelsea in New York City, where he lives with his wife and two sons.

ERICA KAUFMAN is the author of *INSTANT CLASSIC* (Roof Books, 2013) and *censory impulse* (Factory School, 2009). she is also the co-editor of *NO GENDER: Reflections on Life and Work of kari edwards* (Venn Diagram, 2009) and of *Adrienne Rich: Teaching at CUNY, 1968–1974* (Lost & Found, 2014). kaufman lives in the woods and works at Bard College.

KENNETH KOCH (1925–2002) wrote many collections of poetry, fiction, plays, and nonfiction. His poetry has been collected in two major volumes, *The Collected Poems of Kenneth Koch* (shorter poems) and *On the Edge: Collected Long Poems.* Koch's fiction was gathered in *The Collected Fiction of Kenneth Koch*, and he was the author of three groundbreaking books on poetry and the teaching of poetry. Koch was awarded numerous honors, including the Bollingen Prize and the Rebekah Johnson Bobbitt National Prize for Poetry, bestowed by the Library of Congress in 1966, and was a finalist for both the National Book Award and the Pulitzer Prize. He was the recipient of awards from the American Academy of Arts and Letters and the Fulbright, Guggenheim, and Ingram Merrill foundations. In 1966 he was inducted into the American Academy of Arts and Letters. Kenneth Koch lived in New York City, where he was a professor of English at Columbia University.

WAYNE KOESTENBAUM has published eighteen books of poetry, criticism, and fiction, including *Notes on Glaze*, *The Pink Trance Notebooks*, *My 1980s & Other Essays*, *Hotel Theory*, *Best-Selling Jewish Porn Films*, *Andy Warhol*, *Humiliation*, *Jackie Under My Skin*, and *The Queen's Throat* (a National Book Critics Circle Award finalist). He is a Distinguished Professor of English, Comparative Literature, and French at the CUNY Graduate Center in New York City.

RACHEL LEVITSKY is the author of *Under the Sun* (Futurepoem, 2003), *NEIGHBOR* (UDP, 2009), the novel *The Story of My Accident Is Ours* (Futurepoem, 2013), and several chapbooks, including *The Adventures of Yaya and Grace* (Potes & Poets, 1999), *Renoemos* (Delete, 2010), and with the artist Susan Bee, *Hopefully, the Island* (Belladonna*, 2016). She is a founding member of Belladonna* Collaborative.

BRENDAN LORBER is a writer and editor. He's the author of several chapbooks, most recently, *Unfixed Elegy and Other Poems* (Buttered Lamb Press). He's had work in *American Poetry Review*, *Fence*, *McSweeney's*, and elsewhere. He lives atop the tallest hill in Brooklyn, New York, in a little castle across the street from a 500-acre necropolis.

HARRY MATHEWS has published novels, collections of poetry, critical writings, and autobiographical works. He has been associated with the so-called New York School of poets, and with the Oulipo, a Parisian group of writers, mathematicians, and scholars who use strict non-literary constraints in composing literary works. Mathews was inducted into the group in 1973 at the instigation of Georges Perec.

BERNADETTE MAYER is the author of over 27 collections, including most recently *Works and Days* (2016), *Eating the Colors of a Lineup of Words: The Early Books of Bernadette Mayer* (2015), and *The Helens of Troy, New York* (2013), as well as countless chapbooks and artist-books. From 1980–1984, she served as the director of the St. Mark's Poetry Project, and has also edited and founded *0 to 9* journal and United Artists books and magazines.

ANGE MLINKO is poetry editor of *The Nation* and the author of four collections of poetry, including *Marvelous Things Overheard* (FSG, 2013). Her poems and criticism have appeared in *The Nation*, *Poetry*, *Paris Review*, *Granta*, *London Review of Books*, and numerous other journals. In 2009, she was the recipient of the Poetry Foundation's Randall Jarrell Award for Criticism. In 2014, she was named a Guggenheim Fellow. She is an Associate Professor of English at the University of Florida, Gainesville.

FRED MOTEN is author of *In the Break: The Aesthetics of the Black Radical Tradition*, *Hughson's Tavern*, *B Jenkins*, *The Undercommons: Fugitive Planning and Black Study* (with Stefano Harney), *The Feel Trio*, *The Little Edges*, and *The Service Porch*. He lives in Los Angeles and teaches at the University of California, Riverside.

HARRYETTE MULLEN is a poet and professor at the University of California, Los Angeles. Her books include *Urban Tumbleweed* and *Sleeping with the Dictionary*, a finalist for the National Book Award, the National Book Critics Circle Award, and the *Los Angeles Times* Book Award in poetry. *Trimmings*, *Muse & Drudge*, and *S*PeRM**K*T* were collected into *Recyclopedia*, for which Mullen received a PEN Beyond Margins Award. She has been awarded a fellowship from the Guggenheim Foundation, as well as an Academy of American Poets Fellowship and a grant from the Foundation for Contemporary Arts.

EILEEN MYLES is the author of more than 20 books, including *I Must Be Living Twice: New & Selected Poems*, *Snowflake / different streets*, *Inferno*, *The Importance of Being Iceland*, *Sorry, Tree*, and *Chelsea Girls*. She is the recipient of a Guggenheim Fellowship in nonfiction, a grant from the Creative Capital/Andy Warhol Foundation, four Lambda Book Awards, and the Shelley Prize from the PSA. She lives in Marfa, Texas and New York.

MAGGIE NELSON is a poet, art critic, lyric essayist, and nonfiction author of books such as *Bluets*, *The Argonauts* (winner of the 2015 National Book Critics Circle Award in Criticism), and *The Red Parts: A Memoir*. She was awarded an Arts Writers grant in 2007 from the Creative Capital/Andy Warhol Foundation, a National Endowment for the Arts Fellowship for poetry in 2011, and a MacArthur Fellowship in 2016. She currently teaches in the CalArts MFA writing program.

CHARLES NORTH's tenth book of poems, *What It Is Like*, headed NPR's Best Poetry Books of 2011. With James Schuyler he edited the anthologies *Broadway* and *Broadway 2*. *States of the Art*, selected prose, is due in 2017. North has received two NEA Fellowships, four Fund for Poetry Awards, a Poets Foundation award, and a Foundation for Contemporary Arts Grant.

ALICE NOTLEY's most recent books of poetry are *Benediction* and *Certain Magical Acts*. She is the 2015 recipient of the Ruth Lilly Poetry Prize. She lives in Paris, France.

AKILAH OLIVER was the author of two poetry collections, including *A Toast in the House of Friends* (2009), and four chapbooks. Born and raised in Los Angeles, she was an artist-in-residence at Beyond Baroque Literary Arts Center and received grants from the California Arts Council and the Rockefeller Foundation. At the time of her death in 2011, she was a professor at the Pratt Institute in the Humanities and Media Studies Department and a PhD candidate at the European Graduate School in Saas-Fee, Switzerland.

RON PADGETT's *How Long* was a Pulitzer Prize finalist in poetry and his *Collected Poems* won the *LA Times* Prize for the best poetry book of 2014 and the William Carlos Williams Award from the Poetry Society of America. His most recent translation is *Zone: Selected Poems* by Guillaume Apollinaire. Padgett wrote the poems in Jim Jarmusch's film *Paterson*.

ARLO QUINT is the author of *Wires and Lights* (Rust Buckle, 2016), *Death to Explosions* (Skysill, 2013), and *Drawn In* (Fewer & Further, 2010). He collaborated with writer Charles Wolski on *Check Out My Lifestyle* (Well Greased, 2012).

DAVID RATTRAY (1935–1993) was a poet and translator who worked as an editor for *Reader's Digest* General Books. He completed his undergraduate studies at Dartmouth, and trained at Harvard and the Sorbonne. Fluent in Greek, Latin, French, and German, among other languages, Rattray is best known for his translations of work by the 20th-century French writers Antonin Artaud, René Crevel, and Roger Gilbert-Lecomte. His book of collected stories and essays, *How I Became One of the Invisible* (Semiotext(e), 1992), has circulated among poets as a secret history and guide book to the mystical-poetic-outlaw tradition of Western literature, spanning the scholarly classics to the contemporary avant-garde.

ED SANDERS is a poet and activist who resides in New York. In 1962, he opened the Peace Eye Bookstore and started *Fuck You: A Magazine of the Arts*. His books include American Book Award winner *Thirsting for Peace in a Raging Century: Selected Poems 1961–1985*, *Poems for New Orleans*, *Investigative Poetry*, and *The Poetry and Life of Allen Ginsberg*. Sanders has received fellowships from the Guggenheim Foundation and the National Endowment for the Arts.

PAUL SCHMIDT (1934–1999) was a translator, poet, playwright, and actor who studied at Colgate and Harvard University in Russian Studies. He published the poetry collections *Night Life* and *Winter Solstice*, as well as *Arthur Rimbaud: Complete Works*, a translation. Schmidt wrote three plays, including *Black Sea Follies*, which won a Helen Hayes Award and Kesselring Prize for best play. He taught translation and theatre at the Yale School of Drama until he died in 1999.

SALLY SILVERS has been choreographing experimental dances & musicals (3 at Sundance Theater Festival), performing, filmmaking (2 prizewinning dance films), writing & publishing (poetry, theory, dance articles), teaching (improvisation, composition, repertory), dancing in the new and historical works of Yvonne Rainer (2006–2011), collaborating with writer Bruce Andrews & many other musicians, & earning awards—including a Guggenheim Fellowship and NEAs, among others— since 1980. (www.sallysilversdance.com)

DALE SMITH has published five books of poetry and a critical monograph, including, most recently, *Slow Poetry in America*. He is the co-editor of *An Open Map: The Robert Duncan/Charles Olson Correspondence* and *Imagining Persons: Robert Dun-*

can's Lectures on Charles Olson. From 1999–2004 he published with Hoa Nguyen the journal and book imprint *Skanky Possum*. He teaches at Ryerson University, Toronto.

LORENZO THOMAS was born in Panama and moved with his family to New York in 1948. He is the author of five poetry collections: *A Visible Island* (1967), *Dracula* (1973), *Chances Are Few* (1979, reissued in 2003), *The Bathers* (1981), and *Dancing on Main Street* (2004). Thomas was the recipient of a National Endowment for the Arts grant and the Houston Festival Foundation Award. Thomas was part of the Black Arts Movement in New York City and a member of the Umbra workshop.

EDWIN TORRES is the author of eight poetry collections, including *Ameriscopia* (University of Arizona Press), *Yes Thing No Thing* (Roof Books), and *The PoPedology of an Ambient Language* (Atelos Books). Anthologies include: *Angels of the Americlypse: An Anthology of New Latin@ Writing*, *PostModern American Poetry* (Vol. 2), and *Aloud: Voices from the Nuyorican Poets Café*.

JOHN TRUDELL, a Santee Sioux, was born February 15, 1946. During the early '70s, he ran Radio Free Alcatraz and was chairman of the American Indian Movement. In 1979, twelve hours after burning an American flag on the steps of the FBI headquarters in DC, his pregnant wife, three children, and mother-in-law were killed in a suspicious fire. Trudell turned to poetry as a way of therapy and published several books and albums of his words. He walked on, December 8, 2015.

ANNE WALDMAN, poet, performer, teacher, curator, editor, magpie scholar, activist, is the author, most recently, of *Voice's Daughter of a Heart Yet to be Born, Jaguar Harmonics, Gossamurmur*, and co-editor of *Cross Worlds: Transcultural Poetics (An Anthology from Kerouac School of Disembodied Poetics at Naropa University)*. Her feminist epic *The Iovis Trilogy* won the PEN Center Award for Poetry. She has also received the Shelley Award, a Guggenheim Fellowship, and the Before Columbus Foundation Poetry Award for lifelong achievement. She often performs with the family band: Fast Speaking Music. (website: annewaldman.org)

LEWIS WARSH's most recent books are *Alien Abduction* (Ugly Duckling Presse, 2015), *One Foot Out the Door: Collected Stories* (Spuyten Duyvil, 2014), *A Place in the Sun* (Spuyten Duyvil, 2010), and *Inseparable: Poems 1995–2005* (Granary Books, 2008).

He is editor and publisher of United Artists Books and teaches in the MFA program in creative writing at Long Island University (Brooklyn).

MAGDALENA ZURAWSKI's poetry collection, *Companion Animal*, was published in 2015 by Litmus Press and won the 2016 Norma Farber First Book Award from the Poetry Society of America. Her novel, *The Bruise* (FC2, 2008), won both the Ronald Sukenick Innovative Fiction Prize and the Lambda Award for Lesbian Debut Fiction. Her online column on teaching aesthetics after Ferguson can be viewed at *Jacket2*. Zurawski teaches in the Creative Writing Program at the University of Georgia.

PHOTO CREDITS

The following photographs appear courtesy of The Poetry Project archives: "Allen Ginsberg reads in the Sanctuary, ca. 1976" (p. v), Bernadette Mayer (p. 19), Allen Ginsberg and Kenneth Koch (p. 38, Ann Marie Rosseau), Ed Sanders (p. 103, by Karen Levy, 1987), Lorenzo Thomas (p. 173), Anne Waldman (p. 261, by Kai Sibley), Edwin Torres (p. 275, by Anna Siano), Harry Mathews (p. 286, by Sigrid Estrada), Will Alexander (p. 320, by Sheila Scott Wilkinson), and Eileen Myles (p. 374, by Dona MacAdams).

Charles North and Paul Violi (p. 1), photographer unknown, courtesy of Charles North.

Red Grooms (p. 8) by Jerry Atnip.

Paul Schmidt (p. 13) and Bruce Andrews / Sally Silvers (p. 386) by Jacob Burckhardt.

David Rattray (p. 29) by Mary Geis.

Barbara Henning and Harryette Mullen (p. 47), courtesy of Barbara Henning.

David Henderson (p. 60) by Alexandra Weltz-Rombach / parkafilm.cc.

Alice Notley (p. 72) by Anselm Berrigan.

John Godfrey (p. 88, 2004) by John Sarsgard.

Victor Hernández Cruz (p. 118) by Esteban Figueroa. Courtesy of Coffee House Press.

Bernadette Mayer (p. 130) by Marie Warsh.

Kenneth Koch (p. 140), Charles North (p. 200), and Anne Waldman (p. 209) by Laure Leber. Courtesy of The Poetry Project archives and the photographer.

Samuel L. Delany (p. 156) by Kyle Cassidy.

Renee Gladman (p. 164, 2001) by Kevin Killian.

Fred Moten (p. 184) by Lamont Hamilton.

Stan Brakhage (p. 191) by Kai Sibley. Courtesy of Marilyn Brakhage.

Vincent Katz and Alex Katz (p. 219), New York City, May, 2006. Photograph by Vivien Bittencourt.

Illustration of Larry Fagin (p. 229) by George Schneeman. Courtesy of Katie Schneeman.

Tina Darragh (p. 238) by Cathy Eisenhower.

Lewis Warsh (p. 244) by Dan Wonderly.

Jack Collom (p. 251) by Jennifer Heath.

Brenda Coultas (p. 298) by Bob Gwaltney.

Akilah Oliver (p. 310) by Dave Kite.

Ron Padgett (p. 333) by Lawrence Schwartzwald.

Wayne Koestenbaum and Maggie Nelson (p. 344), New York Public Library, 2016. Courtesy of Maggie Nelson.

John Trudell (p. 353) by Nels Israelson, courtesy of Drive Music Publishing.

Ted Greenwald (p. 362) by Charles Bernstein.

The editors would like to thank Rebecca Alson-Milkman, Marilyn Brakhage, Mary Geis, Peter Hale, Karen Koch, Joan McCluskey, Aldon Nielson, Joe Rausch, Bob Rosenthal, Ana Ruiz, Katie Schneeman, Christopher Wiss, Coffee House Press, and The Poetry Project, as well as the authors and photographers, for their assistance with permissions and photographs.